THE LIBERAL MIND IN
A CONSERVATIVE AGE

Also by the author

Radical Visions and American Dreams: Culture
and Social Thought in the Depression Years

THE LIBERAL MIND IN A CONSERVATIVE AGE

*American Intellectuals in
the 1940s and 1950s*

RICHARD H. PELLS

1817

HARPER & ROW, PUBLISHERS, New York
*Cambridge, Philadelphia, San Francisco, London
Mexico City, São Paulo, Singapore, Sydney*

For Shannon

FIRST EDITION

Designer: Sidney Feinberg

Library of Congress Cataloging in Publication Data

Pells, Richard H.
   The liberal mind in a conservative age.

   Bibliography: p.
   Includes index.
   1. United States—Intellectual life—20th century.
2. Intellectuals—United States—Attitudes—History—
20th century. 3. Liberalism—United States—History—
20th century. I. Title.
E169.12.P45 1985   973.91   84-47594
ISBN 0-06-015351-2   84 85 86 87 88 10 9 8 7 6 5 4 3 2 1
ISBN 0-06-091204-9 (pbk.)   84 85 86 87 88 10 9 8 7 6 5 4 3 2 1

Contents

Preface

This is a book about intellectuals. More specifically, it is a book about the way certain American writers in the 1940s and 1950s interpreted and tried to cope with the major events of their time. I have chosen to call these writers "liberal" but I intend to use that word in its loosest possible sense. During these years, the terms liberal and conservative had already begun to shed whatever precise political meanings they may have once possessed. Moreover, several of the intellectuals I discuss continued to describe themselves as socialists or social democrats, while others had grown weary of politics of every sort. A few were even well embarked on a journey to the right, although they did not arrive at their final destination until the 1970s. Nevertheless, given the American political landscape between 1941 and 1960, most of them still occupied the territory from the center to the left—this at a moment when their countrymen and the leaders of their government were becoming increasingly conservative in foreign policy and domestic affairs.

Yet their liberalism, however broad or vague, was not the principal characteristic of their books and articles. Nor did I select these men and women for study because of their particular philosophies, specialties, career patterns, or proximity to people in power. Rather, I decided to write about them because they seemed to me to be fulfilling the essential function of the intellectual in a modern society. Whether they were known officially as sociologists, political theorists, historians, economists, literary critics, or magazine editors, they succeeded in translating their fields of expertise into a form of general communication; they used the language of their disciplines to address the most important issues of the war years and the postwar era.

My book, therefore, is not meant to be a comprehensive survey of American culture in the 1940s and 1950s. I make no effort to treat literature, the arts, music, religion, methodological schisms within university departments, mass circulation magazines and newspapers, or the fluctuations in public taste and opinion. Still, because I think the intellectuals in this book did focus on the central problems of modern American life, the strengths and deficiencies of their analyses may serve as a measure of how effectively or how poorly the nation adapted to a new age. So though I chose to write only about intellectuals, I found myself inevitably writing about larger cultural and social developments as well.

Like their fellow citizens, American intellectuals confronted a series of crises for which their prior experiences furnished few guidelines. In the space of twenty years, they had to deal with the military and technological impact of a second global war that in its ferocity and destructiveness far outdistanced World War I, with a tenuous peace that rapidly disintegrated into an interminable political and ideological conflict between the United States and the Soviet Union, with a cascade of investigations into "subversive" influences in every area of domestic life, and with the complex and contradictory effects of an unprecedented and apparently permanent prosperity.

But the intellectuals brought to this turbulence a special set of memories and assumptions. Although they did not constitute a single or unified generation, some having risen to prominence in the midst of the Depression while the rest launched their careers during or after the war, they all shared a disenchantment with the political and cultural radicalism of the 1930s together with the felt need to ask new questions about and explore the new tensions of a "postindustrial" society. Thus their work was suffused with the conviction that the troubles of the postwar years were very different from those of the past. Whether they concentrated on the specter of totalitarianism abroad or the centralization of power at home, whether they sought to redefine or move beyond the perceptions and programs traditionally associated with liberalism, whether they scrutinized the role of the mass media or the monotony of modern work or the emptiness of life in suburbia or the failures of education or the pressures of conformity, they insisted on the uniqueness of their concerns if not the originality of their arguments.

Because of these suppositions, they neither proposed nor trusted any sweeping solutions to the difficulties of their time. At most, they urged their contemporaries to resist wherever possible the seductive blandishments of the state, the bureaucracies, the media, and the organizations for which almost everyone now labored. In this way, they hoped the citizen might assert his individuality and protect his freedom within the constraints of the existing social order.

Such precepts hardly amounted to a grand or utopian vision of the future. Yet they unexpectedly created the vocabulary and the mental framework with which the next generation of Americans assaulted the nation's political institutions and social values in the 1960s. Inadvertently and often unhappily, the postwar intellectuals became the parents and teachers—literally and spiritually—of the New Left, the partisans of the counterculture, the civil rights activists, and the movement to end the conflagration in Vietnam. And just as inadvertently, though less unhappily, they introduced in the 1950s the attitudes that informed the rhetoric of neoconservatism in the 1970s and 1980s. Their significance, then, lies as much in their legacy to their successors as in the issues they raised in their own era.

In the course of these pages, I am frequently skeptical about their ideas and positions. I believe that many of them were too eager to embrace established political and economic practices, too reluctant to reevaluate the diplomacy of the Cold War, too enamored with the role of leaders and experts, too cooperative with McCarthyism, and too obsessed with the psychological and moral agonies of the middle class—a preoccupation that led them to neglect the systemic diseases of urban decay, racism, and poverty.

But I also admire enormously much of what they said. I consider them neither complacent nor mean-spirited defenders of

the status quo. On the contrary, because of their hostility to and
liberation from the ideological dogmas of the prewar Left, their
preference for asking questions instead of inventing answers, and
their desire to act as free-floating intellectuals rather than as
spokesmen for a mass movement, I think they offered more provocative and imaginative criticisms of their society than one can
find in the manifestos of either the 1930s or the 1960s. Indeed,
I regard Hannah Arendt's *The Origins of Totalitarianism,* David
Riesman's *The Lonely Crowd,* William Whyte's *The Organization
Man,* John Kenneth Galbraith's *The Affluent Society,* Paul Goodman's *Growing Up Absurd,* Daniel Bell's "Work and Its Discontents," Dwight Macdonald's *Against the American Grain,* Louis
Hartz's *The Liberal Tradition in America,* Daniel Boorstin's *The
Image,* and C. Wright Mills's *The Power Elite* as superior in quality
to any comparable collection of works produced in America during other periods of the twentieth century. Consequently, those
of us who came afterward remain in their debt even as we try to
transcend their perspective.

In conceptualizing and completing his own work, every author
acquires other, more personal debts. Various institutions provide
money and time to contemplate and to write. In my case, I am
grateful for having received a Rockefeller Foundation Humanities Fellowship, numerous grants from the University of Texas
Research Institute, and two Fulbright-Hays Senior Lectureships
to teach at the universities of Amsterdam and Copenhagen—all
of which enabled me to plan, rethink, and carry out this project.
    Yet writing is never an entirely solitary enterprise. Along the
way, people contribute insights, suggestions, encouragement,
the benefit of their own experiences and points of view. I should
like to thank here those who have been especially important to
me.
    In Austin, informal conversations with Sidney Monas and Ed-
ward Cohen helped to sharpen my knowledge of particular episodes that engaged the attention of the intellectual community
during the 1950s. More generally, Laura Richardson and Gail
Caldwell at differing times prodded, challenged, argued, contradicted, railed, and thereby made me examine in greater depth

how I felt about what I thought.

In Amsterdam, Arthur Mitzman shared with me his recollections and intuitions about the emergence of the New Left at the dawn of the 1960s, and he let me peer into his divided consciousness as an American intellectual living abroad. Maarten Brands heightened my sensitivity to the ways Washington's foreign policy has shaped and exasperated postwar Europe. Similarly, Marijke Woorts forced me to look at the United States through European eyes, a task the writers of the 1950s weren't always thrilled to undertake; if the encounter didn't change my mind, at least I better understood hers.

In Copenhagen, Paul Levine read the manuscript and offered valuable advice. Annette Wernblad not only read the manuscript as well, but also deployed her wisdom and wit on several occasions when I needed it most.

More than anyone else, however, Shannon Davies gave me her intelligence, her honesty, and her confidence about the worth of what I was doing. Her judgments, critical or favorable, influenced the outlook and style of nearly every page. She was by turns articulate, stern, intense, and amused from beginning to end. Those are the reasons this book is for her.

1

The Intellectuals at War

When enough time has passed, events blur, facts fade, and memories overtake reality. What we remember most vividly becomes for each of us our version of the truth. We recall not the details of an experience, but its essence—some image or moment or scrap of conversation that we think discloses meaning, captures how it was. These recollections get enshrined indelibly as anecdote and case history, dramatized in the retelling as if our past lives were slide shows, either tragic or comic depending on the particular episode recalled and our current point of view.

Memories filter out subtlety, shading, complexity. They distort and oversimplify. But they also convey a special accuracy. It is just because we discriminate in our remembrances between the incidental and the essential that what we choose to recall illuminates our most profound experiences and our truest feelings. Through our imperfect recollections, we reveal to ourselves and to others what the past meant in our lives and how it shaped our present circumstances. Even more, in our differing memories of the same event we grasp how much and how little we have in common with other people and other cultures. Lovers recognize this eventually. Countries rarely do.

In modern times there has been no experience, and no memory, more universal than war. Given the twentieth century's ambition to surpass its predecessors in every field of human endeavor, it seems only fitting that twice in twenty-five years the entire planet (or nearly all of it) should have plunged into combat. The Romans and the Crusaders may have supposed they were embroiled in a series of "world" wars, and the empire builders of the seventeenth and nineteenth centuries presumably indulged in global fantasies, but the "advanced" industrial nations of the twentieth century reserved for themselves the honor of total conflagration.

World War I appears in retrospect a mere skirmish compared to World War II. The "great war" of 1914–1918 was indisputably the first modern war because it relied almost exclusively on the achievements of science, technology, and industrialization. This was a war fought not with arrows or knives or pistols or cavalry charges, but with weapons that were remote and impersonal: machine guns, artillery, tanks, and gas. There was little hand-to-hand combat, no real scope for individual courage or effort. Instead, the enemy was often invisible; soldiers, huddled in trenches or shrouded in dust and mud, rarely saw who or what they were shooting at. As a result, mutilation and death were inflicted by chance; those who were maimed or killed just happened to be in the wrong place at the wrong time when the shell burst or the mine exploded. The archetypal battlefield of World War I is a nightmare landscape within which human beings have no control: They are in "no man's land."[1]

Consequently, one's wound or death could not be justified as a contribution to a cause, nor could it be explained by the customary allusions to honor or glory or sacrifice. The injury was surprising, unexpected, both in physical and psychological terms. No one was responsible for what happened, and no one could offer consolation. Any attempt to do so sounded either embarrassing or obscene. This loss of individual control, the irrelevance of rational interpretation, the failure of political or religious or philosophical language to make personal catastrophe intelligible became the primal experience of modern warfare— just as the war itself became the perfect metaphor in postwar literature for life in the twentieth century.[2]

World War II expanded upon the mechanization and impersonality of the first world war, but with one notable difference. Though the first war had cost eight million lives on the western front alone, most of these were combatants, soldiers killed in what were quaintly called "battles." However interminable the butchery, civilians and cities were normally spared. Despite the lurid atrocity tales, designed by official propagandists to somehow buttress morale at home, the killing of a villager or the gutting of a rural church was inadvertent and accidental. World War II, in contrast, was waged against civilian populations as a matter of conscious and systematic national policy on all sides. The saturation bombing of cities (indeed their very identification as military targets), the wholesale uprooting of nationality and ethnic groups, the deliberate destruction of land and people, all in the hope of breaking the enemy's will to resist—these were the distinguishing strategies of World War II.

It is no wonder then that the images of the second war summon up instances of mass terror: the air raid sirens and the sounds of German bombs falling in the background of Edward R. Murrow's radio broadcasts from the rooftops of London during the Battle of Britain; the retaliatory demolition of German cities culminating in the fire bombing of Dresden; the newsreels of refugees fleeing on trains for unoccupied zones or wandering narcotically down blighted country roads; the extermination furnaces and open graves; the pervasive rubble of bricks and garbage through which soldiers marched and children played; the cosmic casualty figures (six million Jews, twenty million Russians, an estimated total of fifty-five million killed both in Europe and the Far East) that numb the mind.[3] It is also no wonder that the concentration camp and the mushroom cloud emerged as the ultimate symbols for this war: the supreme weapons with which to terrorize and annihilate defenseless people. Nor is it inappropriate that the most famous painting of the twentieth century, Picasso's *Guernica*, should seize upon the dress-rehearsal obliteration of a Basque town by German bombers during the Spanish Civil War to memorialize the agony of all civilians at the mercy of modern war.

There is some irony in all this colossal destruction. By World War II, the belligerents had regained some control over violence. Death in war could again be "explained": One died not by chance but because one was a Pole or a Russian or a Jew, or because one lived in Rotterdam or Cologne or Hiroshima. It was all very rational, if no more comforting, to the survivors. In thirty years, the world had progressed from no man's land to selective genocide.

World War II was regarded by the Allies as a just war, a necessary war, a shared war against Hitler and Mussolini and Togo, those evil demons of the twentieth century. It is not usually remembered as a war of organized terrorism against civilians. At least it is not remembered that way by Americans, whose cities were unbombed, whose land was unoccupied, and whose casualties occurred in the empty North African desert or in the act of liberating the ancient villages of Italy and France or deep in the jungles of some previously unknown Pacific island.

But Europeans and Asians recall a different war. Their memories, however distilled from the chaos of violence and fear, correspond to their reality. A middle-aged Filipino traveling through Europe is bemused at being mistaken persistently for a Japanese; he fought as a guerrilla with the Americans in the hills around his farm for four years, refuses to visit Japan, and resents the Japanese tourists who now flood his country. In the Netherlands, anyone old enough to remember 1940 will recount with enduring bitterness the bombing of Rotterdam, 80 percent of the city destroyed in a few hours, with the Germans threatening the same fate for Amsterdam unless the Dutch surrendered—which they promptly did. Holland has never forgotten the years of Nazi conquest, and the memories are intensely personal: the sophisticated and realistic Dutch woman who is quite sure her mother slept with German soldiers to increase the family rations and who would do so herself under similar circumstances without hesitation or regret, though she is physically repelled by German men; the respectable official of an educational agency who reveres the codes and standards of modern Dutch life because she carries with her eternally the "smell" of hunger during the terrible last winter of the war when her countrymen were dying of starvation and tore down the remnants of the old Jewish ghetto in Amsterdam (vacant after the deportations) for shelter and firewood; the eminent professor who proudly shows off the auditorium at the University of Leiden in which the rector of the law school publicly denounced the Nazis in 1941 for persecuting his Jewish colleagues, whereupon the Germans closed the school and shipped the rector to a labor camp; the young woman born five years after the end of the war who still cannot speak to her lover's parents because she suspects them of having collaborated with the Nazis during the occupation. Reminders of the war are everywhere in Amsterdam. A newsreel records the sight of pathetically unprepared Dutch soldiers riding to the front on bicycles to defend their country against German planes and armored columns. A photographic exhibit of the prewar city documents the presence of a large Jewish population, in silent contrast to the absence of Jewish faces (unless they are tourists) on the streets of contemporary Amsterdam. Meanwhile, the most magnetic attraction in the Netherlands for both natives and visitors is the Anne Frank House, that poignant memorial to a people erased by the war.

Yet it is no different on the other side. The personal, historical, and physical testimonials to the war abound in Germany as well: the gleaming, streamlined cities of Cologne and Hamburg, monuments to modernity but monuments also to the air raids that pulverized most of the architectural past; the rippling machine gun craters still visible on the renovated façades of apartment houses in Berlin, mementos of the street fighting during the final days of the Third Reich; the half-burnt church in the center of West Berlin, surrounded by sleek new department stores and office buildings and travel agencies, a remembrance of the war deliberately preserved so that all should recall the carnage; the now successful chemist who led a double life during the war, serving in both the German army and the German resistance movement, and whose American-born daughter bears the name of his Danish lover executed by the Gestapo; the life-long Berliner who "understands" the lingering prejudice against Germans but who can also remember herself as a two-year-old child being hurled by an aunt into a car just after a Russian soldier had killed her mother with a single bullet to the brain; the museum at Dachau (situated incongruously in a lovely suburb of Munich) with its map of the concentration camps, black dots marking the countless locations throughout Europe, shadowing the continent like a plague of insects before which no one could plausibly plead innocence or ignorance.

The American memory is different because it corresponds to a different reality. The United States emerged from World War II as the strongest economic and military power on the planet because it had escaped physical destruction. Even in the one instance where American territory was violated—the attack on Pearl Harbor—the Japanese were careful to concentrate on the naval base rather than the city. For millions of Americans, the war brought not terror and suffering, but renewed prosperity and a better way of life after ten years of staggering economic depression. The years of combat overseas meant full employment and high earnings at home, a chance for individuals and families to clear up old debts and make a new start. The need to convert the economy from civilian to military production, to expand existing plants and build new factories, transformed American cities from ghost towns with a shortage of jobs to boom towns with a shortage of manpower. Especially for those who had missed out on the great bonanza of the early twentieth century—sharecroppers and tenant farmers, immigrants and their children, women, blacks— the war offered steady work, social advancement, and self-respect, none of which they were eager to relinquish after 1945. In the end, the United States won the war because it was able to outmobilize and outproduce its enemies. The American victory depended not so much on military ingenuity as on economic organization, industrial and scientific innovation, the skilled allocation of technological and human resources unprecedented in the nation's history.

It is understandable, therefore, that Americans should remember themselves not as victims of the war, but as beneficiaries of the war machine. Despite the lack of crusading fervor and missionary slogans reminiscent of World War I, Americans fought the second war with a striking sense of unanimity. If people did not believe they were engaged in a struggle to make the world safe for democracy, if they did not welcome yet another war to end all wars, they did seem to get immense personal satisfaction out of contributing to a common cause, however undefined. The community drives to collect paper and scrap metal, the participation in car pools to save fuel and rubber, the civil defense exercises in coastal cities long after the rumored danger of enemy air raids had passed, the radio and magazine advertisements reminding consumers that a particular brand name (temporarily absent from the marketplace) remained an indispensable link in the war effort, the multiethnic and multiracial platoons in Hollywood war movies that glamourized the innate cooperativeness of the quintessentially average American—all these reflected the enthusiasm of people joining together in a noble enterprise.

By the close of the war, Europe lay in ruins but the United States had entered a new social and technological age. Where Europeans faced the task of reconstructing their cities and reviving their decimated populations, Americans began their long march to the suburbs, the proper setting for a postwar baby boom. Where Europe continued to rely on railroads and electricity, Americans anticipated the benefactions of air travel and atomic power. Where radio and movies remained the chief instruments of European communications, Americans soon awakened to the glories of television and computers. And where Europeans sought economic recovery through a respite from international tension and balance-of-terror diplomacy, Americans would sustain their prosperity by preparing for the next war.[4]

For Europeans and Asians, the sacrifices of wartime were devastating and the future seemed bleak. For Americans, the sacrifices were inspiring and the postwar prospects appeared bountiful. So while the second world war, even more than the first, came to represent the one common experience of the twentieth century, the participants could share neither the event nor the recollection.

The American memory of the war is peculiarly parochial, disconcertingly innocent. At the outset of the conflict, Americans seemed incapable of comprehending what was to come. At the end they remained curiously untouched by what had happened. This special immunity from physical destruction and mass terror shaped not only the way ordinary citizens responded to and remembered the war, but also the way American intellectuals interpreted its meaning and its purposes. Like lovers who are bewildered but unmarked by the collapse of an affair, neither the American people nor the American intelligentsia knew what the rest of the world was talking about. At just the point where reality and memory might together have yielded insight, the war reinforced insularity. And it left Americans poorly equipped to understand or cope with a world after war.

The Cult of Leadership

Two years after German tanks, planes, and soldiers hurtled into Poland, the United States entered World War II. But America had become a virtual participant long before the attack on Pearl Harbor. By 1939, the issues of the Depression were already giving way to the anticipation of combat. The complicated problems of unemployment and economic collapse, the experimental impulse of the New Deal, the radical ideas and programs that captivated the imagination of many intellectuals in the 1930s, had all faded at the end of the decade. In their place, the country began to rearm, the Roosevelt administration devoted its energies increasingly to diplomacy, and the Left rediscovered the attractions of patriotism. As German armies conquered country after country in a week or a month, writers displayed an unaccustomed nostalgia for the American small town, that mythical home of the ubiquitous common man, and a swelling respect for the nation's historic institutions. There had always been a tendency among intellectuals in the 1930s to sanctify the "people" and to affirm the underlying vigor of the national character, but now America seemed even more a haven of democracy, civil liberties, and elementary decency. When Paris, the very symbol of culture and enlightenment, surrendered to the Nazis in June 1940, American writers and artists suspended their arguments with one another and with their countrymen, and prepared to fight the newest barbarians. The intellectual community marched to war in 1940 imbued with a desperate sense of solidarity and purpose. A year later, the bombs at Pearl Harbor completed the unification of the nation. On the day the United States joined the war, Americans were finally at peace with themselves for the first (and possibly the last) time in the twentieth century.

A nation that wishes to wage a total war requires the participation of nearly everyone. Concurrently, a population that believes in the necessity of total war wants to contribute in whatever ways it can. This raises a dilemma for certain groups and individuals whose talents are not noticeably useful in handling weapons, laboring in defense plants, or working on atomic bomb projects. If one's skill lies primarily in the production of books and ideas, the teaching of students or the writing of essays or the editing of magazines, how is it possible to share in the war effort?

Many artists and academics discovered they were not entirely irrelevant to the war machine. Since they were highly educated and often fluent in at least one foreign language, they seeme ideally suited for the "intellectual" work of wartime, which to the military and the government meant intelligence or propaganda. A significant number of authors, professors, and Hollywood film makers found a home in the Office of Strategic Services (the legendary precursor of the CIA), the Office of War Information, and other branches of military intelligence. Men like Harold Rosenberg, H. Stuart Hughes, Lewis Coser, Frank Capra, John Ford, and John Huston became expert in unraveling enemy codes, divining the geopolitical implications of enemy strategy, and explaining to civilians at home "why we fight." Meanwhile, John Kenneth Galbraith helped regulate the cost of the fight in the Office of Price Administration. Others (among them Saul Bellow, Irving Howe, Irving Kristol, Clement Greenberg, Robert Warshow, Dashiell Hammett, James Jones, and Norman Mailer) enlisted or were drafted into the armed forces as either soldiers or resident journalists. Most remember their sojourn in the government or the military as one of the most exhilarating times of their lives. In the case of Jones and Mailer, it was also indispensable for their postwar fiction; faithful to the example of Hemingway, each believed he had to experience war if he ever hoped to supplant Papa as the Great American Novelist.

Those who remained in the universities (especially the elite graduate institutions like Berkeley, Chicago, Harvard, and Princeton) found themselves the indirect beneficiaries of both fascism and the war, their departments having become shelters for the extraordinary wave of European scholars who had fled Hitler and Mussolini during the past ten years. The same cultural cross-fertilization occurred among painters and poets, playwrights and composers, novelists and literary critics, in New York and Hollywood. Most important, however, American scientists

now enjoyed an unprecedented opportunity to work with eminent European refugees on any experiment that might conceivably assist the Allied cause. Supported by elaborate research
facilities and extensive transfusions of government money,
American and European scientists could together pursue their
ideas in circumstances that approached fantasy. They repaid this
massive investment in their brains by bequeathing to both the
war effort and the postwar world the wonders of radar, the com-
puter, and the atomic bomb.[5]

For intellectuals involved in less grandiose activities, the war
still furnished outlets for vicarious participation. They could continue to combine the roles of practical critic and effusive cheerleader inherited from the immediate prewar years. Sensitive to
the military emergency following Pearl Harbor and the not un-
imaginable prospect that America might lose the war, trauma-
tized by the German and Japanese victories in 1942 but recalling
the way in which writers had too eagerly embraced the Wilsonian
crusade during World War I, they tried to offer "responsible"
advice to the Allied leaders while retaining some political independence from their own increasingly powerful government.

Nowhere was this balancing act more artfully performed than
in the weekly pages of the *New Republic*. The magazine had
emerged from the 1920s and 1930s as the preeminent spokesman for left-of-center programs. Throughout the early 1940s, as
other writers either devoted their time and energies to the war
effort or restricted their attention to cultural concerns, the *New
Republic* remained the journal where one could find the most
articulate analyses of political events, economic trends, and foreign affairs.

Nevertheless, it no longer boasted the glittering array of
philosophers, literary critics, and social theorists who had once
graced its luncheon table and editorial columns. Gone were the
John Deweys, the Edmund Wilsons, the Lewis Mumfords. The
wartime *New Republic* reflected the political and economic views
of four men: Bruce Bliven, a professional journalist who had
served as chief editor since the late 1920s; Max Lerner, a historian and veteran liberal commentator; George Soule, a dedicated
Keynesian who wrote most of the articles on the economy; and

Michael Straight, who covered Washington and whose family financed the magazine. Though Bliven still opened the pages of the journal to cultural discussions (the luminous names of Malcolm Cowley, Van Wyck Brooks, and Stark Young remained symbolically on the masthead; Alfred Kazin served as literary editor during 1942; Otis Ferguson and later Manny Farber contributed movie reviews), the *New Republic* seemed wary of freewheeling debate, much less sustained criticisms of America's war objectives. Bliven wanted the magazine to be "useful," to be read by those in charge of concrete government and military policies.[6]

Whether the journal achieved this goal is questionable. But it could presume some influence among a special segment of the population. From 1939 to 1946, the *New Republic*'s circulation climbed slowly from 28,000 to 41,000. These figures contrasted favorably with those of its nearest competitors: *Partisan Review* claimed only 7000 subscribers at the end of the war while the *Nation* matched the *New Republic*'s circulation at 45,000. On the other hand, *Harper's* readership grew during the war from 110,000 to 138,000; the *Atlantic,* from 103,000 to 156,000; *Newsweek,* from 328,000 to 730,000; *Time,* from 760,000 to 1.5 million. By 1946, *The New Yorker* had 230,000 subscribers while the *Saturday Evening Post* flourished with 3.4 million and *Life* reigned as champion of the magazine world at 5.2 million. Nevertheless, according to the *New Republic*'s own demographics, more than half the journal's readers were professional people, 70 percent had graduated from college, and 50 percent of these held advanced degrees. The largest age group consisted of upwardly mobile subscribers in their twenties and thirties. They lived primarily in Washington, D.C., or in the cities of the most politically significant industrial states: New York, California, Illinois, Pennsylvania, Massachusetts, Michigan, and Ohio (the *New Republic* was apparently least appreciated in the provinces of Wyoming and Nevada). In effect, the journal's typical reader was relatively affluent, urban, middle class, politically sophisticated, and culturally aware (the magazine assumed this last characteristic because the respondents to one of its polls acknowledged listening to the radio an hour per day and attending movies at least once a month).[7] The audience for its ideas were reasonably well placed, if not certified members of a power elite.

At the outset of the war, however, the *New Republic* functioned neither as an advocate of specific programs nor as a spokesman for a particular constituency. Instead, the magazine was initially enthralled by the sheer size and diversity of the war effort itself. In the eyes of its editors and contributors, this was to be a truly democratic war in which everyone might benefit from the common emergency. "Never before has national unity approached so close to national unanimity," exclaimed the historian Arthur Schlesinger, Sr. The current American mood, he wrote approvingly, was "quiet" and "grim" but "determined," in striking contrast to the revivalistic fervor and "hurrah spirit" of World War I.[8] Malcolm Cowley reported from a small New England village that the "community had been drawn together" by the war; while it might have otherwise degenerated into a mere suburb of Boston, it now seemed a "better and friendlier town in wartime than it was in peace."[9] From this perspective, the war had clearly improved upon Thornton Wilder's rustic fantasies; all America was being transformed into Our Town.

It was also becoming a gigantic war factory, a phenomenon equally appealing to the *New Republic.* Within a few short months, one observer enthused, the American people were devoting "all their time, strength and thought to the creation of an unparalleled military machine." Enchanted by this "stupendous story of incessant activity," the writer's own heart began "to swell at his country's achievements."[10]

Yet for all its tributes to the far-flung industriousness and patriotic sacrifices of ordinary citizens, the journal invariably fastened its sights on where the action really was. The war had thrust the United States into a position of "world leadership"; it was not only a matter of survival but the "American destiny" to emulate and surpass the Nazis in military, technological, and diplomatic ingenuity and speed—a dubious model for which the *New Republic* felt no need to apologize.[11] To carry out such a global mission, Washington was necessarily becoming the center of activity—the source of jobs, policies, decisions. For the *New Republic,* the inner sanctum was the presidency. "All paths in Washington," a regular columnist intoned, "lead ultimately to the White House.

Roosevelt is the key figure in the newly created World-Capital-on-the-Potomac."[12]

Consequently, the magazine most often addressed its editorials and essays not to other intellectuals or to its average subscribers, but to those who held administrative power. This preoccupation with important decision makers was not inspired simply by a yearning to capture the attention of the influential. It coincided with the *New Republic*'s wartime philosophy about leadership, itself a legacy from the Depression years when liberals and radicals placed their faith in economic planning boards, specialists in social engineering, government agencies, and official spokesmen for class interests. But the war, even more than the Depression, deepened the *New Republic*'s dependence on authority figures of all sorts both at home and abroad.

Bluntly, the journal insisted that democracy could not endure nor could the war be won without "concentrating power in the executive."[13] The nation had to act "decisively"—a favorite catchword of the *New Republic*'s editors and columnists—and it needed "tough" managers.[14] In the words of "T.R.B.," the journal's normally skeptical reporter on domestic political intrigue, such tenacity could be achieved "only by a strong centralized government largely controlled by the administrative branch." At least until victory was achieved, the legislature must "confine itself to a secondary role."[15]

The *New Republic* magnified the role of the presidency in part because it had a dismal opinion of senators and congressmen. In the judgment of the editors, Congress sheltered not only a group of conservatives who obstructed the war effort and whatever remained of the New Deal; its members were also inefficient, inferior, and generally incompetent. Worst of all, Congress had the temerity to represent "local districts or special interests" while President Roosevelt was striving heroically to serve the "whole people."[16] When the nation's very existence was imperiled, the journal complained, why did Congress "persist in trying to decide important details concerning the conduct of a war which it has neither the constitutional authority nor the ability to manage?" The president and the military had the sole responsibility for "careful, integrated decisions" regarding the war, not a Congress that too often behaved "like a schoolroom of unruly boys venting resentment against the teacher."[17] In exceedingly moralistic tones, the magazine demanded that Congress "chasten and discipline itself."[18] Toward this end, the *New Republic* periodically compiled lists of approved legislators (Samuel Dickstein, Lyndon Johnson, Estes Kefauver, Vito Marcantonio, Gerald Voorhis) and those it wished to retire (Hamilton Fish, Howard Smith, Martin Dies, Everett Dirksen, John Rankin, Karl Mundt, J. Parnell Thomas).[19]

Congress was not the only object of the *New Republic*'s frustration and scorn. If legislators should stop interfering with the White House and the military on questions of war strategy, the state department should stop meddling with foreign policy— another subject the president knew most about. In the editors' view, the state department was afflicted by a "tory mentality," by inertia and complacency when it came to pursuing international democratic goals.[20] It continually sought to appease the most unappetizing regimes: Vichy France, Franco's Spain, Latin American dictators like Vargas of Brazil. Sometimes the journal's disdain seemed motivated as much by the state department's style as by its policies: Those who entered the foreign service were "light-minded little snobs, protected by the taboo about the sacredness of diplomatic secrets" that, given their awesome conspiratorial talents, enabled them to "wreck the prospects of democracy in country after country throughout the world, and finally to compromise democratic victory itself."[21] Hence the president should take "decisive" action to change the department's personnel and practices as the one way to clean out the reactionary "deadwood" and protect his "strong and glowing vision" of world order.[22]

Apparently it never occurred to the editors that the state department might already be carrying out Roosevelt's policies, that the real problem lay in the White House where the president himself deliberately refrained from antagonizing reactionary regimes because he wanted to preserve their neutrality in the war. On this, as on other matters, the *New Republic* assumed that Roosevelt's innate liberal instincts were being undercut by closet conservatives in his own administration. The editors rarely paused to ask why, if the presidency now possessed so much power, its goals seemed so easily thwarted. But then to pose such a question might have led the magazine to a discomforting conclusion: that FDR was not quite the "progressive" savior it imagined; he too might secretly harbor "tory" values.

The editors' habit of relying on Roosevelt to champion their programs raised another more disturbing dilemma. The *New Republic*'s sour estimation of congressional abilities, its impatience with career diplomats, and its worship of presidential power reflected the editors' heightened fear that the reform impulse of the 1930s might become the first casualty of the war. But the issue here is not whether they were wrong to criticize conservatives in the legislature and the foreign service, or whether they may have deluded themselves about the extent of Roosevelt's domestic and international liberalism. Rather, it is that the implications of their statements could be chilling when applied to later controversies like the Cold War and Vietnam, where the executive branch claimed omniscience as a way of silencing all opposition to its policies. Similarly, the language they used to disparage the foreign service and Congress could also take on a different meaning when heard in the context of Joseph McCarthy's assault on the "striped-pants boys" in the state department who he alleged were loftily indifferent to the Communist menace; or in the self-righteous rhetoric of pressure groups like the Moral Majority, with their own hit lists of obstreperous politicians. The *New Republic* was inadvertently providing the intellectual justification for both an "imperial presidency" and a witch hunt psychology, developments it would eventually regret.

At the time, however, these possibilities were unforeseen. With no reservations, the journal saw its wartime role as combating those "ruling economic and political groups" whose "vested ideas" led to delays and inaction at a moment of mortal crisis for the nation.[23] Again, the editors carefully exempted the president from this circle of "ruling groups" to be distrusted. If anything, the *New Republic* criticized Roosevelt for not exercising *more* authority, for being too amiable and too ready to compromise with rather than fight conservative legislators, recalcitrant diplomats, and the corporate barons who were now filling government positions.[24] The president's resolve clearly needed stiffening, so the journal argued that liberals must organize to influence Roosevelt from the left as a way of counteracting the pressure presumably being leveled at him from the right.[25]

In this epic contest for the president's ear, one might find allies even among those formerly consigned to the obstructionist camp. During 1942, the *New Republic* consistently praised any conservative spokesman who accepted the basic objectives of the war and who perceived the importance of centralized power. The litmus test for such accolades was a demonstrated willingness on the part of conservatives to limit their opposition to technical matters while conceding the president's authority to define and implement overall policy. Max Lerner, for example, applauded Wendell Willkie's conversion from implacably opposing TVA to vigorously supporting the war effort. Along with other enlightened Republicans like Henry and Clare Boothe Luce, Harold Stassen, Donald Nelson, and George Ball, Willkie shrewdly grasped which way the political winds were blowing; he understood, in Lerner's view, that the "axis of power was shifting in America from the economic to the governing elite." Because he was "drawn to power," because he realized that the New Deal and the war had brought about an "administrative revolution," Willkie and his Republican counterparts recognized the necessity for "realistic businessmen" like themselves "to move directly into the key administrative posts." Though Lerner warned that they still conceived of "international order" as synonymous with their ability to retain control over world-wide economic affairs, though he saw the future dangers in such a coalition between New Deal liberals and sophisticated conservatives, he welcomed Willkie and company as "honorable allies" in "our" joint struggle.[26]

The *New Republic* admitted other converts into the congregation beyond the nation's borders, some of them neither potentially liberal nor conspicuously enlightened. Reviewing the results of the conferences at Cairo and Teheran in 1943, the magazine extolled Winston Churchill as the representative of a "gallant Tory militancy" (Tories being acceptable as long as they were British), Chiang Kai-shek as the embodiment of "conservative nationalism," and Joseph Stalin as the architect of a "stable socialism." But what these disparate rulers really had in common, in the *New Republic*'s eyes, was a capacity to share with Roosevelt the charismatic stature and managerial wisdom required to lay the foundations for a unified and democratic postwar world.[27]

Since executive presence ultimately mattered more than liberal principles, the magazine could sometimes inflate even the most questionable political operator into a visionary commander as long as he attached himself to the Allied cause. A priceless example of this rhetorical expansiveness occurred early in 1942, a month after the bombing of Pearl Harbor and America's entrance into the war. In trumpeting the virtues of T. V. Soong, Chiang Kai-shek's brother-in-law and foreign minister to Washington, one columnist pictured him as China's "Alexander Hamilton." Applying what he once learned in such revolutionary outposts as Harvard, Columbia, and Wall Street, Soong had helped set up and bankroll Chiang's "republic," which was today "fighting Japan with all it has." As a "financial expert and democratic statesman," Soong possessed all the requisite qualities of leadership: He "talks turkey when and as he pleases, and he believes in getting things done." Soong also exhibited the proper bloodlines: His family was "the most amazing accumulation of brains and power in the modern world." Given these multiple attributes, the author was not surprised that the "younger Chinese" who had left their university campuses and "trekked far inland to work for a reborn and free China, worship him." Together with Chiang, that "brilliant soldier," Soong would expertly "attend to the job of postwar rehabilitation." The fact that Soong maintained a permanent residence in Washington suggested to the columnist not the diplomat's less optimistic appraisal of his future role or his more cautious estimate of how grateful the "younger Chinese" might feel toward his family; instead, it simply illustrated the "close relation between the two large democracies." So in fine democratic fashion, the article concluded with the prophecy that under the stewardship of Chiang and Soong it was "China's historic privilege to administer the death blow" to the Japanese invaders (whom the author delicately referred to as the "brown dwarfs").[28]

Apart from the atmosphere of crisis generated by the attack on Pearl Harbor, there was little excuse for such hokum. Chiang and Soong were no newcomers on the world scene by 1942. They were known quantities, as was their fifteen-year struggle with the Chinese Communists, their decade-long ineptitude in trying to expel the Japanese, the unquenchable arrogance of their reign, and the wrenching poverty of their people. But the essay did reflect in an exaggerated way the *New Republic*'s extravagant confidence in the powerful, its propensity to exalt all leaders who might be remotely antifascist regardless of whatever else they stood for.

By the early 1940s, the *New Republic* had come to speak within the intellectual community for a form of administrative liberalism that relied increasingly on the White House, the Cabinet, and government agencies staffed with ideologically sympathetic appointees for social reform at home and victory abroad. But not all intellectuals were so sanguine about the wartime concentration of power in ever fewer hands. Even in the pages of the *New Republic* itself, some contributors voiced doubts about the capacity of the state to restrain its new-found allies in the corporate world, and about the ability of the people to affect the policies of their leaders.

Robert Lynd—whose classic studies of "Middletown" in the 1920s and 1930s had made him one of the most acute observers of contemporary American life, and whose critique of his fellow social scientists in *Knowledge For What?* at the end of the Depression had emphasized the need for intellectuals to focus on problems larger than those of immediate political concern—admitted the necessity for centralized power in wartime but warned of its consequences for democracy. "Both during the war and after," he pointed out, "the issue is identical: Who controls, and to what ends?" In Lynd's opinion, the war accelerated a century-long fusion of government and business. Given the technological requirements of all modern societies, the demand for "organization" and "efficiency" in both political and economic affairs, government officials and the directors of the major corporations had come to be mutually dependent on each other's resources. But "democratic authority" might be unable to contain the ambitions and prestige of either businessmen or bureaucrats. The result, Lynd feared, was an "unmistakable trend toward the monolithic power structure of the totalitarian state." Even worse, "the public does not know what to do about this merging of powers up aloft over its head." The people, Lynd suspected, remained innocent and impotent bystanders; the historical drama would unfold without their advice or participation.[29]

Max Lerner was more hopeful than Lynd about the prospects for democracy. Granted, America's individualistic heritage and historic distrust of centralized power would have to be modified in the present and future. The old verities were obsolete, Lerner declared. The small businessman had been replaced by the corporation; the unprotected worker, by the union; the yeoman farmer, by agricultural combines and farm associations; the civil servant, by administrative agencies; the eccentric local editor, by newspaper syndicates and radio networks; the solitary voter, by political movements and pressure groups; the World War I flying ace, by a mechanized and integrated air force. Nevertheless, Lerner remained at this point a good child of the 1930s, and he continued to assume that all change was "progressive." Thus he assured his readers that these transformations also encouraged the development of what he preferred to call an "affirmative state" which might yet master the tasks of economic well-being and world peace. Still, Lerner shared Lynd's qualms about too much concentrated power. He accepted the positive role of government but urged as much decentralization as possible so that administrators (whom he characteristically described as "men in the strategic posts") might behave with some humility, and become more responsive to the cares of ordinary citizens.[30]

To one *New Republic* contributor, however, the issue was neither the marriage of business and government nor the sensitivity of administrators to democratic etiquette. The central problem, Walton Hamilton argued, was that the management of a modern society—especially one at war—had become so complicated that laymen were inevitably excluded from the inner circle of decision making. They hadn't the knowledge or the clout to participate in interdepartmental negotiations and behind-the-scenes bargaining. Even the president found it hard to cope with the bureaucracy, Hamilton mused. One could hardly talk about "responsible government" when the executive "establishment" had grown "too vast for one man to understand." Nor could Congress, the courts, or the political parties effectively supervise the agencies, bureaus, and commissions that dominated wartime Washington. Meanwhile, government specialists spent their time on "technical" matters and framed their decisions in a language only an expert would comprehend. As a result, Hamilton concluded, it was foolish to suppose that any presidential administration could now "operate as representative government. The will of the people moves in one domain; the real questions of policy lie in another."[31]

Analyses such as these left little room for anything but acquiescence or despair. If the average citizen was truly powerless, if what counted was one's access to the official in charge, then the *New Republic* might be right to devote its editorial energies to winning the ear of the president and his closest advisers. While not a posture calculated to earn the admiration of more radical critics, the journal's perspective did at least appear realistic given the reduced political expectations of the war years.

The only other alternative for certain intellectuals seemed to be a reiteration of the 1930s belief in the transforming potential of the labor movement. Though all of these writers eventually abandoned their faith in the working class after the war, in the early 1940s they continued to regard it as the sole constituency capable of challenging the centralized state.

The young C. Wright Mills, for example, contributed angry book reviews to the *New Republic* assailing the magazine's complacent assumption that "progressive" administrators could be distinguished from "conservative" capitalists. "At the top of every country," Mills insisted in words that anticipated his passionate treatises of the 1950s, "the executives are blended by blood and interest, by idea and status with propertied families and cliques." Political and economic leaders were part of the same hierarchy, with the same values and instincts. Therefore, Mills argued, it was not enough to compete with businessmen for the attention of the president. "The chief social power upon which a genuine democracy can rest today is labor. . . . Unless trade unions unify into an independent political movement and take intelligent action on all important political issues, there is danger that they will be incorporated within a government over which they have little control."[32] Here Mills invoked the language of the Depression years, but his vision was nonetheless prophetic.

Dwight Macdonald—who had functioned at various times in the 1930s as a movie critic, a journalist for Henry Luce's *Fortune* magazine, a Marxist polemicist with a distinct sympathy for Leon Trotsky, and a founding editor of *Partisan Review*—went somewhat further than Mills. He too saw no distinction between government and business, or between the "left" and "right" political parties in either Britain or the United States. In his eyes, both countries practiced imperialism abroad and "domestic liberalism" at home; indeed, the two strategies were intertwined. Hence it was understandable to Macdonald that embodiments of the corporate aristocracy like Wendell Willkie and Henry Luce should support Roosevelt in the war. The president and his Republican allies agreed that "private enterprise" ought to be preserved, and that the United Nations could "police" the postwar world while it was being "refashioned in the image of America." In sum, the "People's Century" of Henry Wallace and the "American Century" of Henry Luce were identical.[33] Yet in Macdonald's estimation, neither philosophy could win the war, much less reconstruct the planet. "Only a socialist government," he submitted, "can defeat totalitarianism" and "the only road to such a state is for the workers to insist on replacing the antiquated capitalism represented by Roosevelt and Churchill with their own government."[34] The working class remained for Macdonald the "one social group with broad enough interests and a sufficient capacity for organization to lead any movement for revolutionary . . . change."[35] Why he continued to suppose that workers throughout the world possessed these qualities, he did not say. But given his mordant assessment of how strong and harmonious were the ruling elites, it perhaps seemed wiser to lapse into a litany of socialist slogans than to pursue these matters more rigorously.

Sidney Hook—the acerbic philosopher from New York University who had written several pioneering books in the 1930s trying to reconcile pragmatism with Marxism, and who still described himself as a socialist—escaped this quandary by uttering a plague on everyone's house. Analyzing the "failure of the Left" in 1943, Hook dismissed writers like Macdonald and Mills as romantic "theoreticians without practical or theoretical responsibility" who had overlooked the simple fact that capitalists were superior to fascists, and that the war must first be won before the Marxist millennium could arrive. But he saved his most caustic barbs for New Dealers, union leaders, and unnamed editors of liberal weeklies who were "so much in the thick of things that they have forgotten their own justifications for engaging in political action." Instead, they magnified "trivial differences" between Democrats and Republicans "into great issues of principle." Worse, they had grown emotionally dependent upon "individual leaders [Roosevelt, Wallace, Churchill] to win their social battles for them." Indeed for most of the American Left, Hook observed, "Roosevelt has taken the place of a program."[36]

What, then, did Hook propose? His solutions actually sounded little different from those of Mills and Macdonald, and they were couched in a vocabulary even the *New Republic* might not automatically reject. Hitler must certainly be defeated, Hook conceded, but in the process the Left could not "lose sight of its programs and the ideals of a democratic socialist world order." To achieve these twin objectives, he urged the creation of an "independent political bloc, outside of the major existing parties," composed of trade unions and their political allies who would insist that the war be fought effectively (which meant without the "restrictions of capitalist property relations") and democratically (which meant with the participation of workers and consumers in the councils of government). Above all, Hook believed that by maintaining its autonomy, by giving "critical political support" to the war effort while remembering its original ideological commitments, the labor movement could better influence both the direction of current policy and the shape of the postwar world.[37]

Yet like Macdonald, Hook carefully avoided the dilemma of what happened if the working class did not especially want socialism. Should the labor movement be satisfied with short-term economic gains, then an independent political party made no sense because the Democrats were perfectly willing to grant concessions to their traditional constituents. And if this were the case, what other groups in society could possibly be counted upon to oppose the coalition of corporate executives and government managers? This was not a question the *New Republic* or its critics cared to consider.

In essence, the debate over how closely the Left should identify its fortunes with the wartime Roosevelt administration was a continuation of the argument in the late 1930s between those liberals and Communists who joined in a Popular Front to defend the New Deal and the anti-Stalinist advocates of a more militant Marxism. Mills, Macdonald, and Hook were clearly correct that a labor movement which relinquished its independence could be disarmed by and absorbed into the government. And they were also right to resist the *New Republic*'s enthusiasm for centralized power. But their own mystical reliance on the working class was strangely similar to the *New Republic*'s idolatry of the president. Each became a symbol of generalized social progress and a medallion to ward off reaction at a time when the war made it difficult to think creatively about new programs and strategies of any kind.

Given this impasse, it was not surprising that Macdonald's coeditors at *Partisan Review* (Philip Rahv and William Phillips) decided to minimize political controversy in the magazine, and concentrate instead on developments in art and literature in the hope of maintaining some measure of intellectual detachment from the swirling demands of wartime. "Our main task," they announced in 1942, "is to preserve cultural values against all types of pressure and coercion."[38] A year later, Macdonald resigned from the editorial board in protest against the journal's apparent disinterest in political and social issues. Like Rahv and Phillips, Macdonald wished to sustain his radical ideals; neither he nor they had any desire to influence those in power. But Macdonald believed that cultural problems were an expression of "deeper historical [and ideological] trends" which could not be safely ignored.[39]

So in 1944 Macdonald launched *Politics*, which (because he

served as "editor, publisher, owner, proofreader, layout man and chief contributor") reflected his own changing attitudes toward domestic and foreign policy over the next five years. *Politics* was indeed a singular magazine. With a circulation of 5000 readers —80 percent male, 90 percent college graduates, mostly young, overwhelmingly urban, without established party affiliations, and predominantly members of the professional middle class—*Politics* existed largely as the voice and conscience of one idiosyncratic writer who refused on principle to join any political camp.[40] Eventually, however, Macdonald followed the path of Rahv and Phillips; he too withdrew from political debate and turned to cultural analysis as the last redoubt of the radical intellectual.

For its part, the *New Republic* responded to its myriad detractors with both scorn and some self-satisfaction at having held fast to practical politics. Throughout the war years, Bruce Bliven castigated those writers who refused "to take any real part in the struggle between fascism and democracy." In Bliven's eyes, intellectuals like Rahv, Phillips, Macdonald, and Hook had become "mere sideline sitters" or worse: "spiritual saboteurs." They seemed content to "snipe" and complain; each declined to be a "man of action"; they had "deliberately cut themselves off from the two great centers of dynamic energy in the world today"— the Roosevelt administration and the Soviet Union. But, Bliven reminded his critics in words drenched in the battlefield imagery of both the 1930s and the war, there was no room for "ivory towers" in the contemporary world; a writer, like an ordinary citizen, must choose sides.[41]

The *New Republic* had proudly chosen. It had committed itself to certain men and institutions, however imperfect, in order to accomplish concrete political goals.[42] The magazine, Bliven asserted, certainly identified with labor and it tried occasionally to think in "long-range terms." But its primary obligation was to advise Roosevelt "from the Left," confident that the president welcomed criticism as long as it was "just and reasonable in tone." Thus the editors believed they should spend most of their time "fighting for short-range and immediate objectives."[43] It was precisely these deeply felt sentiments that separated the *New Republic* so sharply from *Politics* and *Partisan Review*.

What the *New Republic* defined as "activism," as taking a "real" part in the controversies of the day, was very clear if somewhat narrow. The journal functioned during the early 1940s as a spokesman for the latest liberal doctrines: an unlimited support for the war effort, sympathy for the resistance movements in occupied Europe, a willingness to embrace the Soviet Union as an ally combined with the hope that it might sometime become more democratic, a faith in the concept of the United Nations, protection of labor's rights during and after the war, and a reliance on Roosevelt and the executive branch of government for policy making and leadership. Much of the magazine's shrillness on these issues, its emphasis on speed and decisiveness, stemmed from its sense of urgency, especially in 1942 when the outcome of the war really did appear in doubt. In the absence of any major allied victories, the editors focused on the spectacle of American productivity, the heroism of the Russian people in withstanding the advance of the German armies, and the virtues of leaders like Winston Churchill and Chiang Kai-shek, all in order to reinforce domestic morale.

These tendencies seemed understandable, but were such concerns the true province of journals like the *New Republic*? Should not an independent magazine of opinion, written and edited by people who thought of themselves as intellectuals, have been asking harder questions about current institutions and values, rather than serving as a cheerleader for the war and the Roosevelt administration? Instead of constantly reiterating the need for more democracy at home and abroad, might not the *New Republic* have better fulfilled its mission by probing the growing dependence on elites to carry out democratic programs?

The magazine, like most of the liberals whose views it mirrored, rarely considered these problems because they conflicted with a set of political formulas inherited from the 1930s that were amplified during the war. The *New Republic* continued to see the world as divided schematically between "progressives" and "vested interests," democrats and fascists, forceful leaders and benighted obstructionists. In such a contest, it seemed appropriate simply to offer sensible counsel to those whose side you were on.

The trouble here is not the magazine's accuracy in assessing political or military trends, but rather its state of mind—its unwillingness to be too critical, its fear of losing influence with the decision makers. This in turn led to a certain smugness of tone, an intellectual complacency in the *New Republic*'s content and style. Its articles were seldom skeptical about and never iconoclastic toward those in power. On the contrary, the journal was punctilious—almost deferential—to "Mr." Roosevelt and other world leaders. In the editors' estimation, these worthy statesmen instinctively knew what was best. In loose cooperation with the common people, they would extend the boundaries of the welfare state, encourage further social reform, and win the war. Thus their policies could be improved but should not be seriously challenged by Congress, the state department, conservatives, the electorate, or "irresponsible" intellectuals.

The editors of the *New Republic* longed to be insiders. This was what they meant by being "men of action"; this was how they thought they could most effectively contribute to the war effort. But in their romance with leadership, they may have surrendered their freedom as intellectuals. They sought the attention of the powerful; but in gaining a hearing, they suppressed much of what they might have said. Throughout World War II, such self-restraint was well intentioned and perhaps excusable. But after 1945, the desire for influence and respectability on the part of too many writers and artists led to unforeseen disasters.

The Political Economy of Wartime Liberalism

There were moments during the war when liberals both in government and in the intellectual community paused to consider the future. On at least one topic—the shape of the postwar economy—they permitted themselves the luxury of bold speculation. Armed with the theories of Thorstein Veblen, Alvin Hansen, and especially John Maynard Keynes, impressed by the breathtaking sweep of the Beveridge Plan to rebuild Britain after the war, and inspired by the visionary report of the National Planning Resources Board on the problems of reconverting the United States to a peacetime economy which was submitted to

Roosevelt and the Congress in 1943, liberals offered their own prospectus for an American-style social democracy. In retrospect, their expectations bordered on fantasy; their notions about what was imminently achievable and economically desirable sounded both utopian and naïve. At the time, however, their ideas did reflect a passionate—even noble—commitment to a genuinely humane society. In their eyes, after all, the war was being waged not merely as a struggle for national survival, but also as an opportunity to construct a different world. If their ambitions now seem extravagant, this may reveal more about the subsequent loss of imagination and sense of diminished possibilities in what became an increasingly conservative age.

The *New Republic* opened its pages enthusiastically to a variety of liberal proposals. Nothing pleased the editors more than the occasion to "chart a course." Between 1942 and 1944, Bruce Bliven, George Soule, and Max Lerner collaborated on a number of articles and special supplements promoting Keynesian scenarios for a "new America." Though many of these plans differed in minor detail, together they set forth a liberal agenda that promised to move the nation far beyond the New Deal.

Essentially, the creation of a postwar welfare state rested on certain well-defined premises. Among these, the two most cherished were the concepts of permanent full employment and infinitely increasing productivity. What the first ideal implied, according to George Soule, was that "there shall be a job available for every competent person who wants one, and that those who for good reasons do not have jobs shall have other means of support" guaranteed to them by the government.[44] But the second goal—the faith in what one writer called "full-blast production" to ameliorate almost every human difficulty—was far more crucial.[45] "If people are to have more," Soule pointed out, "they must produce more. With economic expansion, every problem is capable of solution; without it, we have major depressions and war."[46]

To cope with the more mundane dilemmas of inflation and recession, liberals relied on a third device: orthodox Keynesianism, or what they referred to as "compensatory fiscal policy." Thus the *New Republic* endorsed a strategy of maintaining "high

taxes and low public expenditures during prosperous periods"
and "low taxes and high public expenditures when depression is
threatened."[47] The editors hoped that such a flexible balance of
taxation, borrowing, and government spending would eliminate
the dreaded cycles of boom and bust typical of prewar capitalism.

The *New Republic* editors regarded full employment, an expanding economy, and Keynesian fiscal controls as prerequisites
for the erection of a liberal commonwealth. But their minds really
took flight when they described the enormous social benefits the
welfare state might deliver. Here their appetite for reform was
insatiable. The menu, as in a particularly bountiful Chinese restaurant, offered every conceivable dish. Bliven, Soule, and
Lerner foresaw the massive rehabilitation of American cities involving large-scale slum clearance and public housing projects,
better forms of sewage and waste disposal, and a purposeful
attack on industrial pollution. They awaited the creation of nation-wide employment exchanges and vocational retraining programs, the extension of Social Security to groups not yet covered
by its provisions (particularly migrant workers and domestic servants), and the abolition of unequal pay scales for blacks and
women. They thought it possible to modernize the country's
transportation network by constructing new highways and airports, as well as by reinvigorating the bus and railroad systems.
They looked forward to the further development of energy resources modeled on TVA and rural electrification, firmer control
over the use of land and water, more regional conservation experiments, and the preservation of that treasured but vanishing
institution—the family farm. They were excited by the chance to
achieve comprehensive medical care and health insurance for
each citizen (Bliven went so far as to predict the early eradication
of polio, heart disease, and cancer). Finally, they anticipated substantial increases in federal aid to education, which would lead to
more nursery schools and kindergartens, free lunches for all
grade-school children, day-care centers for pupils from homes
with working mothers, assurances to war veterans that they could
continue their education, the rapid growth of high school and
college enrollments, the building of new schools as well as the
improvement of teaching skills and salaries—even publicly sup-

ported camps for every child whose parents could not afford to ship him off to the mountains for the summer.[48]

These blessings, the editors argued, would result from Washington's intimate partnership with management and labor. Bliven, Soule, and Lerner did not yearn for direct government ownership or operation of industry and agriculture; whatever interest they once displayed in Marxist solutions had long since waned. Instead, they were outlining the dimensions of a mixed economy in which Washington would temporarily retain wartime price and rent controls, carefully regulate domestic monopolies and multinational cartels, supervise corporate investments overseas, undertake long-term socially useful public works projects wherever the private sector failed to generate enough jobs and productivity, subsidize scientific and technological research, and assume responsibility for the most important economic decisions.[49]

Their aspirations were truly vast, but not implausible given America's prospective economic power at the end of the war. Indeed, it is ironic that the welfare state they envisioned became a reality in western Europe and Scandinavia, particularly in those countries most damaged by the war. Meanwhile, the United States—the nation best equipped after 1945 to provide such social amenities—proved much more resistant to blueprints for reform. The supreme question turned out to be not whether a mixed economy was technically feasible, but whether liberals could devise a political strategy capable of transforming America into an authentic social democracy.

The answer was they couldn't, at least not during the war. However romantic their economic reveries, liberals became more calculating whenever politics intruded. Wishing always to appear tough-minded and pragmatic, they tended to settle for what they could get.

One *New Republic* columnist doubted whether fundamental social changes after the war were really possible. The war experience itself may have undercut liberal hopes, T.R.B. observed in 1943. The average American's perspective was obviously colored by the nation's immunity to physical destruction, he pointed out, especially when compared with Europe's agony. This led to a feeling among American soldiers overseas that the United States remained the "ultimate in desirability"; they wanted to return to the country they remembered. Meanwhile, the rise in living standards at home, the expectation of a postwar economic bonanza stimulated by an accumulation of purchasing power in the hands of defense workers, as well as by potentially huge foreign markets for American investment and surplus goods, all reinforced the assumption that the United States could proceed "essentially unchanged in political, social, and economic organization." Hence, T.R.B. concluded, the American impulse for "radical reform seems to lose its force as the war goes on."[50]

Others were not quite so pessimistic. But the presidential election of 1944 represented a test of how far liberals were willing to go in defying political realities. Their performance was hardly encouraging.

The dominant issue for liberals in 1944 was whether Roosevelt would retain Henry Wallace as his vice-president. During the war, Wallace had become a symbol of their dreams for further economic and social change. In a typically rhapsodic passage, the *New Republic* described Wallace as "by all odds the outstanding American progressive, and one of the two or three most distinguished men of our time. Today, with the President preoccupied by war, Mr. Wallace is the one clear voice for liberalism to be heard in any high place in Washington."[51]

For once, therefore, the editors were intensely critical of both Roosevelt's stewardship and their own emotional allegiance to his policies. The president's efforts to remove Wallace from the Democratic ticket demonstrated, they confessed, that liberals had been mistaken to put "too many of their eggs in the White House basket. The progressive movement will never be secure so long as it depends so largely on the whims and erratic impulses of a single individual who is . . . playing power politics."[52] The trouble, George Soule explained in tones reminiscent of Sidney Hook, was that liberals had relied "too much on the Great Leader, counting on him to do everything."[53]

The *New Republic* further claimed it would not be satisfied merely with the retention of Wallace, however eloquent his crusade for liberal causes. For to shift one's faith from Roosevelt to another leader would be to make the same error. As an alternative, the editors urged the mobilization of public opinion to prevent presidential backsliding, and the election of more liberal representatives and senators who could alter the current dreary political climate in Washington. Above all, they recognized that liberals must commit themselves to programs and principles "more fundamental" than the simple desire "to place a single champion in the Presidential chair."[54]

Unfortunately, the *New Republic* quickly forgot its own advice. After Wallace had been jettisoned at the Democratic convention, the editors surveyed the wreckage of their hopes and decided that not all was lost. They conceded that Roosevelt had once again appeased the conservatives in his party; they also regretted the gradual disappearance of veteran New Dealers from wartime Washington. Nevertheless, they shrugged, "political life is always a compromise between the ideal and the best you can possibly get." And the journal was as prepared as the president to compromise. Given a choice between Roosevelt and the Republican nominee, Thomas Dewey, and given the additional question of what sort of leadership would finish the war and organize the peace, Bruce Bliven did not "see how any progressive American [could] hesitate for a moment" to vote for FDR.[55]

In fact, the *New Republic* exclaimed, though it may not have seemed so to less crafty political observers, the liberals had actually won a great victory at the convention. They had forced the vice-presidential nomination of Harry Truman, a certified New Dealer not quite the equal of Henry Wallace but surely acceptable.[56] Moreover, liberals were "closely allied with millions of trade unionists" who had become politically conscious; they were also in touch with "all minorities who suffer discrimination." Thus in the *New Republic*'s opinion, there was "no good reason why the progressives" ought not be able to "capture" the Democratic party eventually, and "start again on a bigger and better New Deal." Should this buoyant appraisal fail to persuade, Bliven counseled liberals to cheer up because "the tides of history are running our way. All over the world, nation after nation is moving steadily and rapidly in the direction the progressives advocate in this country. . . . Instead of being disheartened, the liberals have every cause to feel reasonably proud of the past and reasonably confident about the future."[57]

Despite this jaunty rhetoric, the *New Republic* editors and most of the liberals for whom they spoke had quietly surrendered to political expediency. The problem was not that they preferred Roosevelt to Dewey. In 1944, they had no other option. It was rather that they had so eagerly subordinated their economic and social demands to the exigencies of a reelection campaign. A reluctant endorsement of FDR may have been justified; such an ardent identification with his political fortunes was far less defensible. For all its concern with postwar reform, for all its talk about exerting leverage and influence, the *New Republic* offered no convincing reason why Roosevelt (or any other Democratic party official) should pay attention to liberal ideas when liberal loyalties were never in doubt. Forsaking true independence, the *New Republic* editors and their counterparts in the intellectual community continued to regard Roosevelt as their ultimate benefactor, whatever his flaws. They occasionally contemplated the glories of a "new" America in essays and public forums. But at moments when unyielding political pressure might have counted, they could not bring themselves to jeopardize their ties to Roosevelt and the remnants of his New Deal for the phantom vision of a postwar social democracy.

The Russian Enigma

Once the United States entered the war, any notion of what the future would be like necessarily involved a consideration of foreign policy. Since a victorious America was certain to emerge from the conflict as the world's dominant military and economic power, the intricacies of wartime diplomacy took on major significance in the minds of the nation's statesmen and political commentators. Yet much of the conversation among liberal intellectuals was fairly rudimentary. There were several precepts on which everyone agreed: the desirability of close tactical cooperation among the "Big Three" (America, Britain, and the Soviet Union); an early opening of a "second front" in western Europe to liberate France, Belgium, and Holland as well as to relieve

Russia of the main burden in fighting Germany; support for the resistance movements in all the occupied European countries; and the need for some plan to preserve the grand alliance after the war ended. Beyond these general objectives, however, the liberal journals made little effort to analyze the conditions that might produce a permanent peace. On the contrary, the problem of competing national interests and the possibility of postwar power struggles were minimized.

Moreover, most American writers (whether liberal or not) had only the haziest idea of what the war was actually doing to Europe. Very few foresaw how different the world would be after 1945. So, many of their assumptions about international harmony, like their proposals for domestic reform, now seem painfully innocent—a combination of virtuous sentiments and wishful thinking. But then we know how badly it all turned out. Perhaps they were better off not knowing.

Nevertheless, there was one issue that consumed much of their time and interest: the current intentions and future role of the Soviet Union. This preoccupation with Russia was hardly unusual; American intellectuals had been trying to figure out what they thought of the Soviet state since the Bolshevik triumph in 1917. The image of Russia had undergone numerous changes in the preceding twenty years. In the 1920s and early 1930s, a growing number of writers and artists were fascinated with what they liked to call the "socialist experiment." During these years, the Soviet Union was variously depicted as a youthful and energetic society engaged in a stirring industrial and cultural revolution, a concrete example of effective social and economic planning, a true proletarian democracy, a powerful nation guided by wise leaders who pragmatically applied Marxist principles, a workable alternative to capitalism, and a model the Depression-plagued countries of the West would do well to follow. After 1935, as the repressiveness of Stalin's regime became more obvious, and as old Bolsheviks confessed their political sins in the Moscow trials while thousands of less prominent citizens simply disappeared, these favorable estimates declined. In the late 1930s, a small but increasingly influential band of anti-Stalinist intellectuals, gathered principally around *Partisan Review,* helped

deflate the Soviet mystique. But no single event was more shattering to Russian prestige than the announcement of the Nazi–
Soviet pact in 1939. Thereafter, few writers could continue to
believe that Russia was special, that she would never engage in
treacherous diplomacy or balance-of-power politics.[58]

Still, the Communist movement had displayed real heroism
and gained considerable credit in opposing fascism before 1939,
particularly in the Spanish Civil War, where the Soviet Union was
nearly alone in extending military aid to the Loyalist government,
and where individual Party members from many countries went
to fight and often to die. The movement recaptured some of its
moral authority after the Nazis invaded the Soviet Union in June
1941—not only because the Red Army and the Russian people
resisted far more ferociously than anyone expected despite the
awesome damage inflicted on their land and cities, but also because Communists in large numbers joined and frequently led
the underground organizations throughout Europe. Thus by the
time America declared war, the image of Russia had substantially
improved, though it was now to have quite different connotations
from those that flourished in the 1930s.

Most noticeably, the Soviet Union was no longer considered a
model of socialism or a prototype of an alternative society.
Among those liberals who admired the courage of the Russians
in defending their homeland, there was no attempt to translate
such sympathetic portraits of the Soviet war effort into a Marxist
morality play. The *New Republic,* for example, described Russia in
1942 purely as a valued ally "doing a magnificent job" in the
military sphere, and therefore worthy of "trust." After the war,
the editors predicted, the "Russian system" rather than returning to its revolutionary origins "should be able to live as amicably
in the same world as our own."[59]

In their more optimistic moods, writers pointed out the potential similarities between Russia and the West. Max Lerner expressed a widely shared hope that the war experience might draw
the Soviet Union closer to the "standards of Western democracy."[60] Indeed, some commentators asserted that the Russians
had never strayed very far from the world of John Stuart Mill. The
worst one could say about Russia, according to another *New*

Republic contributor, was that it had tried to achieve the "avowed ideals of nineteenth-century liberal democracy" with "methods that are distasteful to the liberals."[61] Henry Wallace did not even find the Soviet "methods" especially "distasteful." In his view, Russia had already developed into an "economic democracy" while the United States remained a "political democracy." Apart from this minor distinction, both nations were striving in concert "for the education, the productivity and the enduring happiness of the common man."[62] Should there be any lingering ambivalence about this collaboration, the *New Republic*'s Washington editor, Michael Straight, advised the Soviets to make it clear that they were using their military power "only in defense of democracy against a fascist rebellion; with that [objective] every liberal will agree."[63] Finally, if these assessments of Russia's fidelity to Western ideals seemed unpersuasive, some American intellectuals could always dispense with political principles altogether, and fall back on adulatory allusions to the "historic fight" of a "simple people" to repel the Nazi invaders.[64]

Liberals were not alone in extolling the heroism of Russian peasants and the democratic instincts of Kremlin bureaucrats. From the innermost sanctum of American conservatism, *Life* magazine raised its voice (and its cameras) in praise of the patriotic Russians who had united under the tough but benevolent leadership of that pipe-smoking man of the people—"Uncle Joe." Throughout the war, *Life* presented an idyllic picture of the Soviet Union suggesting that Communists, like the sturdy British, could be worthy junior partners in sustaining a future Pax Americana.

In 1943, Hollywood registered its own unqualified approval with two films that managed not only to fictionalize Soviet history and society, but also to get many of those responsible for making these movies in political trouble ten years later. *The North Star,* produced by no less a Hollywood sage than Samuel Goldwyn (who, at least in this instance, forgot his dictum about sending messages by Western Union), boasted a script by Lillian Hellman, a musical score by Aaron Copland, and lyrics by Ira Gershwin. Its director was Lewis Milestone. The film itself purported to show the innate nobility of Russian villagers guarding their farms against German tanks and planes, but the brutalities of wartime faded ineluctably into a romantic celebration of agrarian endurance—the Joad family transported to the eastern front.

The North Star, however, did not pretend to examine politics or ideology. *Mission to Moscow* elevated both to the level of myth. Based loosely on the experiences of Joseph E. Davies, America's ambassador to Russia in the 1930s, and allegedly made at the request of the Roosevelt administration, *Mission to Moscow* rivaled Leni Riefenstahl's Nazi-inspired *Triumph of the Will* as a master-piece of propaganda—perhaps, as James Agee remarked, the "first Soviet production to come from a major American stu-dio."[65] On the one hand, the film was suffused with Stalinist homilies, including an authoritative explanation of the Moscow Trials as the occasion to rid the country of Trotskyite saboteurs. On the other hand, the movie presented Russians as really no different from your average American, except that in the Soviet Union everyone spoke with an accent left over from the Yiddish theater. Compared with these media fantasies about Russia, the cheerful musings of liberal intellectuals sounded astute and dis-passionate.

Besides, a number of liberals regarded the Soviet Union less as a participant in the Western movement for democratic but non-Communist reform than as a nation with increasingly con-servative and traditional objectives. Thus they portrayed Russian foreign policy as essentially nonrevolutionary and unthreatening to the West. Paradoxically, they themselves continued to talk about creating new societies after the war while at the same time praising the Russian desire for national security and world-wide stability. Yet these orthodox diplomatic aims they too had come to embrace.

Indeed, from many of their articles it was difficult to tell if the Soviet Union had any postwar ambitions at all. In 1942 and 1943, the *New Republic* repeatedly insisted that Russia wanted only bor-ders secure enough to withstand future invasions. It was "per-fectly clear" to the journal's editors that "Russia's policy is defen-sive, not aggressive."[66] So far, everything Stalin had said or done proved (at least to them) that "he has no intention of Bolsheviz-ing Europe and attaching it as an appendage to Russia."[67] The

Soviet Union was not interested, according to this view, in acquiring new territories or intervening in the domestic politics of nations beyond her boundaries. Even if she were, she would surely fail. "After all," the *New Republic* comforted its readers, neither Moscow nor Washington nor London could dictate the postwar destinies of the liberated countries; "man himself will in the end everywhere decide what sort of regime he will live in."[68]

Of course, it soon occurred to liberals that Moscow might have a few additional goals in mind. Although the Soviets had "sincerely renounced imperialism," George Soule observed, they did covet lands they considered "historically Russian," particularly those that could provide "strategic protection against attack."[69] Having "largely solved her internal economic problems," Max Lerner was certain, Russia would not need "foreign war adventures." Still, he predicted, the Soviet leaders "will want us to keep our hands out of the internal affairs of the postwar countries in Eastern Europe." And despite the economic solutions to which Lerner referred, Russia would apparently require American financial and technological assistance "in the tasks of reconstruction."[70]

But liberals continued to keep their composure regardless of reports from the battlefield. As late as the winter of 1944, with the Red Army firmly entrenched in eastern Europe, Jerome Davis (a regular commentator on Soviet affairs) remained convinced that Russia did not wish to "foist Communism off on other nations by force, revolution or propaganda." In fact, Moscow "would even prefer not to have Communist governments in border states"; instead, the Soviet Union "definitely" wanted postwar regimes that were "democratic and friendly," and that also did not endanger her military safety.[71] Phrased in this fashion, such objectives could scarcely alarm the West. Nevertheless, it did seem that "man himself," at least in eastern Europe, might encounter a few difficulties in determining his own political future.

As the war unfolded in 1943 and 1944, however, liberals began to acknowledge that there were signs of disagreement between the Soviets and the West. All the Allies said they were committed to the creation of democratic governments in Europe, but the

New Republic gently suggested that "there may be differences in the interpretation of democracy." If this were the case, then military and geopolitical considerations would settle the issue. Given the Red Army's steady advance into Poland and Hungary, the editors admitted that "we cannot effectively oppose anything the Soviet Union may insist on doing in the Baltic or Eastern Europe," though there was still no evidence "that its demands in this area will be displeasing to us."[72] Anyway, America and Britain were hardly in a good "tactical" position to quarrel with Stalin about the postwar regimes of countries so close to Russia's strategic interests (and whose prewar rulers were so "deeply reactionary"), while at the same time demanding that Washington and London should decide the fate of western Europe, Italy, Latin America, the Middle East, and Asia.[73] According to Frederick Schuman, the *New Republic*'s resident specialist in realpolitik, the only way to maintain international harmony was for the Big Three to respect each other's spheres of influence.[74] This was not a very inspiring solution to the potential conflicts among the Allies, but it certainly sounded practical.

Occasionally, the *New Republic* could seem positively Machiavellian (or maybe just desperate) in its search for principles the Big Three might share. Heinz Eulau, a frequent analyst of Soviet foreign policy for the journal, argued that all the Allies were inherently conservative and preoccupied with postwar stability. "Stalin," he believed, "desires chaos and revolution in Europe no more than Churchill and Roosevelt do." Specifically, this meant that both Russia and the "Anglo-American bloc" would not tolerate indefinitely the "strong left-wing tendencies at work throughout the European continent." Neither the Soviet Union nor the West was ecstatic about the long-term political implications of the resistance movements; each member of the Big Three wanted to make sure its own security was not threatened by social upheaval and ideological turmoil in the countries its armies occupied. Therefore, Eulau contended, just as America and Britain sought to restrain the underground organizations in western Europe and Greece, so Russia would be foolish to "give up the influence which is falling into her lap" in eastern Europe.[75] Eulau was quick to deny that Russia contemplated the "sovietization" of the Balkan states. Besides, the "overwhelming majority of the common people" in the East did not "fear" Moscow's management; they found it "natural." So Eulau concluded optimistically that "Soviet influence" in eastern Europe "may . . . turn out to be a stabilizing factor," achieving much the same results that America and Britain yearned for in presiding over the postwar fortunes of the West.[76]

Though ingenious, such interpretations conveniently avoided the question of what the Europeans themselves might desire. By concentrating on spheres of influence and balance-of-power diplomacy, the *New Republic* appeared realistic while glossing over any problems that could eventually destroy the grand alliance. Essentially, the journal's editors and contributors anticipated the assessments of Russia's postwar goals set forth both by Henry Wallace in his 1948 presidential campaign and by revisionist historians in the 1960s: The Soviet Union was obsessed with military security and economic reconstruction; it demanded friendly but not necessarily Communist governments on its borders; and it insisted on dominating affairs in eastern Europe while permitting America to do the same in the West. Underlying these propositions was the recognition that, because of the way the war was fought, Washington and London could do little to affect the future regimes of eastern Europe in any case. But what liberals overlooked or didn't want to face before the war's end was the possibility that "friendly" governments might not turn out to be democratic, that indeed Russia would never feel safe until Communists ruled the countries of eastern Europe. Nor could liberals foresee the methods Stalin would use to enforce his ideas about Soviet security. Thus, journals like the *New Republic* assumed that the continuing unity of the Big Three was crucial to world peace, without imagining how the policies of the great powers could conceivably conflict with Europe's own needs and aspirations.

By the time of the Yalta conference in February 1945, however, liberals could no longer ignore the obvious fissures in the alliance. The *New Republic* consoled itself that the Big Three were still working together and had agreed to resolve their differences "somehow or other." But on the question of Poland and the Balkans, the magazine confessed, Yalta "represents a substantial victory for Stalin."[77] Still, not all the returns were in; the ultimate configuration of the eastern European governments depended "on how the decisions are implemented."[78]

Heinz Eulau was more direct. The Russians expected the postwar world to be administered by "the cold considerations of power politics," he asserted, so they were "preparing to remain the arbiters of their own fate through a balance of power favorable to themselves." As far as the future regimes in eastern Europe were concerned, the "decisive test of [their] political reliability is not 'democracy,' but their willingness to cooperate with the Soviet Union." Eulau believed that these governments might still be regarded as "socially progressive in the sense that they propose to introduce far-reaching reforms," and he remained persuaded that Moscow wanted to "maintain peace through a concert of the three great powers." But he was clearly most impressed by the Soviets' lack of illusions at Yalta, by their readiness to snap the "whip over [their] satellites," and by their military and diplomatic aggressiveness.[79] These, presumably, were the latest lessons Russia could teach the West.

If so, they dramatized how much the image of the Soviet Union had altered since the 1930s. By the close of the war, no one spoke of Russia as an embodiment of socialism. The wartime alliance had not revived interest in Marxist ideals. At best, American liberals admired Russia as a powerful military partner rather than as an ideological symbol. She was seen as shrewd, decisive, pragmatic, and tough-minded—values liberals wished their own leaders would emulate. But the affirmative portrait of the Soviet Union as a typically conservative nation-state, the emphasis on the diplomacy of the Big Three, and the acceptance of Keynesian models for future economic reform gave these intellectuals little reason to interest themselves in postwar radical movements or programs. In effect, the war experience (both domestically and internationally) accelerated the demise of the Left. At the time, few writers noticed or lamented its passing.

The War as Holocaust

Among the many victims of World War II, radicalism was only a minor casualty. Its expiration was somewhat less newsworthy than the death of optimism, rationality, and the assumption that there were certain moral limits civilized nations would not dare to exceed even in war.

Most observers, especially in the United States, preferred not to think about these losses. It was easier to suppose that a country's domestic and foreign policy could be explained in traditional political and economic language, that governments were run by reasonable if not always effective leaders, and that human behavior remained fairly comprehensible. Given the persistence of such ideas, American intellectuals continued to discuss presidential politics, Keynesian economics, and international diplomacy in tones that were sober and sensible. The world might no longer be safe but it was still predictable. On only a few occasions did the unfathomable savagery of the war disrupt their equanimity. At these moments, the notion that the struggle was "good" or "progressive" seemed fatuous. The true monstrousness of World War II became unmistakable.

In December 1942, an article appeared in the *New Republic* by Varian Fry, who had spent the two years before Pearl Harbor in Vichy France helping prominent refugee intellectuals and scientists, some of them in Nazi prison camps, escape to the United States. His activities were often dangerous, but he learned much about the conditions of life for those who had become political and ethnic pariahs in occupied Europe.[80] Now Fry presented to the readers of the *New Republic* a knowledgeable description of what was happening to ordinary people in the countries conquered by the Nazis. The details, he remarked simply, "add up to the most appalling picture of mass murder in all human history." Fry outlined in stark images the methods by which millions of Jews, gypsies, Poles, Russians, homosexuals, and political dissidents were being slaughtered: starvation, hanging, executions by firing squads before open graves the victims themselves had been forced to dig, deportation in cattle cars to concentration camps where human beings were destroyed in medical experiments or with poison gas or by the injection of air bubbles into their bloodstream, followed by the extraction of their hair and teeth fillings and the burning of their bodies in crematoria. This was not a mere atrocity tale or propaganda reminiscent of World War I, Fry pointed out; it was a story of "systematic extermination" which seemed hardly possible in the twentieth century. But, he insisted, "we must face the terrible truth" that men in power in the modern world were perfectly capable of committing genocide as a matter of national policy.[81]

A year later, the *New Republic* published a special supplement on the massacre of the European Jews. For once, the journal abandoned its temperate prose style. Like Fry, the editors recoiled from "the thought that a whole people may be in process of annihilation, but nothing is to be gained by a refusal to face reality, however grim and painful." And so they submitted their own exposé on organized butchery. "A man may travel from Amsterdam to Warsaw," the essay declared, "pass through scores of cities where great and historic Jewish communities have existed for a thousand years, and not encounter a single Jew." Half the Jews of Europe had already perished; the rest "exist from day to day under the shadow of an inexorable doom." The plight of the Jew, the journal argued, was fundamentally different from the non-Jew. The latter might also be imprisoned and tortured by the Nazis, but he was "sustained by the hope of survival and of ultimate victory." The Jew was sentenced to death for no other reason than his Jewishness, and "there is nothing he can do to escape this fate." Denouncing those who could do something but refrained, the *New Republic* condemned the "moral weakness which has palsied the hands of our statesmen" as "one of the major tragedies in the history of civilization." The unwillingness of the British and American governments to offer temporary asylum to Jews not yet captured by Hitler, the continued ban on Jewish emigration to Palestine, the lip service paid to the bromide that only the Allies' triumph would salvage European Jewry, sickened the editors. If the Nazis were allowed to "achieve . . . the total destruction of Jewish life in Europe," the journal asserted, the world "will have suffered a moral disaster so overwhelming that military victory will be unable to avert its consequences." The war itself would no longer have any political or human significance.[82]

The editors could not bring themselves to pursue the implications of this idea. They needed to believe that World War II was fought for some purpose beyond national survival, that its goals were rational and just, that the damage caused by the Allies was necessary and not simply an expression of man's primitive urge to destroy everything in sight. In their judgment, "the fate of the Jewish people was one of the issues in this war"—along with the preservation and expansion of the New Deal, the future of democracy in Europe, and the ability of the Big Three to remain united after the war ended.[83] But they could not shut their eyes completely to the horror that lurked just beneath the surface of their wartime aspirations—the nightmare vision of evil and insanity that might yet mock their fondest dreams of social progress.

Clearly, the extinction of the Jews was a matter of public record by 1943. Yet people could not deal intelligibly with such barbarism without assigning blame. Once the enormity of the carnage in Europe was fully known, journals like the *New Republic* demanded that the Nazis be tried after the Allied victory as war criminals. Then, at the very least, specific individuals would be found liable for the consequences of their acts.[84] If one could say precisely who was responsible, the world might not seem so utterly mad.

The gas chambers and the crematoria were regarded as uniquely German atrocities. It was more difficult, however, to maintain a belief in rationality if all the combatants engaged in indiscriminate bloodshed. Whenever they troubled to examine the military tactics of World War II, American liberals were equally disturbed by the strategic bombing of civilian populations. Still, for most of the war they insisted that the methods employed by the Allies were morally distinguishable from those of the Axis.

In 1944, for example, the *New Republic* tried to differentiate between the Nazi reliance on "robot" missiles to terrorize Britain, and the Allies' use of air power over Germany. The robots, the editors argued, could not be guided to any particular target; they maimed and killed wherever they happened to land. Thus "the robot bomb is a weapon of random murder with no military significance. It is far more savage than our saturation bombing of German cities, which has military purpose and gives civilians a chance to take cover in air-raid shelters."[85]

This subtle distinction eluded Dwight Macdonald. In his stubborn view, each side had deliberately chosen to fight a "war of annihilation." Both the Allies and the Nazis depended on science, bureaucratic organization, and mass production to attain victory. These techniques, Macdonald felt, transformed the entire war into an impersonal and irrational holocaust, with defenseless civilians as the main prey whether or not they had time to scurry into air-raid shelters. At the end of the struggle, he declared in the early summer of 1945, three apparitions confronted one another in Europe: "the dying Nazi horror and the surviving Allied horror; the horror of conscious, rationalized destruction of the fabric of Western culture and ethics; and the horror of vast technological power exerted in warmaking by nations with no positive aims and little social consciousness."[86] For Macdonald, World War II had been emptied of purpose by the way it was waged. The war's true nature consisted of violence for its own sake—"the maximum of physical devastation accompanied by the minimum of human meaning."[87]

On the mornings of August 6 and 9, 1945, the world may have momentarily understood what Macdonald was talking about. Within a few hours of each atomic blast, 75,000 people in Hiroshima and 35,000 in Nagasaki lay dead. An additional 130,000 Japanese perished from burns and radiation in the next five years. The American decision to use its most catastrophic weapon seemed to confirm the lessons learned from the concentration camps and the policy of saturation bombing: that this was indeed a war of extermination in which both sides were morally culpable.

Decades later, one commentator pointed out the intimate relationship of the atomic bomb to the war. "The attacks on Hiroshima and Nagasaki," Kai Erikson observed, "were not 'combat' in any of the ways that word is normally used. Nor were they primarily attempts to destroy military targets, for the two cities had been chosen not despite but because they had a high density of civilian housing. Whether the intended audience was Russian or Japanese, or a combination of both . . . the attacks were to be a show, a display, a demonstration." Then Erikson posed a question for those who considered themselves ethically superior to their enemies, but who were nonetheless prepared to utilize their own instruments of mass terror: "What kind of mood does [a nation] have to be in, what kind of moral arrangements must it make, before it is willing to annihilate as many as a quarter of a million human beings for the sake of making a point?" America had won the war but it had not escaped untarnished after all. It had its own brutality to contemplate, its own amends to offer to the world. And Americans would require a new vocabulary to make the consequences of their deed comprehensible: "Once words are found for what the victims suffered, we will also need words for what the victors were all too ready to do."[88]

In 1945, the words would not come; the full implications of the atomic bomb could not be grasped. Bruce Bliven groped for consolation; he hoped atomic power, under the control of the United Nations, would be used for good and not for evil.[89] T.R.B.'s response was less feeble. "In a short week," he mused, "man learned that he had at last found how to blow himself up." So the end of the war brought no peace: "Among my friends I find a curious new sense of insecurity, rather incongruous in the face of military victory."[90]

It remained again for Dwight Macdonald, writing in *Politics,* to address the issue squarely. "This atrocious action," he charged, "places 'us,' the defenders of civilization, on a moral level with 'them,' the beasts of Maidanek." Macdonald was not surprised that peace seemed an anticlimax or that men lacked the mental equipment to deal with the mushroom cloud. The atomic bomb, he contended, rendered concepts like "Good" and "Evil," "democracy" and "progress," obsolete. "Can one imagine," he asked, "that The Bomb could ever be used 'in a good cause'? Do not such means instantly . . . corrupt *any* cause?" Didn't the bomb, like the Nazi death camps, warp and dehumanize everyone involved? In Macdonald's estimation, the use of both atomic fission and poison gas were the end results of remote technological and governmental processes over which the average individual had no control, but in whose name they were always employed. For this reason, he submitted, the "Bomb is the natural product of the kind of society we have created": a society where "vast numbers of citizens can be organized" to create weapons of universal destruction "without even knowing they are doing it." Such a situation suggested to Macdonald that the world was rapidly achieving a "perfect automatism," an "absolute lack of human consciousness" in which projects proceeded inexorably "regardless of ideologies or personalities" until the final solution or the final explosion occurred. These cataclysms appeared utterly mechanical, he asserted; "it is *Götterdämmerung* without the gods."[91]

Nevertheless, Macdonald did believe that certain people could be held accountable. To him, the moral responsibility for Hiroshima and Nagasaki rested with those scientists who developed the bomb, and the political and military leaders who decided on its use. Ignorance of how prolonged or deadly the effects of radioactivity would be did not prevent the scientists from "completing their assignment, nor the army from dropping the bombs." Regarding themselves exclusively as specialists and technicians, assuming that the details of scientific discovery and military planning were "morally neutral," sacrificing their larger obligations as human beings to the narrow task of defeating the enemy, the scientists and generals and politicians were all equally guilty in Macdonald's opinion. The outcome of their gigantic labors, he concluded, was "the most magnificent scientific experiment in history, with cities as the laboratories and people as the guinea pigs."[92]

Macdonald's rage was justified. Yet somehow neither his nor anyone else's revulsion could encompass the murderousness of World War II. A year after the war ended, Mary McCarthy criticized John Hersey (who had recently published an essay in *The New Yorker* on the survivors of Hiroshima) for treating the atomic bomb as if it belonged to the "familiar order of catastrophes—fires, floods, earthquakes." Hersey's traditional journalistic techniques—interviews, human interest stories, statistics—seemed to her irrelevant, an "insipid falsification of the truth of atomic warfare."[93] But what was "true"; what was "relevant"; how should one respond? Macdonald himself confessed that he no longer considered naturalistic description or political analysis "adequate, either esthetically or morally, to cope with the modern horrors."[94]

Perhaps there never would be words to convey what one felt at the instant of revelation. Nor afterward could memory summon the appropriate language. Confronted by the inconceivable, people might have nothing they could think of to say. Alfred Kazin recalled his own speechless reaction sitting in a London newsreel theater where he and others watched the first films of the newly liberated Belsen concentration camp. Maybe this was the most authentic, or at least the most human, response to the "modern horrors":

> On the screen, sticks in black-and-white prison garb leaned on a wire, staring dreamily at the camera; other sticks shuffled about, or sat vaguely on the ground, next to an enormous pile of bodies, piled up like cordwood, from which protruded legs, arms, heads. A few guards were collected sullenly in a corner, and for a moment a British Army bulldozer was shown digging an enormous hole in the ground. Then the sticks would come back on the screen, hanging on the wire, looking at us.
>
> It was unbearable. People coughed in embarrassment, and in embarrassment many laughed.[95]

On the Eve of Victory

As the Allied armies inched closer to the heart of Germany and Japan, American and European intellectuals began to contemplate more realistically the prospects of a world without war. Although everyone welcomed the approach of peace, some writers viewed the future with decidedly mixed emotions. World War II had not only claimed millions of lives and reduced great cities to rubble; it had also shattered many assumptions about the ways people and nations would necessarily change under the impact of the struggle. Liberals and Marxists alike had described the war as "revolutionary"; they expected profound readjustments in every country's political and economic institutions. Now they appeared far less convinced that such transformations were likely. Instead, they looked forward to the postwar years with a sense of uncertainty and confusion.

Nothing seemed to be working out quite as predicted. A number of intellectuals had anticipated that the resistance movements would reshape European politics after the war. Hannah Arendt, herself a refugee from fascism and therefore presumably more knowledgeable about Continental affairs than her American counterparts, suggested in *Partisan Review* that the wartime collapse of the European nation-state and the class structure on which it rested could lead to new political and social arrangements. In her estimation, the antifascist underground organizations might eventually seize power with the promise to achieve a truly integrated federation of all the European countries and a socialist reconstruction of each nation's economy. Nonetheless, Arendt admitted that the imminent "return of the Governments-in-exile may quickly put a stop to this new feeling of European solidarity, for the very existence of these governments depends on the restoration of the status quo. Hence their inveterate tendency is to weaken and disperse the resistance movements with the aim of destroying the political renaissance of the European peoples."[96] Moreover, she realized that a division of the postwar world into spheres of influence dominated by the United States and the Soviet Union, coupled with the already apparent inclination of the resistance movements to concentrate on purely domestic rather than Continental issues, would eliminate any hope of an indigenous European revolution. For the moment, Arendt was unsure whether the resistance organizations could triumph over conventional power politics, but she did suspect that the dream of European unity might very well disintegrate as each country became a client state of either Moscow or Washington.[97]

George Orwell shared Arendt's misgivings about the possibilities of building a new world on the ruins of the old. Reassessing the political situation in Britain in 1945, he acknowledged to the readers of *Partisan Review* that he had previously "over-emphasized the anti-Fascist character of the war, exaggerated the social changes that were actually occurring, and under-rated the enormous strength of the forces of reaction." Like many of his contemporaries on both sides of the Atlantic, Orwell assumed at the outset of the war that the Allied nations would have to move to the left in order to survive, that victory and revolution were inseparable. Now he conceded with some amazement that, while winning the war, the Allies had not embraced any form of socialism. Britain adopted a semi-planned economy, yet "there has been no real shift of power and no increase in genuine democracy. The same people still own all the property and usurp all the best jobs." At the same time, the United States appeared to be stronger and more capitalist than ever. Looking back over several years of mistaken judgments and misplaced commitments, Orwell concluded that "the first admission [intellectuals] ought to make is that *we were all wrong.*"[98]

Dwight Macdonald was less willing than Orwell to repent, but he sounded equally bewildered by the effects of World War II on American life. Far from delivering the nation into the arms of either Keynesian visionaries or reactionary militarists, he observed, "the war has brought national prosperity on an unprecedented scale; the cream has naturally gone to big business and the rich, but there has been plenty of milk left over for the workers and farmers; guns *and* butter have been produced, to the surprise of both leftist and conservative prophets." As a consequence, the earlier conviction that the "common people" would engineer a "series of popular revolutions" which were to be "socialist as to economics and democratic as to politics" had nearly vanished. "The chances of anything like that happening in this country in the foreseeable future," Macdonald snorted, "would seem to be as close to nil as at any time in our history."[99]

Macdonald blamed these depressing developments largely on the nature of the war itself, but he also deplored the absence of any effort to justify its objectives on moral or ideological grounds. "It is notable," he remarked, "that everything possible [was] done by our leaders to *de-politicalize* this war." The Office of War Information portrayed Hitler as "a bully, a murderer, a thief, a gangster," but rarely as "a *fascist.*" Nor did it try to define what democracy meant beyond a few patriotic allusions to the American way of life. In the meantime, Macdonald complained, the Soviet Union never pretended to fight "for any international socialist ideals, but simply for national survival." The Allies thus chose to wage the war without reference to "basic values and ultimate ends"; they submitted to the "brute force of events" and refused "to look too far ahead." In Macdonald's opinion, this flight from "positive principles" contributed to a general loss of faith in social ideas and coherent programs among writers as well as national leaders.[100] The result was a political and intellectual vacuum just as the world prepared to celebrate the end of the war.

What most astonished Arendt, Orwell, and Macdonald was the persistence of traditional institutions, particularly the resilience of capitalism in England and the United States. While the Depression of the 1930s and World War II had forced the British and American governments to intervene more directly in economic matters, neither crisis had proved a catalyst for revolution. The prospects for socialism seemed greater in western Europe after the war only because the problems of reconstruction were more formidable. But even there, the impending conflict between the United States and the Soviet Union might soon strangle the impulse for social change.

Yet whether one was pessimistic or merely perplexed about the future, it was clear to intellectuals that America alone had benefited from the war. Not only was its economy thriving, but its political system had remained stable throughout the struggle. The personal and social upheavals familiar to Europeans and Asians appeared incomprehensible to people in the United States. Americans could afford to fight the war without worrying about its long-term political or ideological meaning because they assumed the future would be both a continuation of and an improvement upon the present. The majority of Americans neither expected nor desired substantial changes in their institutions. They liked themselves the way they were. Few in Europe or the Far East could say the same.

Yet America was not completely immune to fate or uncertainty. Whatever the effects of the Depression and war, the one fixed star in the national firmament for the past twelve years was Franklin Roosevelt. Whether they worshiped or despised FDR, a generation of Americans counted upon his presence in the White House. When he died in April 1945, the future even for the United States no longer seemed so assured.

The reaction of writers did not differ from that of ordinary citizens. T.R.B. found himself in tears, overcome by a childlike feeling of "loss and bewilderment."[101] Bruce Bliven eulogized Roosevelt as "one of the greatest leaders who ever lived" because with his help the scales of history "were balanced at last in the right direction." But Roosevelt's chief appeal, Bliven believed, was as a "father image" to millions of people at home and abroad, a "rock of security and confidence in a world of chaos."[102]

That was exactly the trouble, Dwight Macdonald reflected. Roosevelt "had indeed become the Father of his Country, using the term in the Freudian rather than the Fourth-of-July sense." In Macdonald's judgment, FDR served as "the Father especially of the left-of-center section of American society. This was an unhealthy state of affairs, both politically and psychologically," because it encouraged liberals and the labor movement to rely on Roosevelt's wisdom and protection rather than on their own ideas and will power. As long as Roosevelt lived, they behaved like adolescents—unwilling to take chances, unable to assert their independence. But "rebellion against paternal authority," Macdonald pointed out, "is the road to maturity for society as for the individual." Perhaps with Roosevelt's death, America "will now grow up."[103]

Macdonald may have been unfair both to Roosevelt and to the liberals. But objectivity was never his strongest suit. Anyway, he was right about the future. In the next few years, Americans might not become entirely mature, but they would certainly shed their innocence.

2

The Shattered Peace

Despite the death of Franklin Roosevelt and the uneasiness with which certain intellectuals regarded the postwar era, most Americans instinctively understood how enviable their prospects were when compared to those of other people in other lands. In the fall of 1945, the United States was triumphant, powerful, and bursting with vigor. Among the major combatants in World War II, America had made the fewest sacrifices and reaped the greatest rewards. Its armies controlled the most important industrial regions on the globe: western Europe and Japan. Its political influence could be felt daily in Latin America, North Africa, the Middle East, India, and China. Only the Soviet Union and eastern Europe stood outside the American orbit. Meanwhile, the nation's economy flourished as the healthiest and most productive in the world, ready to undertake the pleasurable task of sustaining prosperity rather than the grim burden of resurrecting charred villages and bombed-out cities. Above all, the United States alone had entered the atomic age—an awesome accomplishment that presumably guaranteed the nation's military and technological dominance for decades. Blessed with all these advantages, the American people and their leaders could reasonably expect to redesign the postwar world in accordance with their own perceptions and values.

The euphoric mood of 1945 was reminiscent of 1919, one writer remembered. Once again "the whole face of the world seemed changed, and a long period of peace and promise must surely lie ahead. One felt a whole new world was opening up before one." Just as at the end of World War I, intellectuals and artists could anticipate a new release for their creative energies; the legendary excitement of the 1920s would be revived and perhaps exceeded. Europe might lie in ruins, but this time there was no need to go abroad: "We could move Paris to New York and begin it all over again here." The United States had become the center not only of power but also of culture and ideas.[1]

Within five years, America's serenity and optimism had evaporated. By the summer of 1950, the nation had suffered a series of shocks that undermined its self-esteem and sense of omnipotence. Half the planet appeared indifferent or hostile to American ambitions. The Soviet Union, having rebuilt its damaged economy and tightened its grip on eastern Europe, was now an equal competitor in the contest for global supremacy. No event dramatized this parity more graphically than Russia's explosion of its own atomic bomb in 1949. In the same year, the open door that American diplomats had struggled to maintain in China since the beginning of the century slammed shut with the victory of the Communists and the flight of Chiang Kai-shek to Formosa. In the rest of Asia, as well as in the Middle East and Latin America, the United States confronted a future filled with instability and revolution. To compound the insult, many western Europeans also sounded distrustful of America's benevolence, and yearned for neutrality in a divided world. At home, the nation enjoyed a prosperousness surpassing the wildest fantasies of the 1920s, but the interminable tensions of the Cold War bred an atmosphere of such insecurity and panic that this unprecedented affluence seemed curiously unsatisfying. Worst of all, even while the American people were still cherishing the military masterpieces of World War II, they found themselves fighting yet another war in Korea—a war that, for the first time since 1812, they discovered they could not win.

Faced with the collapse of so many illusions, a large number of Americans engaged in a thunderous debate between 1945 and the early 1950s about what went wrong. The participants included politicians with innumerable axes to grind and scores to settle; generals and industrialists dedicated to the preservation of the free world and free markets; metaphysicians masquerading as foreign service officers and intelligence experts; ex-radicals who had switched their allegiance from the Comintern to the FBI and the congressional investigating committees; labor leaders and Hollywood luminaries presenting themselves as newly minted specialists on the Communist menace; newspaper reporters and gossip columnists with the inside dope on sabotage and subversion; clerics fulminating from pulpits, revival tents, and television studios on the perils of atheistic Marxism; professors and university administrators who staunchly defended the academic freedom of those with whom they already agreed. Yet despite this clamor for explanations and scapegoats, much of the discussion missed the point. The question was not who might be responsible for America's failures in foreign policy, but whether the nation should ever have assumed it could determine the character of the postwar world.

The intellectual community did not wish to be excluded from the great debate. But it too entered the battle armed with a set of untested convictions time and reality would demolish. At the close of World War II, many writers—particularly those of the liberal persuasion—believed in the following propositions: To inspire a movement for domestic reform, America required a strong, charismatic president whose forceful style mattered as much as his political programs; to achieve a prosperous economy and avoid the twin disasters of depression and inflation, the nation's leaders needed to commit themselves to some form of Keynesian planning; to ensure international peace and stability, Europe and the underdeveloped countries would have to be reconstructed under the auspices of the United Nations, while the wartime cooperation between the United States and the Soviet Union must be perpetuated at all costs.

These ideas bore little relation to the actual problems of the postwar years. However articulate and authoritative a president might sound, he alone could not overcome congressional opposition or public apathy. Without a vibrant, independent constituency that did not have to count on the personality or rhetoric of a particular president, sweeping social change was most unlikely. And the absence of such a liberal movement was one of Franklin Roosevelt's more dubious legacies.

Additionally, the intellectuals' faith in Keynesian solutions to economic difficulties rested on their supposition that the predicaments of the 1930s would continue to plague the country after 1945. During the war, liberal journalists and social critics worried about the chronic dangers of mass unemployment, widespread poverty, corporate resistance to the rights and very existence of trade unions, and a chaotic cycle of booms and busts. But postwar America had to deal with quite different dilemmas. The need to prevent another economic crack-up faded before the effort to control the constant rise in prices for consumer goods. The haunting fear of joblessness gave way to the issue of how government could protect the purchasing power of a surprisingly affluent labor movement and middle class.

In fact, the nation's economic structure underwent a transformation more profound than writers had imagined in their most elaborate blueprints for a "new America." Few foresaw the harmonious marriage of government, business, the military, and the unions that became an accustomed feature of American life after 1945. Nor did they anticipate the phenomenal breeding of babies, which in turn generated a demand for every conceivable product and service industry could provide. Nor were they prepared for substantial alterations in corporate behavior: the speed with which businesses converted to and expanded civilian production to satisfy the insatiable desires of a population released from the wartime restrictions on what it might buy; the willingness to diversify and experiment with different kinds of merchandise; the gradual shift from pitched battles on the barricades with militant workers over wages and hours to quiet negotiations with labor leaders over fringe benefits and pension plans enshrined in long-term strike-free contracts; the dependence on government subsidies for airports, highways, foreign trade, scientific research, and education, each of which helped improve the technological and managerial efficiency of the private sector; the reliance on national defense as the uniquely American version of deficit financing and Keynesian pump-priming. Most of all, liberal intellectuals could not know in 1945 that these developments would soon make prosperity the crucial factor in remolding the nation's political and social institutions.

Finally, the rest of the world refused to conform to the expectations of American writers. The wartime alliances swiftly disintegrated; the United Nations appeared helpless and irrelevant; democracy seemed permanently confined to western Europe; and
the United States wrestled with the Soviet Union to see who
could best fill the military and political vacuum left over from
World War II. International relations turned out to be neither
amicable nor orderly. Instead, they were marked by ideological
combat, a fierce rivalry for spheres of influence, anticolonial
upheavals in the Third World, and a nuclear arms race that
threatened to vaporize everyone on the planet.

Since events at home and abroad diverged so sharply from
what intellectuals envisioned in 1945, they were as eager as their
fellow citizens to figure out what happened and whom one could
blame. During the next three years, writers quarreled among
themselves about foreign policy, domestic politics, and liberal
values. For a time, they searched frantically for alternatives to the
growing belligerency between the United States and the Soviet
Union. By the late 1940s, however, the intellectual community as
well as the American people had reached a new consensus, at
least on international affairs. The guiding assumptions of World
War II were replaced by the stern orthodoxies of the Cold War.
These remained largely unchallenged and unshaken until they
decomposed in the jungles of Vietnam.

The New President

All presidents undergo reevaluation after they leave office. But
Harry Truman's subsequent reputation has fluctuated more
dramatically than most inhabitants of the White House. Over the
years, Truman has been cast as a bumbler, a demagogue, a decisive statesman, a man of the people, an early prophet of the Great
Society, a political wizard, and a simple-minded warmonger.
Every politician facing disaster on election day has comforted
himself with the memory of Truman's miraculous victory in 1948
(though two of his recent admirers, Gerald Ford in 1976 and
Jimmy Carter in 1980, were unable to duplicate his feat at the
polls no matter how many times they invoked his name). After a

suitable interlude, historians and journalists have come to consider Truman a superior president whose virtues were sadly unrecognized during his reign and whose flaws now appear more charming than dangerous. Many of the same judgments are being advanced retrospectively on behalf of Dwight Eisenhower—perhaps because, as one less appreciative commentator recalled, Ike "managed to get through eight consecutive years in office . . . without doing anything catastrophic," which is more than one can say for most of his successors.[2] The favorable reassessment of past presidential performances is often reinforced by the feeling that they were more adept than we in coping with, or eluding, the world's disarray.

For these reasons, some historians seem almost mystified by the attacks upon Truman in his own time. They cannot understand why conservatives should have criticized his foreign policy, since its distinguishing feature was a firm opposition to Communist expansion. Nor can they fathom the liberals' hostility to his domestic record, since Truman clearly wanted to enlarge the New Deal. And they are bemused by the intellectuals' antipathy to Truman's brand of leadership, since he sought to be a strong and dynamic president. Those who sympathize with Truman's achievements eventually conclude that his contemporaries must have disliked his mannerisms and personal style, that they were blinded by their idolatry of Franklin Roosevelt and therefore underestimated Truman's real worth.[3]

Unquestionably, Truman suffered in comparison with FDR. Liberal intellectuals especially found his public personality vaguely depressing after twelve years of Roosevelt's buoyancy and magnetism. Just as they were later embarrassed by Lyndon Johnson's Texas drawl and his inability to master television (in contrast to their enthusiasm for John F. Kennedy's New England twang, his elegant demeanor, and his witty press conferences), so they complained that Truman could not deliver a speech or formulate an idea without flattening his vowels, jerking his arms like a marionette, and lulling his audiences to sleep. "There is no bugle note in his voice," the *New Republic*'s T.R.B. lamented in 1945, and "little evidence that he has shown of being able to lift and inspire the masses."[4] In this view, Truman was a crushing disappointment. He possessed neither the flair for leadership nor the talent for phrasemaking so necessary in a modern president.

Not only did Truman lack Roosevelt's eloquence and vision, he also surrounded himself with men most writers dismissed as cronies and bores. His appointees seemed "humdrum" and "prosaic" to T.R.B., not at all like the "gay, audacious" New Dealers who flocked to Washington in 1933.[5] I. F. Stone, the most indefatigable scourge of official pomposity in the Washington press corps, whose columns appeared in such liberal bastions as *PM* and the *Nation,* was similarly unimpressed by the "big-bellied good-natured guys" Truman installed in his Cabinet. To Stone, the nominations of Tom Clark as attorney general and John Snyder as secretary of the treasury heralded not the ascendancy of the common man but the arrival of a "new mediocrity." Roosevelt's sophisticated entourage had been supplanted by people "one was accustomed to meet in county courthouses," not in the postwar capital of the free world.[6]

Some observers feared that Truman's mundane personality and his dependence on political hacks, his loyalty to the Democratic party rather than to liberal ideals, were contributing to the intellectual deterioration of Washington itself. After a year of Truman's tenure, T.R.B. could not discern any "new ideas" or "thinking of importance" emanating from either the White House or Congress. "Where are all the bright young men who were here ten years ago?" he wondered. The New Dealers, the brain-trusters, the innovative lawyers and economists "used to inspire so much hope." Now the spirit of the capital was "slow and plodding. There's a sterility about Washington—perhaps about the whole country."[7]

Yet no matter how much writers deplored Truman's style, they objected far more strenuously to his policies. What opponents ultimately found offensive in Lyndon Johnson was not his accent but his war in Vietnam. What angered many intellectuals about Harry Truman was not so much his inarticulateness as his blunders in domestic and foreign affairs. They held him accountable for squandering the inheritance of the New Deal and World War II. Whether or not their appraisal was accurate, their assaults on the Truman administration were motivated less by the prejudice some historians have imputed to them, and more by the sense that Truman had violated the principles of liberalism. From 1945 to 1948, the intellectual community criticized Truman more often for what he did than for who he was.

Within a year of Roosevelt's death, his legendary political coalition had fragmented. In 1946, Truman confronted a swarm of problems he seemed powerless to solve: the exodus from Washington of veteran New Dealers like secretary of the interior Harold Ickes, a restive and increasingly conservative Congress, unconstrained inflation, a cascade of strikes by workers for higher wages, generalized discontent among farmers and the middle class.

If these predicaments were not enough to overwhelm Truman, he was scolded by writers for his apparent indifference to social reform. As promulgated by journals like the *New Republic,* the postwar liberal agenda called for the adoption of Keynesian strategies to achieve full employment, the maintenance of price and rent controls, an expanded Social Security system, federal aid to public education, a national health care program, and extensive civil rights legislation.[8]

Truman, however, declined to embark on a new domestic crusade. Instead, he antagonized what remained of Roosevelt's constituency by proposing a bill that threatened to draft striking railroad workers into the army. In response, the *New Republic* denounced Truman for having dreamed up the "most vicious piece of anti-union legislation ever introduced by an American President."[9]

Nevertheless, the magazine continued to regard Truman as marginally preferable to other putative leaders. But he clearly needed help. Thus the editors urged their readers to support liberal Democrats in the upcoming congressional elections. For the moment, the *New Republic* rejected the idea of forming a third party because "any such movement now would guarantee a Republican victory."[10]

With or without a third party, the results of the 1946 congressional election were extremely disheartening to liberals. For the first time since 1930, Republicans won majorities in both the House and Senate. Although the *New Republic* claimed that this

conservative resurgence could not be interpreted as an indictment of the New Deal, the editors conceded the current exhaustion of "progressive" ideas. Traditional Democrats had stayed
home, the journal explained, because they were disgusted with
Truman's obvious ineptitude in curbing inflation and managing
the postwar economy.[11] For advocates of reform, the portents
were bleak. Contemplating the possibility of a Republican president in 1948, many liberals were no longer certain they could
rescue Harry Truman from political oblivion.

Liberal intellectuals may have been dismayed by Truman's
domestic gaffes, but they were even more upset by his conduct
of foreign policy. Here Truman's shortcomings as a world leader,
in contrast to Roosevelt's grasp of global complexities, seemed
most pronounced. It was not that writers believed Truman had
incited a conflict with the Soviet Union immediately after he took
office. Rather, they accused him of lacking Roosevelt's skills at
mediation. In their eyes, Truman's glaring weakness was his refusal to seek a rapprochement with the Russians. His unyielding
rhetoric and his simplistic view of international relations made an
already tense situation far worse. Truman's decision to "get
tough" with the Soviet Union offended liberals because such a
stance offered no prospect of reconciliation; it subverted the
unity of the Big Three while raising the specter of a new and
potentially more destructive war.

Yet few writers could suggest an alternative to the impending
collision between America and Russia beyond the plea for a rational dialogue and greater understanding on both sides. By the end
of World War II, liberal intellectuals had lost much of their previous naïveté about Soviet intentions and the likelihood of cooperation among the superpowers. Still, journals like the *New Republic*
continued to assert that "Russia and the United States need each
other." The Soviet Union required American "money and machinery to help rebuild her shattered economy." Conversely, the
United States had to reach some sort of accord with the Russians
in order to avoid the menace of a future war. Soon after Roosevelt's death, therefore, the editors urged Truman to reaffirm "the
fact that the United States has no fundamental quarrel with
Russia and certainly none that cannot be settled by friendly discussion."[12]

But what exactly was there to discuss? The *New Republic*'s entreaties were unassailable in theory; they simply hadn't much
foundation in diplomatic, political, economic, or ideological reality. The editors were not entirely oblivious to this dilemma. Although they persistently exhorted America and Britain to support the "democratic forces" in postwar Europe, they admitted
that it was difficult to determine just who the democrats were,
especially in the countries under Soviet control. Democracy, after
all, could not be defined exclusively in terms of the American
experience, the journal warned its readers; it had a different
meaning in different places.[13] In the case of Poland, for example,
the *New Republic* dismissed the Western-endorsed government-
in-exile as composed mainly of "feudal reactionaries." So long as
Russia abided by the agreements made at Yalta and Potsdam to
hold "free and secret" elections, this was a sufficient demonstration of her democratic impulses to placate the editors—at least
for a while.[14]

In the meantime, during the transition period before elections,
they thought the West was hardly in a moral position to impose
its own narrow conceptions of democracy on the countries of
eastern Europe. The *New Republic* did not deny that Moscow was
exerting "terrific pressure" on the lands occupied by the Red
Army, that Russia was establishing regimes it could easily manipulate, and that it was using "techniques of political control which
are objectionable to democratic nations." But the Soviet Union's
disregard for democratic niceties in eastern Europe was balanced
in the editors' opinion by Washington's resolve to "keep the
atomic bomb our exclusive property"—though what these two
policies had in common was not instantly clear. More to the
point, since the West had never displayed much antagonism to
the prewar dictatorships in eastern Europe or to Franco's fascist
regime in Spain, it appeared hypocritical to the *New Republic* that
the Truman administration would now complain so stridently
about the absence of formal democracy in the Soviet sphere. The
journal concluded that Russia should be criticized when it
flagrantly insulted liberal principles, but Moscow also deserved
applause when it sponsored "coalition governments" committed
to "agrarian reform" and the nationalization of a country's industrial resources. Soviet methods in eastern Europe might not be

"democratic in the Western parliamentary sense," the journal confessed, but Moscow was encouraging economic improvements "which are favorable to the eventual emergence of democracy."[15]

The *New Republic*'s logic often sounded circuitous on these issues because the editors were trying desperately to find some philosophical rationale for an accommodation between the United States and the Soviet Union. The trouble was that neither nation presently had any practical motivations for such a détente. They cooperated during World War II not because of some political or ideological affinity, but because of the threat posed to each by Nazi Germany. No comparable reason for preserving their wartime alliance now existed. Thus the liberals who wrote for or read the *New Republic* took refuge in abstractions about "democracy," "fascism," "reaction"—words left over from the Depression and the war that no longer had much relevance when applied to current international problems. In actuality, there was little America and Russia could "understand" about or "discuss" with one another.

Occasionally, the *New Republic*'s editors recognized the sublime implausibility of what they were proposing. By 1946, weary of being ignored, they began to accuse both Truman and Stalin of destroying the peace. The Russians created uneasiness and distrust in the West, the journal argued, by their authoritarian rule at home, their unilateral actions in eastern Europe, and their unpredictable diplomatic behavior throughout the world.[16] Not to be outdone, the Truman administration heightened Soviet fears by opposing all "popular movements" on the grounds that they might be "Communist-led," and by endorsing Winston Churchill's hyperbolic image of a Europe divided by an "iron curtain," which barred any opportunity for "peaceful coexistence" among the great powers.[17] Given this dismal scenario, the *New Republic* despaired of finding a solution to the intensifying struggle between an "intransigent Soviet nationalism" and an "emergent American reaction." Disdaining compromise, each nation was hurtling toward an "unjustifiable, inexcusable and altogether dangerous break. And both sides are to blame."[18]

While the *New Republic* did not think Truman completely responsible for the deterioration of American–Soviet relations, neither was the journal satisfied that he possessed the wisdom or the sensitivity to explore new diplomatic strategies. Just as he failed to control the peacetime economy and galvanize the Roosevelt coalition at home, so he could not imagine a reprieve from the Cold War abroad. In both domestic and foreign affairs, Truman had inherited a set of excruciatingly difficult problems. With this, his critics sympathized. But to those liberals for whom the *New Republic* spoke, Truman simply seemed incapable of coping with the postwar world. By the end of 1946, they were actively searching for another political champion—someone who would miraculously combine Roosevelt's passion for social reform with his vision of international accord. It was not long before a suitable messiah appeared.

The Liberals and Henry Wallace

On September 12, 1946, Truman's secretary of commerce delivered an iconoclastic speech on foreign policy at New York's Madison Square Garden. Within a week, secretary of state James Byrnes vociferously objected to the president that such speeches interfered with delicate negotiations between the United States and the Soviet Union currently taking place in Paris. Truman, who had initially approved the contents of the address, now retracted his support. On September 19, he fired his secretary of commerce.

Normally, this intramural dispute between Cabinet officials would have little effect on American intellectual life. But the secretary of commerce was no ordinary bureaucrat. He was instead the last remaining spokesman in the Truman administration for the New Deal and the preservation of the wartime alliance. He was also a man with a sense of mission. Save for the internal conflicts within the Democratic party, he might himself have been president. His departure, therefore, touched off a fierce controversy over the next two years about America's role in the world. Ultimately, he came to symbolize the national yearning for an alternative to the Cold War.

Henry Wallace sprang from an illustrious family of Iowa farmers who in the early twentieth century had experimented with new methods of cross-breeding and more scientific techniques of tilling the soil. As "progressive" farmers, they believed in efficiency, innovation, planning, cooperatives, and free trade. Wallace never forgot these creeds. He converted what he learned in Iowa into a social philosophy equally applicable to domestic and international concerns. Yet far from being an eccentric theorist, Wallace spoke from a position of power—first as Roosevelt's secretary of agriculture and then as vice-president from 1940 to 1944. Though eventually displaced by Harry Truman, Wallace returned to the Cabinet as secretary of commerce—until the fateful day he found himself without a job or a public platform.

His unemployment was brief. Wallace's views were well known. At home, he had long advocated a Keynesian approach to economic problems which emphasized higher productivity, full employment, price ceilings to restrain inflation, a wide range of federally financed social services, and civil rights legislation for black people. Abroad, he stood for friendship between the United States and Russia, the acceptance of semipermanent spheres of influence so that Washington and Moscow might each feel secure, international controls over atomic energy, reciprocal trade between the West and the Soviet bloc, and a policy of peaceful competition among the superpowers to test the relative merits of capitalism and socialism. Like his colleagues in the administration, Wallace did not think America should tolerate Communist expansion beyond eastern Europe, nor did he approve the suppression of civil liberties within Russia itself. Nevertheless, his opinions were sufficiently heretical by 1946 that many prominent Americans (corporate executives, southern Democratic congressmen, conservative Republicans, militant anti-Communists, members of the diplomatic establishment) distrusted his presence in the Cabinet and cheered his dismissal. In the eyes of liberals, however, Wallace had made precisely the right enemies.[19] So in October 1946, barely a month after his resignation, the *New Republic* announced that Wallace would become its chief editor (Michael Straight now served as publisher and Bruce Bliven shifted to "editorial director"). From this new rostrum, Wallace promised to expand the magazine's coverage and readership, while refocusing its articles to take into greater account the possibilities of political action.[20] Once again, he had a portfolio.

Wallace's reign at the *New Republic* certainly altered the magazine, though whether he improved its quality is debatable. During his year as editor in 1947, the journal's circulation climbed from 40,000 to 100,000 subscribers. Wallace clearly enhanced the *New Republic*'s prestige and impact: It became the authoritative voice of those liberals whom Truman's domestic and foreign programs had alienated. But the magazine's style also grew more journalistic, less analytical and speculative. The *New Republic* began to concentrate almost exclusively on political and economic problems, even in its book reviews. Extended discussions of literature and the arts nearly vanished. An increasing number of contributors regarded themselves not as intellectuals but as activists, direct participants in the events they wrote about. And Wallace himself was the supreme example of the author as crusader. His editorials carried political weight because he was obviously preparing for future political battles. Unfortunately, his hunger to rejoin the fray too often resulted in the journal telling its readers what it wanted them to hear, rather than what they might need to know.

Whatever the deficiencies of the *New Republic* in 1947, its editors and subscribers could always count on the Truman administration to perpetrate some new outrage. No event in the entire postwar period evoked more wrath among liberal intellectuals than the proclamation in March of the Truman doctrine as the cornerstone of American foreign policy. Originally conceived as an offer of economic and military aid to the governments of Greece and Turkey (which were fighting and losing their respective civil wars with native guerrillas, reformers, revolutionaries, and other bothersome malcontents), the doctrine rapidly escalated into a justification for thwarting Communist expansion everywhere on the globe. Specifically, it defined Soviet aggression not only as the Red Army marching across national borders, but also as a form of internal subversion sponsored by the Kremlin. Presuming that revolutionaries were inevitably the agents of Moscow's imperialist ambitions, the Truman doctrine implied that America possessed the right and the obligation to intervene on behalf of pro-Western anti-Communist regimes whenever their survival seemed endangered. In effect, the United States cast itself in the role of world policeman, seeking to prevent forcible social change in other countries no matter what the local conditions, and committing the nation's energies to a limitless defense of the international status quo.

Liberals were appalled. The Truman doctrine expounded a view of the world they had been resisting since the end of the war. More important, they now had a concrete issue that crystallized their opposition to the president. In the *New Republic*, Henry Wallace condemned the doctrine as a "widening of the conflict against the Soviet Union." Angrier and more eloquent than he would ever be again, Wallace believed Truman's new policy meant that "every reactionary government and every strutting dictator will be able to hoist the anti-Communist skull and bones, and demand that the American people rush to his aid." Having embarked on this path, he declared, the United States was abandoning forever the goal of international cooperation. In sum, Wallace argued that the Truman doctrine bypassed the United Nations, hardened the division of the world into two hostile camps, and invited an arms race which could only lead to another war.[21]

To avoid this frightful outcome, Wallace proposed a sophisticated and surprisingly pragmatic revision of American diplomacy. On the one hand, he urged a "world reconstruction program, underwritten by American resources and administered by the UN." The ostensible purpose of such largess was to rebuild those countries devastated by World War II, as well as to help underdeveloped lands enter the twentieth century. But Wallace's altruism was tempered by his assumption that a massive injection of dollars into the world's bloodstream would restore economic stability, raise purchasing power overseas, and eventually result in more foreign outlets for American exports and investments. Thus the United States could conveniently dispose of its industrial and agricultural surpluses, and escape another depression.[22]

On the other hand, Wallace and the *New Republic* called for substantial American trade with Russia and eastern Europe in order to more effectively influence events in the Communist world. The editors did not suppose that the influx of American merchandise and capital would change the politics of eastern Europe or halt its drift toward socialism. But they were suggesting that the United States might better protect its interests through the shrewd use of economic assistance, thereby making the Soviet bloc increasingly dependent on Western technology, products, money, and attitudes.[23]

Given the political climate of postwar America, these recommendations generated no visible enthusiasm in the White House or the state department. Instead, Wallace and his fellow liberals were ridiculed as hopelessly innocent and utopian. Yet ten years later, the Eisenhower administration translated many of their ideas into the language of peaceful coexistence, with dutiful allusions to the "spirit of Camp David." During the early 1970s, Richard Nixon and Henry Kissinger embraced somewhat the same policies, describing them as "détente." In this respect, Henry Wallace was far ahead of his time.

In another sense, however, the times were ahead of him. At the very moment Wallace and the *New Republic* prescribed a program of international aid as an antidote to the Truman doctrine, the American government presented its own remedy for Europe's economic distress. With the unveiling of the Marshall Plan, much of the liberal hostility to Truman's foreign policy was defused. Suddenly, Wallace lost his most compelling issue. In his contest with Truman, he never regained the initiative.

At the outset, liberals felt ambivalent about the Marshall Plan, not only because it preempted their arguments but also because its intentions were unclear. Advertised as an effort to rehabilitate the war-ravaged economies of countries on both sides of the Iron Curtain, the Marshall Plan seemed basically designed to improve conditions in western Europe. Indeed, the Truman administration defended the plan before Congress as a device to eliminate poverty and political instability in the West, thereby vaccinating America's allies against the social viruses on which Communism presumably thrived. At the same time, the government publicized the Marshall Plan as a means of re-creating foreign markets for American products, thus making the entire scheme sound more palatable to conservatives.

These conflicting rationales disconcerted Truman's critics. T.R.B.'s mixed reaction illustrated their predicament. While he praised the administration's offer of massive relief, food, and loans to western Europe, he distrusted America's underlying motivations. He thought it ironic that the government should exploit anti-Russian sentiments as well as the fear of a future recession in order to justify "one of the most generous international programs in history."[24] Editorially, the *New Republic* considered the Marshall Plan incompatible with but immeasurably superior to the Truman doctrine. The magazine hoped Russia and eastern Europe might participate so that the continent would not be further divided, with each bloc of countries subservient to the financial and military stewardship of Washington or Moscow.[25] Henry Wallace wished the Marshall Plan success if it permitted "capitalism and communism [to] live in the same world without going to war." But should it degenerate into another anti-Soviet weapon, Wallace was ready to resume his attack on Truman's foreign policy.[26]

The difficulty liberals experienced in deciding how to evaluate the Marshall Plan intensified once Russia opposed its extension to eastern Europe. Now, one had either to endorse the plan as a genuine though limited attempt to raise the standards of living in western Europe alone, or reject it as an instrument of America's Cold War diplomacy. Wallace found himself in a particularly unenviable position. While he did not want merely to echo Soviet suspicions of American benevolence, neither could he approve a program that perpetuated international disunity. Wedded to his vision of "one world," he concluded by late 1947 that the Marshall Plan was simply "an enlarged and glorified non-military application of the Truman Doctrine." As a substitute, he reiterated his sympathy for the "hungry people of Western Europe" and pleaded that something be done for them under the auspices of the United Nations.[27]

The meagerness of Wallace's alternative to the Marshall Plan revealed how formidable a task he faced in reviving liberal resistance to the administration's current diplomatic stance. Having already advocated a program of world-wide economic reconstruction on the grounds that it would guarantee America's domestic prosperity, and having earlier accepted the proposition that spheres of influence were necessary to ensure the peace, Wallace had no new international ideas to suggest. Increasingly, he and his disciples fell back on the tactic of disparaging Truman while ritualistically proclaiming their faith in the United Nations, amicable discussions among heads of state, and the elusive ideal of a harmonious world.

Still, throughout 1947, Wallace seemed remarkably adept at persuading himself (and perhaps the *New Republic*'s readers as well) that America longed for his leadership. No matter where he traveled, no matter what his audience, he invariably pronounced the political trends favorable for a new party.

At the beginning of the year, Wallace presided over the formation of the Progressive Citizens of America—an organization of dissident liberals, trade unionists, veteran Communists, and Hollywood artists. The PCA pledged itself to an impeccably reformist agenda: It denounced monopoly and racial segregation, protested the growing red scare and its assault on civil liberties, urged welfare legislation and the protection of labor's rights, called for the preservation of the family farm and more economic planning by the federal government. On international affairs, the PCA denied its allegiance to any "foreign power" (meaning Russia), but it also refused to modify its positions simply because these might coincide with the Kremlin's diplomacy. Politically, the organization encouraged liberals to remain united in order to exert pressure on the Democratic party and make it reverse its commitment to the Cold War. In Wallace's view, the PCA was ultimately dedicated to the unexceptionable goals of "peace, prosperity, and freedom in one world."[28]

Having unfurled his banner, Wallace traversed the countryside searching for signs of enthusiasm among the citizenry. Not surprisingly, he encountered partisans in every region. In a series of breathless dispatches to the *New Republic* during the summer of 1947, Wallace expressed his amazement at how well he was received. From the Midwest he described the "new spirit" stirring among the people; they were "open-minded," looking for "convincing answers," ready to "resume their forward march toward a progressive America." All they required, he told himself, was a political movement to give their energies "shape and direction."[29] In Texas and California, Wallace was entranced by the cheering crowds: 10,000 in Austin applauding "every assertion of liberalism"; 27,000 in Los Angeles chanting their opposition to the Truman doctrine and the Marshall Plan; a total of 100,000 "vibrant" Americans, each of whom he managed to address "face to face." In both these states, he reported some interesting discoveries: discrimination against blacks and Mexican-Americans was "passing" in Texas and southern California, while in Hollywood the "witch-hunting and the anti-Communist crusade have spent their strength and are on the decline" (the Hollywood Ten would surely have welcomed this news). After lectures at the University of Texas and Berkeley, he prophesied that the new generation of students was certain to produce many "splendid ideas"; evidently, they had not yet graduated into the conformists and organization men of the 1950s. Armed with such insights, Wallace insisted that those who relied on public opinion polls and the judgments of Washington columnists were "missing the biggest story in American politics today." In his estimation, if the people found no satisfaction in the policies of the Republicans or Democrats, they would inevitably turn to a third party that reflected the "growing liberal sentiments of [most] Americans."[30]

Wallace's journey obviously confirmed what he wanted to believe. Much like Richard Nixon in 1968 and 1972, Wallace appeared before safe and sympathetic audiences already converted to the cause. His unwillingness or refusal to scrutinize his adoring constituency more skeptically revealed how badly he had lost touch with political reality. His excessive optimism about the possibilities of a third party led him to wildly overestimate the "progressive" mood in both America and the world. Wallace also deluded himself about his capacity to withstand the potential shifts in Democratic strategy. Should Truman become more liberal on domestic issues while remaining a militant proponent of the Cold War, Wallace might find his flock rapidly diminishing. Yet this mixture of reformism at home and anti-Communism abroad was precisely the political and ideological recipe necessary for Truman's victory and Wallace's defeat.

Nevertheless, with images of twelve million votes quivering in his mind, Wallace relinquished his editorship of the *New Republic* in January 1948 and declared himself a candidate for president. He continued writing for the magazine until July when he withdrew entirely so that his successors might be free to endorse anyone they wished. Upon his departure, Wallace promised to conduct a campaign "based on principle, not on political expediency." Specifically, this meant that he would not repudiate Communist help in order to make his candidacy respectable in the eyes of red baiters or Cold Warriors. Moreover, he announced that the abolition of racism was going to be his primary domestic concern. Finally, Wallace repeated his conviction that Russia and America were jointly responsible for the present international tension, and that only a strong United Nations could promote economic recovery and preserve the peace. By adhering to these positions, Wallace hoped his campaign might demonstrate the existence of "another America," which sought not to master the planet but to share in its transformation.[31]

These were admirable, even courageous, ideals. For all his naïveté, Wallace had stubbornly defended throughout his tenure at the *New Republic* the Rooseveltian legacy of social reform and international cooperation in an increasingly illiberal era. But just as he launched his climactic crusade, his support was about to wither. Neither Wallace nor the liberals to whom he appealed could know how swiftly they would be overwhelmed by the emerging political and intellectual consensus of 1948.

The Cold War Generation

In the three years following the end of World War II, a number of prominent intellectuals subjected both the *New Republic* and Henry Wallace to a mounting barrage of criticism. Although they did not feel especially fond of Harry Truman's domestic and foreign policies, they were even less enamored with the Soviet Union or the vaporous notions of "one world." Neither were they sanguine about the United Nations (Dwight Macdonald dis-

missed this worthy organization as "quite simply, a bore"), international control over atomic weapons, or alliances between liberals and Communists.[32] Indeed, they hadn't much confidence in
social reform of any sort. Nor did most of them crave political
influence. Having never trusted in the programs of liberalism,
and having shed much of their faith in the dogmas of Marx, these
intellectuals seemed at first displaced from American life.

Yet their ideas formed the nucleus of a national agreement on
the nature and purposes of the Cold War. Regarding themselves
initially as exiles in their native land, they assimilated more
quickly than they might have desired. Even as they continued to
treasure their radicalism and their sense of alienation, they were
becoming—however inadvertently—the champions of existing
institutions at home and the defenders of American power
abroad.

Their essays and opinions appeared most often in two magazines: *Partisan Review* and *Commentary*. *Partisan Review* was born in
1934 as a publication of the New York John Reed Club—itself an
offspring of the Communist party. After 1937, in its second and
more famous incarnation, the journal had divorced the Party (or
vice versa, such details being shrouded as usual in mutual recrim-
ination and contempt), while proclaiming its commitment to socialism in politics and modernism in the arts. By 1946, both
allegiances had grown vague, consisting largely of reverential
nods to assorted demigods: Marx, Trotsky, Freud, Eliot, Joyce,
Proust, Kafka, and Dostoevsky. Still, *Partisan Review* flourished as
the most sophisticated voice of those intellectuals who sought an
alternative to both Stalinism and conventional liberalism, and
who cared as much about twentieth century literature and painting as about contemporary politics.[33]

From 1946 through 1955, *Partisan Review* published bimonthly
(except for a period between January 1948 and the summer of
1950 when it appeared each month). Philip Rahv and William
Phillips, two of the magazine's founders, remained as editors;
Delmore Schwartz and William Barrett, a philosopher at New
York University, were the associate editors; its "advisory board"
included Sidney Hook, James Burnham, and Lionel Trilling.
Though its circulation hovered around 10,000, the journal was

required reading for intellectuals, not least because at one time or another it printed the work of almost every major American writer. In any issue one might find an essay, story, or poem by Edmund Wilson, Saul Bellow, Paul Goodman, Meyer Schapiro, Alfred Kazin, Leslie Fiedler, Daniel Bell, C. Wright Mills, Arthur Schlesinger, Diana Trilling, Pauline Kael, James Agee, Irving Howe, Harold Rosenberg, Richard Chase, Ralph Ellison, James Baldwin, Norman Mailer, Bernard Malamud, Robert Brustein, Mary McCarthy. No other magazine could match in impressiveness *Partisan Review*'s roster of contributors or equal its claim to intellectual indispensability.

Commentary tried. Launched in November 1945 as a monthly under the sponsorship of the American Jewish Committee, its editor throughout the postwar era was Eliot Cohen—an experienced inaugurator of little magazines in the 1930s, all of them noted for early deaths. *Commentary* was Cohen's most spectacular success, in part because of his dynamism, the talents of his staff, and the bankroll of the A.J.C. Clement Greenberg, the dedicated expositor of abstract expressionism, served as associate editor. Robert Warshow functioned as managing editor while writing some of the most provocative essays on films and popular culture in the postwar period. Nathan Glazer (the sociologist who later collaborated with David Riesman on *The Lonely Crowd*) and Irving Kristol (the political theorist who eventually resurfaced as a godfather to the neoconservatives) were soon appointed assistant editors. According to Cohen, *Commentary*'s debut in the shadow of the atomic bomb and the concentration camps represented an "act of faith" in the redeeming power of the intellect. It also signified a reaffirmation of "our possibilities in America."[34] From the beginning, the journal attempted to fulfill these two—not always compatible—obligations: It tried to both encourage social criticism and provide a means by which writers might feel at home in the United States.

Because *Commentary* addressed itself primarily to a middle-class Jewish clientele rather than just to other intellectuals, its tone was less elevated than that of *Partisan Review*. Whereas *Partisan Review* often sounded as if it were carrying on an intimate conversation with an audience of peers who immediately grasped its allusions and concerns, *Commentary*'s articles seemed more instructional, more interested in dispensing information or exposing readers to ideas with which they might be unfamiliar.

But whatever their differences in orientation or style, *Commentary* and *Partisan Review* shared some of the same contributors and many of the same attitudes. They also reflected a common cultural heritage. Both journals regarded their liberal competitors as unimaginative, superficial, and excessively polite. The *New Republic*, the *Nation*, and *PM* allegedly lacked a sense of irony and an appreciation for the absurd. Their editors still believed in the existence of ideological systems (liberalism, Marxism, fascism); the writers for *Partisan Review* and *Commentary* took comfort only in individual creativity and the capacity of the private intelligence to assert itself against the world. The *New Republic*, especially under Henry Wallace, seemed insufferably innocent, insensitive to the complexities of culture or politics. Rahv and Phillips, Cohen and Greenberg, thought of themselves as quintessentially urban, refreshingly cynical, and above all erudite. Liberals apparently considered America their ancestral home and the "people" their natural brethren. The intellectuals who clustered around *Commentary* and *Partisan Review* were instinctive outsiders, descendants of immigrants and ghetto dwellers, New Yorkers with an inbred distaste for the hinterlands, suspicious of populist sentimentality as a prelude to pogroms. Thus, while the *New Republic* or the *Nation* provided a refuge for whatever was left of the Protestant mentality, *Commentary* and *Partisan Review* became outlets for the expression of an unmistakably Jewish consciousness.[35]

Indeed, their quarrel with liberals—whether Trumanesque or Wallaceite—seemed as much a matter of background and temperament as principle. Most of the contributors to *Commentary* and *Partisan Review* had been born between 1905 and 1925, and were reared or educated in New York City.[36] Where the *New Republic* looked to Washington as the source of political energy, many of the writers for *Commentary* and *Partisan Review* still lived in New York, in what Alfred Kazin called the postwar capital of the cultural world—"triumphant, glossy, more disorderly than ever, but more 'artistic,'" a center of "the old European intellect, of action painting, action feeling, action totally liberated, personal, and explosive."[37] The majority now ranged in age from their twenties to mid-thirties, some (like Rahv, Phillips, Hook, and Trilling) having begun their careers before the war, but most just starting out to make a name for themselves after 1945. On the whole, they were younger, less established, and more ambitious for recognition than those who published in the liberal journals.

The cultural and political terrain they sought to occupy was already changing, and this affected their prospects as well as their style. Irving Howe has pointed out that "the New York writers came at the end of the modernist experience, just as they came at what may yet have to be judged the end of the radical experience, and as they certainly came at the end of the immigrant Jewish experience. One shorthand way of describing their situation, a cause of both their feverish brilliance and their recurrent instability, is to say that *they came late.* "[38] Deeply influenced by the Marxist movements of the Depression years and the destruction of European Jewry during the war, they cultivated an intensity (and a rudeness) in their writing that set them apart from the more decorous liberals. Their essays were at once polemical and pessimistic, cosmopolitan and self-consciously flamboyant, theoretical and impatient with abstractions. They indulged themselves in ideological pyrotechnics more for the sake of showing off the agility of their minds than in the hope of arriving at some doctrinal truth. Their analyses of literary and artistic trends were suffused with moral and social passion, yet they also loved to demonstrate how widely and perceptively they had read. They abhorred specialization, so became specialists in every subject. Essentially, their work was meant to be as much a performance, a personal tour de force, as a presentation of their ideas or current positions. Most of all, as Howe remembered, "they could talk faster than anyone else, they knew their way around better, they were quicker on their feet."[39]

But for all their intellectual acrobatics, and their feelings of being newcomers dependent more on their wit than on their familial roots in America, the contributors to *Commentary* and *Partisan Review* evolved during the postwar years into articulate exponents of a new orthodoxy on foreign affairs. Despising all forms of mass conformity and totalitarian politics, they found themselves supplying the philosophical ammunition for the Cold War. Paradoxically, the country seemed more receptive to their ideas than to those of its native sons—the liberals who shunned the anti-Communist crusade.

The Retreat from Socialism

In the late 1930s, those intellectuals who felt estranged from both the politics of Stalinism and the middle-brow culture of the Popular Front began to reevaluate the entire socialist experience. Among the most disenchanted of the revisionists were Max Eastman, Sidney Hook, Dwight Macdonald, Edmund Wilson, Philip Rahv, and William Phillips. Each had his own reasons for questioning the continuing validity of Marxism in the modern world, but on the importance of certain issues they all agreed.

Because socialist theory had become so fatefully entangled with events in the Soviet Union, and because the revolutionary spirit in Russia had so rapidly shriveled under Stalin's despotic rule, these writers were driven to ask whether the Marxist prophecy did not itself contain authoritarian implications. Although they disputed among themselves the character of Soviet society —unsure whether it was still a workers' state, however distorted, or merely a mutation of capitalism presided over by a new ruling class of bureaucrats and technicians—they focused their attention on several crucial problems. Must the success of a revolution always depend on the ability of a single party to control the pace and define the goals of social change? Did the Leninist reliance on centralized power inevitably lead to the Stalinist dictatorship? Was it sufficient simply to abolish private enterprise and nationalize a country's economic institutions, or were the ideals of democracy and personal freedom intrinsic to the meaning of socialism? Could radicals continue to speak of a conflict between capitalism and socialism, or need they invent new terms to describe what was happening in Nazi Germany and Stalinist Russia? Might intellectuals have to dispense completely with the language and vision of Marxism, or were some portions of its philosophy still relevant to life in the twentieth century?

In the waning years of the Depression, their answers to these questions were tentative and often equivocal. Mostly, they sought to retain as much of the socialist heritage as possible, though their Marxism increasingly seemed more a habit of mind or a turn of phrase than a set of enduring convictions. But the issues they raised smoldered during the war, and exploded after 1945 with volcanic force. Now discussions about the nature of Soviet society and the consequences of Marxist ideology were no longer considered the abstract concern of a few theorists; it became a matter of national survival to know precisely what one thought of Stalinism. The pressures of the Cold War thus injected a note of extreme urgency into the debate among intellectuals. For the first time, it was almost possible to believe that an essay in *Partisan Review* carried the same weight as a memorandum from the state department to the White House. Whatever his other interests or intentions, the anti-Stalinist intellectual discovered that he was a recognized and valued expert on the subject of Communism.

No one embraced this role with greater relish than James Burnham. A philosopher by training and a metaphysician by temperament, Burnham had been sporadically involved in the doctrinal wars of the 1930s. Never too comfortable with any radical creed or party, he had briefly sworn his allegiance to Trotskyism. But his true obsession lay not with the plight of the proletariat; rather, he was fascinated from the beginning with the structure and uses of modern power.

After departing the Trotskyist movement in 1940, Burnham devoted himself to an extended reappraisal of Marxist ideas, contrasting them with the lessons learned from both twentieth century political theory and the actual behavior of contemporary nation-states. He presented his conclusions in *The Managerial Revolution* (1941) and *The Machiavellians* (1943), each of which asserted that recent history should be read not as a tale of class conflict leading inexorably to the triumph of socialism but instead as a testament to the natural concentration of authority in the hands of elite executives and administrators, themselves the masters of two or three superpowers contesting for world domination.[40] Though Burnham had originally insisted on the similarities between Roosevelt's New Deal, the Third Reich, and the Soviet Union, his analysis continued to sound compelling after the war when Russia seemed increasingly indistinguishable from Nazi Germany, with Stalin's motives and appetites supplanting those of Hitler. In comparison with these noxious regimes, America's own "managerial revolution" looked exceedingly tame.

Burnham always succeeded in infuriating his intellectual colleagues chiefly because his interpretations, if accepted, left them with little reason to maintain their radical commitments. Burnham himself was growing more conservative; by the mid-1940s, he had already traveled half the distance to his eventual destination at William Buckley's *National Review*. In 1945, however, he paused one last time to deliver an obituary over the grave of the Bolshevik revolution. His essay, published as "Lenin's Heir" in *Partisan Review*, revived the argument about whether there was anything at all to be retrieved from the ashes of Marxism.

Contrary to the familiar Trotskyist tenet that Stalin had corrupted the ideals and programs of socialism, a position which implied that the true purposes of the Russian revolution were still worthwhile and might some day be resurrected, Burnham portrayed Stalin as Lenin's legitimate descendant. In fact, the son had surpassed the father. Far from being an unimaginative bureaucrat, a primitive theoretician, or a crude manipulator of slogans and people, Stalin was in Burnham's estimation a veritable genius in political and military strategy. Impervious to the moral and social conventions that constrained the mediocre leader, Stalin had been perfectly willing to murder thousands of his opponents in order to strengthen his rule, and to sacrifice millions of his countrymen to win the war against Germany. Now he was embroiled in diplomatic combat with the West, and again he demonstrated much more "boldness and dash" than his adversaries. Indeed, Stalin's "wizardry" in the Cold War especially impressed Burnham. Not only were the Soviets consolidating their control over eastern Europe while assisting the Communists in China; they had also persuaded people throughout the world to adopt a bizarre double standard in evaluating Russian policy. The Kremlin advertised itself as the steadfast champion of democracy, Burnham marveled, "while it maintains . . . the most anti-democratic regime in world history; aggression and annexation are denounced in the midst of Soviet aggression and annexations. . . . 'Slave labor' is howled about by the state whose economy rests integrally on fifteen or more millions of slave laborers in its work and concentration camps. The most totalitarian state that exists and that has ever existed not only claims to be, but is everywhere accepted as—the world leader in the struggle against totalitarianism."[41] In this house of mirrors, only the audacious Stalin knew what was real and what was illusory.

Yet Burnham did not intend merely to reverse the customary image of Stalin. He wanted his readers both to understand the imperialist designs he believed implicit in Stalinism, and to discard whatever remained of their attachment to socialist doctrine. But in pressing his argument, Burnham revealed his own Marxist ancestry—particularly his tendency to inflate momentary episodes into historical laws.

For Burnham, nothing Stalin did was accidental, arbitrary, or improvised. Seeking to uncover a coherent "pattern" in Soviet conduct, Burnham ascribed to Stalin a fixed geopolitical ambition: the "domination of Eurasia." Anyone who talks about "Eurasia" as if it were a real locale has already transported himself to a cosmic wonderland, devoid of people, regional politics, religious discord, and ethnic animosities. Nevertheless, Burnham's ominous metaphors summoned up the deepest fears of the Cold Warriors. The source of Soviet power emanated from the "Eurasian heartland," he intoned; then flowed outward, almost hypnotically, like a turbulent and unharnessable river, "west into Europe, south into the Near East, east into China, already lapping the shores of the Atlantic, the Yellow and China Seas, the Mediterranean, and the Persian Gulf."[42]

Beyond the obvious message this apocalyptic language conveyed to American policy makers, Burnham extracted an even more universal principle from the Soviet experience. "Under Stalin," he submitted, "the communist revolution has been, not betrayed, but fulfilled." Moreover, the essential continuity between Lenin and Stalin, the conquest of power by a "conspiratorial movement" leading ineluctably to the institutionalization of "slavery and terror and suffering," illustrated for Burnham a "general law of revolutions": Those who begin by promising to liberate mankind end by imposing a despotism on their own people. Stalin, not Trotsky, was Lenin's authentic heir. "Stalinism," Burnham declared, "is communism."[43] What had transpired in Russia should therefore serve as a warning to anyone who still believed in radical social change. In Burnham's view, there was no option save to repudiate the Marxist dream, now and forever.

Burnham clearly wanted his thesis to have an impact on American diplomacy, as well as on the attitudes and behavior of American intellectuals. In 1947, he emphasized the practical implications of his ideas in *The Struggle for the World,* a tract apparently widely read in Washington, which endorsed the Truman doctrine and the theory of containment as the only way to check Soviet expansion.[44] In addition, Burnham expected writers to play a starring role in this epic battle. If people "everywhere" thought of Russia as a defender of democracy and an opponent of imperialism, then these assumptions must be demolished. Who could better puncture the Communist myth than American intellectuals, once the victims of such delusions? Burnham conceived of the Cold War not only as a political and military conflict, but also as an ideological contest for men's minds, particularly the minds of western Europeans. He thus instructed his comrades in the intellectual community to engage in a dialogue with their counterparts overseas, and win them to America's side in the "struggle for the world." Toward this end, Burnham helped launch the American Committee for Cultural Freedom at the close of the decade—an organization of philosophers, political theorists, and literary critics dedicated to combating Soviet propaganda in the West. Yet even now it was hard for Burnham and others to shake off the mental habits of the Depression years. Just as writers had been taught to scorn neutrality in the class war of the 1930s, so they were again being urged to man the front lines in the Cold War of the 1950s.

Whatever influence an author might hope to wield in Washington or western Europe, he could not be said to have made his mark among the New York intellectuals until an article of his elicited instant replies, rebuttals, and rejoinders. By this measure, Burnham's essay scored a direct hit.

Dwight Macdonald took time out from editing his own magazine to exchange insults with Burnham in the pages of *Partisan
Review*. Their long-running feud actually began in the late 1930s
when both were disciples of Trotsky; it escalated after Burnham
published *The Managerial Revolution*. Now Macdonald, posing on
this occasion as an amateur psychoanalyst, accused his old antagonist of secretly admiring Stalin. In his ceaseless quest for a
father figure, Macdonald charged, in his infatuation with the
"power and success" of great leaders regardless of how morally
repugnant their actions, Burnham displayed a masochistic need
to "submit to authority." Worse, his latest opinions were in Macdonald's eyes a "public menace" because by elevating Bolshevism to a malign conspiracy bent on dominating the planet, by
proclaiming that all revolutions must invariably degenerate into
autocracies, Burnham was either recommending surrender or
advocating Armageddon.[45] Macdonald, not surprisingly, was dismayed by both possibilities.

Burnham and *Partisan Review*'s editor, William Phillips, replied
to Macdonald, hurling the harshest gibes they could recollect
from their radical pasts. Each chided Macdonald for being intellectually "irresponsible," for having never understood what it
meant to "think politically," for adopting a "moral stance" and
confusing "personal feelings" with a "serious" analysis of contemporary problems. In their judgment, Macdonald treated an
idea as if it were a "plaything," which made for "lively journalism" but impractical politics. To clinch the case, Burnham called
up the heavy artillery, reminding readers of what no less a father
figure than Trotsky himself had once remarked: "Every man has
a natural right to be stupid; but Dwight Macdonald abuses the
privilege."[46]

Curiously, neither Burnham nor Phillips explained what was
wrong with relying on moral values or personal inclinations in
deciding where one stood on political issues. Nor could they
admit that it might be precisely Macdonald's "irresponsibility,"
his instinctive aversion to ideological cant, and his love of intellectual play that made him both a good writer and a trenchant
critic. Conversely, Macdonald's efforts to unmask Burnham's hidden motivations did not really answer Burnham's arguments.

Despite this acrimony, Burnham's article provoked a painful reexamination of socialist doctrine among American intellectuals in the immediate postwar years. "We must . . . ask ourselves," Phillips acknowledged, "why so many predictions and revolutionary expectations" dear to the Left "have been belied by history." Though he denied Burnham's principal contention that Stalin was a logical outgrowth of the Bolshevik revolution, though he believed the Soviet regime had nothing in common with the classic "spirit of socialism," Phillips conceded that the old Marxist formulas no longer accounted either for the emergence of totalitarianism as a new political phenomenon or for the current paralysis of radical movements throughout the world.[47]

Phillips's coeditor, Philip Rahv, tried during the late 1940s to derive a few of his own lessons from the Soviet experience. He too pictured the Stalinist bureaucracy not as a revolutionary vanguard but as a "new ruling class, the master of a new social order as hostile to capitalism as it is to socialism." Its monopolistic control over state power and its suppression of all political opposition ultimately deprived the Russian people of any means to revolt against or even modify the dictatorship. For Rahv, the only way radicals outside the Soviet Union could recover from the totalitarian disease was to disavow the authoritarian implications in Marxist thought, and pledge themselves to a "revitalized politics of democratic and libertarian socialism."[48]

As the years wore on, however, he sounded increasingly pessimistic about the possibility of resurrecting socialism in any form. By 1949, as reflected in a laudatory review of George Orwell's *1984,* Rahv's mood had grown melancholy and fatalistic. He praised the novel for capturing "with finality" the "lost illusions" of an entire generation of radical intellectuals, their shared sense of "Utopia betrayed." Orwell's *1984* seemed especially frightening to Rahv because it analyzed the "psychology of capitulation," the capacity of modern dictatorships to extinguish "private life" through "a methodology of terror that enables them to break human beings by getting inside them." In Rahv's view, what made twentieth century despots like Hitler and Stalin so "implacable" was their abolition of the individual's right to martyrdom, their ability to render personal courage and rebellion meaningless. The totalitarian state, its secret police and Grand Inquisitors, had devised techniques to convert suffering into acquiescence: "The victim crawls before his torturer, he identifies himself with him and grows to love him. That is the ultimate horror."[49] And from this horror, Rahv could imagine no deliverance.

Macdonald, Phillips, and Rahv had all wished to retain at least some minimal faith in radical ideas. Yet their language, like Burnham's, became far more vivid when they described what had been lost. They were truly moved not so much by a need to reevaluate Marxism as by a passion to document its awesome failures. Capitalism had not collapsed (indeed in America it seemed more potent than ever); the working class had not carried out its revolutionary mission; socialist rhetoric had been twisted into a rationalization for dictatorship. Thus by the end of the 1940s, their minds and their essays were filled less with the dream of a social democracy than with the harrowing imagery of totalitarianism.

Hannah Arendt and the Totalitarian Mystique

Most American intellectuals could only glimpse the approaching menace of totalitarianism from afar. Perhaps that was why they seized upon the symbolism of hypnotic rivers, implacable forces, terror stalking the earth and taking over the individual's psyche, as if they were confronting an invasion from outer space. Perhaps that was also why they relied increasingly on Europeans to guide them through alien territory, turning particularly to those writers who had encountered the monster at close range: George Orwell, André Malraux, Arthur Koestler, Ignazio Silone —and above all, Hannah Arendt, the Jewish refugee from Nazi Germany who spoke with greater authority than anyone else because she knew more intimately than anyone else exactly what there was to fear.

Arendt's experience was typical of many émigré intellectuals. Trained in philosophy under Martin Heidegger and Karl Jaspers during the springtime of the Weimar Republic, she fled Hitler's Germany in 1933, lived in Paris (where, as a social worker, she helped German Jewish children migrate to Palestine), escaped to the south of France after the Nazi occupation in 1940, and finally arrived in New York in 1941 bearing impressive academic credentials but faced with all the other formidable problems of adapting to a new language, new customs, and a new culture.

Arendt found herself in a country that took pride in its indifference to tradition, that felt miraculously free of the demons haunting the European imagination. Yet by the late 1940s, she was emerging as a towering figure among American writers because her preoccupations were increasingly theirs. Like Delmore Schwartz (but without his detours into manic-depression), Arendt drew people to her with the force of her mind, the energy of her conversation, the breadth of her knowledge. She became a powerful intellectual presence in the lives of Robert Lowell, Randall Jarrell, Alfred Kazin, Mary McCarthy—and when her essays began to appear in American journals like *Partisan Review,* she grew in influence as a diagnostician of contemporary political ills.[50]

Because she was an immigrant permanently cut off from familiar surroundings and friends, because she knew at first hand the meaning of displacement and instability, Arendt sought to comprehend what had happened to her by explaining what had happened to her civilization. She had personally witnessed the disintegration of European society, and she spared her American audience none of its hideous details. In her mind, the classical, predictable, well-ordered universe of Plato, Augustine, and Kant had irreparably fractured. The philosophers of modernity were Marx, Nietzsche, Freud, Heidegger, Kafka—they illuminated for Arendt a world torn apart by conflict, violence, irrationality. They helped her understand, as much as anyone could, the calamities of her lifetime. They provided a vocabulary and a set of metaphors she used to describe the collapse of nation-states, the uprooting of people, the assault on the individual that began with the rise of mass movements and ended with the concentration camps. With their insights, she set out to make a chaotic history at least *appear* coherent—to account somehow for the madness that had tormented Europe and now threatened America's sense of security.

Arendt's intellectual strength lay in her sensitivity to political disruption and cultural breakdown, her awareness of what was unprecedented and almost unfathomable in the social disloca- tions of the twentieth century. She insisted that the horrors of the present were qualitatively and fundamentally different from any- thing known or experienced in the past. It seemed fitting, though also ironic, that she should preach this message in a country which had always thought of itself as a novel experiment, as a liberation from the old ways of thinking and feeling. But Arendt wanted to demonstrate what was terrifying about the new, what catastrophes attended the rupture of tradition. And she hoped as well to discover for herself some political moorings, some endur- ing principles to protect her and her adopted countrymen from the crack-up of modern society.

In 1951, Arendt published her first book in English. Its impact was immense, not least because it offered a systematic and per- suasive interpretation of those problems with which American intellectuals had grappled for the previous five years. Majestic in its scope, astonishing in its control over a vast array of ideas and issues, *The Origins of Totalitarianism* is one of those books whose grandeur and brilliance are undiminished even when a battalion of revisionists later "prove" the author wrong. For all its histori- cal and philosophical erudition, it is in addition a personal state- ment about the requirements for survival in the modern world. In most of the ways that count, Arendt's work remains the politi- cal masterpiece of the postwar era.

Despite her debt to Marx, Arendt had never been enticed by the radical dream. Indeed, she approached her subject from a profoundly conservative perspective, though on political matters she displayed little sympathy for the Right in either Europe or the United States. But she clashed primarily with Marxists. Where they normally stressed the issues of economic organization and social class, Arendt was more concerned with the implications of mass psychology, the centralization of power, and the role of violence and terror in solidifying a regime's authority. To her, these were the crucial problems of modern life; these were what made the present so sharply divergent from the past. Arendt did not think that any of the familiar Marxist categories could ade- quately explain the origins or structure of the totalitarian state.

Nor did she assume that the commonplace theories of law, morality, or human behavior (like sinfulness, self-interest, greed, and
cowardice) offered more satisfactory interpretations. "We actually have nothing to fall back on," she lamented, to help us
"understand a phenomenon that nevertheless confronts us with
its overpowering reality and breaks down all standards we
know."[51] Yet because she regarded "the rise of totalitarian governments [as] the central event of our world," Arendt felt deeply
the need to acquire as much knowledge as possible about its
causes, evolution, and distinguishing characteristics.[52]

Arendt repeatedly insisted that totalitarianism was a genuinely
novel force in human history. In her view, the totalitarian state
differed "essentially from other forms of political oppression
. . . such as despotism, tyranny and dictatorship." It could not be
equated with conventional autocracies (like Franco's Spain or
Mussolini's Italy), nor with nineteenth century imperialisms
(which sought only to exploit the economic resources of the
underdeveloped world). "Wherever it rose to power," she asserted, it created "entirely new political institutions and destroyed all social, legal and political traditions of the country."
Her basic definition, then, emphasized its willful break with every
aspect of the past: "Totalitarian government always transformed
classes into masses, supplanted the party system, not by one-
party dictatorships, but by a mass movement, shifted the center
of power from the army to the police, and established a foreign
policy openly directed toward world domination."[53] Thus it had
nothing in common with conservatism (which was based on a
respect for law, property, and long-standing social institutions),
or with liberalism (which conceived of politics as a competition
among parties, each presumably expressing the aspirations of
individual citizens), or with socialism (which saw class relationships as the foundation of economic and political life).

Still, for all its uniqueness, the totalitarian impulse had its roots
in the turbulent conditions of late nineteenth and early twentieth
century Europe. Arendt believed that totalitarianism was tied
inextricably to the decomposition of Western society, especially
the failure of the traditional nation-states to cope with the strains
of imperial adventure and transnational ambitions. It was also

linked to the growth of anti-Semitism, the Jew serving as symbol and scapegoat for those who were dissatisfied with political parties, governing elites, and modernist culture.

Arendt considered the problem of anti-Semitism central to her analysis. By showing how the position of the Jew shifted in response to major political and social changes, by tracing the way in which the attitudes of Europeans toward Jews congealed into a myth and then an ideology, she hoped to disclose the mechanisms that eventually produced the totalitarian state.

Anti-Semitism seemed to her neither an accident nor an aberration; it was a direct result of historical transformations over which the Jews themselves had no control. It coincided with the decline of nationalism, and "reached its climax at the exact moment when the European system of nation-states and its precarious balance of power crashed."[54]

Jews had been important to nineteenth century governments as financiers, advisers, and diplomats. Their influence derived from their contacts with Jews in other nations, and from their ability to act as emissaries of one country to another, roles that could have significance only at a time of inter-European solidarity. But Jews formed no class of their own, Arendt pointed out, nor did they belong to any larger social group within a nation—they were not industrialists, workers, landholders, or peasants. Their status depended almost exclusively on their usefulness to the state; their identity was bound up in the services they, and no one else, could render. When in the late nineteenth and early twentieth centuries European nations attempted to solve their economic difficulties by building empires, Jewish wealth ceased to be indispensable. When during and after World War I each country's reliance on intricate negotiations and delicate alliances gave way to a policy of trying to annihilate one's enemies, and when the war itself led to the rise of transnational movements that had no allegiance to any particular government, Jewish diplomatic and political skills shrank in value.[55]

In these new circumstances, Arendt contended, the position of the Jews in Europe became ever more vulnerable. They remained prominent—indeed all too conspicuous—as journalists and intellectuals, artists and professionals, affluent cosmopolitans, sophisticated proponents of modern culture, the visible symbols of an international society from which ordinary individuals felt excluded but toward which they bore growing resentment. Nevertheless, the Jews lacked real power, and they no longer enjoyed the patronage of postwar governments whose own weakness and instability were increasingly obvious.[56] Hence in Arendt's opinion the breakdown of the nineteenth century European political order left Jews dangerously exposed to all the grievances and animosities that began to flourish in the twentieth century.

Because the Jews had identified their fortunes so thoroughly with the traditional nation-state, they now found themselves the foremost victims of its deterioration. "Each class . . . which came into conflict with the state" in the early twentieth century, Arendt observed, "became anti-Semitic because the only social group which seemed to represent the state were the Jews." Even worse, since Jews were unable to escape their "Jewishness" through religious conversion or by disappearing into another class, since they were defined by the societies in which they lived as a special group with innate attributes, they could be held "guilty" not because of anything they did but because of who and what they were. Had Jews committed a specific crime, Arendt suggested, they might have been punished. Their Jewishness, however, was regarded as a "vice"—and vices "can only be exterminated." Ultimately, anti-Semitism exemplified for Arendt the general tendency of European politics in the twentieth century to move beyond "actual experience" into the realm of "ideology" transcending law, parties, governments, existing social and economic institutions, and national boundaries.[57] The growing hatred of Jews, therefore, was Arendt's metaphor for the progressive collapse of all those familiar structures that had once made European life manageable, and now made it terrifying.

The spread of anti-Semitism was symptomatic of other upheavals taking place at the same time. Arendt's larger purpose was to show the political consequences of Europe's dissolution under the blows of imperialism and war. The construction of colonies overseas did little to mitigate class conflicts within the home country, she argued. If anything, the competition for empire contributed to the outbreak of World War I, which further jeopardized the internal cohesiveness of each nation. Furthermore, the war's very destructiveness obliterated differences between countries and among individuals; throughout Europe, the common experience of violence and irrationality was in her mind a necessary prelude to the emergence of mass movements dedicated to redrawing boundaries and erecting alternative institutions.[58]

Indeed, for Arendt the most ominous result of the war, the abortive revolutions that followed in its wake, and the peace treaties that promised self-determination but brought havoc to eastern and central Europe was the creation of a permanent refugee population—millions of people floating across borders, unprotected and unwanted by any government, economically irrelevant and socially burdensome, introducing yet another "element of disintegration" into the politics of postwar Europe.[59] Arendt was describing here a situation ripe for political explosion: war veterans with no stake in parliamentary institutions and no attachments to parties, professional associations, or trade unions; ethnic and religious minorities thinking of themselves as eternal outsiders subject not to laws but to bureaucratic whim and arbitrary decrees; declassed individuals detesting those whom the state seemed to tolerate and assist (like the Jews). These disparate groups constituted a furious and potentially savage mob, ready at any moment to shatter whatever remained of the old order.[60] All the "masses" needed was direction, organization, leadership.

The genius of totalitarianism, Arendt believed, lay in its pledge not to restore stability or reintegrate the mob into a national community, but to remake the whole of European society along entirely new lines. Totalitarian movements, appearing first in the guise of pan-Slav or pan-German crusades, then crystallizing in the Bolshevik revolution of 1917 and the Nazi paramilitary gangs of the 1920s, completed what imperialism and the war had begun. In one form or another, she observed, the totalitarians sought to undermine the prestige of both the state and the parliamentary system on the grounds that neither truly represented the interests of the people. They portrayed themselves not as a party but as a movement "above" politics, superior to the courts, and indifferent to national frontiers. They wished to mobilize the masses into a revolutionary force aimed not merely at seizing the machinery of government in order to implement a specific program, but at liquidating all class divisions, traditional parties (whether conservative, liberal, or socialist), and every social group (again, like the Jews) that benefited from and tried to defend the status quo.[61]

Echoing social psychologists like Erich Fromm, Arendt also surmised that totalitarianism was attractive because it guaranteed an end to the masses' rootlessness and displacement: It reunited them as members of a "race," the "people," or an international proletariat. Hoping to escape the feeling of being lonely and "isolated individuals in an atomized society," Arendt declared, unable to play a normal economic or political role in the countries where they resided, yearning for the comradeship afforded by "sheer numbers," contemptuous of liberal theories about the glories of individualism and the rights of man, the masses were predisposed to give their unlimited loyalty to any movement that provided opportunities for participation in public life, and that endowed them with a "divine" or historical mission.[62]

Thus in Arendt's judgment, totalitarian movements succeeded whenever they could appeal to a politically inexperienced mob that had no concrete and obtainable goals nor any sense of class affiliation, whenever the established parties of a particular country entrusted their survival to the mercurial will of the majority rather than to fixed constitutional procedures, and whenever a populace had come to rely more on myth and propaganda than on rational political debate for an understanding of its problems.[63] All of these conditions prevailed in Russia in 1917 and in Germany by the late 1920s. They therefore gave rise to Stalinism and Nazism, the two supreme models for Arendt of twentieth century totalitarianism in practice.

Arendt's depiction of Nazi and Soviet society confirmed and enlarged upon the assessments advanced by Burnham, Phillips, Rahv, Koestler, and Orwell. Yet her portrait, even more than theirs, became the standard interpretation because it supplied a rationale for the totalitarian state. Where they had emphasized its terroristic features alone, or its corruption of socialist principles, or its tendency to follow a natural law of development and behavior, she insisted that totalitarianism had quite conscious objectives. Its explicit purposes and motivations could be detected by paying attention to the function of ideology, the methods of organization, the nature of the bureaucracy, and the role of the Leader.

Arendt did not consider totalitarian ideology simply a distortion of some prior social philosophy or economic program. It was designed to reinterpret the past, analyze the present, and predict the future in terms that would reveal secret "truths" and hidden "meanings," that would offer an internally consistent and thus convincing explanation for otherwise chaotic events. Whether it stressed the significance of race or class, the "folk" or the workers, hardly mattered to Arendt; she was not really interested in the substance of either doctrine. For her, the persuasiveness of Nazism and Stalinism depended on the skill with which each proposed a version of reality that did not have to be modified on the basis of political or personal experience, and that did not have to take into account the impact of chance or coincidence in human affairs. The task of ideological thinking, she asserted, was to make the universe appear logical, uniform, and coherent.[64]

Yet no ideology could long be effective unless its adherents were permanently shielded from the "normal" world. The totalitarian movement, Arendt argued, deliberately created a layer of hierarchical organizations to separate militants from sympathizers, and sympathizers from nonbelievers. This complex arrangement allowed the elite party member to transmit the movement's propaganda to fellow travelers, who would in turn convert the most "fantastic lies" into acceptable "political reactions or opinions" for consumption by the larger society. Eventually, she pointed out, the "whole atmosphere is poisoned with totalitarian elements": Ordinary citizens were conditioned by front organizations to listen respectfully to Nazi or Stalinist doctrines, while the movement itself was protected from having to test its theories in the laboratory of daily life.[65] It was, of course, all an elaborate façade until the movement attained power. Then the administrator replaced the party member and the sympathizers; ideology became an instrument not to organize the masses, but to implement policy.

Arendt characterized the archetypal totalitarian bureaucrat—the Nazi Gauleiter or Stalinist commissar—as the impersonal bearer of truth, the incarnation of latent trends, the anonymous agent of historical forces. He saw himself as a disciplined functionary, willing to carry out his duties without question or thought, adept at the mechanics of organization and control, because he already knew what was "correct." He had invested his whole identity in the movement; he was the movement's purest abstraction; he represented a new species, the immaculate embodiment of Aryan or Communist ideals.[66]

Above all, he was a servant of the Leader. In Arendt's estimation, Hitler and Stalin were neither geniuses nor madmen, neither demagogues nor mandarins. Unlike orthodox dictators, they did not merely resolve disputes among subordinates or blame functionaries for policies that failed. Neither did they project themselves as quasi-military governors dedicated to the preservation of law and order. On the contrary, they assumed complete responsibility for everything done in their names by the bureaucracy, while at the same time posing as the dignified spokesmen of still-conventional nation-states to the outside world. According to Arendt, the totalitarian Leader claimed infallibility in order to permit his subjects to commit any crime, swallow any dogma, betray any ally.[67] He alone justified the principle that everything was possible.

The ideologue, the fellow traveler, the bureaucrat, and the Leader invented the totalitarian state. But for Arendt, as for her contemporaries, the essence of totalitarianism lay in its reliance on terror as a permanent technique of government. Routine despots had employed violence to suppress rebellions, exiled dissidents to labor camps and penal colonies, reduced the people of conquered nations to virtual slavery, and generally made sure no opposition arose to threaten their reign. What Arendt found distinctive about the Nazi and Stalinist regimes was their continuing use of terror against an *already passive and obedient* population. A person singled out for persecution need not have engaged in sabotage or articulated a subversive idea. The state could arbitrarily designate someone an enemy of the favored race or class regardless of his effort to establish his innocence. Nor could any institution save him from his predetermined fate. The job of the totalitarian police and the courts, Arendt noted, was not to uncover crimes or prove conspiracies, but to arrest and sentence whichever groups the government chose to banish from society. Since in this situation there were no prescribed penalties for explicit offenses, the victim was dispatched to an eternal hell where his life or death no longer mattered to anyone.[68]

The real purpose of totalitarian terror, however, was not just to frighten and coerce the populace, but to abolish all traces of personal dignity, to eliminate individual spontaneity, to fashion a perfectly predictable society in which human beings could be treated as interchangeable and superfluous. Earlier dictatorships seemed content to manage external events, Arendt asserted; the totalitarian state sought to invade the inner life of each citizen, extinguish private feeling and ambition, remold people into automatons with preconditioned reflexes so that their conduct would always be reliable even as they shuffled to their annihilation. In her eyes, the totalitarian ideal was realized only in the concentration camps, where everyone was expendable, where guards behaved like puppets and victims marched without resistance to the gas chambers. This destruction of individuality—achieved through sudden imprisonment, constant purges, and mass exterminations—allowed both Nazism and Stalinism to achieve unlimited power over every aspect of man's experience and behavior.[69]

But despite their success in mastering their own populations, Arendt declared, a Hitler or Stalin ultimately craved dominion over the entire planet. Here again she distinguished between the goals of a classic autocracy and the needs of a totalitarian state. In her view, Nazi Germany and the Soviet Union were inherently expansionist not because they longed to carve out empires or exploit the economies of other countries, but because their very survival depended on their capacity to subdue the nontotalitarian world. Hitler and Stalin recognized that if they did not pursue global conquest, they would lose whatever power they had already amassed. Thus, Arendt submitted, the totalitarian state must maintain its momentum or it would deteriorate into an ordinary government bound by treaties, laws, and customs. The Leader had to prevent this normalization; political stability was antithetical to the notion of an international "movement," which in its perpetual evolution could ignore momentary setbacks, and whose final triumph might last a thousand years. For this reason, Arendt was extremely pessimistic that Stalin (any more than Hitler before him) would be satisfied with the territory already under his command, or that the usual diplomatic concessions could transform Russia into either a traditional dictatorship or a democratic society.[70]

Indeed, Arendt offered no specific recommendations about how the West should deal with the Soviet Union. Her solutions to the problem of totalitarianism were implicit in her explanation of its origins. Arendt's analysis of the historical changes that produced Nazism and Stalinism reinforced her conservative values. The ideas and institutions that had broken down in the late nineteenth and early twentieth centuries were precisely those she wished to repair and preserve. In her mind, Europe's tragedy began at the moment nations turned themselves into empires, political parties surrendered their legitimacy to mass movements, and rational debate over concrete social and economic issues gave way to mythic or ideological interpretations of the universe. Somehow, Arendt hoped to halt this process. She yearned to revive an era when governments served as the guarantors of legal rights and constitutional procedures, when several parties coexisted to represent the ambitions of various groups and classes, when societies were composed of citizens rather than displaced mobs, when the individual did not hunger for membership in an organic community, when public affairs never intruded upon private life. If Americans and Europeans did not appreciate the virtues inherent in these venerable political doctrines, she feared, the totalitarians would make good their promise to reorganize the world. Against those who called themselves the sovereigns of the future, she hurled the accumulated wisdom of the past.

In retrospect, it is easy—perhaps too easy—to see the weakness in some of her arguments. Arendt deliberately constructed a model of totalitarian behavior based on but abstracted from historical experience. As a result, she was often more persuasive in describing the political and social turmoil that preceded the emergence of the totalitarian movements. Her account became increasingly theoretical as it concentrated on totalitarianism in action. This was particularly evident when she tried to explain why she thought totalitarian states had to expand beyond their borders. The motivations she attributed to the Leaders, their insistence on ceaseless motion as a means of staving off normality and decay, sounded too mystical to be completely convincing.

Moreover, Arendt tended to blur the differences between Nazism and Stalinism, selecting those features in each that best illustrated her general conclusions. This left the impression that Hitler and Stalin were identical, that their policies and intentions were exactly the same—a notion that could encourage Americans to apply to the Cold War the "lessons" they had presumably learned from the. events leading up to World War II. In fact, because many politicians and intellectuals did overemphasize the similarities between Nazi Germany and the Soviet Union, America's postwar diplomacy rested on the premise that Russia was unalterably committed to world domination, and that efforts to negotiate with Stalin were pointless since totalitarian appetites could never be appeased. Arendt shared these assumptions, regardless of other ideas she may have had about the contest between the West and the Soviet Union.

Above all, her conception of totalitarianism was peculiarly static. She seemed unable to imagine the possibility of sustained conflict within the governing elite, or the presence of pluralistic interest groups competing for influence in the larger society. Nor could her theory allow for totalitarian mismanagement and incompetence. Arendt's vision of totalitarianism stressed its robotlike efficiency, its absolute control over every sphere of human activity, its immunity to internal modifications, its refusal to tolerate disagreement or resistance of any kind. Thus in her opinion, a totalitarian state must either continue to grow or collapse; it must either spread its power throughout the world or be defeated (usually in war). There were no other alternatives.

Such an appraisal seemed true of Nazi Germany, but was it equally relevant to the Soviet experience? Five years after Arendt's book appeared, Russia embarked on a halting, contradictory, restricted, but not ungenuine experiment in "de-Staliniization." More important, its monolithic sway over the Communist bloc had already been defied by Tito's Yugoslavia—and would be challenged again in East Germany, Hungary, Czechoslovakia, China, and Poland. Arendt's thesis could account for the Kremlin's attempts to suppress these convulsions, but not for the changes that did occur both in the "satellite" countries and within Russia itself.

Still, whatever its methodological flaws or lack of political foresight, Arendt's book illuminated the endemic brutality and moral emptiness of totalitarianism. Couched in the dispassionate language of the social sciences, it was in reality a powerful jeremiad —and a moving autobiography by someone who continued to believe in the old-fashioned principles totalitarianism had nearly destroyed. Arendt spoke for her generation on both sides of the Atlantic; when her book was published in 1951, it verified what many influential American and European intellectuals had been arguing since 1945. About the nature of totalitarianism, they had nothing more to add. Now the only question that remained was how best to combat its current manifestation in the Soviet Union.

Containment and Consensus

Once American intellectuals began to accept the idea that Russia was not a socialist but a totalitarian society, and that Stalin had succeeded Hitler as the principal threat to democracy, they became increasingly concerned about how intimately they should involve themselves in the Cold War. Was it their responsibility to provide practical advice on the problems of political and military strategy, or should they maintain some detachment from the quarrel between the West and the Soviet Union? Must they associate themselves completely with America's domestic values and diplomatic objectives, or could they give conditional support to the nation's foreign policy while continuing to criticize its social and economic institutions? To what degree could they participate in a global crusade against Communism and still preserve their independence as intellectuals?

These were hardly new dilemmas by the late 1940s. Writers had been accustomed to "taking sides" since the Depression— first, in the conflict at home between the working class and the bourgeoisie; then, in the world-wide clash between democracy and fascism. The identity of the combatants had now changed, Russia having supplanted both the "bosses" and the Nazis as embodiments of everlasting villainy. But the intellectuals' frame of mind remained the same. Within a few years after the end of World War II, they were again marching off to battle.

This time they required little encouragement from a political party or the Truman administration. No government agency purchased their souls at a discount. Long before the CIA started subsidizing book publishers, journals, conferences, and exchange programs, many intellectuals elected on their own to function as the voice of America to the rest of the world. If anything, the government eventually realized that its own interests were better served by letting writers speak for themselves. One need not pay for what came free of charge. If intellectuals did not always adhere to the latest official position, if they often disagreed with specific policies, they usually endorsed America's general international goals. And as they reached a consensus on the Cold War, their attitudes and statements grew firmer, more authoritative, more predictable. They knew what they thought; the phrases flowed easily from the typewriter or the lectern; their arguments sounded well rehearsed. From the government's point of view, no more could be asked for or bought.

For certain writers (especially the contributors to *Commentary* and *Partisan Review*), the decision to align themselves, however reluctantly, with America's diplomatic aims was a moral necessity. In their eyes, the spread of Communism imperiled both democracy and their own survival as intellectuals. As a result, they could be both contemptuous of and vituperative toward those who seemed insufficiently alarmed by these hazards. Indeed, they occasionally indulged in the sort of inflammatory rhetoric that became all too commonplace in the next several years.

As early as 1946, when the Cold War had not yet benumbed

the language of intellectuals, and when the House Un-American Activities Committee was still a joke, *Partisan Review* printed a lengthy editorial entitled "The 'Liberal' Fifth Column." Though actually written by William Barrett, the essay was unsigned and therefore carried the imprimatur of the entire editorial board.

The quotation marks around "liberal" were as intentional as the allegation that the *New Republic,* the *Nation,* and *PM* constituted a highly "vocal lobby willing to override all concerns of international democracy and decency in the interests of a foreign power." Together with Henry Wallace, Eleanor Roosevelt, and Claude Pepper (then a liberal Democratic senator from Florida), these journals were purportedly conducting a conscious "campaign of concealment, misrepresentation, and deception" on behalf of the Soviet Union. "Never during the disastrous period of fellow traveling in the thirties," Barrett claimed, "were the Russian zealots so highly placed in American life." According to *Partisan Review,* the "liberals" evaluated each political issue on the basis of whether it helped or harmed the Kremlin. They echoed Russia's demand for "security" on her borders while ignoring the consequences of Stalin's control over eastern Europe; they depicted themselves as champions of "democratic liberties" for all people except those who lived under the dominion of the Red Army; they advocated a policy of "appeasement" toward Moscow while refusing to recognize that Soviet totalitarianism had initiated the Cold War and was now the chief menace to world peace. In effect, the editorial jeered, they were neither liberals nor socialists; they wanted neither democracy in Russia nor revolution in Europe. Because their proposals amounted to a "sanction" of the Stalinist dictatorship, "the 'liberals' [could] only be described as Russian patriots."[71]

In the midst of this assault, *Partisan Review* paused to remind liberals that they too could be obliterated by the Cold War, whoever won. "A world-wide victory of Stalin," Barrett warned, "would mean their immediate extinction. On the other hand they would fall as the first victims of a terror of the Right as American public opinion [became] solidly mobilized against Russian aggressions." In a contest between the United States and the Soviet Union, American Communists would be "dealt with" for what they actually were: "outright foreign agents." Meanwhile, the "pink . . . friends of Russia" would find political and civil liberties suppressed for themselves and everyone else. Thus by their support for Russia, the liberals were endangering their own freedom and that of other intellectuals as well.[72]

That *Partisan Review* could accuse liberal journals, writers, and politicians of being either covertly disloyal or willful collaborators with Soviet power, that it could use slogans like "fifth column" and refer to "Russian patriots" flourishing in the highest circles of American life, was disgraceful if not tragic for a magazine devoted to what it liked to think were high standards of cultural discourse. That the editors could then admonish liberals about potential repressions from the Right seemed sadly ironic. In an essay such as this, *Partisan Review* was leveling the very charges in the very words that later became so familiar in the search for "security risks," in the proceedings of government loyalty boards, in the FBI investigations and HUAC hearings, and in the pronouncements of Joseph McCarthy. Why worry about inquisitions and witch hunts from the Right when some intellectuals appeared quite ready to vilify other intellectuals as secret traitors?

Partisan Review's hysteria might be excused as a reflection of the growing tension all writers felt over the Cold War. In their calmer moments, the editors insisted that they only wished to clarify the inherent differences between democracy and totalitarianism. For their part, they no longer believed that intellectuals could remain aloof from the concrete issues of foreign policy. Nor could writers abstain from choosing sides once again. Because Stalinism was the mortal enemy of both democratic and socialist ideals, and because the millions of people already conquered could not be expected to overthrow the Soviet dictatorship, the editors announced their commitment to the "Western democratic powers" as the sole force capable of resisting Russian expansion. This was not simply a matter of expediency. *Partisan Review* now considered the political, economic, and cultural institutions of "democratic capitalism" vastly preferable to any other social system currently in existence. Only in the West could one "speak of civil liberties, intellectual freedom, and the possibilities of human advance." While the editors did not suggest that the "independent Left" ought to "cease its struggle against capitalism," they regarded socialism as "inconceivable" unless and until the democracies halted the totalitarian infiltration of Western political life.[73]

When cast in these terms, it was difficult to imagine when or how the struggle for socialism would ever be resumed. Indeed, by 1947, as the prospects of radical social change grew dimmer, and as the basic propositions of the Cold War were more widely embraced by intellectuals of all political persuasions, the central questions about American diplomacy became increasingly tactical. Even here, however, the boundaries of permissible disagreement were narrowing. Since a substantial number of writers and politicians presumed that the Soviet Union would automatically extend its power to other countries unless checked by some countervailing force, they might quibble over the details of Western foreign policy but they saw no reason to ask whether their perceptions of Russian behavior were accurate. On the contrary, if the measures they prescribed managed to deflate Moscow's global aspirations, their assumptions about the need to keep exerting pressure on Russia were only reinforced. The more effective America appeared to be in deterring Soviet rapaciousness, the more such success confirmed what they already believed.

These self-fulfilling prophecies were best illustrated in the theory of "containment" as it developed among several prominent journalists, scholars, and foreign policy experts in 1947. The discussion also revealed that, whatever the differences in emphasis, each participant arrived at his conclusions from a similar premise.

The chief architect of containment was George Kennan. A foreign service officer in Moscow during the war before he became chairman of the state department's Policy Planning Staff, Kennan seemed a classic example of the intellectual as insider. He had dedicated himself to analyzing Soviet intentions, first in an 8000-word memorandum to Washington in 1946 which impressed George Marshall (the new secretary of state) and James Forrestal (the secretary of the navy), then in a private paper for

Forrestal which was ultimately published in the July 1947 edition of *Foreign Affairs* (the journal of the foreign policy establishment in the United States) as well as in *Life* magazine. Entitled "The Sources of Soviet Conduct," Kennan's article supplied the theoretical justification for the Truman doctrine, the Marshall Plan, and eventually the NATO alliance. It not only interpreted the origins of the Cold War, but also offered a powerful rationale for America's decision to curb Russia's imperial ambitions.

Like James Burnham and later Hannah Arendt, Kennan argued that Moscow's compulsion to conquer the world proceeded from its totalitarian social structure and ideology. Soviet diplomacy did not reflect, in his view, a prudent desire for security or an understandable fear of the West's century-long opposition to socialism. Rather, the "internal nature" of the Stalinist dictatorship, its intrinsic impulse to survive and grow, forced Moscow to cultivate the "semi-myth of implacable foreign hostility," assert its monolithic control over eastern Europe, and fanatically deny the "possibilities of permanent and peaceful coexistence" with rival nations. To dramatize how inexorable were Russia's efforts to enlarge its domain, Kennan presented his two most vivid images of Soviet behavior. Since everyone resorted to mechanical or geophysical metaphors when describing a totalitarian state, Kennan asked his readers to think of Russia as a "toy automobile wound up and headed in a given direction, stopping only when it meets with some unanswerable force." Alternatively, Soviet conduct could be compared to a "fluid stream which moves constantly, wherever it is permitted to move" until "it has filled every nook and cranny available to it in the basin of world power." In either case, Russian leaders were "unamenable" to discussions with or persuasion from the outside world; only the construction of "unassailable barriers" would deflect them from their path.[74]

It was characteristic of Kennan, as of his contemporaries, to take refuge in symbolism when trying to decipher the motivations of Soviet foreign policy. But if Moscow's goals were fundamentally irrational, if the Kremlin was inhabited by robots rather than real people, then there was nothing for the West to negotiate about or bargain for. Accordingly, Kennan urged Washington to confront these strange creatures with an "adroit and vigilant application of counterforce at a series of constantly shifting geographical and political points" wherever the Russians showed signs of "encroaching upon the interests of a peaceful and stable world." Kennan's approach required long-term patience and resourcefulness, with no expectations of sudden triumphs. In the distant future, however, he foresaw the possibility of compelling Moscow to moderate its appetites; if all outlets for expansion were blocked, the Soviet empire might either crumble or gradually mellow. To lighten Washington's burden in the meantime, Kennan added one comforting thought: The American people should be grateful to "Providence" for providing them with this "implacable challenge," he suggested; it would test their capacity to carry out the "responsibilities of moral and political leadership that history plainly intended them to bear."[75] In combating the men from Mars, Kennan seemed to be saying, it always helped to have a few supernatural allies (in this case, God and History) on your side.

One of the few writers who questioned at least parts of Kennan's thesis was Walter Lippmann—by now one of the most influential journalists in America with contacts of his own in the government. In a series of twelve articles originally published in the New York *Herald Tribune* during the late summer of 1947 before appearing as a book entitled *The Cold War,* Lippmann sought an alternative both to Kennan's vision of a global struggle between the Soviet Union and the West, and to Henry Wallace's dream of a unified and cooperative world.

Lippmann did not share Wallace's faith in the United Nations. He felt that American policy should be based on the "realities of the balance of power" and the acceptance of a permanent contest between Russia and the United States. In a bipolar world, America would have to utilize all its political, economic, and military ingenuity to achieve its diplomatic objectives. Indeed, Lippmann agreed with Kennan's assessment that Russia would expand indefinitely unless it encountered resistance from the United States.[76]

But while he granted Kennan's argument that Soviet power must be contained, Lippmann disputed the methods Kennan proposed. In Lippmann's judgment, Kennan's policy committed

America to unlimited intervention everywhere in the world, rather than the use of its strength solely on favorable terrain. Moreover, Lippmann submitted, such an extensive strategy could be implemented "only by recruiting, subsidizing and supporting a heterogeneous array of satellites, clients, dependents and puppets" who would form a "coalition of disorganized, disunited, feeble or disorderly nations, tribes and factions around the perimeter of the Soviet Union." At some point, he predicted, America might have to "disown" one of its more dubious client states, thereby acknowledging defeat and "loss of face," or rush to its aid whatever the cost and however "undesirable" the issue. Lippmann preferred that Washington concentrate its resources on western Europe, where there were reliable allies and "natural" similarities in geography and politics, religion and philosophy, social institutions and moral values.[77] (Kennan himself acknowledged all these objections in the 1960s when he recalled that containment was designed primarily for Europe and should not have been applied to Vietnam. Nevertheless, the war in southeast Asia made Lippmann in 1947 sound like the wisest of seers.)

Additionally, Lippmann attempted to unravel the mystery of Soviet conduct by pointing out that Russia's westward thrust occurred not because of its Marxist ideology or its totalitarian instincts, but because "the Red Army defeated the German army and advanced to the center of Europe." Yet having identified Europe (and especially Germany) as the main battleground of the Cold War, and having portrayed the conflict as a normal competition for power and prestige rather than some cosmic crusade, Lippmann offered no realistic recommendations of his own. Instead, he retreated to utopian fantasies about the neutralization of Germany, followed by the evacuation of both American and Soviet troops from the continent. The two nations might continue to duel with each other economically and politically, but the threat of a third world war over Europe would be eliminated. Hence America, he concluded, should dedicate itself to containing Russian military might until the Kremlin agreed to a mutual disengagement.[78]

Unfortunately, though Lippmann was speculating about a future form of coexistence and détente, he nowhere indicated how Moscow might be induced to withdraw the Red Army from Europe or accept a diminished role in the world. Actually, the standoff he anticipated in Europe did not arrive until both countries had armed themselves to the teeth with nuclear weapons— a development that hardly lessened the danger of igniting World War III. Furthermore, Lippmann's inability to devise practical mechanisms for defusing the antagonism between America and Russia left him with little more than suggestions about how to improve the theory of containment. Focusing on Europe might be shrewder than erecting global alliances, but it would not necessarily relax international tensions or transform Russia into a society more congenial to American interests. Thus, as long as most intellectuals and government officials maintained their conviction that Moscow was infinitely expansionist, and that peace depended on a display of American military strength and diplomatic resolve, there could be no real alternative to Truman's foreign policy.

And as long as the Soviet Union behaved in exactly the ways the United States expected, repressing its satellites and menacing western Europe by tightening its pressure on Germany, Americans would have no incentive to revise their ideas about the Cold War. In fact, by 1948 some of the very liberals *Partisan Review* had castigated so savagely for being pro-Russian began to join the chorus in support of the administration's diplomacy. After Henry Wallace resigned as editor of the *New Republic,* the journal's criticisms of American foreign policy subsided. The *New Republic*'s position changed not because Wallace was supplanted by writers more sympathetic to Harry Truman (Michael Straight assumed the post of editor, while Bruce Bliven continued to serve as editorial director), or because the magazine had been convinced by the arguments of George Kennan and others. Rather, events in Europe seemed to corroborate the thesis that Russia was responsible for perpetuating the Cold War and for undermining democratic institutions throughout the world. Given these perceptions, liberals drew back from Wallace's Progressive party and solemnly endorsed the battle against Communism.

The turning point for the *New Republic* came in March 1948, after the overthrow of a social democratic government in Czecho-slovakia, which coincided with the growing apprehension that the French and Italian Communist parties might gather enough votes in their respective elections to take power on their own. For the first time, the journal conceded that the United States might actually be "losing the Cold War"—a notion previously incon-ceivable to the editors.[79] Upon contemplating this possibility Michael Straight announced that the *New Republic* was no longer ambivalent about the Marshall Plan. While Henry Wallace still attacked America's unilateral aid program as a device to further divide the world, Straight felt that the plan was the sole "means of establishing western Europe's self-reliance and . . . its political independence."[80]

The *New Republic*'s support of America's diplomatic aims was intensified in the summer and fall during the Soviet blockade of Berlin. Russia had provoked a confrontation, the editors con-tended, that compelled the United States to respond with an airlift of food and clothing. But much more than Berlin's survival was at stake; the city could not be abandoned without jeopardiz-ing other "outposts" like Vienna. Therefore, the *New Republic* exhorted Washington to "consolidate western Germany economically" and "build it up as a military bulwark against a possible Soviet advance on Western Europe."[81] In addition, the United States must proceed "at top speed" with the formation of an Atlantic alliance that would rely not only on the Marshall Plan but also on "American military commitments and military sup-plies."[82]

As the *New Republic*'s sense of urgency mounted, so did the harshness of its rhetoric. The journal's characterizations of So-viet policy sounded increasingly indistinguishable from those of James Burnham, Philip Rahv, and George Kennan. The custom-ary references to Russia's need for security disappeared, along with the suggestion that the Red Army was introducing socialism to eastern Europe. Instead, the editors charged that Stalin had "forced a purge of all Communist Parties" in order to ensure their "absolute loyalty and discipline," engineered the "ruthless sovietization" of the countries on his borders, and liquidated "all the economic and social bases of real or potential opposition to him" throughout the Soviet bloc.[83] Consequently, the *New Republic* agreed that a quarantine against Stalinism was not only strategically imperative but morally justified.

Once wedded to the Cold War, the magazine welcomed any portents of victory. In November, Arthur Schlesinger applauded the success of the Marshall Plan in "healing the European failure of nerve. It has brought to life, not only the will-to-recovery, but the will-to-resist . . . the Soviet offensive against Europe." According to Schlesinger, the solidification of the Communist dictatorships in eastern Europe, when compared with Washington's economic assistance to its allies, had punctured the "fantasy" that western Europeans could remain neutral, and had "done much to build up [their] confidence in the fundamental sanity of American intentions." But these achievements merely emphasized the need for more rigorous measures. The Cold War could not be won, Schlesinger declared, unless "every responsible European government" accepted the "duty of making rearmament its first priority." Such an "immediate" military escalation would, of course, be "underwritten" by the United States.[84]

Though Schlesinger did not specify what this policy entailed, both he and the *New Republic* were anticipating the creation of NATO. When the Alliance was formally organized in 1949, the journal praised it as the military analogue of the Marshall Plan. As long as western Europe appeared vulnerable to millions of Russian soldiers, the United States had an obligation to protect its friends by constructing a multinational army fortified with American weapons and American troops stationed on European soil.[85]

Thus, well before Russia's explosion of its own atomic bomb and Mao's triumph in China in 1949, or the outbreak of the Korean War in 1950, the *New Republic*'s conversion was complete. Its lingering desire to find an alternative to the Cold War had been swept away by the crises of 1948—especially the coup in Czechoslovakia, the Berlin blockade, the anxiety about Communist strength in Italy and France, and the fear that the Red Army might someday march to the Atlantic.

Each of these issues represented a challenge to the deepest values of liberalism. American intellectuals could rationalize the

Stalinist repressions in eastern Europe, at least for a while, on the grounds that Russia was "socializing" a region that harbored reactionary regimes and native fascist movements before World War II. But Czechoslovakia had been the one industrial democracy in eastern Europe during the 1920s and 1930s, and writers throughout the West admired its postwar efforts to maintain a coalition government of liberals and socialists. The coup proved that the Soviet Union would not tolerate the existence of *any* non-Communist state in eastern Europe, no matter how "progressive" its institutions or "friendly" its feelings for Moscow.

The Communist threat to western Europe was far more disturbing. Italy, France, even Germany despite the Hitler years, were countries with which intellectuals had established strong cultural and personal bonds. They may never have seen the Balkans, much less Asia, but at various times in their lives they had traveled through western Europe, read its novels, haunted its museums, wandered its streets, talked endlessly in its cafés, carried on love affairs in (and with) its cities. London, Amsterdam, Paris, Rome, Vienna, Copenhagen, Berlin were their second homes—filled with neighborhoods, shops, people, and experiences they could visualize in minute and passionate detail regardless of how long it had been since they last visited. Just as many writers remained skeptical about World War II until the Nazis invaded Holland, Belgium, and France in 1940, so they turned into fervent champions of the Cold War when the survival of the Western democracies seemed imperiled again in 1948. Whatever their other differences, Philip Rahv and Arthur Schlesinger, James Burnham and Dwight Macdonald, George Kennan and Walter Lippmann, Hannah Arendt and Michael Straight all believed that the preservation of the Atlantic community was a cardinal requirement of American diplomacy, equivalent to defending one's own family.

Because of this emotional investment in the fate of western Europe, it was not surprising that the *New Republic* should add its voice to the consensus on foreign policy. And once most intellectuals had committed themselves to the containment of Communism abroad, their political allegiances at home became equally clear.

The Election of 1948

During the spring and summer of 1948, liberals were still hunting desperately for a presidential candidate they could approve. Besides Henry Wallace, they had briefly flirted with Supreme Court Justice William O. Douglas and Dwight Eisenhower before each declined to run.

One name conspicuously missing from this list was Harry Truman. The president remained an incorrigible mediocrity in the opinion of liberals despite their rising sympathy for his foreign policy. Throughout this period, the *New Republic* reiterated the standard complaints about Truman's intelligence and abilities: He was a small-time machine politician abjectly dependent on cronies, conservatives, and military chieftains; his speech-making was pitifully inadequate; he lacked the necessary stature and vision to lead the Western alliance; he had alienated the labor movement, mishandled inflation, and helped throttle civil liberties with his loyalty-oath program; he should not be renominated because his prospects for reelection were utterly hopeless; his candidacy would guarantee the defeat of liberal Democrats in Congress, and bury the remnants of the Roosevelt coalition forever.[86]

Yet within a few months, the majority of liberal activists and intellectuals changed their minds about Truman. By the fall, they had transformed themselves from the president's severest critics into his most ardent advocates. Such a sudden metamorphosis might appear inexplicable were it not for the impact of international events on domestic politics. Truman became increasingly acceptable to writers as the strains of the Cold War grew more oppressive, and as he himself began to revive the reformist impulses of the New Deal in his campaign. With the approach of election day, no other candidate, least of all Henry Wallace, seemed preferable to Truman.

As the president's prestige climbed, Wallace's support crumbled. The liberals' dissatisfaction with Wallace had been festering for over a year. In 1947, a number of prominent politicians and ex-New Dealers (Chester Bowles, Hubert Humphrey, Eleanor

Roosevelt), Washington lawyers (Joseph Rauh, Paul Porter), labor leaders (Walter Reuther, David Dubinsky), and writers (Reinhold Niebuhr, Arthur Schlesinger, John Kenneth Galbraith, Joseph and Stewart Alsop) organized the Americans for Democratic Action as a counterweight to Wallace's Progressive Citizens of America. The ADA's domestic program was respectably left of center: It called for an enlargement of the welfare state, the protection of civil liberties, and the extension of civil rights to black people. It differed fundamentally from Wallace in its insistence that the Soviet Union was the principal threat to peace, and in its refusal to work with Communists in a political coalition. Essentially, the ADA wanted to cleanse liberalism of any totalitarian taint.[87]

By 1948, the ADA's dual commitment to social reform and anti-Communism became an attractive stance not only for liberals but also for the Truman administration. When the Progressive party convened in July to nominate Wallace officially, its own domestic agenda was barely distinguishable from the platform the revitalized Democrats had offered several weeks earlier. The Progressives sounded all the requisite liberal themes. They demanded stronger measures to ban segregation, regional development projects patterned on the Tennessee Valley Authority, a higher minimum wage, the continuation of farm price supports, government assistance to small businessmen, a vast public housing program, and federal funding for education and medical care.[88] Yet since the Democrats favored many of the same proposals, there seemed little reason to vote for Wallace on these grounds alone. Quite the contrary, the *New Republic* pointed out. However much Wallace had forced the Truman administration "farther to the Left," his candidacy could now weaken the movement for reform by dividing liberals and ensuring Republican victories at every political level. Thus because Wallace's campaign made the president's reelection more difficult and Thomas Dewey's triumph more likely, the journal reprimanded its former editor for embarking on a "dangerous . . . adventure" and advised its readers to consider the choice of Truman as a lesser evil.[89]

The Democrats had effectively preempted Wallace's position on domestic issues, thereby driving away many of his potential constituents. But it was the Cold War, and the fear of Communist influence on American politics, that really demolished the Wallace candidacy. Wallace's attempts to promote cooperation between the United States and the Soviet Union, and his tendency to blame the Truman administration for wrecking the wartime alliance, seemed preposterous in the context of Stalin's repressions in eastern Europe, the coup in Czechoslovakia, and the Berlin blockade. Moreover, Wallace's unrelenting opposition to the Marshall Plan—the one diplomatic initiative Truman's most vehement critics admired—persuaded liberals that Wallace was either indifferent to Europe's postwar plight or an apologist for the Kremlin's foreign policy.

This last accusation plagued Wallace throughout his campaign. As a matter of both principle and expediency, he could not disavow his Communist clientele. Wallace detested red baiting and tried to maintain some minimal unity among his left-wing disciples. He also realized that the Communists were often his most dedicated and tireless campaign workers. They raised money, licked envelopes, rang doorbells, solicited signatures on petitions to place his name on state ballots, sat through every stupefying meeting, and kept the mimeograph machines in decent repair. Nevertheless, their very indispensability presented Wallace with a predicament he never escaped. His reliance on Communist activists and advisers dismayed his liberal followers and prompted their desertion. Yet the fewer liberals who remained in his movement, the greater his dependence on the Communists—and the more susceptible he became to charges that the Progressive party was merely a front for Moscow.

James Wechsler—a veteran of Communist politics on university campuses in the 1930s, but now a respected liberal journalist whose credentials ranged from membership in the ADA to a column in the New York *Post*—helped refine the techniques with which Wallace's crusade would be deflated throughout the election year. Wechsler ridiculed the Progressive party as "the latest in the long line of fellow-traveling enterprises designed to recruit a new generation of well-intentioned citizens from the plains of Hollywood and the grime of Park Avenue." Willfully ignoring the similarities between the Nazi and Stalinist regimes, the Progressives denied that "an unchecked Soviet sweep across Europe imperils the future of freedom," and sought instead to appease Moscow's expansionist dreams. Wallace's foreign policy might be simple-minded, Wechsler submitted, but his insensitivity to democratic values was even more distressing. Wechsler insisted that the crucial choice before the voters had nothing to do with capitalism or socialism. Rather, the election required an "affirmation or rejection of the traditional liberal attitude toward personal liberty."[90] With Truman cast in the starring role as a defender of freedom, and Wallace reduced to a cameo performance as a spokesman for "appeasement," who could doubt where the audience's sympathy must lie?

Irving Howe was equally caustic about Wallace's entourage. Reviewing a book by F. O. Matthiessen (an enthusiastic Wallace supporter but also the author of *The American Renaissance,* a classic study of early nineteenth century literature), Howe energetically dissected the typical left-wing intellectual's state of mind. Matthiessen's account of his recent six-month teaching appointment in eastern Europe revealed to Howe the "slightly sad, slightly ridiculous eagerness to sidle up to 'the people' " so reminiscent of the Popular Front in the 1930s. In Howe's eyes, Matthiessen was a relic, still enthralled by rallies with "stirring songs" and "fraternal laughter," by the spectacle of "comrades" marching "arm in arm," by "the pulpy *schwärmerei* of progressivist festivity," all of which Matthiessen described in "that falsely-charged prose style of the fellow-traveler atremble before the glories of the 'new world'—a style that might be called *vibrato intime.*" Unfortunately, Howe added, Matthiessen had been seduced by the "pseudosocialist rhetoric" of those who "jailed, exiled, and murdered" genuine radicals abroad. The eminent literary scholar also neglected to notice that the Wallace movement at home was a "completely contrived creature of Stalinism."[91]

Wechsler and Howe at least entertained the possibility that most of Wallace's partisans were naïve. James Burnham regarded them simply as stupid, if not malign. Never one to use a stiletto when an ax would better serve, Burnham disclosed that the Progressive party had no rational or legitimate ideas. He then proceeded to discount whatever the Progressives said they did believe. It might well be, he conceded, that Wallace appealed to people who were fed up with the two major parties, or who were suffering from inflation, or who were unhappy with the inequities in American society, or who were troubled by racial discrimination, or who were afraid of war. Nonetheless, Burnham dismissed these motivations as "without political significance." The only "political fact" that did matter to Burnham was Wallace's fidelity to *Pravda*'s line on foreign affairs. In Burnham's judgment, all one needed to know about the Wallace movement was that it represented the "pro-Soviet party in the United States. That is all. There is nothing else." Actually, there was an additional "fact" Burnham thought important to emphasize. Where the *New Republic* worried that voting for Wallace would enhance the chances of Dewey's election, Burnham suggested a simpler equation: "A vote for Wallace is a vote for Stalin."[92] On this lofty note, the intellectuals' assessment of Henry Wallace concluded.

The Democrats themselves were rarely as dogmatic as Burnham, but they skillfully exploited Wallace's Communist connections during the campaign. Truman persistently reminded the voters that *his* liberalism did not include a tolerance for Soviet aggression. The ability to pose as a vigorous Cold Warrior gave Truman a distinct advantage in 1948. To seem indulgent of Communists was Wallace's heaviest liability—a point conveniently underlined on the eve of the election when the House Un-American Activities Committee provided the setting for Whittaker Chambers's sensational testimony that the New Deal sheltered subversives like Alger Hiss (whom Wallace, as secretary of agriculture, had once employed), and the justice department announced its intention to prosecute the leaders of the Communist party under the Smith Act. Crippled by international crises, political diatribes, the stirrings of McCarthyism, and his own inflexibility, Wallace eventually received only one tenth of the votes he envisioned at the start of his quest for the presidency.

Liberals returned to Harry Truman, however, for reasons other than their disenchantment with Henry Wallace. By the late summer and autumn of 1948, they decided the president's record on social and economic issues was commendable after all. It now appeared that Truman stood for every program they had craved

since 1945. Far from being muddled and incompetent, he was
emerging as the articulate champion of national health insurance,
slum clearance and urban redevelopment, rent and price controls, tax cuts for low-income families and higher levies on corporate profits, expanded benefits under unemployment compensation and Social Security, government aid to education, and an
increase in the minimum wage. Liberals were also gratified by
Truman's efforts to repeal the Taft-Hartley law, passed by the
Republican-dominated Congress in 1947 to reduce some of
labor's power to carry on lengthy strikes. Most of all, they hailed
Truman as the first president since the days of Reconstruction to
use his executive authority to eliminate segregation in the armed
forces and in government agencies, and to propose extensive
civil rights legislation (specifically an anti-lynch law, abolition of
the poll tax, measures to protect the rights of blacks to vote in
the South, a permanent Federal Employment Practices Commission, and a legal assault on discrimination in interstate transportation). Thus when Truman recalled Congress into special session in August, a stroke of political theater designed less to enact
reform than to dramatize the obstinate conservatism of the
Republicans, Michael Straight cheered the president's "bold and
liberal leadership"—an accolade previously reserved only for
Franklin Roosevelt and Henry Wallace.[93]

The startling revelation that Truman, not Wallace, might be
the authentic heir of FDR was confirmed in the fall campaign.
Truman's style, it turned out, was tough and decisive, just what
liberals always fancied when they shopped for leaders. In his
disparagement of Wall Street moneychangers and "do-nothing"
Republican congressmen, Truman sounded to T.R.B. "as far to
the left as Roosevelt ever was in his most leftish days."[94]

Given these newly flattering portraits of Truman's personality
and programs, the final choice was almost anticlimactic. Though
some liberal organs like the *Nation* and the New York *Post* remained ambivalent about the election, the *New Republic*—once
the most outspoken critic of the administration's domestic and
foreign policies—endorsed Truman in September. The journal
rediscovered that there was a "real and deep" contrast between
the two major parties, and that Truman had committed the

Democrats to a "militant liberalism" which deserved the "full support" of the magazine and its readers.[95]

When people are deciding whether to continue or end a love affair, they usually know what they want to do in advance and they invent the reasons afterward. Like many liberals in 1948, the *New Republic*'s editors were emotionally predisposed to divorce Wallace and embrace Truman well before they announced their choice. Their acceptance of the Cold War, coupled with their desire to elect a candidate who might actually resuscitate the New Deal, made them increasingly unresponsive to Wallace's entreaties. Then, in the campaign, Truman pleased the liberals just enough (while Dewey scared them more than enough) to permit them to vote for the president without embarrassment. The rationales followed in due course, but they weren't intended so much to persuade as to ratify. The liberals yearned to join the consensus, and they longed to have a "leader" in the White House. In each case, they got what they wanted.

Or did they? Like everyone else, the intellectual community was astounded that Truman won the election, and that the Democrats regained control of Congress. As they reviewed the results, several writers leaped to the conclusion that the American people had delivered the president and his party a mandate for sweeping social change. The "evidence" at the polls indicated to *Commentary*'s Eliot Cohen a hunger among Americans for a "middle-of-the-road social democracy."[96] Similarly, Truman's victory demonstrated to the *New Republic*'s T.R.B. that the populace had certified its allegiance to the most "radical" platform in presidential history.[97] These developments persuaded Michael Straight that the American people were demanding "nothing less than a new era of reform," and nothing less would they accept.[98]

Unfortunately, there was very little proof in the election itself that the people were expressing their radicalism or even urging an expansion of the welfare state. Nor did the political climate during the next two years merit such euphoric assessments. If anything, Truman may well have triumphed because the electorate perceived him as the most *conservative* of the candidates—in the sense that, as the guardian of Roosevelt's legacy, he appealed to those groups (workers, blacks, immigrants and their children, small farmers, the urban middle class) who remembered the Depression, felt grateful to the Democratic reforms of the past, and feared a Republican dismantling of the New Deal. What the majority of Americans really seemed to have wanted was not a social democracy, but the continuation and strengthening of prosperity. In 1948, Truman appeared safer than Dewey, more familiar, less likely to overturn the economic gains of the postwar years. The Democrats had become the party of orthodoxy; the Republicans, the party of change.

Thus when Truman introduced the "Fair Deal" in 1949, a package of substantial social programs designed to implement the promises of the campaign, his more far-reaching proposals were quickly stalemated in a Congress still dominated by the coalition of Republicans and southern Democrats that had blocked most domestic measures since the late 1930s. Though Truman managed to obtain a low-income housing bill, an increase in Social Security benefits and the minimum wage, and higher price supports for farmers, he was unable to extract from Congress any legislation on health care, education, or civil rights. The supervision of the economy remained Truman's primary responsibility; the problems of society were entrusted to future administrations.

Truman could not be the leader liberals hoped for because he lacked the mandate they assumed. But even if their estimates of the nation's political mood in 1948 had been more accurate, the prospects for social change virtually disappeared by 1950. In the closing years of the decade, the United States was haunted more than ever by the Cold War. The administration focused most of its attention on whether to build a hydrogen bomb in response to the Soviet atomic explosion, on how to deal with the new Communist regime in China, and on where America's proper line of defense ought to be drawn in the Far East. At home, liberals disputed among themselves the degree to which democracy and civil liberties should be restricted in the wake of the Hiss case, the government's prosecution of the Communists under the Smith Act, the arrest of Julius and Ethel Rosenberg, and the HUAC investigations of subversion in the academic and entertainment worlds. All of these pressures sapped the energy of Truman's

Fair Deal, but the reform impulse finally perished (along with 55,000 American soldiers) on the beachheads and nameless hilltops of Korea.

Still, despite these distractions and disasters, most American intellectuals had agreed on a liberal agenda to which they subscribed for the next two decades. In addition, they had reaffirmed their faith in the Democratic party as the principal instrument for social progress in the United States. Above all, they had arrived at a common outlook on foreign policy. The Cold War might seem frustrating and interminable. The nation's preoccupation with international crises might paralyze its efforts to cope with domestic problems. The spirit of liberalism might give way to a distrust of controversial ideas. But writers could now explain (at least to their own satisfaction) the enormous discrepancies between what they expected in 1945 and what had happened by 1950. Having shed their optimistic wartime illusions, they were left to explore the perplexing realities of postwar American life.

3

🔔

Accommodation and Ambivalence: Political and Economic Thought in the Cold War Years

Like most humans, Americans prefer their past to be coherent and easily intelligible. Complications and ambiguities mar the historical record and clutter personal recollections. Writers share this desire for clarity with their fellow countrymen. Hence they have often reduced their own experiences in the twentieth century to a didactic tale of youthful alienation and exile, followed by a gradual (and presumably more mature) acceptance of their native land. Their overall trajectory is plain, even if each generation of intellectuals differs from its predecessors. Starting out as exuberant reformers in the Progressive era, writers are supposed to have gained wisdom as rebels during the 1920s and as radicals in the 1930s, before reconciling themselves to society in the 1950s. In this view, the consensus they achieved on foreign policy after 1945 led directly to a unified perspective on domestic affairs as well. By the 1950s, they had finally grown up and settled down.

No doubt such a pilgrimage from adolescence to adulthood appears comforting and comprehensible to the participants, their chroniclers, and their readers. But sometimes the story is amended to suggest darker implications. Told this way, the cultural rebellion of American intellectuals in the 1920s and their political radicalization in the 1930s yielded not to postwar maturity but to a decline in artistic experimentation, a loss of faith in revolutionary ideologies, and a middle-aged capitulation to existing institutions and values. Writers who had eagerly embraced the bohemian life after World War I and moved to the left in response to the Great Depression were then catapulted by the horrors of Stalinism and the orthodoxies of the Cold War to the safer harbors of conservatism and complacency in the 1950s. Whereupon, in the serenity of the Eisenhower interregnum, they ceased to serve as critics of American society, becoming instead its explicators and apologists. Meanwhile the problems of poverty, racism, and urban decay simmered under the surface of middle-class affluence until a new and angrier generation of radicals in the 1960s assaulted America's tranquility at home and its imperial ambitions abroad.

As with all clichés, both these versions of the nation's intellectual history in the twentieth century are not totally mythical. Many writers were attracted to modernism in the 1920s and Marxism in the 1930s; they could justifiably regard themselves as opponents of America's political and economic arrangements. After World War II, they did surrender much of their passion for social improvement; they did assume that most of the nation's domestic difficulties had been or were being eradicated; they did turn away from the ideological clamor of the Depression years to the subtler private anxieties of the 1950s.

The very names of the magazines they edited and wrote for reflected their changing commitments and roles. Recoiling from the symbolic villains of the 1920s (Puritans, Victorians, Philistines, H. L. Mencken's "booboisie," the benighted inhabitants of Winesburg and Gopher Prairie), searching for alternative communities uncontaminated by the mentality of Harding and Coolidge (Greenwich Village, Provincetown, the Left Bank of the Seine, the cabarets of Berlin), the expatriates launched journals like *Broom, Secession, transition, This Quarter,* the *Modern Quarterly—* all of whose titles proclaimed an intention to sweep away the genteel past, depart from the old formulas, concentrate on the immediate present, revel in modernity. During the Progressive years and again in the 1930s, intellectuals cultivated their image as reformers or revolutionaries on behalf of immigrants, workers, sharecroppers, the poor. Their enemies were bosses, plutocrats, and fascists—each customarily adorned in top hat, cutaway tails, and a vest emblazoned with a dollar sign. The names of the representative magazines emphasized the need for partisanship —for fashioning alliances with some group, class, or political constituency: the *Masses,* the *New Masses,* the *Nation,* the *New Republic, Partisan Review.* After 1945, there seemed to be no one in America to blame or to champion, no arch-enemies to denounce and no movements to join. Thus two of the major postwar journals were christened *Commentary* and *Dissent,* as if intellectuals could only comment upon and dissent from but never hope to transform the prevailing social order.

This apparent diminution of artistic and political energy was in part a product of and reaction to external circumstances. Whether writers matured or merely aged, they felt compelled to discard their earlier creeds in the midst of the Cold War and the distortion of the socialist dream into a totalitarian nightmare. Weary of the Marxist slogans and radical activism of the 1930s, disappointed by the American labor movement's abandonment of its Depression-style sense of mission, bored by the absence of dramatic social controversies in the 1950s, and increasingly mistrustful of all political movements that incited mass emotions (especially if they resulted in right-wing crusades like McCarthyism), intellectuals sounded ever more skeptical about grandiose projects to remodel economic institutions or human nature.

Their retreat from radicalism, however, was motivated not only by a disenchantment with Marxist polemics and a recently acquired suspicion of collectivist programs. While the Soviet Union may have damaged the cause of socialism irreparably, the visible affluence of postwar America made even the most benign leftist proposals appear obsolete. A nation that dreaded another depression at the end of World War II found itself wrestling after 1945 with the mysteries of inflation, mass consumption, and long-term economic growth. Given the country's rising standard of living and comparative social stability, it was reasonable to believe that the fundamental problems of American capitalism (particularly those of poverty and unemployment) had been permanently solved. The smooth functioning of a Keynesian economy, fueled by massive federal expenditures on national defense and atomic research, seemed to eliminate the inevitability of class conflict and the necessity of a socialist revolution. Prosperity had become the supreme and incontestable fact of contemporary experience.

These political and economic developments in turn altered the way writers thought of their place in society. Intellectuals were starting to enjoy the rewards of affluence and the perquisites of power. Where many had lived on the margins of the American economy in the 1920s and 1930s, free-lancing for little magazines and barely surviving on publishers' advances, they were now offered jobs in universities as professors or writers in residence. The world was opening up to them; their opportunities were expanding; corruption, they learned, need not accompany success. As Irving Howe remembered, his generation began to realize that "publishing a story in *The New Yorker* or *Esquire* was not a sure ticket to Satan," and that "the academy, while perhaps less exciting than the Village, wasn't invariably a graveyard for intellect"; the commercial magazines and the universities might actually provide other kinds of havens where "serious people could do their own writing and perform honorable work."[1]

On a more exalted level, because the United States had become an increasingly complex society which only well-educated and highly trained experts could fathom or administer, some intellectuals discovered that their talents were useful to the government, the corporations, the foundations, and the military. Economists and social scientists could function as specialists, problem solvers, advisers to policy makers, managers of crises, technicians of postindustrial civilization. Philosophers and literary critics who felt the United States must compete with Communism culturally as well as strategically traveled to international conferences where they instructed their audiences on the underlying benevolence of American diplomacy and the moral superiority of American ideals.

Yet even in these capacities, most writers did not really long to bask in the presence of the politically eminent, nor did they hope to enlarge their bank accounts. Their influence was limited; their incomes remained modest; the buffet tables were usually uninspiring. The postwar intellectuals had not compromised their integrity but they had risen to the position of a relatively privileged class, with institutional affiliations and obligations that made them more dependent on and more grateful to the established social order. For the first time in their lives, they acquired some status and prestige in the eyes of their countrymen; they had a stake in society that seemed worth protecting. As a consequence, they may have been less willing to ask troublesome questions about America's domestic passivity or its international preoccupations.[2]

Still, the combined effects of the Cold War and the nation's prosperity did not automatically convert ex-radicals into self-satisfied defenders of the American Dream. Although intellectuals grew more conservative, politically and economically, their accommodation to the postwar world was frequently tentative and incomplete. In the books and essays of Reinhold Niebuhr, Lionel Trilling, Sidney Hook, Arthur Schlesinger, Daniel Boorstin, Seymour Lipset, and especially Daniel Bell, one could detect a mixture of contentment and uneasiness with the organization and values of contemporary American society. In the scholarship of Richard Hofstadter and Louis Hartz, readers were treated to a surprisingly unflattering reassessment of the country's liberal past and present. And in the work of John Kenneth Galbraith and Dwight Macdonald, the current infatuation with Keynesian economics and centralized power was subjected to a sardonic attack.

While none of these writers explicitly challenged the reign of American capitalism, neither had they entirely renounced their role as critics of American life. Apart from Macdonald (who seemed temperamentally incapable of repressing his irreverence or despair), their disaffection was muted, indirect, half-concealed. But it lurked beneath the surface of their sophisticated prose like a nagging conscience—hinting at something different, something better. No longer rebels or revolutionaries, they took refuge in ironic observation, ambivalent commentary, and occasional dissent. Perhaps, given the times, little more could be demanded or achieved.

The Crusade for "Cultural Freedom"

Among the more significant catalysts in redefining the allegiances of American intellectuals was their continuing apprehension about the world-wide appeal of Communism. During the late 1940s and early 1950s, a number of writers were astonished at the endurance of what they considered the myth of Soviet commitments to peace and social progress. Because they had long since disclaimed any connection between socialism and the Stalinist regime, and because they regarded the Kremlin as primarily responsible for exacerbating international tensions, they did not understand how some people in both the United States and western Europe could retain their admiration for Russia. Clearly, the world was in need of reeducation; thousands, maybe millions, had to be disabused of their innocence and reminded of democracy's many virtues.

No one seemed better equipped to undertake this mission than the intellectual who had been exposed to the disease of Communism in the 1930s and was now immune to further infection. Accordingly, the writers gathered around *Commentary* and *Partisan Review* set out to win the hearts and minds of the waverers, the politically confused, the ideologically naïve. For a few years, the Cold War became a form of cultural combat—and a chance for intellectuals to demonstrate their indispensability to America.

The shock of contemporary events—Russia's hardening grip on eastern Europe, the palpable strength of the Communist parties in Italy and France, the crisis over Berlin, the "fall" of China to Mao, the Soviet acquisition of an atomic arsenal, the Korean War—added a note of desperation, if not hysteria, to the essays and speeches of American writers. Several of them refurbished their skills as activists and theoreticians. Drawing on their experience with radical movements and sects in the Depression, they knew how to organize committees, forge intercontinental alliances, issue bulletins to the media, dash off letters to the editor denouncing all restrictions on cultural and political freedom, polemicize against heretics and exhort the already persuaded. In the cacophony of conferences, lecture forums, and panel discussions, some may have spent less time thinking than phrase-making. But with the fate of the world again in jeopardy, the contemplative life seemed as much a luxury as during the most apocalyptic moments of the 1930s.[3]

The sense of an approaching Armageddon was intensified by the far-flung and well-orchestrated activities of the "other side."

Beginning in 1948, the Communists embarked on an international campaign for "peace," complete with congresses of prominent intellectuals in Prague and Paris, the accumulation of innumerable signatures on petitions to outlaw war, and the awarding of "Stalin Prizes" to politicians and artists who had registered their disapproval of such inflammatory schemes as the Marshall Plan, NATO, and the creation of the West German republic. The Communist crusade seemed designed not so much to collect new converts for the Soviet Union as to mobilize a global protest against American foreign policy.[4]

Nowhere was the machinery of Communist propaganda more graphically displayed than at the Cultural and Scientific Conference for World Peace, which took place at New York's Waldorf-Astoria Hotel in 1949. In the eyes of anti-Stalinist observers like Dwight Macdonald, Arthur Schlesinger, Mary McCarthy, Robert Lowell, and Irving Howe, the meeting was obviously controlled by Moscow's minions: The program committee, for example, welcomed the formal statements of fellow travelers but refused to let Sidney Hook deliver a paper deprecating the Marxist notion of "class truths."[5]

Evaluating the conference for *Commentary*, William Barrett dismissed the entire proceedings as a "propaganda spectacle" intended to bewitch a still sizable audience of "indecisive . . . liberals." The Communists, he asserted, had carefully selected the participants to avoid "any possibility of a genuine intellectual exchange." Even the attempt to balance criticisms of Russia with diatribes against the United States sounded fraudulent to Barrett; the result was to "equate the two systems," thereby removing the grounds for political or moral choice, and denying America the right to resist "Russian aggression" in Europe and the Far East. More ominously, Barrett speculated that the Communists remained popular with those segments of the American middle class most susceptible to contrived publicity and manufactured opinion. To him, the audience looked principally composed of professionals, college students, and delegates from Hollywood and Broadway—in sum, the producers and consumers of mass culture. On the whole, the conference left Barrett with the "melancholy impression that there is no American organization ade-

quate in resources, energy, or direction" to fight "Stalinist propaganda on a satisfactory intellectual level." In its "mortal struggle" with Communism, he concluded, the United States was making a "great mistake" not to "use" its writers.[6]

At this point, it scarcely occurred to Barrett or the other critics
of the conference that American intellectuals ought not to emulate their Communist adversaries by functioning as equally profi-
cient propagandists. On the contrary, they rushed into combat
with inordinate zeal, determined to match every Communist con-
clave and committee with one of their own.

Often, however, their supreme enemy appeared to reside less
in Moscow than in western Europe. The Party hacks were a minor
nuisance compared to the skeptical and nonaligned intellectuals
of Paris, Rome, and Berlin. In the view of Americans like Barrett,
Hook, William Phillips, and James Burnham, the truly unforgiv-
able heresy of the early 1950s was not Stalinism but neutralism.

Throughout this period, *Commentary* and *Partisan Review* persistently complained about the European inability to see that America was preferable to Russia. Returning from two conferences on
religion and philosophy in Amsterdam, Sidney Hook castigated
his European counterparts for their "nervous timidity" in shun-
ning the controversies of the Cold War. Unwilling to grant that
the world was presently an ideological "battlefield," and fearing
future reprisals should the Red Army march to the Atlantic, they
refused to engage "in any cultural action which might bring them
into open opposition to Communist totalitarianism." Because
they entertained the "preposterous" idea that "total cultural terror" in the Soviet Union was no worse than the "evils of capitalism" in the United States, and because they insisted on "being
above partisanship in the current death-struggle of the free mind
in Europe," they became for Hook unwitting "accomplices of
Stalinism" in the contest for the "soul of the West." Their neutrality demonstrated both their "political cretinism" and their
failure of nerve as intellectuals. The paramount duty of philosophers and theologians, Hook submitted, was not to take cover in
their specialized disciplines, nor to debate the comparative merits of capitalism and socialism, but to publicize the "elementary

truth that what divides the world today is . . . the issue of political freedom versus despotism."[7]

Hook elsewhere admitted that America was hardly a "paradise of liberty," especially for black people, yet he seemed mystified by the European blindness to the differences between a flawed democracy and a "totalitarian Inferno." Neither he nor William Phillips could imagine how anyone might pretend that the United States was as much a political and cultural menace to European values as the Soviet Union. The reluctance of western European intellectuals to unite in a "common fight" against Stalinism must be the twin result, they guessed, of insidious Communist propaganda and America's distorted image abroad.[8]

How to explain such obdurate anti-Americanism? One could always blame the country's novelists for giving the world an inaccurate picture of American life. In 1940, Archibald MacLeish rebuked the writers of the 1920s because they had "irresponsibly" ridiculed the political ideals and cultural assumptions that swept America into World War I, thereby depriving the nation of the faith and self-confidence it needed to enter World War II. Ten years later, Sidney Hook offered a similar lament. Europeans, he discovered, were "shockingly ignorant" of American realities because they relied on "impressions derived from reading the novels of social protest and revolt" like John Steinbeck's *The Grapes of Wrath*, as well as on the portraits of national "degeneracy" and "inanity" to be found in the works of William Faulkner and Sinclair Lewis. In effect, Hook was suggesting that American writers had not sufficiently taken into account the longrange political consequences of their criticisms. To compensate for these one-dimensional and excessively harsh appraisals, he recommended that Washington mount an "informational" campaign in which the "sober facts" about American life, both good and bad, would be communicated to Europeans. Hook was certain this could "produce a revolution" in their attitudes toward the United States, and generate a new spirit of solidarity among Western intellectuals.[9]

In this strenuous rivalry for the European mind and soul, James Burnham was far more frank than Hook or Phillips about what American writers might have to do and say in order to prevail. Addressing an international audience in Berlin in 1950, and trying to sound as hard-headed as possible, Burnham urged that the language of the West be cleansed of its sentimental allusions to peace and democracy. The Communists, he charged, had consistently manipulated the "rhetoric of public goodness" and "looted" the slogans of liberalism. Since they represented themselves as forward-looking, progressive, racially tolerant, anti-imperialist, pro-labor, and ardently pacifist, Western intellectuals should candidly declare that "the working class is no better than some other classes, that not every war is worse than any peace," and that "the popular will is as much a fiction as the divine right of kings." To compound these blasphemies, Burnham announced that he for one was not "under any and all circumstances against atomic bombs." He did oppose those bombs "stored . . . in Siberia or the Caucasus, which are designed for the destruction of Paris, London, Rome, Brussels, Stockholm, New York, Chicago, . . . Berlin, and of Western civilization generally." But he was indubitably "*for* those bombs made in Los Alamos, Hanford, and Oak Ridge" that "have been the sole defense" of western European liberty. Having dispensed with the "pious litany" of pacifism and all genuflections to "the common man," Burnham informed his listeners that there was no room left for indifference in the duel between "human freedom" and "monolithic totalitarian enslavement." European writers must cast aside their "illusions of neutrality" and join with Americans in a "moral, psychological and political counteroffensive" against Communism.[10]

Armed with this martial vocabulary, Barrett, Hook, Phillips, and Burnham naturally found it difficult to comprehend why Europeans seemed unenthusiastic about choosing sides. Slowly recovering from one conflagration, European intellectuals might not have felt quite so eager to enlist in another "death-struggle." Nor could they be expected to acquiesce in accusations that their nonpartisanship was a sign of cowardice or "political cretinism." Indeed, given Burnham's encomium to America's bombs, one sympathizes with the "nervous timidity" of European writers (not to mention ordinary citizens), as well as with their desire to flee as far as they could from the "battlefield."

Moreover, their hostility to American capitalism may not have arisen simply out of ignorance or misconceptions purveyed by alienated novelists. No public relations effort could extinguish the genuine yearning in Europe for some measure of political and cultural independence from the United States. In this respect, the disposition to criticize America did not mean that European intellectuals were oblivious to the sins of the Soviet Union. Neither did it make them "accomplices of Stalinism." Rather, when Europeans voiced misgivings about the United States, they were exercising the very freedom whose imminent demise their American colleagues kept bemoaning. Like most family quarrels, the rift between European and American writers could grow shrill and self-righteous, but this indicated how much each side asked of the other, not how few principles they shared. Ultimately, the preservation of democratic values and cultural diversity might have depended more on the inclination of intellectuals—in both Europe and the United States—to question some of the dogmas of the Cold War, instead of organizing global "counteroffensives" and decrying the perfidy of those who remained aloof.

Yet detachment proved hard to maintain, especially in the context of the Korean War. The decision (sanctioned, after all, by the United Nations) to repel what appeared an obvious instance of Communist aggression lent credence to the argument that writers could not abstain from ideological combat—quite the opposite. In these precarious circumstances, the West required from its intellectuals a commitment to use their skills in converting the undecided and winning away followers from the Communist cause.

Thus on the eve of Korea, the *New Republic* echoed the chant of the Cold Warriors, proclaiming that "the world's battle" was not between two superpowers but between "two universal faiths." Appreciating this, the Russians relied on an international clergy of Communists to preach their sermons; America must develop an identically effective ministry to proselytize on behalf of the democratic creed.[11]

A few months after the shooting began, William Barrett was pleased to report that most intellectuals no longer disputed the complexities of the Cold War. The "police action" in Korea, he observed, had "cleared the air" in America; "almost overnight a lot of political discussions became obsolete." Barrett felt vindicated: "At last the authorities seem to be waking up to realize how badly the U.S. has been beaten so far in the battle of ideas." Now the "chief problem of politics" was how to wage "the diplomatic and propaganda war." Unhappily, Russia could still invoke the more powerful slogans, particularly in the impoverished Far East where the canons of liberalism sounded unintelligible and irrelevant, and in Parisian cafés where the bourgeois values of self-government and due process were belittled as trivial and empty abstractions. Barrett therefore thought it necessary for the United States to contest the influence of Marxism by inventing new and better catch phrases. In his estimation, the most appropriate aphorism for the West's "counter-crusade" was "No Slavery!"[12]

Apparently, it escaped the notice of both Barrett and the *New Republic* that they were resurrecting a Communist bromide of the 1930s—the notion that ideas should be treated as "weapons" in whatever struggle currently raged. But with men dying from real weapons in Korea, this hardly seemed the occasion to recall the dangers of reducing intellectual life to a competition between opposing camps for the most rousing mottos. It was instead a time when writers formed again into political columns and fortified their doctrinal positions.

Accordingly, an illustrious collection of American and European intellectuals assembled in Berlin in June 1950 to inaugurate the Congress for Cultural Freedom. The participants included Ignazio Silone, André Malraux, Arthur Koestler, John Dos Passos, Arthur Schlesinger, James T. Farrell, Carson McCullers, Tennessee Williams, Sidney Hook, and James Burnham. Reinhold Niebuhr, A. J. Ayer, and Eleanor Roosevelt sent messages endorsing the proceedings. Over the next several years, the congress successively elected Benedetto Croce, John Dewey, Karl Jaspers, Jacques Maritain, and Bertrand Russell as its honorary presidents.[13]

Sidney Hook described the conference as an "exciting affair," largely because news of the Korean War had just arrived and the delegates were uncertain whether, in the event the Russians took advantage of the crisis to invade Germany, they might all wind up as prisoners of the Soviet secret police. Thus, Hook exclaimed, "this was no ordinary meeting of a learned society," but a "political affirmation." He conceded that, in such a tense but heady atmosphere, the "analytic quality" of the discussions "left something to be desired." Nevertheless, the level of discourse barely mattered. The conference was called to demonstrate the militant unity of Western intellectuals, not to exchange philosophies. As Hook pointed out, the most important papers propounded the basic thesis that at certain crucial junctures "instead of saying 'Neither-Nor' and looking for other viable alternatives, we must recognize an 'Either-Or' and take one stand or another." Condemning those writers whose distaste for anti-Communist theatrics led them to minimize the totalitarian peril, the congress "created a nucleus" of internationally famous writers "who will have no truck with 'neutrality' in the struggle for freedom."[14]

It turned out, however, that the congress would "have truck with" the CIA. The two guiding impresarios of the congress were Michael Josselson (a veteran of the Office of Strategic Services during World War II) and Melvin Lasky (who had worked with the American Information Service in postwar Germany). They secretly collaborated with the CIA in the 1950s and early 1960s in disbursing funds through fake foundations to help subsidize both the activities of the congress and its London-based magazine, *Encounter*.[15] Still, the anti-Communist convictions of the congress did not originate with the CIA; these had already congealed long before intelligence operatives began spending Washington's money on cultural warfare.

Nor could the CIA take credit for the rapid and widespread acceptance of the program set forth in Berlin. In 1951, the American Committee for Cultural Freedom was established as an affiliate of the European congress. Its membership was equally impressive. In addition to the familiar names of Burnham, Hook, and Farrell, the ACCF enrolled Norman Thomas, J. Robert Oppenheimer, Arthur Schlesinger, John Kenneth Galbraith, David Riesman, Daniel Bell, William Phillips, Diana Trilling, Irving Kristol, Eliot Cohen, Nathan Glazer, Norman Podhoretz, James Wechsler, Richard Rovere, and Elia Kazan. Most were unaware of the cordial relationship between their leaders and the CIA.

What this array of notables on both sides of the Atlantic did indicate was a willingness on the part of certain writers to fight the Cold War in tandem with their governments. On this issue at least, Western politicians and intellectuals assumed they shared a common purpose. But the alliance was tenuous; in the end, the state could no more harness its writers than they could influence military or foreign policy. And as some intellectuals discovered while resisting the terrorism not of Moscow but of HUAC and Joseph McCarthy, such a union did not really serve the interests of either political or cultural freedom.

The Celebration of America

From the late 1940s through the 1950s, partly as a reaction to the Cold War but also as a reflection of their new attitudes toward and position in American society, a number of writers devoted themselves to a full-scale reassessment of capitalism and democracy. Their revised portraits of life in the United States were mostly sympathetic. They recounted the benefits of liberalism in promoting social improvement without inhibiting personal freedom and self-development. They praised the tactics of bargaining and compromise, the virtues of pluralism and interest-group competition, the superiority of Keynesian economics and a limited welfare state. They agreed that the problems of modern America were no longer ideological but technical and administrative, and that these could be solved by knowledgeable experts rather than by mass movements. Their affection for the United States was not unbounded; they recognized the persistence of racial bigotry, the uneven distribution of wealth and power, and conservative longings to dismantle the New Deal. But they clearly preferred to emphasize the strengths of the political and economic system, not its deficiencies. Whatever their conscious intentions, they became in effect the celebrants of their native land.

Among the most prominent exponents of this reorientation were Arthur Schlesinger, Lionel Trilling, Reinhold Niebuhr, Daniel Bell, Seymour Lipset, Daniel Boorstin, and Oscar Handlin. During these years, their stature in the intellectual community rose steadily, not only because of the quality of their minds and the excellence of their work, but also because they seemed to flourish equally well in a variety of environments: in elite universities and research institutes, on the lecture circuit, in the world of specialized as well as mass circulation magazines, even in political campaigns.

Their articles and books received respectful attention and sometimes awards. Arthur Schlesinger taught history at Harvard and published admiring biographies of Andrew Jackson and Franklin Roosevelt, but his service as a speechwriter and adviser to both Adlai Stevenson and John F. Kennedy supported his claim to being the exemplary intellectual-as-social-activist. Sections from his key political treatise of the period, *The Vital Center* (1949), first appeared in *Partisan Review,* the *Nation, Life,* and the *New York Times Sunday Magazine.* Lionel Trilling prided himself on being the first Jew to be hired by the English department at Columbia; he also supplanted Edmund Wilson as America's most influential literary critic, especially after the publication of *The Liberal Imagination* (1950)—a compilation of his essays on culture and politics initially written for *Partisan Review,* the *Nation,* the *New Leader, Kenyon Review,* the *American Quarterly,* and the *New York Times Book Review.* Reinhold Niebuhr was a professor at the Union Theological Seminary, as well as a founding father of the Americans for Democratic Action; his major contribution to the postwar reevaluation of liberalism, *The Irony of American History* (1952), emerged from lectures delivered at Northwestern University and Westminster College in Fulton, Missouri. At different times, Daniel Bell was labor editor for Henry Luce's *Fortune* magazine, a fellow at the Center for Advanced Study in the Behavioral Sciences, and a member of the sociology department at Columbia. His authoritative study of American political and social life in the 1950s, *The End of Ideology* (1960), began as a series of articles written throughout the decade for *Commentary, Encounter, Partisan Review,* the *New Republic,* the *New Leader,* the *Saturday Review of Literature, Antioch Review,* the *American Journal of Sociology,* and *Dissent.* Like Bell, Seymour Lipset was a sociologist at Columbia before moving on to Berkeley; portions of *Political Man* (1960), his account of the social cohesiveness of American democracy, were originally published in the 1950s in *Daedalus,* the

American Political Science Review, the *American Sociological Review*, and *Encounter*. Daniel Boorstin was a historian at the University of Chicago who periodically wrote for *Commentary;* his renewed appreciation for America's pragmatic past was most eloquently expressed in *The Genius of American Politics* (1953) and *The Americans: The Colonial Experience* (1958), the second of which won the American Historical Association's Bancroft prize. Oscar Handlin enjoyed a distinction similar to Lionel Trilling's as the first Jewish appointee to Harvard's history department; he was a student (perhaps at first hand) of immigration and assimilation, a contributor to *Commentary,* and a recipient of the Pulitzer prize for *The Uprooted* (1951)—a poetic and poignant interpretation of the immigrants' experience in the new world.

Thus their ideas, reinforced by their multiple credentials, carried weight with other intellectuals, magazine and newspaper editors, academics, journalists, and segments of the general public. To the degree that one could measure the impact of their work, they provided what became the standard explanations of America's political ingenuity, economic success, and social stability in the 1950s.

None of them wished to be regarded as having surrendered their critical faculties. Several felt it necessary to swear their continuing fidelity to radical or at least reformist goals.

Seymour Lipset, for example, announced at the outset of *Political Man* that he considered himself "a man of the left." He identified with those liberals who sought to "extend democracy" and "reduce the punitive aspects of stratification"; in his view, they were the worthy heirs of the nineteenth century "socialist revolutionaries." Their task in the United States, however, was easier than one might suppose since, according to Lipset, "the values of socialism and Americanism are similar." Despite its image as the world's "wealthiest capitalist nation," the United States was also committed to the diffusion of economic and cultural opportunities through an expansion of its educational system.[16] This, of course, was not precisely what Marx had in mind, but such beneficent objectives could hardly be scorned.

Daniel Bell described his position more cautiously in *The End of Ideology*. The perspective he chose to adopt was "anti-ideological, but not conservative." Though he frowned upon utopian forms of thought, he understood that people needed "some vision of their potential, some manner of fusing passion with intelligence." So he recommended an "empirical" strategy that specified "*where* one wants to go, *how* to get there, the costs of the enterprise, and some realization of, and justification for the determination of *who* is to pay." Along the way, Bell proposed to question not only radical ideologies but "existing society" as well. After all, he pointed out in words that echoed the sentiments of most of his colleagues, "one can be a critic of one's country without being an enemy of its promise."[17]

Yet for all their testimonials to the Left and their advocacy of additional social reforms, they could not disguise their disenchantment with traditional radicalism. For most of these writers, economic problems had become far less important than political, psychological, and moral issues in the postwar years. Now the advantages of planning and the socialization of property appeared insignificant beside the greater need to safeguard democratic procedures and civil liberties. These insights led them to the inevitable conclusion that Marxism was irrelevant to the solution of contemporary dilemmas, that the Left's historic fondness for the ideals of community and cooperation had obscured the more important value of individual freedom, and that revolutions were neither practicable nor desirable in the modern world. But by this late date, few were saddened by the obsolescence of socialist ideas. If the grim lessons of the twentieth century meant intellectuals had to discard Marx, Arthur Schlesinger shrugged, "let us by all means discard Marx."[18]

This repudiation of the Old Left was made easier by the vitality of capitalism, particularly after World War II. In contrast to Europe, America's immense resources, the unparalleled affluence of the middle class, and the capacity of the economic system to satisfy the material needs of the people, all seemed to belie the Marxist prognosis and eliminate the justifications for socialism in the United States. In addition, intellectuals recognized that the New Deal had robbed radicals of their programs and their constituency. Arthur Schlesinger was especially impressed with the already substantial accomplishments of the "liberal democratic state" fashioned by Franklin Roosevelt. In Schlesinger's view, the New Deal and its successors had "redressed the balance of social power," sponsored a "systematic redistribution of wealth" that "helped confound Marx's prediction of increasing proletarian misery," figured out how to "control the business cycle" and stabilize the economy so as to prevent another depression, and drowned revolutionary rhetoric in a "torrent of consumer goods."[19]

Such analyses helped writers explain the American workers' singular disinterest in the socialist agenda. The average laborer, Schlesinger asserted, cared less for revolutionary maxims than for short-term improvements in his social and economic situation. As a result, he rarely displayed the impulses attributed to him by Marx.[20] Moreover, as Daniel Bell pointed out, the working class had been heavily composed of immigrants who were more eager to "win acceptance" in the United States and "become respectable" than to revamp the nation's institutions. This ambition tended to make workers "conservative" and resistant to demands for political militancy.[21]

According to Schlesinger, Bell, and Seymour Lipset, the American labor movement's emphasis on moderation and practicality perfectly suited the prosaic desires of the typical worker. The unions had given up all attempts to nationalize private property. They concentrated instead on those reforms that might immediately benefit their members: better housing, newer schools, nation-wide health insurance, a more "humanistic" atmosphere inside the factory. No writer thought these goals unworthy or mundane. But, as Lipset remarked approvingly, they did not "require or precipitate" the sort of "extremism" on the part of labor leaders and corporate executives that had characterized the battles of the 1930s. On the contrary, Schlesinger and Bell observed, the unions were now displaying maturity, assenting to the "role of partnership in government," building a liberal coalition within the Democratic party, and wisely extending the principles of collective bargaining from the boardrooms to the political arena. Only "by 'sharing' power rather than seeking the radical transformation of society," Bell submitted, could the labor movement remain a "force for social change."[22]

At bottom, the dismissal of socialism, the hosannas to capitalism and the New Deal, and the emphasis on the labor movement's inherent conservatism all permitted these writers to deal with America as they thought it was rather than as they might have once wished it to be. They could not breathe life into the corpse of the Old Left, or hold on to radical doctrines that no longer bore any relation to postwar life. In their estimation, the times called not for revolution but for realism.

The rejection of socialist theory and the urge to analyze American society with rigorous honesty made some intellectuals equally skeptical about certain aspects of liberalism. Like Schlesinger, Lipset, and Bell, Lionel Trilling wanted to preserve his critical detachment from the prevalent orthodoxies, whether radical or reformist. As he saw it, liberalism had become the reigning political philosophy in the United States, impervious to challenges from the Left or Right. Trilling in fact was less bothered by the irrelevance of Marxism than by the propensity of conservatives to substitute "irritable mental gestures" for coherent debate. Still, he did not think his fellow liberals should be content to "occupy the intellectual field alone." Since "we cannot very well . . . contrive opponents who will do us the service of forcing us to become more intelligent, who will require us to keep our ideas from becoming stale, habitual, and inert," liberals would have to perform these tasks for themselves. The most useful work intellectuals could undertake, he counseled, was not to confirm liberalism "in its sense of general rightness" but to put "under some degree of pressure the liberal ideas and assumptions of the present time."[23]

Such a reexamination did occur, but it led to somber conclusions. A number of writers criticized liberalism not for its economic shortcomings, but for trying to achieve too much. Wishing to appear practical and unsentimental, unable to forget the savagery of the Nazi and Stalinist experience, they emphasized the folly of man's efforts to completely remodel the world. Their language reflected this subdued outlook. "The key terms which dominate discourse today," Daniel Bell noted, were "irony, paradox, ambiguity, and complexity." His generation also found wisdom in the concepts of "pessimism, evil, tragedy, and despair."[24] Many of these attitudes were inspired by a revival of religious sensibility after 1945. By the 1950s, Americans could watch their favorite clerical celebrities on television, Fulton Sheen and Norman Vincent Peale competing in the ratings with Milton Berle and Howdy Doody. Among intellectuals, the most influential spokesman for a tough-minded Christianity was Reinhold Niebuhr. Though he himself had been attracted to socialism in the 1920s and 1930s, he persistently chided liberals and Marxists for ignoring the "reality of original sin" in their ambition to transform human behavior. Neither creed took into account "the tragic character of history," or recognized that people could do as much harm as good in the modern world. Secular ideologies, Niebuhr asserted, did not fully comprehend the "disharmonies" and "maladjustments" intrinsic to man's existence on earth; only religion could provide a vision of life that transcended the presumptions of politics.[25]

Niebuhr's vocabulary, if not his theology, had a profound effect on Arthur Schlesinger. Throughout *The Vital Center,* an otherwise skillful defense of postwar liberalism, Schlesinger peppered his prose with Augustinian (and Freudian) references to the tensions, uncertainties, and anxieties that afflicted people in the twentieth century. The most frightening feature of totalitarianism, in his opinion, was its attempt to "liquidate the tragic insights which gave man a sense of his limitations." In response, Schlesinger insisted that the problems of society could not be ascribed entirely to unjust political and economic institutions, that human beings were fallible and often corrupted by the "dark, slumbering forces" in their own psyches, that the optimistic faith in progress and perfectibility must be abandoned. Liberals, he complained, had "left no room" in their philosophy for the "awful reality" of Hitler and Stalin. So in order to understand the destructive impulses of mankind, they needed to recall the "old and chastening truths of Christianity."[26]

Novelists, poets, and literary critics could also assist in the renovation of liberalism. Lionel Trilling dedicated *The Liberal*

Imagination to the idea that politics and literature were intimately connected, though not in the direct or propagandistic ways cherished by radicals in the 1930s. Trilling did not crave more novels of social protest. Instead, he stressed the political relevance of those artists (particularly Proust, Joyce, Lawrence, Eliot, Yeats, Kafka, and Gide) who most acutely portrayed the "variousness, possibility, complexity, and difficulty" of human life. Like Freud and Niebuhr, these authors understood the subtlety and frequent irrationality of man's activities; an appreciation of their work could give liberals a modesty and a toughness they presently lacked.[27]

Niebuhr, Schlesinger, and Trilling all regarded the liberal mind as excessively rational and therefore simplistic. In its obsession with organization and efficiency, liberalism minimized the role of emotions and the play of imagination. Even worse, liberals could sound as utopian (and as arrogant) as socialists: Both overlooked the extent to which people were unmanageable and unpredictable, and both assumed that society could be made to conform to some preconceived plan or ideal. Such innocence about history and human nature no longer seemed charming to the postwar intellectuals; they preferred a political philosophy that was sensitive to the illogical and accidental elements in social life.[28]

The attack on liberal optimism and rationality coincided with the growing feeling after 1945 that many problems were ultimately insoluble. "I cannot imagine a free society which has eliminated conflict," Schlesinger confessed. Security, he declared, "is a foolish dream"; crises "will always be with us." Men were entangled in eternal dilemmas; they could normally expect "anxiety and frustration, not progress and fulfillment."[29] The best one could hope for in domestic and foreign policy, according to this view, was the gradual alleviation of suffering rather than the creation of a new world.

None of these writers were preaching passivity or stoicism. They continued to believe in the necessity of social reforms and governmental initiatives. But what emerged from the essays and books of Trilling, Schlesinger, and Niebuhr was an existential injunction that people should commit themselves to political action despite the high probability of failure.[30] Trilling labeled his position "moral realism," which he defined as the willingness to work for change combined with an awareness of "the dangers" that "lie in our most generous wishes"—especially the tendency to reduce other human beings to "objects of our pity, then of our wisdom, ultimately of our coercion."[31]

Thus a mature liberalism ought naturally welcome the instructions of religion, literature, psychiatry, and history. Since there were no simple answers or millennial solutions to contemporary difficulties, since the attempt to alter society might well unleash man's not-so-latent capacity for brutality and fanaticism, liberals could reconcile themselves to the humble but still important job of modifying existing institutions without worrying that they had betrayed the passions of their youth.

Those less inclined to grant the pessimistic conclusions of religion or literature had other reasons for lowering their political aspirations. While European history in the twentieth century had disclosed the lethal consequences of utopian fixations, the current realities of American life made all doctrinal absolutes appear anachronistic. The "radical intellectual who had articulated the revolutionary impulses of the past century and a half," Daniel Bell asserted, now saw no purpose in "chiliastic hopes," messianic dogmas, or "apocalyptic thinking." Few contemporary issues could be "formulated any more . . . in ideological terms" because such explanations had lost "their power to persuade." Thus Bell announced that "ideology, which once was a road to action, has come to be a dead end." With no class enemies to slay and no mass movements to romanticize, ex-radicals should concern themselves with the "unheroic, day-to-day routine of living," disavowing all blueprints for social change and acknowledging the virtues of "pragmatic compromise."[32]

Fortunately, America seemed the country best suited to carry on without ideologies of any kind. The United States had prospered for two hundred years, some writers argued, not only because of its vast natural wealth but also because its cultural traditions encouraged experimentation and a shrewd distrust of all political abstractions.

Daniel Boorstin (briefly a disciple of Marx in the 1930s) displayed the greatest enthusiasm for America's indifference to ideology. The "genius" of the nation's political parties, he exclaimed, lay paradoxically in their ignorance of political theory. Statesmen and citizens had always shown more interest in how the society actually worked than in its philosophical premises. A practical people who saw themselves as the "lucky beneficiaries of an especially happy environment" needed no myths, faiths, or slogans to account for their success, Boorstin declared; the "crude facts of history have been good enough."[33]

If the United States was indeed a land in which formal principles mattered less than a casual empiricism, then intellectuals were equally free to weigh political and social issues on their specific merits, without reference to the claims of any organization or sect. The revolt against ideology could therefore be liberating. Potentially, it permitted writers to avoid rigid or archaic patterns of thought, to ask new questions, to analyze creatively the unprecedented problems of modern society. The very act of criticism depended on the intellectual's ability to emancipate himself from all systems of belief.

More often, however, the repudiation of ideological formulas led writers in the 1950s to glorify established political procedures, to applaud rather than evaluate America's cheerful practicality. These tendencies were particularly evident in their glowing praise for such estimable institutions as the two-party system, with its promotion of tolerance and compromise as the supreme values of a liberal society.

Anyone wishing to bring about or resist change in the United States now had to operate within the framework of the Democratic or Republican parties, Daniel Bell insisted. This obligation compelled certain standards of public behavior: the implicit agreement among various factions not to convert "concrete issues" into "ideologically tinged conflicts" that might only polarize the nation, the adherence to a spirit of "pragmatic give-and-take" rather than the indulgence in a "series of wars-to-the-death," a common realization that "democratic politics" meant "bargaining between legitimate groups and the search for consensus."[34]

The protagonists on the American political stage must be "responsible," Arthur Schlesinger cautioned. They should consent to parliamentary tactics and "piecemeal" transitions that would not "disrupt the fabric of custom, law and mutual confidence" on which national unity and personal freedom depended. Schlesinger admitted that the politics of expedient wheeling and dealing could seem "dull" after "living dangerously in the exciting land of either-or," but democracy's survival involved the willingness of its citizens to "enter the unromantic realm of more-or-less."[35]

Their journey was facilitated, according to Bell and Seymour Lipset, by the capacity of each major party to mobilize a broad coalition of regional, economic, and special-interest groups. No matter what frustrated Marxists or baffled Europeans might say, the hybrid character of the American parties, their refusal to define issues explicitly or confine their appeal to particular classes, their invariable decision to select "a man of the center" as their presidential nominee, all reduced the intensity of political debate and contributed to social cohesion.[36]

If as a result, the policies of Democrats and Republicans frequently appeared identical, Lipset was not deceived. He realized that the decline of radicalism did not imply the end of political or economic controversy. The Democrats continued to represent the needs of the "lower-income" groups while the Republicans remained the spokesmen for the "more privileged" segments of the population. But this American version of the "class struggle," Lipset submitted, would always be "a fight without ideologies, without red flags, without May Day parades."[37]

Thus what Bell and Lipset, like Boorstin and Schlesinger, admired most was a political system that turned candidates into brokers and parties into agencies of "mediation," that refrained from moral or doctrinal divisiveness by taking on problems "one at a time."[38] The hostility of all four writers to dogmatic creeds and their defense of political pragmatism stemmed from their postwar reverence for those elements that had held the nation together during its shakiest moments in the recent past. Where in the 1930s they might have valued ideological strife and social upheaval, they now desired a politics of stability and moderation. The 1950s was for them a decade not only of lowered aspirations but also of lowered voices.

The intellectuals' advocacy of political compromise had implications for economic policy as well. In their view, the antagonism between government and business nurtured during the Depression need not persist; statesmen and corporate executives could jointly travel the middle of the road. The point was to avoid economic extremism, to keep one's eyes fastened on what Arthur Schlesinger called the "vital center" of American life.

For Schlesinger, as for Daniel Bell, the ideal arrangement was a "mixed economy," where Washington guaranteed full employment and dispensed social services while ensuring a favorable environment for "private investment and adequate consumption," all of this to be accomplished without excessive regulation or bureaucratic interference. Their patron saint was not Marx but Keynes; their goal was no longer the introduction of socialism but the construction of a welfare state on the foundations of a capitalist economy.[39] The principal attraction of these proposals, as Reinhold Niebuhr and Seymour Lipset noted, was to achieve an "equilibrium" between government and business, balancing the power of one against the other, thereby reinforcing the stability of society as a whole.[40]

An additional advantage of the mixed economy was its spectacular success in raising the standard of living for the majority of Americans, which further smothered the causes of social unrest. In this respect, as in so many others, the United States appeared strikingly different from Europe. The crucial distinction between the two continents was not the presence or absence of opportunities for social mobility, Lipset declared. Rather, real income was more widely and equitably distributed in America than in Europe. Consequently, the "gap between the living styles" of the various classes in the United States seemed "much narrower." In effect, Lipset asserted, America was a more egalitarian society not because people could climb the economic ladder with greater ease, but because capitalism itself had expanded throughout the twentieth century, creating new white-collar jobs in the cities for impoverished farmers and manual laborers, giving them the means to purchase the commodities and prestige symbols that signified membership in the middle class.[41]

Although Schlesinger, Bell, Niebuhr, and Lipset were careful not to depict the mixed economy as a panacea for all the country's problems, they did regard it as an essential pillar of a democratic and pluralist society. Indeed, their social preferences coincided with their political and economic values: In each area, they stressed the benefits of concrete negotiations, loose and informal alliances, the middle way.

To Daniel Bell, America was neither a class nor a mass society. On the one hand, he argued, the power of decision making in the modern corporation had passed from long-established families whose wealth and property were largely inherited, to a new generation of managers whose authority derived from their technical skills and professional competence. This transformation of American capitalism meant that one's access to the boardroom depended not on lineage but on education, ambition, and efficient performance—qualifications potentially available to anybody. Nor could a successful manager transfer his expertise to his heirs; positions were open to all according to ability. Thus in Bell's judgment, America had no "ruling class" in the Marxist or aristocratic sense.[42]

On the other hand, Bell derided the notion that America was an individualistic, "atomized" society where each person could overcome his loneliness and isolation only in mass movements or through the mass media. Instead, he insisted that Americans were inveterate "joiners," participating endlessly in "pressure groups" and every form of "voluntary community activity," all of which diminished the need for mass organizations and ideological causes with their moralistic, irrational, and utopian obsessions.[43]

A number of writers besides Bell looked upon America's pluralistic tradition as the perfect antidote to the sectarian politics of the 1930s and the totalitarian impulses of the postwar world. First, voluntary associations offered a variety of allegiances, no one of which could dominate the political or economic landscape. "The persistent sprouting of all sorts of religious, cultural, and social groups," Oscar Handlin suggested, enabled the individual to choose freely among numerous affiliations, often accepting membership in and scattering his loyalties among several organizations. Second, Handlin contended that this "freedom of association . . . shielded the citizen against the naked exercise of power by his government. In the United States, the individual was not compelled alone to confront the state. Between the isolated man and his government stood a wide array of intermediaries."[44] Schlesinger and Lipset agreed with Handlin. In their estimation, the spontaneous proliferation of neighborhood, ethnic, and occupational groups acted as a "buffer" for the average American, offsetting the capacity of the government, the corporations, and the media to manipulate opinion. Moreover, they gave people a "sense of belonging" and a "meaningful role in society," thereby preventing the "pulverization of the social structure essential to totalitarianism."[45] Finally, Handlin, Bell, and Lipset all considered voluntary associations indispensable to the democratic process because they encouraged ad hoc alliances and "group [rather than class] struggles"; the result was a greater tolerance for political opponents, a pragmatic striving for specific economic gains, and "institutionalized" (not messianic) campaigns to rectify social inequality.[46]

In sum, the voluntary association became in the minds of these intellectuals the social analogue to the two-party system and the mixed economy. Each represented an alternative to, or at least a compromise between, America's ritualistic glorification of individualism and the collectivist ideals of contemporary socialism. Modern America might well be "compartmentalized, superficial in personal relations, anonymous, transitory, specialized, utilitarian, competitive, acquisitive, mobile, and status-hungry," Daniel Bell conceded, but it remained superior to the closed, stratified, and hierarchical communities of the past or the totalitarian models of the future. What Bell thought most valuable in the United States was its defense of the "right to privacy," its willingness to reward achievement rather than ancestry, and its trust in a "plurality of norms and standards, rather than [in] the exclusive and monopolistic social controls of a single dominant group."[47] Similarly, Arthur Schlesinger admired America because it was so "loosely organized," because it permitted "gaps and rivalries," because its political, economic, and social institutions were *not* coherent or consistent. "Liberty," he concluded, "gets . . . fresh air and sunlight through the interstices of a diversified society."[48]

Occasionally, these laudatory descriptions summoned up the

image of America as a halfway house in a world divided between capitalist chaos and socialist uniformity. But they also revealed the intellectuals' desire for a social order that was neither intrusive nor anarchistic, that provided opportunities for cooperative action and crevices for personal freedom. In a nation devoted to centrist politics, a Keynesian economy, and interest-group competition, the individual should have little cause to feel alienated from or suffocated by his fellow citizens.[49] However elusive and intangible this portrayal of the good society might seem, such ideas were hardly trivial or unpersuasive. And they did suggest a set of democratic values different from and superior to the images associated with totalitarianism.

Nevertheless, these writers may have too quickly assumed that their vision was already a reality in postwar America, rather than an assortment of goals still to be won. Their overriding preoccupation with those institutions and behavior patterns that produced a stable society led them to minimize the necessity for radical criticism and continuing reform. During much of the 1950s, they and many other American intellectuals seemed less interested in the dynamics of social change than in the factors that contributed to a national consensus: political pragmatism, widespread prosperity, the acceptance of the welfare state by both liberals and conservatives, a relatively contented middle class, "responsible" labor leaders who preferred bargaining to the barricades, a common recognition of man's limitations, and the concentration on present tasks rather than millennial myths.

No one exhibited these tendencies more transparently than Seymour Lipset. Throughout *Political Man,* he detected elements of stability in the most unlikely phenomena, and he was continually able to translate the most unpromising institution or social ill into a democratic asset.

Did union officials ignore the rank and file? Too much internal democracy provoked factional disputes and pointless wildcat strikes, Lipset replied.[50]

Were American voters apathetic? "It is possible," he speculated, "that nonvoting is now . . . a reflection of the stability of the system, a response to the decline of major social conflicts." While a high voter turnout was "not necessarily bad," any sudden increase in the size of the electorate "probably reflects tension and serious governmental malfunctioning." Worse, it "introduces as voters individuals whose social attitudes are unhealthy," whose lack of education left them with "cynical ideas about democracy and political parties," whose impatience with parliamentary coalitions coupled with their authoritarian penchant for strong leaders all threatened to disrupt the normal routines of governance.[51]

Were Washington bureaucrats remote and impersonal? Perhaps, Lipset acknowledged, but they also tempered the "strains of party strife" by removing "conflicts from the political to the administrative arena." Additionally, because bureaucrats demanded "objective criteria" for settling problems, they played "major mediating roles" in society. Hence, Lipset asserted, "the pressures to extend bureaucratic norms and practices" to all areas of public life actually strengthened the "democratic consensus."[52]

It was not that Lipset abhorred political combat and social cleavage. These too had a place in an orderly nation. "A stable democracy," he declared, required some "manifestation" of conflict "so that there will be struggle over ruling positions, challenges to parties in power, and shifts of parties in office." Even better, such battles often gave the "have-nots" a greater sense of "loyalty . . . to the system." By allowing them to participate in and improve their lot through ordinary political channels, they might eventually lose their fervor for reform and join the "conservative ranks." Still, both Lipset and Daniel Bell insisted that every contending group must abide by the "rules of the game." There were boundaries of political conduct no party or organization should be permitted to exceed. But as long as conflicts did not endanger the nation's basic institutions and ideals, as long as movements remained "legitimate" instead of becoming revolutionary, they could contribute to the "integration" of American society.[53]

Such prescriptions sounded reasonable enough. Yet they also revealed how loyal to established procedures these intellectuals had themselves become in their migration from the left to the political center. Their fear of revolutionary upheavals, combined with their quasi-theological insights about the human potential for barbarism and destruction, persuaded them that neither the "people" nor mass organizations could be entrusted with power, that a cohesive and well-run society required responsible elites and stable institutions to control man's inherent irrationality. Where the *New Republic*'s editors during and after the war had focused too much on the president as the catalyst for reform, some liberals now concluded that it was the function of leaders (whether in government, the business community, or the unions) to exemplify for the multitudes the virtues of moderation and compromise. But writers like Schlesinger, Bell, and Lipset tended to deny or underestimate the possibility that social movements could pursue equally specific and pragmatic goals—and that their existence was often essential simply to put pressure on and overcome the resistance of experts, managers, and administrators.[54]

Similarly, though the denigration of ideology helped free intellectuals from the shibboleths of Marxism, it also made them indifferent to questions about the ultimate worth of capitalism and the underlying values of American life. An exclusive attention to immediate problems, the emphasis on practical and incremental reforms, may have been wise given the political realities of the 1950s. But such a diminished perspective induced many writers to concentrate on the techniques of intergroup bargaining rather than the content of social programs, to describe the mechanics of political conflict in the United States rather than examine the substantive issues that could tear the country apart at some future date. Few intellectuals were able to give up their faith in older radical doctrines yet continue to subject American institutions to systematic analysis and criticism.

The disillusion with mass movements and socialist theory, however, arose less from an unconscious failure of nerve among postwar intellectuals than from their conviction that prosperity was now a permanent feature of American life. If the country's economic difficulties were merely technical, then there seemed no need for a thorough—much less an ideological—investigation of modern capitalism. But the belief in eternal affluence, like Hannah Arendt's portrait of totalitarianism, translated what might have been a temporary set of conditions existing in a particular historical period into a static model of social and economic behavior good for all time.

The point here is not that intellectuals in the 1950s should have foreseen how severe the problems of inflation and recession would become, any more than Arendt should have anticipated de-Stalinization. The trouble was that they did not look closely enough at or emphasize more strongly the circumstances surrounding America's prosperity at the moment they were writing —especially the intimate connections between business profits, full employment, defense contracts, and the Cold War. Moreover, in their picture of an infinitely expanding economy and a loosely organized society open to pluralistic competition and individual initiative, they understated how much inherited wealth remained in the hands of Rockefellers, Du Ponts, and Fords. In addition, they discounted the ability of the new corporate managers to transmit their power and social position to their children in the form of educational and professional opportunities unavailable to the offspring of farmers, shopkeepers, salesmen, clerks, blue-collar workers, and the poor. Finally, for all their praise of voluntary associations and their assumption that freedom lurked in the nooks and crannies of American life, they rarely asked which groups possessed real power to affect national policy, or what liberty actually meant in a nation still stratified by wealth, class, and color.

Such queries might have been incompatible with the spirit of consensus. But it was the primary duty of intellectuals to raise and debate them nonetheless. Some did. Too many writers, however, wound up exchanging the packaged orthodoxies of the Old Left for a new bundle of dogmas. They remained true believers, only this time in the tenets of realism, pragmatism, pluralism, the two-party system, the mixed economy, and social stability. Ironically, at the very moment they welcomed the "end of ideology," they had become the ideologues of the American Way.

The Liberal Tradition and Its Critics

The postwar veneration of balance and moderation sprang not only from a distaste for revolutionary turmoil and a belief in the durability of America's economic abundance, but also from new and more lenient treatments of the nation's past. During these years, a major reassessment of American history coincided with and reinforced the notion that the current vitality of the United States flowed from its distinctive environment and traditions, and that the hallmark of its political and social life was not change but continuity.

An appreciation of the nation's homogeneity had not always been fashionable. From the turn of the century until World War II, the most influential interpretations of American history had stressed the importance of social conflict in shaping the country's development. These views frequently mirrored and justified the economic and political battles waged during the Progressive era and the 1930s. Frederick Jackson Turner, Charles Beard, Vernon Parrington, and their various disciples all saw the past as a series of titanic struggles between farmers and financiers, workers and robber barons, Jeffersonian reformers and Hamiltonian reactionaries, the "democratic" frontier and the elitist seacoast.

In the 1940s and 1950s, however, when perpetual social strife no longer seemed quite so laudable, and when the Old Masters of American historiography had retired or died, a young generation of historians began to reconsider the very meaning of the American experience. Where Turner and Beard had emphasized sectional and economic divisions, their successors discerned uniformity, agreement, an unconscious but pervasive harmony of interests linking every party, group, and region. The American Revolution, it turned out, was not a revolution at all but a ratification of the gradual changes taking place throughout the colonial period. Jeffersonians and Jacksonians appeared in retrospect less democratic than entrepreneurial. The Populists of the 1890s ceased to be agrarian radicals and became instead rural opportunists seeking to enlarge their profits at the expense of urban workers and middle-class consumers. The Progressive movement during the first two decades of the twentieth century looked more like an exercise in nostalgia than an effort to cope with big-city corruption and industrial blight. In each of these cases, what now mattered was how many values the advocates of reform shared with the defenders of order and tradition.

It required some ingenuity, of course, to fit the Civil War into this monochromatic canvas, but the scholar could usually note the speed with which Americans—North and South—returned after 1865 to the tasks of making money and conquering the West. Thus, regardless of some contradictory evidence here or an aberration there, the central message of the new generation was clear: America enjoyed a historic exemption from the ideological and class convulsions of Europe. Whether one read Daniel Boorstin's *The Genius of American Politics* (1953) or David Potter's *People of Plenty* (1954), one came away convinced that Karl Marx had been forever banished from the promised land.[55]

Still, no author concluded that the nation's past was devoid of subtle tensions, hidden quandaries, paradoxical impulses. On the contrary, the postwar historians rejected the dualistic vision of Turner and Beard in part because they were fascinated by the multiple complexities of American life. This was particularly true of those in the burgeoning American Studies movement who undertook an interdisciplinary quest for the national "character." They drew on every conceivable source—a close textual reading of Puritan sermons, the recently rediscovered insights of Alexis de Tocqueville (whose *Democracy in America* was republished at the end of World War II), the political rhetoric of the Jacksonians, the novels of the nineteenth century, the myths and symbols of popular culture, legends and folk tales, painting and architecture, hand tools and industrial machinery, clothing and furniture—all in a massive attempt to portray the special qualities of the "American mind." Their work disclosed the country's astonishing diversity, as well as the population's persistent ambivalence toward the wilderness, urban civilization, wealth, power, technology, religion, science, eastern refinements, westward expansion, political tacticians, social codes, minority rights, and national progress.

Yet like the more conventional historians, they also insisted on the nation's absolute uniqueness; they too wanted to specify those attitudes and customs that made the United States different from (and by implication superior to) Europe. Perry Miller's two-volume *The New England Mind* (1939 and 1954), Henry Nash

Smith's *The Virgin Land* (1950), John William Ward's *Andrew Jackson: Symbol for an Age* (1955), R. W. B. Lewis's *The American Adam* (1955), Marvin Meyer's *The Jacksonian Persuasion* (1957), Leslie Fiedler's *Love and Death in the American Novel* (1960), and Leo Marx's *The Machine in the Garden* (1964) each told its readers what was "American" about America, how the people had adapted to their new environment, why the nation remained "exceptional" despite the cataclysms of the twentieth century.

Nevertheless, the one characteristic that united the prewar generation and the postwar revisionists was an inclination to identify with some aspect of the nation's past. Turner, Beard, and Parrington aligned themselves with frontiersmen, farmers, small-property holders, and Jeffersonian democrats. Boorstin, Potter, and Miller sympathized with American practicality, economic growth, or the intellectual rigor of the Puritan divines. The historians who came to dominate the profession after 1945 commemorated different heroes and different ideals, but they were still using the past to provide instruction to and reassurance for the present.

Not every postwar scholar took pride or comfort in the past. At least two, Richard Hofstadter and Louis Hartz, chose neither to magnify conflict nor to applaud consensus. In their books, the United States emerged as idiosyncratic but not necessarily as a model for mankind. Indeed, their reading of American history was in many respects more critical than the work of their predecessors before World War II, and certainly less affirmative than the accounts of their contemporaries. Because they managed to transcend the Manichean approach of Turner and Beard, as well as the more recent disposition to celebrate America as an unceasing success story, Hofstadter and Hartz became at once the most detached and the most provocative historians of their generation. And in raising the issues others in the 1950s often avoided, they functioned both as academics and as genuine intellectuals.

Richard Hofstadter, according to his friend Alfred Kazin, was a man "filled with divided loyalties." Half Lutheran and half Jewish (his father was a Yiddish-speaking émigré from Poland), captivated by the raw energy of an expanding America in the late nineteenth century yet suspicious of its legacy in his own time, a student of political and social thought who kept his distance from most of the quarrels and activities that absorbed intellectuals in the 1950s, Hofstadter elected to be an aloof but mordant observer of American life. Yet this coolness was often a pose—a style deemed mandatory for academics, if not for the entire society in the postwar years. In reality, Kazin remembered, Hofstadter "was a derisive critic and parodist of every American Utopia and its wild prophets, a natural oppositionist to fashion and its satirist, a creature suspended between gloom and fun, between disdain for the unexpected . . . and powerfully disturbed emotions that never showed."[56]

Hofstadter taught first at the University of Maryland before going to Columbia in 1946, where he spent the rest of his career. In 1948, at the age of thirty-two, he published *The American Political Tradition*, a collection of acerbic essays on those presidents who were the chief architects of liberalism in the United States. The book established Hofstadter's reputation as an iconoclastic and imaginative historian. But his masterpiece, published in 1955, was *The Age of Reform.* Here Hofstadter analyzed the Populists and Progressives as exemplars of America's recurring passion for social uplift and moral renovation. He poured into the work all of his own mixed feelings about mass movements, especially those vaguely associated with the Left. Hofstadter was both sympathetic to and fearful of these spasmodic crusades to remold the country's institutions and values, and he traced their line of descent through the New Deal to the McCarthyite hysteria of the 1950s. *The Age of Reform* eventually elicited a response similar to the one directed at *The Origins of Totalitarianism.* By the 1960s, its arguments had been corrected, refuted, disproved, and dismissed. Nonetheless, *The Age of Reform* remains a classic indictment of American liberalism—and one of the most prescient books of the 1950s.

At the outset, Hofstadter mildly disclaimed his critical intentions. "The function of the liberal tradition in American politics," he conceded, had been "first to broaden the numbers of those who could benefit from the great American bonanza and then to humanize its workings and help heal its casualties."[57] But in both *The American Political Tradition* and *The Age of Reform,* Hofstadter professed his dissatisfaction with the rosy depictions of the past currently prevalent in popular histories and even in formal scholarship. "I have no desire," he remarked, "to add to a literature of hero-worship and national self-congratulation which is already large." Like Lionel Trilling, Hofstadter believed that in the absence of a conservative counterattack, liberals would have to reevaluate their own ideas and inherited attitudes. In dissecting the language and programs of the Populists and Progressives, he hoped to indicate "some of the limitations" of the reform tradition, "and to help free it of its sentimentalities and complacencies." Hofstadter proposed to be "critical, but not hostile," for as a liberal himself he was "criticizing largely from within."[58]

Hofstadter agreed with the postwar view that the dominant strain in American history was not conflict but consensus. "The fierceness of the political struggles has often been misleading," he submitted; "the range of vision embraced by the primary contestants in the major parties has always been bounded by the horizons of property and enterprise." Except for "small groups of dissenters and alienated intellectuals," most Americans (and particularly practical politicians) had accepted the philosophy of "individualism," the "value of competition," and the "economic virtues of capitalist culture as necessary qualities of man." Jeffersonians and Federalists, Jacksonians and Whigs, Democrats and Republicans might rage at each other "with every appearance of a bitter and indissoluble opposition," but their differences were really minute and their policies in office seemed "indistinguishable." Ultimately, no one wished to advocate theories inimical to the country's "fundamental working arrangements."[59]

But this concord did not delight Hofstadter. Unlike Daniel Boorstin and Seymour Lipset, he was bothered by the political inflexibility and intellectual stagnation it bred. Thus he complained that liberals had rarely understood or tried to confront the problems of their own era. Instead, they had fixed their gaze steadily on "bygone institutions and conditions"; they were always enchanted by pastoral fantasies and obsolete goals. Even in the present circumstances of "concentration, bigness, and corporate monopoly—when competition and opportunity have gone into decline—men look wistfully back toward a golden age."[60]

In Hofstadter's opinion, these chronic longings to recapture a vanished past were best illustrated in the rhetoric of Populism and Progressivism. Wading through the pamphlets, novels, economic treatises, political manifestos, legislative agenda, and presidential pronouncements of the late nineteenth and early twentieth century reformers, he uncovered a reactionary state of mind hidden beneath the pleas for social change.

The Populists and Progressives did not seek to utilize the new forms of industrial organization and managerial expertise for the betterment of society, Hofstadter contended. Rather, they wanted to restore the "economic individualism and political democracy" as well as "a kind of morality and civic purity" that allegedly flourished in an earlier, more pristine America.[61] Already in *The American Political Tradition,* Hofstadter had described Woodrow Wilson as an archetypal liberal (and in many ways the villain of that book). "Neither an aggressive critic nor an intellectual innovator," unable to dissociate himself "from the political values of the society in which he lived," Wilson was for Hofstadter "a spokesman of the past," yearning in both his domestic and foreign policies to reproduce the anarchic conditions of the nineteenth century—or failing that, at least to "preserve the essentials of the status quo."[62] In effect, Wilson served as one of Hofstadter's major symbols for the deceptions and fraudulence of American reform. Hofstadter's own feelings about the whole charade resembled those of H. L. Mencken. In the efforts of the Populists and Progressives to hold on to the myths of agrarian life, to "save personal entrepreneurship . . . and maintain a homogeneous Yankee civilization," he found "much that was retrograde and delusive, a little that was vicious, and a good deal that was comic."[63]

Hofstadter was no more impressed with later manifestations of the reform impulse. He preferred the New Deal's lack of moralistic fervor and its interest in "practical achievement," but Franklin Roosevelt's "ability to get results" was not matched by a capacity to develop "systematic" or "consistent" ideas. Consequently, FDR "provided no clearly articulated break with the inherited faith."[64]

Yet in the end, Hofstadter objected to liberalism not because it was Janus-faced or excessively pragmatic, but because it could become self-righteous and irrational—particularly in its response to alien influences and attitudes (like those carried across the ocean by immigrants and radicals), none of which fit very smoothly into the American consensus. Hence, reformers resisted new ideas not only by looking backward or refusing to think coherently, but also by insisting on "impossible standards" to which everyone was expected to conform. This in turn led to "a form of moral absolutism" and a "ruthlessness in political life" that repelled Hofstadter.[65]

Well before the rise of Joseph McCarthy, Hofstadter in *The American Political Tradition* had noticed the ease with which a liberal era might succumb to venomous demagogues once its deepest values were threatened by domestic turmoil or external pressures. If Woodrow Wilson dramatized the conservative implications of reform, Theodore Roosevelt revealed its neurotic undertones. America's "frantic" industrial growth and sudden encounter with millions of foreigners in its own midst had "heightened social tensions" and left a residue of "bewilderment, anger, and fright," Hofstadter asserted. Roosevelt's function as a public leader was primarily psychological. Like later self-appointed saviors, he set out to "relieve . . . anxieties with a burst of hectic action and to discharge . . . fears by scolding authoritatively the demons that aroused them." To Hofstadter, Theodore Roosevelt was a shrewd charlatan who presented himself as the "master therapist of the middle classes"—a role McCarthy would shortly try to reenact.[66]

Indeed, much of Hofstadter's criticism of the reform spirit rested on his discomfort with its historical results. His books were meant as both a reappraisal of the past and a warning to the present. Like Daniel Bell and Seymour Lipset, he distrusted mass enthusiasms. In his judgment, as in theirs, the appeal of ideologies and the existence of social conflicts were often symptomatic of a society's free-floating frustrations and emotional instability.

But Hofstadter seemed more prone than they to question the benevolence and wisdom of liberal doctrines, whether expressed by elites or popular movements. His main purpose was to point out the extent to which "such tendencies in American life as

isolationism and . . . extreme nationalism, hatred of Europe and
Europeans, racial, religious, and nativist phobias, resentment of
big business, trade-unionism, intellectuals, the Eastern seaboard
and its culture" had all thrived not only in opposition to liberalism "but also at times oddly combined with it." He had studied
the early twentieth century reformers because as the years wore
on, "a large part of the Populist–Progressive tradition . . . turned
sour" and became "illiberal and ill-tempered," foreshadowing
"some aspects of the cranky pseudo-conservatism of our own
time." The modern intellectual, therefore, ought not to "senti-
mentalize the folk" or their leaders, for he might in the future
find his own liberal principles "enlisted in the service of reaction."[67]

Given the ardor with which some intellectuals converted themselves into Cold Warriors, and the difficulties many liberals had
in defending their values against the insinuations and distortions
of congressional investigators and private blacklisters, Hofstadter's words were even more pertinent to the 1950s than to
the dawn of the century. Whatever the flaws in his interpretation
of Populism and Progressivism, he had demonstrated the dangers of investing too much faith in any political or national cause
—especially those that seemed most congenial to one's own liberal convictions. Thus for all his apparent scholarly detachment
from the immediate concerns of his fellow intellectuals, Hofstadter was indirectly challenging the sorts of commitments they
had made, together with the dubious allies they might as a consequence be forced to embrace.

In contrast to the reserve Hofstadter normally displayed, Louis
Hartz looked and sounded as if he'd been sent over by Central
Casting to audition for a minor part in *The Godfather*. Where
Hofstadter's public demeanor was deliberately laconic, Hartz
spoke with the speed and intensity of a tommy gun. In a classroom, he seemed prepared at any moment to break into an impression of James Cagney or John Garfield; one half expected
him to interrupt his lecture with the recollection that as a kid he
never had a decent pair of shoes.

Yet if Hartz's style was pyrotechnic, his knowledge was wideranging. He surveyed the American past with the eye of a Euro-

pean political theorist, and his courses at Harvard consistently stressed the comparisons between the New World and the Old. In 1955, he published *The Liberal Tradition in America,* a book that reflected both his mannerisms and his interests. Part history, part polemic, part meditation, *The Liberal Tradition* was maddeningly allusive in its barrage of names (Americans, British, French, German—politicians, philosophers, agitators, revolutionaries, clerics, assorted historians and literary critics), each of whom represented a particular idea or position Hartz alone had in mind but seemed too impatient to decode. The book was also a brilliant tour de force, as well as an exposé of the American liberal's complacency and provincialism. More than any other historical work of the decade, it synthesized the prevailing interpretations of the nation's past and suggested ways in which the United States might begin to comprehend and live with the rest of the world.

Like Hofstadter, Hartz felt equally uncomfortable with the prewar historians' overemphasis on social discord, and the implications of the postwar insistence on a deep-rooted national consensus. The Beardians, Hartz charged, had turned American history into an incessant clash between "conservatives" and "radicals," thereby consoling themselves that the nation's better instincts would periodically triumph over its "inferior self." The revisionists too often either reversed this equation, pointing out how conservative the radicals really were, or took refuge in the notion that America's pragmatic genius lay in its indifference to all social and ideological struggles. Whichever stance they adopted, most postwar historians continued to view the past with the same insularity as their predecessors. "You merely demonstrate your subservience to a thinker," Hartz wisely observed in reference to the attacks on Beard, "when you spend your time attempting to disprove him. The way to fully refute a man is to ignore him . . . and the only way you can do this is to substitute new fundamental categories for his own, so that you are simply pursuing a different path."[68]

Hartz proposed to follow his own advice in *The Liberal Tradition.* In order to transcend the parochial perspective of both Beard and his detractors, Hartz embarked on a metaphorical and intellectual journey to Europe where he hoped (as had so many other expatriates) he would discover the true dimensions of the "American liberal world." He did not deny that serious divisions had existed in the United States, but he meant to unravel their ambiguous meaning in the context of the European experience. Nor did he underestimate the degree to which Americans agreed on how their institutions should be structured. Still, Hartz believed a comparative point of view might enable him to think more critically about his native land than had the historians of conflict or consensus. Feeling no obligation to support one group against another, and lacking the certitude that America's ingrained practicality could overcome all domestic and foreign obstacles, Hartz was free to diagnose the "weaknesses" of the nation as a totality, while offering "no absolute assurance on the basis of the past that they will be remedied."[69]

Hartz's thesis evolved from "the storybook truth about American history": that the nation was settled by people who fled from, rather than rebelled against, the feudal oppressions of the Old World. In fact, "physical flight" was "the American substitute for the European experience of social revolution." Never having endured the "destruction of a social order to which one belongs oneself," the American had no familiarity with the traumatic effort to "build a new society on the ruins" of the past. Instead, the United States was invented, like Gatsby, out of a platonic conception of itself. The original colonizers as well as their immigrant successors departed Europe at precisely the moment when liberalism was emerging first as a revolutionary philosophy and then as a victorious program for the organization of political and economic life. By escaping the bloody task of overthrowing the *ancien régimes,* Hartz reasoned, Americans were left with only the need to create—or perhaps simply to fulfill the mission history had assigned to them.[70]

In Hartz's opinion, the absence of feudalism in America contributed to the irrelevance of socialism. Since "the hidden origin of socialist thought" in Europe could be traced to the "feudal ethos," and since the most salient fact about the United States was that it had no medieval past, Hartz was hardly surprised at America's imperviousness to the doctrines of Marx or even to the concepts of class. What the pilgrims to this newest Jerusalem erected was an immaculate "liberal community." Their Moses, the man who dominated their political thought, was John Locke.[71]

There was, however, one other factor besides historical timing and ideological commitment that accounted for America's fidelity to liberalism. Many commentators in the 1950s, including Hartz, occasionally lapsed into mysticism when searching for the causes of the national consensus. Returning to reality, Hartz reminded himself and his readers that American liberalism was immeasurably fortified by the "magnificent material setting" of the New World. Democratic ideas flowered in the United States not only because there were no monarchists dreaming of restoration or Bolsheviks storming the White House, but because the success of capitalism eliminated the need or desire for alternatives.[72]

Having established the supremacy of liberalism, Hartz saw the country's past political and social battles as having all been fought within the framework of the Lockian consensus. Here he differed only marginally from the interpretations of his contemporaries. The American Revolution, he agreed, was the "end-product of a chain of historical experience" reaching back to the earliest colonial settlements. Thus it seemed essentially a "mopping up campaign" against whatever vestiges of European feudalism persisted in the New World, and a vindication of America's "inherited" political freedom rather than a profound social disruption. Thereafter, the typical American "conservative" yearned neither for an aristocracy nor for fascism; he desired only the steady expansion of industrial and corporate profits. Meanwhile, the man who might still think of himself as a peasant in European terminology became a rural businessman in the mental universe of the United States. Similarly, the "proletarian" emerged as an "incipient entrepreneur." Both the farmer and the worker, Hartz argued, held the values of the European petite bourgeoisie, which meant that they wanted to preserve rather than destroy private property in order to accumulate more of it for themselves. But in America, neither the Right nor the Left had to make its "common allegiance to democratic capitalism" clear, much less speak in the accents of European liberalism. Lacking a genuinely reactionary philosophy or a powerful socialist challenge, Republicans commended laissez faire, and Progressives inveighed against the "trusts," each happily oblivious to how many ideals they shared.[73]

The most conspicuous exception to this liberal accord was the Civil War. Yet Hartz remained unruffled. He dismissed the attempt by southern intellectuals and politicians to manufacture an authentically conservative ideology as a "simple fraud"; the southerners were seeking not to revive feudalism but to justify slavery. Besides, the North had "tradition" on *its* side. The abolitionists invoked the venerable principles of the Declaration of Independence, forcing the slaveowners to contrive radically new theories to replace the long-standing faith in liberty and equality. How, Hartz wondered, could an aspiring conservative be "iconoclastic"? The answer was the southerners did not really wish to tear down the national idols because they too cared for profit; some even harbored the "bourgeois" ambition to industrialize their own region. But whatever the paradoxes in southern thought, Hartz was struck by how little impact it had on the nation's consciousness, and how rapidly it disappeared after the war. That the country could parry this massive assault upon its creed "not through controversy, not after consideration, but by a vast and unbelieving neglect," proved for Hartz the strength and vitality of the "liberal idea," as well as its "utter dominion over the American mind."[74]

The New Deal simply confirmed in the twentieth century what Hartz had discovered in the nineteenth. At just the point where the American people might conceivably have turned to Marxism for salvation, Franklin Roosevelt adopted the programs (but not the language) of European liberal reform. Facing no serious threat from the Left and only ritualistic carping from the Right, Roosevelt had no incentive to indulge in the rhetoric of class or uphold the sanctity of property. Instead, he "spoke pragmatically of solving 'problems,'" using the distinctively American euphemisms of "economic royalist" and "forgotten man," thereby translating the rigorous categories of European thought into an amorphous "experimental mood." The very success of the New

Deal in avoiding ideological debate during the worst crisis since the Civil War, as well as the readiness of both major parties to embrace Roosevelt's solutions after 1945, seemed to Hartz the clinching evidence of liberalism's hypnotic grip on American loyalties.[75]

On the surface, Hartz's thesis appeared to coincide with the postwar portrait of the nation's history. Certainly, he stressed the role of consensus in defining the terms of political discussion and restricting the effects of social upheavals. But Hartz was in fact arguing a very different case. Far from celebrating America's immunity to ideology, he considered the United States one of the most rigidly doctrinaire countries on earth. The trouble was that most Americans, having had no encounter with other social systems or styles of life, were blind to the substance of their own beliefs.

America's legendary pragmatism, Hartz submitted, was always "deceptive because, glacierlike, it has rested on miles of submerged conviction." When a country took its "general principles" for granted, it could imagine that its problems were merely technical. Thus the founding fathers devised a "complicated scheme of checks and balances" to deal with political and economic conflicts, but such an arrangement could work only in a nation already united by custom and outlook. Similarly, the people's willingness to let the courts adjudicate national policy, the peaceful transmission of power from one administration to another, and the assumption of the pluralists that American society could be adequately described as a "free and easy play of pressure groups" unobstructed by class barriers, were all "inconceivable" to Hartz without a prior acceptance of common moral premises and ideological formulas.[76]

It was not only the nation's failure to recognize its hidden dogmas that disturbed Hartz. Throughout his book, he deplored the *way* Americans worshiped liberalism as naïve, irrational, and presently outdated. Hartz acknowledged that democratic institutions and ideals were still worth defending, but "even a good idea can be a little frightening when it is the only idea a [country] has ever had." He intended no disparagement of liberalism as a political philosophy, yet he could not help worrying that "a doctrine which everywhere in the West has been a glorious symbol of individual liberty" exerted in America a "tyrannical compulsion," which "posed a threat to liberty itself." Particularly when the American people faced "military and ideological pressure" from abroad, their absolute and near unanimous devotion to John Locke could equate the "alien with the unintelligible," convert "eccentricity into sin," and generate mass hysteria in the form of red scares and witch hunts. What this neurotic addiction to liberalism could not do, according to Hartz, was enable America to "live in comfort" in a world of diversity.[77]

Unlike Daniel Boorstin, Seymour Lipset, and Daniel Bell, Hartz regarded the tenacity of America's political traditions not as a sign of stability but as a symptom of arrested adolescence. A people "born equal," blissfully innocent about what true revolutions entailed, would never understand the issues with which Europeans and Asians grappled daily—unless Americans themselves began to grow up by leaving home. Where other intellectuals saw in America's current international involvement the opportunity for an anti-Communist crusade and a reassertion of liberal precepts, Hartz hoped that the nation might at last shed the "peculiar limitations of its own perspective." If America ever expected to "compensate for the uniformity of its domestic life," he declared, it must "look to its contact with other nations to provide that spark of philosophy, that grain of relative insight that its own history has denied it." Instead of trying to "impose Locke everywhere," Americans might allow their political and intellectual horizons to be "drastically widened"—perhaps to the point where they could appraise their own institutions and ideals more objectively.[78]

Hartz did not know whether the United States, through its exposure to other countries and other cultures, would finally come of age. But in his estimation, there was more to be won in the Cold War than the survival of freedom and the American Way. "What is at stake," he concluded, "is nothing less than a new level of consciousness, a transcending of irrational Lockianism, in which an understanding of self and an understanding of others go hand in hand."[79]

Because Hartz and Hofstadter paid attention to the political and social beliefs Americans shared, rather than the regional or economic tensions that drove them apart, both have been labeled "consensus" historians. This classification suggests that they, like Daniel Boorstin or David Potter, mostly esteemed the nation's uniqueness, the continuity of its democratic traditions, and the resourcefulness of its people. Yet the refusal to exaggerate conflict does not automatically make one uncritical. Quite the contrary: Hartz and Hofstadter were neither pleased with nor complacent about the values they perceived as dominant in American life.

In methodology and outlook, their books differed profoundly from the seminal works of American historians before World War II. Yet Hartz and Hofstadter seemed at least in one respect the spiritual children of Frederick Jackson Turner and Charles Beard. They too thought of writing history as a means of communicating with the present, as a vehicle to raise questions and debate issues, even as a catalyst for new ideas. The implications of their analyses were subtle and less overtly political than those of Turner and Beard. They urged no changes in institutions and no specific alterations in national policy. Neither Hofstadter nor Hartz were "activists" in the radical or reformist sense of that word. They were merely subjecting liberalism to the same critical examination other commentators reserved only for socialism. For them, criticism was a form of action—which was precisely what Turner and Beard had also believed. More important still, in their skepticism about *all* official doctrines (not just those identified with the Left or the Soviet Union), Hofstadter and Hartz were maintaining their intellectual independence at a time when many writers—scorning affiliations with a movement or class—had become partisans of and propagandists for the nation as a whole.

John Kenneth Galbraith and the Economics of Affluence

For all their interest in American politics and foreign policy, few writers had any firsthand experience with the way government actually functioned. Whatever eminence they attained as academics, editors, essayists, and cultural ambassadors, however well they knew New York or Boston or Paris or Berlin, most intellectuals did not feel at home in Washington. In their own minds, they remained strangers to the world of high-level decision making—a condition some accepted with satisfaction; others, with dismay or resignation.

John Kenneth Galbraith, however, was not now nor had he ever been (at least since the 1930s) an outsider. By the 1950s, he had already led several different lives. Even more than Arthur Schlesinger, Galbraith seemed from the outset of his career extraordinarily adept at shuttling between government posts, presidential campaigns, mass circulation magazines, and the academic world.

Born and initially educated in Ontario, Galbraith emigrated to Berkeley where he received a Ph.D. in agricultural economics in 1934. During the Depression, he worked briefly for the New Deal's Agricultural Adjustment Administration and the National Resources Planning Board while teaching at Harvard.

Thereafter, Galbraith rarely declined invitations to influence public affairs. In the early years of World War II, he ran the Office of Price Administration before conservatives in Congress drove him to the improbable sanctuary of Henry Luce's *Fortune* magazine, where he became an editor (Luce, to his credit, consistently hired people who could write well, regardless of what he considered their political or economic delusions). In 1945, Galbraith returned to government service, this time to help prepare the report of the United States Strategic Bombing Survey, which involved among other tasks extensive interrogations with captured Nazi officials, the most loquacious of whom was Albert Speer. The report itself concluded that, despite the appalling damage inflicted on German cities from the air, saturation bombing did not substantially disrupt the Nazi economy or break the German will to resist—a lesson studiously ignored in later wars, notably in Vietnam.

Following World War II, Galbraith resumed his position at Harvard, but managed to join in the founding of the Americans for Democratic Action, as well as to compose speeches for Adlai Stevenson in the campaigns of 1952 and 1956. Meanwhile, he published *American Capitalism* in 1952. The book advanced the optimistic theory that trade unions, farm organizations, super-market chains, and consumer groups could exercise a "counter-vailing power" to check the dominance of the modern corpora-tion. Though its arguments were much disputed by conservatives and radicals, *American Capitalism* enhanced Galbraith's stature as one of the leading liberal economists of the postwar era.

Yet despite (or maybe because of) his adventures in Washing-ton and his political activism, Galbraith seemed less inclined to glorify American society than did many of his contemporaries. On the contrary, he scarcely missed an opportunity to deflate whatever orthodoxies currently prevailed. Partly, this was a mat-ter of personal temperament. No one ever accused Galbraith of being amiable, ingratiating, or excessively polite. He treated pomposity or the affectations of civil discourse with terse disdain. (Once, during a meeting of faculty and tutors at Harvard's Win-throp House in the late 1960s, a colleague of obviously distant acquaintance kept addressing Galbraith as "John." After endur-ing several minutes of this ostentatious familiarity, Galbraith turned to the offending gentleman and snapped: "No one calls me John. My friends call me Ken. *You* may call me Galbraith.")

An appreciation for the redeeming qualities of insolence marked his prose style as well. An admirer of Thorstein Veblen, Galbraith enjoyed his own reputation as a heretic and a satirist of received opinion. "One of my greatest pleasures in writing," he recently admitted, "has come from the thought that perhaps my work might annoy someone of comfortably pretentious posi-tion. Then comes the saddening realization that such people rarely read."[80]

His books typically began by summarizing some obsolescent body of doctrine (variously deprecated as liturgy or the "conven-tional wisdom") that was, alas, still honored by politicians, busi-nessmen, and economists—the last of whom Galbraith persis-tently mocked as the "priesthood." He then proceeded to puncture the faith of the true believers with a mixture of ar-gumentation, common sense, and caustic humor. Finally, Gal-braith presented his own ideas or alternatives, which always ap-peared wiser and more realistic than the myths he had just demolished. Throughout, Galbraith eschewed sentimentality or humanitarian rhetoric. Thus he sounded both critical and hard-headed, the perfect stance for an intellectual who championed inconvenient social reforms while pursuing practical politics. Galbraith's distinguishing trait, reflected in the tone and content of his books as well as in his public career, was to combine the roles of insider and nonconformist.

Nowhere were these talents better displayed than in *The Affluent Society* (1958). Galbraith's earlier assumption that different forms of countervailing power could effectively restrain the monopolistic and inflationary tendencies in the nation's economy seemed to support the concept, nourished by other writers in the 1950s, that the United States was a model of pluralism in action. Galbraith eventually regretted the "euphoric" overtones of *American Capitalism*.[81] He wanted no one to misunderstand his attitude toward the nature and consequences of postwar prosperity. "These are . . . days," he complained in the opening pages of *The Affluent Society*, "in which even the mildly critical individual is likely to seem like a lion in contrast with the general mood. These are the days when men of all social disciplines and all political faiths seek the comfortable and the accepted; when the man of controversy is looked upon as a disturbing influence; when originality is taken to be a mark of instability; and when . . . the bland lead the bland." For his part, Galbraith refused to engage in yet another celebration of American wealth. Instead, he cast himself, not without enthusiasm, as a dissenter. There would be "negative thoughts" in his book, he warned, "and they cannot but strike an uncouth note in a world of positive thinking." Apparently, this admonition did not put off too many readers, since after its publication *The Affluent Society* quickly climbed to second place on the *New York Times* best-seller list.[82]

The idol Galbraith chose on this occasion to blaspheme was nothing less than the postwar commitment to productivity as a solution to all economic and social problems. Specifically, he proposed to challenge the notion that "any action which increases production from given resources is good and implicitly important; anything which inhibits or reduces output is, *pro tanto*, wrong." Liberals and conservatives now agreed that unlimited economic growth, underwritten by Keynesian fiscal policy, would sustain full employment, abolish poverty, provide an alternative to the Marxist demand for the redistribution of wealth, reduce social inequities, alleviate the tensions and insecurities associated with booms and busts, minimize the risks of investment, relieve the financial troubles of the states and cities, and improve the standard of living for everyone. No wonder the goal of an expanding economy had become so "deeply embedded" in the postwar psyche, Galbraith mused; it seemed to measure the very "quality and progress of our civilization."[83]

There were expedient motives behind this consensus. Corporate executives had a "vested interest" in the infinite output of goods, Galbraith argued, because (profits aside) "if production is of preoccupying importance," the businessman who held the "established right to the title of producer will be the dominant figure in the social constellation." Since his prestige was bound up in the nation's continuing obsession with productivity, his Republican party spokesmen had finally assented to Keynesian ideas, whatever their nostalgia for a balanced budget and a passive government. Democrats, on the other hand, saw in the promise of full production and full employment a "major claim to votes"; Keynes became for them the touchstone of their political success from the 1930s to the 1950s. Yet in Galbraith's opinion, the common bond uniting conservatives and liberals was their mutual reliance on large defense expenditures to fight Communism, stimulate the economy, and justify the growing size of the state.[84] In short, every group trying to enlarge its own power— the corporations, the military, the politicians, the unions, the federal bureaucracy—had developed a stake in the nation's ongoing productivity.

This represented for Galbraith the current "conventional wisdom." Unfortunately, such pieties were no longer relevant to the conditions of modern American life. Galbraith insisted throughout his book that the problems of affluence were fundamentally different from those of the past. The United States, he asserted, was stubbornly conducting its affairs in accordance with the rules and assumptions of a poorer age; its policies were "rooted in the poverty, inequality and economic peril" of the nineteenth and early twentieth centuries. Unless the country discarded these outmoded attitudes, it would not only overlook the "new tasks and opportunities" of the present, but also when encountering future difficulties "implacably prescribe for itself the wrong remedies."[85]

How might the regnant orthodoxy be repudiated? Galbraith's response was itself slightly antiquated. Summoning up the familiar concept of cultural lag, he contended that established ideas must ultimately yield to the "massive onslaught of circumstance," especially when they could not explain or cope with a world to which they had become "palpably inapplicable."[86]

It was clear, at least to Galbraith, that the time to abandon untenable theories was at hand. By the 1950s, notwithstanding the blueprints of *New Republic* liberals and the speeches of Democratic aspirants for the presidency, Keynesianism had assumed in Galbraith's mind some of the attributes of an enthralling folk tale. "The effect of increasing affluence," he observed, was to "minimize the importance" of traditional economic priorities; "production for the sake of the goods produced" now made less sense. As a source of income for wage earners, productivity remained significant. But the sheer abundance of marketable commodities and the obvious wealth of American society created new issues so far unrecognized and unexamined.[87]

Galbraith therefore became one of the first writers in the postwar years to deal extensively with the *economic* dilemmas peculiar to prosperity. Like his contemporaries, he supposed that the chronic "uncertainties of economic life" had either been eliminated in America or were less "serious" than in the years before World War II. But where the majority of liberal intellectuals continued to emphasize the role of the government, the welfare state, and Keynesian techniques in diminishing the threat of another depression, Galbraith dwelt on the twin specters of inflation and consumer debt—both of which he believed were inherent in an economy dedicated to maintaining high production and employment as the sole signs of its success. The classic methods to halt inflation (increasing interest rates and/or restricting the flow of money, raising taxes or cutting the federal budget, all in an effort to slow down corporate borrowing and consumer spending) inevitably collided with the ethic of productivity, the need to expand the market for industrial and agricultural goods, and the desire to keep vast numbers of people at work. Yet the rise in prices and the dependence on credit, Galbraith declared, could not go on indefinitely. At some point, the purchasing power of the ordinary citizen must decline, the warehouses and retail outlets would be glutted with merchandise few could buy, and the depression everyone hoped to avoid might naturally ensue. Thus by operating the economy "at a level of output where it is not stable—where persistent advances in prices are not only probable but normal," while at the same time rejecting the "vigorous use" of monetary or fiscal controls to retard inflation and debt, America faced new dangers it could not permanently elude.[88]

Inflation was not the only stigma of an affluent society. Galbraith objected just as strenuously to the process by which businesses manipulated consumer tastes and behavior in order to create a steady demand for their goods and services. In an era of prosperity, he submitted, when basic human needs had been satisfied, the historic rationale for unrestrained production appeared less compelling. Now for goods to be sold, "wants must be effectively contrived," largely through "the institutions of modern advertising and salesmanship." Yet precisely because the appetite for most products no longer originated spontaneously with the individual, they could not be construed as urgent requirements of daily life. "A man who is hungry," Galbraith pointed out, did not have to be "told of his need for food"; a person without physical cravings must be persuaded to purchase the latest status symbols. Here Galbraith seemed to imply that any item, the desire for which had been artificially fabricated, was by definition nonessential and probably frivolous. But what he really disliked was the presumption that the goals of society and the well-being of the individual should still be identified with the manufacturers' concern to maximize output and profits.[89]

In fact, the image of the United States as an affluent society was undermined by the calculated starvation of the public sector. Americans viewed the lavish production of some of the most trivial commodities "with pride," Galbraith charged. Conversely, they regarded "some of the most significant and civilizing services" as a "burden" to be discharged "with regret."[90] This disparity between private opulence and social austerity evoked Galbraith's greatest scorn—and the most memorable passage in his book:

> The family which takes its mauve and cerise, air-conditioned, power-steered and power-braked automobile out for a tour passes through cities that are badly paved, made hideous by litter blighted buildings, billboards and posts for wires that should long since have been put underground. They pass on into a countryside that has been rendered largely invisible by commercial art. . . . They picnic on exquisitely packaged food from a portable icebox by a polluted stream and go on to spend the night at a park which is a menace to public health and morals. Just before dozing off on an air mattress, beneath a nylon tent, amid the stench of decaying refuse, they may reflect vaguely on the curious unevenness of their blessings. Is this, indeed, the American genius?[91]

Such prose, however hyperbolic, did not often occur in the works of other intellectuals in the 1950s—certainly not in those that extolled the merits of the mixed economy. Galbraith had portrayed the central paradox of postwar prosperity: its direct contribution to the dismal quality of American life. Given the disintegration of the cities, the neglect of mass transit, the deterioration of the environment, the indifference to education and medical care, and the spectacle of an "advanced" civilization incapable of removing its own rubbish, Galbraith could reasonably conclude that the "expansion of economic output" was hardly a supreme "test of social achievement," much less "the solvent for all social ills."[92]

Ultimately, Galbraith was convinced that the "failure to keep public services in minimal relation to private production" would cause "social disorder" and impair the nation's economic performance. Moreover, a wise society should realize that schools, hospitals, and parks were as indispensable as automobiles. He therefore urged the establishment of a "social balance" between industrial productivity and the amenities furnished by the state. This involved considerably more than the strengthening of the public sector to deal with the fluctuations of a capitalist economy.

It meant, in Galbraith's estimation, the fashioning of new goals and new "symbols of happiness" to replace the exclusive preoccupation with production—even a "major wrench in our attitudes" about what constituted "sound economic behavior" in a society where the "race to manufacture more wants for more goods" had grown not only suspect but self-defeating.[93]

Unfortunately, Galbraith seemed vague about the values to which Americans should now subscribe. Perhaps he was unaccustomed to using hortatory language; perhaps he felt more at ease as a critic than as an oracle. In any case, he suggested tentatively that "compassion" might supersede productivity as the criterion for civilized behavior. The modern corporation, for example, could conceivably pay more attention to the "dignity" and "individuality" of its employees than to the efficient utilization of manpower and resources. Similarly, a "rational" society ought to assist those who wished to stay in their declining communities, rather than sponsor a mass exodus in pursuit of higher-paying jobs. Finally, instead of trying always to protect domestic industry, America's tariff and trade barriers could be lowered to relieve the problems of underdeveloped regions in other parts of the world.[94]

These were worthy objectives, but Galbraith was far more precise when advocating changes in economic policy. In order to prevent social breakdowns, as well as to ensure the stability of the private sector, he offered a set of programs that went far beyond the current liberal agenda.

First, Galbraith recommended the imposition of wage and price controls, especially on those industries where strong corporations bargained with well-organized unions for long-term contracts that invariably resulted in higher costs for consumers. In his opinion, these controls when combined with Keynesian fiscal mechanisms could effectively combat the inflation that otherwise plagued an economy functioning at nearly full capacity.[95]

Second, Galbraith urged liberals to embrace the heresy of a national sales tax, rather than continue to wage interminable and usually fruitless battles in Congress for income tax reform or the passage of more welfare legislation. A sales tax, he argued, could take advantage of America's postwar prosperity by automatically transferring to the government additional funds to be spent for social purposes. Such a levy certainly meant that "private goods" would become more expensive, Galbraith acknowledged, but it would also make "public goods . . . more abundant." This might injure the poor momentarily for they could least afford to pay a sales tax. Eventually, however, their plight (or that of their children) would be alleviated through the nation's larger investment in measures to end their impoverishment and improve their lives.[96]

Not surprisingly, this proposal did not galvanize those American liberals whose political fortunes rested on the support of the labor movement, blacks, and the lower middle class—all of whom would be immediately victimized by a sales tax. Nor were conservatives eager to penalize their affluent constituents in order to expand the welfare state. But the countries of western Europe soon began to rely heavily on a similar instrument—the "value-added tax"—to finance a variety of social programs still regarded as harmful, if not subversive, in the United States.

Third (and perhaps even more visionary, given the premises of the Cold War), Galbraith anticipated a time when federal revenues would not be "pre-empted so extensively" by the "requirements (actual or claimed) of national defense." He saw no logical reason why the country's scientific and technological development had to proceed only "under the inspiration of military need" or commercial feasibility, particularly when this resulted in the stockpiling of weapons "thoughtfully designed to destroy all life." If the incentives for research and innovation could be diverted to civilian goals, Galbraith speculated, Americans might discover that they could maintain their prosperity and have a healthier society without resorting to an economy geared for war.[97]

Fourth, and most disconcerting of all to a nation reared on the Protestant ethic, Galbraith contended that the American people must look for substitutes to production as a source of income and status. In an affluent age, when not everyone had to labor long hours to turn out more products, when the ability to get and hold a job was no longer the ultimate test of one's character, work had lost much of its ancient moral and economic significance. In these circumstances, Galbraith felt that the poor and the jobless need not be made the wards of the government bureaucracy or face permanent destitution. Instead, he called for a substantial increase in unemployment compensation so that it approached the level of an average weekly wage. Further, he encouraged his countrymen to consider the adoption of a guaranteed annual income plan, not only to assist people who had difficulty finding work or who should not be in the labor market at all, but also as a means of securing every citizen's "essential" right to live in "decency and comfort."[98] Here again, Galbraith's proposals (as he expected) were ignored in the United States, though they became commonplace features of European life over the next twenty years.

For the more privileged, Galbraith observed, work had grown less arduous, repetitive, and routine. The requirements of ceaseless physical toil gave way to a concern for better education (largely subsidized by the public sector), pleasant surroundings in the office, jobs that demanded intellectual creativity or the refinement of technical skills, and a more satisfying use of leisure time. These transformations contributed to and coincided with the emergence of what Galbraith labeled a "New Class" in whom he placed his greatest hopes for a more imaginative and humane society. Indeed, the "further and rapid expansion of this class," he proclaimed, "should be . . . next to peaceful survival itself, *the* major social goal" of America. And since the continuing development of the New Class depended on the quality of the nation's schools, a substantial "investment in education" could replace the production of goods as the new and basic "index of social progress" for the United States.[99] Not for nothing had Galbraith remained a professor.

All of these ideas—wage and price controls, a national sales tax, cuts in military spending, a guaranteed annual income, the redefinition of work, education as an alternative to unlimited economic growth—amounted to a radical shift in America's historic values and preferences. It was paradoxical, therefore, that Galbraith (an experienced political infighter with close ties to the Democratic party and the Washington establishment) should contemplate such sweeping reforms, while other intellectuals with less powerful connections seemed more disposed to defend existing institutions.

Yet in a further paradox, Galbraith himself sounded curiously impractical—not because his proposals were utopian, but because he evaded elementary questions of political strategy. How was the country to jettison its anachronistic commitment to productivity? What forces would propel Americans from the past to the future? Galbraith was confident that new conditions would inevitably triumph over old assumptions, an attractive proposition that conveniently minimized the entrenched power of business executives, liberal officeholders, government administrators, labor barons, and military chieftains, all of whom had (as he previously noted) a vested interest in preserving the sanctity of production as a measure of national strength.

At the same time, Galbraith's reliance on highly trained scientists, engineers, intellectuals, and middle-level managers to reject traditional economic policies was reminiscent of Thorstein Veblen's belief that the instinct of workmanship could counteract the wasteful procedures of capitalism. The education of this New Class, Galbraith presumed, would not only serve the "technical and scientific requirements of modern industry," but would also widen personal tastes, thereby "inducing more independent and critical attitudes" toward advertising, the accumulation of unnecessary merchandise, and the reigning values of the affluent society.[100] But Galbraith's trust in a technocratic elite implied again that the country could be transformed without major political conflicts or social upheavals. To this extent, he shared the outlook (and possibly the wishful thinking) of his fellow writers in the postwar years.

Of course, Galbraith's neglect of tactical matters—the mobilization of particular constituencies, the building of new coalitions, the challenge to the Democratic party hierarchy—may in the end have been shrewd. Given his assertion that the primary problems of prosperity were cultural, moral, and psychological, it was hard to envision how any political remedies could truly improve the *quality* of American life.

Still, Galbraith had gone farther than most of his contemporaries. His refusal to accede to military priorities, his disdain for corporate prerogatives, his assault on the conventional economic wisdom of the New and Fair Deals, and his recognition that the gross national product was not the only standard by which to judge human progress, made him one of the most provocative social critics of the 1950s.

Galbraith, however, was no revolutionary. Like Richard Hofstadter and Louis Hartz, he mainly wanted liberals to become less complacent about their intellectual heritage, especially to shed their dependency on Roosevelt and Keynes. Nor did Galbraith wish to divorce himself from worldly affairs. Soon he reentered the political arena, working in the 1960 campaign of John F. Kennedy, and then accepting an appointment as ambassador to India—a somewhat incongruous post for an expert on affluence. Nevertheless, Galbraith always retained his interest in policy making even as he attacked the assumptions of the policy makers. It was a delicate balancing act the majority of writers seemed unable to duplicate, then or since.

The Politics of Dwight Macdonald

By the 1950s, the intellectuals' relationship to society was taking several different forms. Writers could devote much of their time to the defense of democratic ideals in the Cold War—as in the case of Sidney Hook, James Burnham, and William Barrett. Or they might embark on a sympathetic reexamination of the nation's political and economic institutions—following the example of Arthur Schlesinger, Daniel Boorstin, Seymour Lipset, Daniel Bell, and Reinhold Niebuhr. As still another option, they could seek to criticize and even to transcend the past and present liberal frame of mind, while remaining liberals themselves—a strategy pursued by Lionel Trilling, Richard Hofstadter, Louis Hartz, and John Kenneth Galbraith. There were other choices, but these seemed the most common.

Dwight Macdonald was temperamentally incapable of pursuing a strategy or following anyone's example. That may be why so many of his colleagues thought him "unserious," apolitical, inconsistent, and generally irritating. No doubt Macdonald was a nuisance because he continually questioned what everyone else believed. Moreover, his own positions kept changing at a time when a number of writers were again busy taking "stands." In effect, Macdonald was an eccentric subject to no ideological classification, a dissident unconcerned about influencing those in power, an agnostic who ultimately denied the claims of all political systems. Yet these were precisely the attitudes that made him not only a more interesting but also a more "radical" intellectual than most of his counterparts.

During the late 1940s and early 1950s, Macdonald wrestled with almost all the political issues that absorbed other American writers. If anything, he took politics too seriously in the sense that he cared what effect governments actually had on their citizens. He could also dispute the fine points of doctrine with anybody, having committed himself at various junctures to Trotskyism, anarchism, and pacifism. But Macdonald was by nature an empiricist rather than an ideologue; he could not restrain his skepticism about grand designs, particularly when they wound up corrupting individuals, culture, and elementary standards of moral conduct.[101] Thus he experimented with many political philosophies while giving his full approval to none. And he constantly moved on.

This inability to settle on one political creed was reflected in his prose style—another source of annoyance to his contemporaries. Macdonald started out in the late 1920s as a film critic (an occupation to which he returned in the 1960s), and the skills he developed then stayed with him even when he was discussing broader cultural and social problems. He specialized in extended essays and book reviews, first as editor of his own magazine (*Politics*) in the 1940s, and later as a regular contributor to *The New Yorker, Encounter,* and *Partisan Review* in the 1950s. Yet whatever the forum, Macdonald normally treated someone else's argument or a government policy as if he were responding to a particularly pretentious Hollywood epic. He derided the ideas of an author, a political leader, or a cultural spokesman by performing a vivisection on their language and imagery; how they wrote and talked was for Macdonald the essential indication of what they truly thought. He frequently interrupted with satirical asides, personal recollections, and cantankerous footnotes.

Throughout, he treated his subject as an illustration of some larger political or esthetic phenomenon currently debasing the sensibilities and intelligence of the average citizen. Macdonald's technique was frequently devastating. It was also a method guaranteed to infuriate writers who preferred advocacy to criticism, a "constructive" outlook and a set of fixed principles to perpetual dissent.

In fact, Macdonald did have firm political convictions, some of which resembled those of other postwar intellectuals. He shared their disillusion with Marxism, for example, though for slightly different reasons. Macdonald found the working class not merely pragmatic or conservative, but "rabidly nationalistic." Meanwhile its leaders, far from being major participants in a liberal coalition, had "quite lost touch with the humane and democratic ideals [they] once believed in." The collapse of the labor movement's revolutionary potential, together with the rise in American living standards as a result of the permanent "war economy," was not a situation Macdonald greeted with joy. But he did agree that there was no chance in the foreseeable future to revive socialist ideas in the United States.[102]

Similarly, he detested totalitarianism, though as much for its impact on culture as for its intrinsic expansionist tendencies. Macdonald's opposition to Stalin began with the Moscow Trials in the mid-1930s. Thereafter, he attacked the Soviet Union not because he feared the Red Army's invasion of western Europe, but because the Kremlin persistently used "censorship . . . exile and imprisonment to punish dissident thought." Even worse, since the government controlled all the channels of communication and could manipulate public opinion at will, the Russian intellectual never contemplated the possibilities of "open resistance" or tried to publicize "subversive" ideas. Instead he censored himself. The consequence, in Macdonald's view, was a culture more tasteless and mediocre than anything emanating from Hollywood.[103]

Indeed, for all his criticism of the mass media in the United States, Macdonald recognized that the American writer could, if he had the determination or the cash, "ignore the commercial market and produce decent work." Echoing Arthur Schlesinger,

Macdonald granted that in a capitalist economy there were "crannies in which the artist and intellectual can survive, as well as conflicting forces of which he can take advantage." In the Soviet Union, there were no "loopholes," no alternatives except to obey the Kremlin's latest edict on art and philosophy. This led Macdonald to admit at least one beneficial effect of private enterprise: "A citizen with property" had a "firmer . . . base of resistance to the encroachments of the State."[104]

Thus Macdonald, like many other intellectuals in the 1950s, felt compelled to affirm his allegiance to the West. He too saw the Cold War as a "fight to the death between radically different cultures." But the necessity for choice did not blind him to the uncomfortable similarities between America and the Soviet Union. Both countries, he asserted, pursued imperialist foreign policies and suppressed indigenous revolutionary movements; both had leaders who "lie like troopers and equivocate like lawyers"; both were unjust societies "where the few have too much and the many too little"; both idolized science, technology, and mass production; and both were preparing mindlessly for World War III. Nevertheless, one could make distinctions. The United States bribed western Europe with exports and foreign aid, Macdonald conceded; Russia absorbed the Baltic nations by force and installed Stalinist regimes. The American people did not appreciate their civil liberties; the Soviet citizen had no freedoms at all. In the West, there were political parties, trade unions, and cultural movements "independent of the State," which in turn meant that the democracies remained "open to change and growth" in contrast to Russia's "perfectly dead, closed society." Because of these differences, Macdonald concluded that the totalitarian trends in the United States could still be reversed. He therefore preferred the "imperfect" West as a "lesser evil," and announced in 1952 that he would "critically" support some of America's diplomatic, economic, and military initiatives in the Cold War.[105]

This was hardly a stirring endorsement. Macdonald had chosen the West reluctantly, but he did not become an admirer of its political institutions or a propagandist in its cultural battle with the Soviet Union. Nor did he suppose that the difficulties of postwar life could be relieved by modifying liberalism or revising Keynes. In his eyes, World War II had transformed the very structure of modern society, East and West. Like Louis Hartz and John Kenneth Galbraith, Macdonald insisted that the problems of the present were absolutely unique and that traditional remedies would not work, yet he was less hopeful than they that the creation of new attitudes might by itself alter national policies.

Macdonald's pessimism and his rift with his peers in the 1940s and 1950s sprang from the way he interpreted the conditions under which people were forced to live. Where Schlesinger, Boorstin, Lipset, and Bell characterized the Western democracies and especially the United States as pluralistic and stable, Macdonald emphasized the rigid management and hierarchical organization typical of all the industrial nations after 1945. As a result of World War II and the unremitting tensions of the Cold War, he declared, Western (no less than Soviet) society had grown so "rationalized and routinized" that it seemed a "mechanism which grinds on without human consciousness or control." While America and Russia terrorized the planet with bellicose rhetoric and atomic bombs, the individual citizen had "almost the same chance of determining his own fate as a hog dangling by one foot from the conveyor belt of a Chicago packing plant." Human beings were reduced to instruments of diplomacy, trapped by incomprehensible policies they felt helpless to change. The "concentration of political power at the top" of every country, Macdonald charged, the exclusion of ordinary people from the inner sanctums of decision making, left them with no sense of personal responsibility for the actions of "their" governments, and no inkling of how to oppose centralized authority.[106] Given this bleak assessment of contemporary life, the competition among pressure groups, the negotiations between political parties, and the rewards of a mixed economy had little meaning for Macdonald.

Furthermore, he could conceive of few institutional alternatives. "Reform, reconstruction, even revolution," he contended, "must begin at a much more basic level" than either the Old Left or the postwar liberals imagined. But in a world dominated by "vast super-states" whose continuing prestige depended on their complex bureaucracies, Macdonald saw no sign that "any considerable number of my fellow men are now in a mood to break up such monstrosities" into "small communities" which might be genuinely "human in scale."[107]

The thrust of Macdonald's argument forced him ultimately to abandon politics altogether. Having lost faith in the working class as an agent of social change, no longer inspired by the theories of Marx yet equally dubious about the glories of capitalism, hostile to every government which spoke in the name but ignored the opinions of its citizens, Macdonald fell back on the principle that the solitary individual must at least part of the time refuse to cooperate with the state, the corporations, and the military machine. "It is not the law-breaker we must fear today," he remarked at the close of World War II with the menace of totalitarianism and the manufacture of the atomic bomb obviously in mind, "so much as he who obeys the law." Rather than trust any ideology or political program, human beings should resist the domestic and foreign policies of their leaders whenever these conflicted "too intolerably with their personal moral code." What forms might this rebellion assume? Macdonald urged his readers to "begin thinking 'dangerous thoughts' about sabotage," consider ways to cause "friction" in the bureaucracy, trust their own consciences, and function as "whole" men rather than as servants of a national cause. "The mental attitude known as 'negativism' " was in his estimation an appropriate response to the modern world.[108]

None of these recommendations, however, offered a strategy to alter society, nor was this really Macdonald's intention. Drawing on a mixture of anarchist and existential sentiments nurtured in the wartime resistance movements, Macdonald was convinced that only through acts of moral protest could the individual protect his private integrity even as he accepted his political impotence.

Macdonald's withdrawal from politics was motivated as well by his feeling that abstractions like the United Nations, the Proletarian Revolution, the Common Man, Democracy, and World Government meant "nothing one way or another to any specific human being." Thoroughly rejecting the collectivist outlook of the 1930s, Macdonald considered it nearly impossible for a true "radical" in the postwar era to "place himself in relation to international affairs, or to any kind of thought or action which goes beyond his own personal experience." Accordingly, the two public figures he most revered, after Leon Trotsky, were Mahatma Gandhi and Dorothy Day (the founder of the Catholic Worker movement). Macdonald respected Gandhi not so much for his pacifist ideas or his political goals as for his insistence on "dealing directly with people, reasoning with them face to face as individuals, not as crowds." Gandhi was a "person, not a mask or a radio voice or an institution"; he understood the "concrete, homely 'details' of living which make the real difference to people but which are usually ignored by everybody except poets." For the same reasons, Macdonald cherished Dorothy Day: She was more a "doer than a thinker"; she believed in direct action rather than systematic planning and rigorous organization.[109] What counted for Macdonald in the case of both Gandhi and Dorothy Day was their distrust of dogma, their moral sensibility, and their willingness to take individual responsibility for the consequences of their behavior instead of seeking comfort in historical laws or authoritarian pronouncements. Again, these attributes had more to do with matters of personal style than with political theories or economic nostrums.

By the 1950s, Macdonald had shifted his attention entirely to "the kind of social-cultural reportage and analysis" that interested him more than "political writing." It was now, he observed modestly, the "small" questions that seemed to him significant: "What is a good life? How do people really live and feel and think in their everyday lives? What are the most important human needs? How can they be satisfied best, here and now? Who am I? How can I live lovingly, truthfully, pleasurably?" Neither liberal reformers nor orthodox socialists, Macdonald had decided, were dealing adequately with the crucial modern problems of work, leisure, child rearing, sex, and art.[110] These then should be the true concerns of the radical intellectual. The writer's duty was to retain his skepticism about all political and economic doctrines, serve as the critic and conscience of his society, and concentrate on the psychological and cultural issues that had become paramount after World War II. When Macdonald ceased publishing *Politics* in 1949 and moved to *The New Yorker,* he was not only acknowledging the change in his own perspective, but pointing to the dilemmas that would occupy many intellectuals in the next decade.

Yet whatever paths writers elected to travel, their destination appeared uncertain. Whether they celebrated, criticized, or remained ambivalent about their native land, it was often easier for them to identify the political and economic precepts they no longer thought valid than to indicate clearly a new set of goals more suitable for postwar American life.

On various occasions after 1945, almost every intellectual announced his disenchantment with the values and objectives of prewar radicalism. The revolt against "ideology" was more than anything else a revolt against Marxism. The Cold War, the hatred of Stalinism, and the surprising health of American capitalism each provided a superlative rationale for repudiating the axioms of the Old Left. Even if a particular writer had never been a socialist in the 1930s, he now felt obliged to dispense with all notions about the nationalization of property, the virtues of centralized planning, the revolutionary impulses of the working class, and the positive impact of mass movements. It also seemed necessary for him to differentiate between the United States and Europe, "proving" that the history of America had always been a conspicuous exception to the Marxist prophecy.

Intellectuals encountered difficulty only when they tried to supply alternative ideas. For writers like Arthur Schlesinger, Sidney Hook, Daniel Boorstin, James Burnham, Seymour Lipset, and Daniel Bell, this task was less burdensome because they tended to elevate existing American customs and institutions to a set of normative ideals. For the most part, they were more interested in explaining how the society functioned than in suggesting what it should think or want. The retreat from ideology did permit them to concentrate on the realities of political and economic life in the United States. At the same time, their high regard for pragmatism and stability, together with their dread of fanaticism and upheaval, were reasonable and humane reactions to the catastrophic experiences of the twentieth century. But these attitudes also led to an unwarranted (and frequently unintended) sense of complacency in their work, as well as to a singular lack of vision about what the future could hold. The present, it seemed, was good enough.

Richard Hofstadter, Louis Hartz, John Kenneth Galbraith, and Dwight Macdonald were far less satisfied with contemporary American beliefs and practices. Nevertheless, they too sounded murky when imagining a different political or economic system. Hofstadter and Hartz pondered the deficiencies of liberalism, and warned against a demagogic or irrational adherence to outmoded faiths. Both hoped that the American people might show greater sophistication in coping with their domestic problems, and develop a more mature consciousness in their relationship to the rest of the world. Yet neither attempted to describe precisely what new political ideas their countrymen should embrace. Macdonald's indictment of American politics was more sweeping than that of Hofstadter or Hartz, but his call for individual resistance and private dissent—however attractive as a moral stance—scarcely disclosed the ways in which the power of the state might be challenged or limited. Only Galbraith proposed an explicit series of reforms, and even he relied on the traditional device of education and the gradual emergence of a "new class" to overcome the current economic wisdom, while declining to specify how this political and intellectual transition was in fact to occur.

Perhaps such speculations about the future were too much to expect from a generation justifiably weary of ideological scenarios for social change. In any case, a significant number of writers began to emulate Dwight Macdonald, losing interest in political and economic theory, and turning instead to those issues which affected the very quality of American life. That intellectuals might follow the example of Macdonald, when he had no wish to lead anyone anywhere, seemed the ultimate irony in an ironic age.

4

Conformity and Alienation:
Social Criticism in the 1950s

One of the major consequences of America's postwar prosperity was that writers turned their attention to the social predicaments of the middle class. Their interest in the subject was not unprecedented. During the Progressive era, journalists, social critics, academics, and city planners had sought to reform the urban-industrial environment on behalf of the native bourgeoisie. The crusade against political machines, the exposés of graft and corruption, the desire to "Americanize" the immigrants as swiftly as possible were all motivated by the assumption that middle-class values ought to guide national policy. After World War I, the enlightened burgher cherished by the Progressives became in the minds of the expatriates a Philistine and a Babbitt from whom they could only flee in disgust. Still, the novelists and intellectuals of the 1920s retained their fascination with the middle class; for all their scorn, they sometimes seemed unable to write about anything else. The Depression encouraged the Left to hope that the middle class might join with the workers and the poor—if not for a revolution, then at least for a New Deal. Indeed, the history of radicalism in the 1930s, particularly during the height of the Popular Front, might be viewed as a case study of how socialist ideas in the United States were gradually diluted to fit the tastes and aspirations of the bourgeoisie. In each of these episodes, the middle class served as a symbol for whatever the intellectuals at any moment admired, courted, or despised.

By the 1950s, however, the middle class was less a repository for political or artistic fantasies than an inescapable presence in American life. The signs of its dominance were everywhere: in the election returns that made Dwight Eisenhower and Richard Nixon the new spokesmen for the average citizen of the affluent society as Franklin Roosevelt and Harry Truman had previously articulated the grievances of the Depression-scarred common man; in the credit-card economy, which kept millions of consumers surfeited with goods and permanently in debt; in the cloverleafs, express roads, and interstate highway systems, which facilitated the mobility (and also the rootlessness) of an increasingly white-collar population for whom job transfers and commuting distances were emblems of success; in the indistinguishable suburban ranch houses, each with its obligatory picture window, fake-wood-paneled den, outdoor barbecue pit, manicured lawn, and privacy fence; in the exploding birth rate, the child-centered nuclear family, the mounting concern over education as a means of social advancement, and the rigid division of labor and roles between husbands and wives; in the growing reliance on television and high fidelity phonographs as the principal forms of information and amusement; and in the booming sales of alcohol and tranquilizers to soothe the multiple anxieties that still discomforted the prosperous bourgeoisie.

For intellectuals in the postwar years, there were no longer any shelters from the middle class. One could hardly sustain the illusion that the man in the gray flannel suit was a reformer or an incipient revolutionary. Nor could writers depart for bohemia; the price of a picturesque cottage in Provincetown or on Martha's Vineyard was now exorbitant, the reigning spirit of Greenwich Village seemed ever more commercial, and the United States was successfully exporting both its products and its culture to Europe. Under these conditions, the intellectual had no choice but to confront the problems of the American middle class as harbingers of the fate toward which the entire world was apparently hurtling.

The compulsion to scrutinize the attitudes and life-styles of the bourgeoisie led intellectuals in the 1950s to markedly different conclusions from those of their predecessors in the 1920s. Nearly

every observer in each decade grumbled about the political passivity of the middle class, its avoidance of social causes, its fear
of public controversy, and its preoccupation with personal gain.
Yet where these complaints gave writers in the 1920s a justification for satire and flight, some commentators in the 1950s suspected that political apathy was a mask for private discontent. In
a wealthy society, overt ideological and social quarrels rarely
erupted; class antagonisms remained muted; the real difficulties
of life were minimized or ignored in the electoral campaigns. But
this did not mean that America was a land without strain, un-
resolved conflicts, or nagging frustrations.

In fact, several writers besides Dwight Macdonald recognized
that the central issues of the 1950s had to be addressed in novel
ways, that one could not expect political parties or mass movements to express much dissatisfaction in a time of breathtaking
prosperity. "Almost all the problems that were once called 'political,' " a contributor to *Commentary* remarked, "now belong to a
different context, psychological, sociological, and cultural."[1] At
the end of *Political Man*, Seymour Lipset acknowledged that his
title might well be inappropriate: "Since domestic politics, even
liberal and socialist politics, can no longer serve as the arena for
serious criticism from the left, many intellectuals have turned
from a basic concern with the political and economic systems to
criticism of other sections of the basic culture of American society, particularly of elements which cannot be dealt with politically."[2] Thus some of the most characteristic essays and books of
the postwar years—Dwight Macdonald's *Against the American
Grain*, Mary McCarthy's *On the Contrary*, Daniel Bell's "Work and
Its Discontents," Norman Mailer's "The White Negro," Paul
Goodman's *Growing Up Absurd*, Clement Greenberg's *Art and Culture*, Robert Warshow's *The Immediate Experience*, Daniel Boorstin's *The Image*, William Whyte's *The Organization Man*, David
Riesman's *The Lonely Crowd* and *Individualism Reconsidered*, C.
Wright Mills's *White Collar* and *The Power Elite*—concentrated less
on the plight of the disadvantaged or the programs of various
administrations than on the psychological, moral, and cultural
tensions plaguing the middle class.

From one point of view, these writers' disinterest in the details of political and economic policy seemed another example of the intellectual community's unwillingness to engage in a systematic critique of postwar America. Yet seen from another perspective, their lack of curiosity about legislative proposals and their relative indifference to presidential campaigns freed them to examine for the first time the dilemmas of a postindustrial society. Since they believed (like the rest of their contemporaries) that the tasks of capital accumulation, economic development, and modernization had all been completed, since they supposed that the historic afflictions of hunger and poverty were being eradicated, they could contemplate those problems that had no obvious institutional solutions.

Liberated from the assumptions of the 1930s, many intellectuals in the 1950s attacked the social order not because it was politically unjust or economically oppressive, but because it seemed impersonal, bureaucratic, and inhumane. No longer awaiting the inevitable collapse of capitalism or the revolutionary fury of the working class, they began to assess the moral impact of mass consumption and material success. Less haunted than the prewar generation by the specters of unemployment and economic disintegration, they evaluated the uses of leisure time, the manipulative effects of advertising and popular culture, the quality of human relationships in an age of affluence. Frightened by the totalitarian implications of state ownership and centralized planning boards, they explored the sense of powerlessness and alienation felt by the ordinary citizen whose voice was never heard at the highest levels of government.

Given their trust in the permanence of prosperity, they considered it more urgent at present to study the plight of the privileged than to catalogue the hardships of the poor. Accordingly, they analyzed the monotony of factory labor and white-collar office work, the middle-class yearning for comfort and security rather than adventure and risk, the emptiness of life in modern suburbia, the traumas of adolescence, the absorption of the individual into a mass society.

Above all, having rejected the notion that political ideologies and organized social movements would provide some form of salvation for themselves and their society, the postwar intellectuals reemphasized the virtues of privacy and personal fulfillment. Where the search for community had captured the imagination of the Left in the 1930s, the search for identity inspired the writers and artists of the 1950s. Where social critics had once insisted on the need for collective action, they now urged the individual to resist the pressures of conformity.

Such concerns indicated how far writers had journeyed from the ideas of Marx to those of Tocqueville, Sartre, and Freud. In their eyes, the contemporary obsession with status and prestige had replaced the traditional issues of class and property. Opinion molders and tastemakers seemed more powerful than the men who owned the means of production. The possession of great wealth appeared less significant than the ability to make the crucial decisions about war and peace. The primary danger was no longer social inequality but standardization and uniformity, not economic exploitation but the moral consequences of abundance.

These were not the sorts of problems that liberal reformers or socialist theoreticians could readily address. Yet as a result of having jettisoned the ideals and commitments of the 1930s, some intellectuals in the 1950s were able to offer a profound and far-reaching indictment of modern American life, often more challenging and provocative than anything found in the social thought of the Depression years. Writers like Dwight Macdonald, Paul Goodman, Norman Mailer, Mary McCarthy, Daniel Bell, Clement Greenberg, Daniel Boorstin, William Whyte, David Riesman, and C. Wright Mills continued to function as critics, persisting in the quest for alternative values if not for alternative institutions. Although they had ceased (apart from Mills) to be "radical" about political or economic affairs, they remained subversive on questions of culture and society.

And they left a legacy for the future. In their works, one discovered a country filled with paradox and potential discord. Here was a population choking on material goods but vaguely uneasy about its addiction to consumerism, a thoroughly urban civilization whose most respectable inhabitants scampered to the suburbs to evade the deterioration and eventual collapse of their most spectacular cities, an opulent and highly mobile nation with large segments of its citizenry still imprisoned in poverty and ghettos, a middle-class society whose children resigned themselves without enthusiasm to their prospects inside the giant corporations and bureaucracies that dominated the economy, an apolitical and inward-looking people whose government harbored global ambitions beyond the influence or control of the average voter.

This was a portrait of America that could have radical implications in another time and under other circumstances. Indeed, most of the moral and cultural quandaries depicted in the articles and books of the postwar intellectuals were transmitted intact to the 1960s. But in the following decade these no longer seemed the subtle contradictions of an economically stable if emotionally insecure nation. Rather, they were at the heart of the political and social crises ripping the country apart. And they shaped the perspective of people too young to have experienced the strains and ambivalences of the postwar years. So, far from being part of a silent generation of complacent apologists, the writers of the 1950s became (whether they wished to or not) the prophets of rebellion and the sires of the New Left.

The Problems of Prosperity

In 1957, Lewis Coser admitted in a symposium on the "American scene" in *Dissent*—the magazine he cofounded with Irving Howe to revive the principles of democratic socialism—that most of the participants were trying "to cope with new problems . . . neither the tradition of socialism nor . . . liberalism has quite prepared us for."[3] Many intellectuals shared Coser's feeling that American life in the 1950s was perplexing, that the customary explanations of social conflict did not illuminate the peculiar troubles of a postindustrial society. The problems of prosperity, as John Kenneth Galbraith had pointed out, were ambiguous, difficult to define, harder still to cure. They required a different language, different perceptions, an investigation of private moods as much as public behavior. One needed to look behind the façade of economic productivity and political consensus, search out the sources of anxiety and unrest, understand why the individual appeared curiously melancholy about his job, his suburban refuge, and his picture-book family. Americans had built a utopia on earth, beyond the most extravagant dreams of Marxists and liberals. Why, then, did the results seem so hollow? Why did the rewards of affluence fail to satisfy?

Often, the answers intellectuals offered were more impressionistic than analytical. Writers sounded as bemused by the economic achievements of the United States as their fellow citizens. Thus, Mary McCarthy wondered whether her countrymen suffered not from too much luxury but from "asceticism" and "unworldliness." After all, she noted, Americans put up with conditions that were "from a materialistic point of view, intolerable. What the foreigner finds most objectionable in American life is its lack of basic comfort. No nation with any sense of material well-being would endure the food we eat, the cramped apartments we live in, the noise, the traffic, the crowded subways and buses. American life, in large cities at any rate, is a perpetual assault on the . . . nerves." Nevertheless, Europeans continued to believe that money and possessions brought contentment. Americans realized that until "you have had a washing machine, you cannot imagine how little difference it will make to you." The real question in McCarthy's opinion was how the United States might "create a cushion of plenty without stupefaction of the soul and the senses."[4]

Clearly, America was far from resolving this dilemma. Instead, the postwar abundance bred unexpected and inexplicable disappointments. "We are an unhappy people," Dwight Macdonald lamented, "a people without style, without a sense of what is humanly satisfying. Our values are not anchored securely, not in the past (tradition) and not in the present (community). There is a terrible *shapelessness* about American life. Prosperous Americans look more tense and joyless than the people in the poorest quarters" of Europe.[5] The consequences of this discrepancy between material wealth and spiritual impoverishment could be psychologically devastating. As Delmore Schwartz suggested, "one can hardly help but be terrified when riches and success bring greater conflict and unhappiness, instead of gratification and peace. . . . To find that the overwhelming fulfillment of hope and desire leave one in disillusion or despair is one of the most demoralizing of experiences."[6] Schwartz, perhaps the most promising poet of his generation, whose early triumphs could not prevent the periodic plunges into depression and paranoia that ultimately destroyed his talent, probably knew better than anyone else how paltry were the emotional compensations of fame and good fortune.

Given this conviction that Americans lacked inner tranquility despite their economic advantages, it came as no shock to Dwight Macdonald that people longed less for riches than for "peace of mind," that they craved "reassuring, soothing messages" from clerics, therapists, and self-help books (the titles of which—*Relax and Live, The Conquest of Fatigue and Fear, How to Control Worry, Cure Your Nerves Yourself*—were symptomatic of what Lewis Coser called the "private nightmares" and "sense of desperation" he saw all around him).[7] Nor was Delmore Schwartz startled that the "vocabulary of psychoanalysis" currently dominated ordinary conversation. Nearly everyone diagnosed himself as neurotic, Schwartz observed; personal relationships were filled with references to "tensions, resentments, and insecurity."[8] Similarly, the term "alienation" had become a "semantic beacon," Nathan Glazer acknowledged; it supposedly described the individual's generalized "feeling of isolation, homelessness, . . . restlessness, anxiety."[9] Indeed, as Leslie Fiedler reminded the readers of *Commentary,* the phenomenon of alienation—once regarded by Marxists as a product of social forces—was now seen as the result of "buried disturbances in the individual psyche," as well as a "basic determinant of the human condition."[10]

The intellectuals' emphasis on private maladies rather than institutional shortcomings reflected their own sense of helplessness in the face of remote and omnipotent governmental structures. Writers were as apathetic as the average citizen, Dwight Macdonald argued, and "for the same reason . . . : you can't work up much interest—politically, at least—in a process which you feel you can't affect."[11] But the concentration of power in Washington was not the only cause of personal malaise. Americans lived in a "bureaucratic culture," claimed a contributor to *Dissent.* Employed in "huge organizations administered by distant impersonal authorities," laboring at "highly routinized" jobs, residing in nondescript suburbs that were "nobody's hometown," the "bureaucratic man" could not "control by his own individual effort anything necessary to his life, liberty, or pursuit of happiness."[12]

Americans therefore found themselves both the beneficiaries and the victims of power and success. No wonder they seemed ambivalent, bewildered, outwardly serene and inwardly distraught. The intellectuals of the 1950s had identified one of the basic incongruities about the postwar affluence. However much politicians might praise the American standard of living, Lewis Coser noted, "there remains the fundamental problem of the standard and quality of life."[13] It was precisely on this issue that writers leveled their most critical judgments.

One area where intellectuals believed the American Dream had patently failed was in providing meaningful work for blue-collar laborers and the middle class. The guarantee of upward mobility and unlimited opportunities to those who were thrifty, able, inventive, determined, and persevering seemed counterfeit in an era of large corporations, mammoth factories, intrusive bureaucracies, specialized jobs, and clear divergences in skill and income. At the same time, the presumption that the individual could find fulfillment at the office or on the assembly line appeared equally absurd. The age of the proud and solitary craftsman had long since vanished; the industrial demands of the twentieth century transformed artisans into appendages of the conveyor belt.

None of these perceptions were new. Writers had been assailing the evils of mechanization, the speed-up, and the efficiency expert for decades. But now, when the labor movement cared more about higher wages and better pension plans than about the dehumanization of modern work, and when socialism no longer held out the hope of liberating the proletariat from the chains of production, intellectuals concluded that the way people spent their hours on the job was itself a permanent testimonial to America's distorted priorities.

Among those who derided the "myth of the happy worker," Daniel Bell might seem out of place as a critic of industrialization.

Yet the same author who applauded the demise of radicalism and celebrated America's democratic traditions had devoted a number of years to studying the sociological and psychological troubles of labor. However strongly he championed liberal politics and the mixed economy, Bell was less than thrilled by the conditions under which most Americans earned their livelihoods. His articles in *Commentary* and *Dissent* in the 1940s and 1950s, culminating with the publication of "Work and Its Discontents" (a lengthy essay that appeared first as a book in 1956), amounted to a merciless indictment of management procedures, the cult of personnel relations, and the worship of output and profits over human needs. When he included the essay as a chapter in *The End of Ideology,* it contrasted sharply with the themes and tone of the rest of the book. In the middle of a work dedicated to the proposition that American institutions were reasonably beneficent, Bell had paused to question his own premises. The result was a brooding discourse on contemporary American values that undercut much of his praise for the political and economic system.

Bell traced the origins of America's present attitudes toward work to the nineteenth and early twentieth century insistence on rationalizing all facets of labor in the interest of technological efficiency and greater productivity. Thus corporate barons and industrial engineers consolidated raw materials, steam and electrical energy, assembly lines, and unskilled manpower under one gigantic roof. Here they scientifically calculated every second of activity, imposed a mechanical sense of time and pace, and broke down each task into a specified and endlessly repeatable set of physical motions. In the new order, laborers were supposed to attend solely to the details of their job; they had no voice in shaping company policy. The executives, designers, and sales managers were responsible for all industrial planning, and they concerned themselves not with the men in the plant but with the "logic of cost . . . and competition." Eventually, the only factors that counted, according to Bell, were "market decisions." Nor did he think that the working conditions for secretaries, file clerks, and accountants were more enviable: "In offices the installation of rapid high-speed calculators, tabulators, and billing machines" turned white-collar employees into the same mechanized "drones" as their blue-collar counterparts.[14]

To make matters even gloomier, factory and office workers could rarely hope to improve their jobs, much less rise through the ranks of the corporate hierarchy. Their children might find better occupations, Bell conceded, but the parents usually stayed where they were. And this "sense of having a fixed place," he realized, was psychologically as well as economically "grinding."[15] It also conflicted with the idea—to which Bell and others normally subscribed—that America was a paradise of social mobility.

As a way of distracting workers from depression or anger at their circumstances, management deployed legions of sociologists, industrial therapists, and personnel experts to minister to the emotional needs of the hired help. Bell saved his fiercest barbs for this endeavor, partially because of what it suggested about more general trends in American life. The vogue of "human relations," he charged, reflected a shift both in business tactics and in the wider culture "from authority to manipulation as a means of exercising dominion. . . . The older modes of overt coercion are now replaced by psychological persuasion. The tough brutal foreman, raucously giving orders, gives way to the mellowed voice of the 'human-relations oriented' supervisor. . . . In industrial relations, as in large areas of American society, accommodation of a sort has replaced conflict." Unfortunately, this approach was in Bell's eyes a "substitute for thinking about the work process itself." Instead of trying to adapt the machines to the men, the "human engineer" sought to "adjust the worker to his job," all the while refusing to take the laborer's viewpoint or difficulties seriously. "Few industrial sociologists," Bell declared, "seem to be aware . . . that one of the functions of social science is . . . to explore alternative (and better—that is, more human) combinations of work and not merely to make more effective those that already exist."[16]

Ironically, the positions Bell adopted on other matters were vulnerable to the very same objections. Still, it was remarkable to hear an advocate of pragmatism, negotiation, and compromise worry about the effects of psychological manipulation and the suppression of conflict. Similarly, Bell's dictum that social scientists should pose alternatives to established arrangements and procedures introduced a note not usually found in his own work. But Bell, like his contemporaries, seemed more willing to act on these sentiments when he was discussing cultural and personal issues, rather than when the subject involved domestic politics or the Cold War.

Bell's gravest complaint about the debilitating nature of modern work, however, was its inherent inability to offer satisfaction to the employee. Individuals had no interest in their jobs, he contended, because the tasks they were called on to perform required little intelligence or creativity and promised no inner gratification. Work became an "irksome chore to be shirked," or to be finished as quickly as possible. Nonetheless, unhappiness on the job led not to militant strikes, union efforts to "reorder the flow of work," the questioning of managerial prerogatives, the repudiation of mass production, or a "radical challenge to society." Instead, Bell asserted, workers either indulged in "hostile gestures" in the shop ("conspicuous loafing," constant evasions of authority, industrial sabotage, slowdowns, "crazy racings against the clock to vary the deadly monotony"), or they narcoticized themselves with "escapist fantasies."[17]

Mostly, though, the only compensation for the drudgery of work was the acquisition of a house, a car, a refrigerator, a television set. Paradoxically, a worker's diligence was measured by how much money he could spend on commodities and on the pursuit of leisure; "success at one's job [became] less important than success in one's style of life." Yet even this turned out to be unrewarding, Bell suggested. Work and play had to be integrated, not divorced; to enjoy life at night one needed "the zest of a challenging day, not the exhaustion of a blank one." Without such connections, Bell was convinced, the laborer would remain passive and frustrated on and off the job.[18]

Although Bell directed his diatribe at the "capitalist industrial order" in the United States, he did not imagine that the socialist regimes in Europe and Russia had discovered a way of making work more attractive or meaningful. In fact, his thesis implied that the problems of modern labor exemplified the larger crises in every advanced society.[19]

But if Bell was actually describing the inevitable consequences of modernization, and if socialism offered no solution since the workers' "control over the entire economy" was "unfeasible," then what could be done to enrich the hours spent on the job? Bell, like Galbraith, believed the only answer was to discard "the concept of efficiency"—to alter the rhythms and pace of work to suit the needs of the employee rather than to serve the goals of productivity and mass consumption. The steady output of goods and services, as well as the maximization of profit, were far less significant to Bell than the creation of "spontaneity and freedom" in the factory and in the office. Hence he welcomed the possibilities of decentralized plants, the enlargement of tasks and responsibilities, and especially the benefits of automation in making the worker less specialized, more knowledgeable about a variety of jobs, more aware of his contribution to the entire enterprise. Ultimately, Bell hoped, the value of work would be defined not "by the slide rule and stop watch," nor by the demands of the marketplace, but by its ability to give the employee "a new concept of self."[20]

For a man who distrusted utopian ideas, Bell was offering some fairly millennial proposals. Yet just as *The End of Ideology* summarized the political attitudes of many intellectuals in the 1950s, so "Work and Its Discontents" reflected their social and cultural preoccupations. Bell neglected to explain how the changes he recommended could be brought about—or to indicate what movements might persuade the owners and managers of American industry to relinquish their control over costs, production schedules, and the tempo of the assembly line. But these omissions were characteristic of Bell's generation. Nevertheless, whatever its deficiencies, Bell's essay contained a brilliant analysis of the relationship between the dissatisfactions in work and the disappointments of life in the United States. It still stands as a model of social criticism in a decade that allegedly wanted only statements of affirmation.

The individual's lack of fulfillment on the job might not have seemed so serious a problem were there other ways for him to gain a sense of accomplishment and self-esteem. Even if one's occupation no longer served as an index of moral character, it remained an indispensable mechanism for residential mobility and social prestige. The weekly wage and the monthly salary provided the wherewithal for families to pursue the American Dream—at least in its twentieth century incarnation. With money, they could acquire the external signs of success: a comfortable home in a classier neighborhood with superior schools for the children. In the United States, making it meant moving on; the feeling of achievement would presumably derive not from the plant or the office but from a down payment on a castle in the suburbs.

Between 1946 and 1958, 85 percent of all the nonfarm housing in America was erected outside the central cities. Conversely, most of the new construction in the downtown areas during these years was commercial rather than residential. Whereas suburban growth in the late nineteenth and early twentieth century had coincided with the expansion of the nation's cities, the postwar flight to the Levittowns and Park Forests took place in the context of urban decline. Increasingly, the suburbs became not exclusive sanctuaries filled with distinctive estates for the very rich, but dreary subdivisions of cheaply built, similarly priced, and often identical houses developed for the middle class by realtors and land speculators interested in quick profits. The spiritual core of these suburbs was no longer the country club but the shopping center and the school.

Middle-class families deserted the cities largely because of high apartment rents, the need for more space to accommodate their swelling brood of children, a deteriorating educational system, traffic jams, dirt, noise, dangerous streets, and what they regarded as undesirable (i.e., poor and racially different) neighbors. But the postwar bourgeoisie had also imbibed the traditional American hostility to city life. From the Jeffersonian mistrust of urban crowds, through the Populist nostalgia for the rural past, to the movies' idealization of the small town (the ancestral home of Andy Hardy and Longfellow Deeds), the land had always been romanticized at the expense of the metropolis. Political rhetoric and the mass media taught Americans that the city was not a place of excitement and creativity, but a violent, unhealthy, corrupt, and lonely environment from which people should flee at the earliest opportunity.

Regrettably, cities were also the source of wealth, power, industry, commerce, culture, and communications. The new suburbs, however, offered the middle class the best of both worlds. Those who could afford to move would enjoy decent housing, a modest garden in the back yard, regular garbage pickups, police protection, and "progressive" schools, while at the same time retaining their access to the economic and cultural advantages still to be found downtown. Suburbia represented a merger of the urban and rural ideals; it permitted people to make a living in the city and a life in the suburbs.

Few intellectuals in the 1950s entertained these reveries. As the quintessential inhabitants of the city (despite their maintenance of "summer homes" upstate or in the country), they could barely fathom the appeal of suburbia. Who in his right mind would exchange an all-night delicatessen for a weekend contest with crab grass? Were PTA meetings and the Little League adequate substitutes for evening concerts and spontaneous excursions to the art gallery? Why give up the cozy French bistro down the street to joust with mosquitoes round the barbecue pit? Were the rumble of subways and the odor of bus fumes any more annoying than the screeching of crickets? Throughout the decade, writers warned that there was no promised land at the end of the exodus to the suburbs.

The failure of suburbia to compensate for whatever else was wrong with American society became a standard refrain in the essays of many intellectuals. Advertised as the locale where the middle-class breadwinner might "prove . . . conclusively that not only he personally, but his whole scale of values . . . can produce the good life," where success in the guise of home ownership could be publicly displayed for all to see and respect, the suburb was supposed to provide a restful oasis from the pressures of urban competition and economic advancement, a veritable utopia in which the average American would momentarily forget the "brute reality of what has to be done" to get ahead.[21] Yet according to its critics, the suburbs offered no such shelter. On the contrary, the problems of the suburbanite seemed more intractable; his anxieties more intense.

As several commentators noted, the new suburbs simply exacerbated the nation's social cleavages, solidifying class and racial divisions in housing and education.[22] But the resident of suburbia felt no sense of community with his fellow migrants. Populated by perpetual transients for whom moving day was a certification of achievement, the suburb could never be a cohesive neighborhood where people had common interests, fixed values, and on-going affiliations. Instead, the suburbs were merely makeshift way stations where the man of the house ate and slept before commuting to work while waiting for reassignment to another part of the country. If anything, the cities remained monuments to permanence and collective living; in the suburbs, the middle-class property owner aspired only to an "isolation . . . from the rest of mankind" that was "necessary to [his] mobility."[23]

Hence, writers were not surprised to discover that the members of the suburban family seemed more estranged from one another, that the separate schedules of parents and children left no time for expressions of intimacy, that the frantic obsession with "keeping busy" transformed the ranch house into a "hotel" from which husbands, wives, and offspring daily emerged to "do battle" with their peers at work, in car pools, and on the playground. In such frightful circumstances, the creation of shared human relationships appeared less important than the compulsion to impress the neighbors. To a number of observers, the interminable striving for status deprived suburbanites of the chance to play diverse roles and "establish more complicated identities." Dedicated to the refinement of their public image, they invariably surrendered "something of themselves" in the attempt to keep up the lawn and the shrubbery.[24]

Yet despite their strenuous efforts, middle-class families could not escape in the suburbs the life they left behind in the cities. The bills piled up; the frenzy to work and succeed persisted; the financial and psychic burdens of the urban rat race were inescapable no matter where people sought refuge. In the estimation of one writer, the American suburbs were founded on a "gigantic illusion, that flight is possible, that the costs of bourgeois values can be avoided, that bourgeois means will not contaminate bourgeois ends, that a bourgeois utopia can be built out of bourgeois cruelty."[25] For intellectuals in the 1950s, the fable of the suburban castle owed its origins less to the brochures of real estate brokers than to the prophecies of Franz Kafka.

The intellectuals' disdain for suburbia revealed a certain snobbery, together with an unwillingness to admit how emotionally gratifying the purchase of a ranch house could be to a generation haunted by memories of immigrant slums, cramped apartments, and the feeling of physical claustrophobia that marked the impoverished 1930s. Open space and residential mobility symbolized freedom as well as privacy; after years of living in close quarters, one could luxuriate in the distance from neighbors, siblings, relatives, parents. The suburbs were impersonal, but that was their greatest attraction. When "community" meant familial interference and social congestion, who would not prefer a little isolation, the ability to retreat to a room of one's own? There might well be "cracks in the picture window" and banality on the "crab grass frontier," yet this was a small price the suburbanite seemed ready and eager to pay. Writers could sneer, but the middle class continued to negotiate its mortgages and relish its escape from the city.

The postwar baby boom accelerated the growth of suburbia. Many families reluctantly decided to leave the city in order to promote the well-being of their children. Even those who considered themselves politically alert and culturally sophisticated were as susceptive to this rationale as the benighted middle class.

In an article for *Commentary* on Chicago's liberal intelligentsia, Isaac Rosenfeld satirized the ambivalence of his own peers. On the one hand, he observed, the local avant-garde dutifully subscribed to *Harper's*, glanced at *The New Yorker*, and bought the *New York Sunday Times* for the Book Review. They also listened to classical music, scurried to the latest foreign movies, covered their living room walls with shelves of paperback books and reproductions of Van Gogh, took up guitars and recorders, discoursed learnedly on the technology of high fidelity phonographs, and made liberated proclamations about the "color question." On the other hand, they were incurably child-centered; they raised their brats according to the dictates of "Spock and Gesell with an assist from Bruno Bettelheim," and they spent half their waking hours debating the merits of various baby-sitters and pediatricians. In fact, Rosenfeld declared, "one sure way of telling whether you are visiting an academic or non-academic household is by the behavior of the children, and the extent to which you can make yourself heard above their clatter. If it is still possible to conduct a conversation, you are in a non-academic household."[26] Apart from excessive permissiveness, the urban intellectual's anxious concern for his progeny seemed indistinguishable from that of the bourgeois suburbanite, whose flight from the city he would soon emulate.

Indeed, the problems at work and in the suburbs paled before the dilemmas of how best to bring up children, endure their adolescence, and manage their education. Since most writers were teachers as well as parents, they devoted much of their attention in the 1950s to the shifting moods, values, and intentions of the young. On the whole, they disliked what they saw. If children were any barometer, the quality of American life would not shortly improve.

Nearly everyone recognized the economic and cultural significance of the population explosion following World War II. By 1949, a contributor to *Commentary* pointed out, the United States had cultivated "an accent on youth which has no parallel in modern Western nations." Advertisers and the mass media directed their messages to the youthful consumers who increasingly controlled the family budget. More important, parents retained their faith in the American Dream "by transmitting to their offspring their personally unfulfilled hopes." Whatever disappointments they had suffered in their own lives, adults took comfort in a "philosophy of sacrifice for a future embodied in their children."[27]

The idea that the child's achievements might make up for parental failures was hardly new in America. But in the postwar years, such notions placed a heavier burden on the schools than ever before. Where people in the nineteenth and early twentieth century had regarded hard work or the ownership of property as the key to success, the middle class now considered education (or more accurately, the acquisition of degrees and credentials) an indispensable ingredient for social and material advancement.

The emphasis on formal training, additionally stimulated by the baby boom and the GI bill of rights (which enabled the veterans of World War II and Korea to resume or complete their educations, thereby keeping them off the labor market until they obtained the skills to enter business or the professions) led to spiraling enrollments in high schools and colleges after 1945 This in turn spurred the demand for more and better teachers, facilities, and methods of instruction. Then in 1957, Russia's dramatic launching of two unmanned space satellites touched off a feverish controversy in America about whether the nation's students were retarded in science and engineering. As a result, education became a government priority. With the passage of the National Defense Education Act in 1958, federal funds for student loans and scholarships, supplemented by allocations from state and local agencies as well as from private foundations, enormously expanded the country's financial investment in its schools. By the end of the 1950s, education had blossomed into a major industry, and also a valuable adjunct to the corporations, the military, and the state.

Yet what did all this money buy? In the opinion of many critics, the classrooms contained more hardware but the students appeared less interesting. Throughout the 1950s, magazines and newspapers berated the young as members of a "silent generation"—politically apathetic, intellectually passive, caring less for social causes than for economic security, preoccupied with their private lives, looking as if they'd just stepped off the set of *Ozzie and Harriet* or *Father Knows Best.*

Intellectuals were especially dismayed by the absence of political activity on college campuses. Though most writers felt little nostalgia for the 1930s, they could not help contrasting the students of the 1950s unfavorably with their predecessors in the Depression years (which usually meant when the writers themselves were young). Nevertheless, the very factors that had stifled the appeal of radicalism among adults reinforced the conservative instincts of their offspring.

Thus George Rawick unhappily acknowledged in *Dissent* that the collapse of the Progressive party after 1948, the present torpor of the labor movement, and the affluence of the middle class had made socialism sound "neither 'right' nor 'wrong' " but "irrelevant" to the young. They imitated their elders in rejecting ideologies and took pride in being "anti-political."[28] Other commentators like Mary McCarthy, Robert Lynd, and Isaac Rosenfeld suggested that the students of the 1950s were indifferent to radical politics because they saw nothing in postwar American life against which they should revolt, or even feel strongly about.[29] Moreover, in the wake of the red scare, the few who might have been inclined toward activism now refused to jeopardize their future careers by getting their names on a "list" that could bar their admission to graduate or medical schools, or prevent them from landing jobs in law firms and corporations. Ultimately, as Rawick understood, the combination of quiescence and fear left contemporary students without the "certainties" that characterized the generation of the 1930s. Not only were the answers harder to find, "the questions seem impossible to formulate." But the children only reflected their parents' confusion. Until there was a basic transformation in American attitudes, Rawick cautioned, "we should not expect too much social or political ferment in the colleges."[30]

In this group portrait, the young emerged as neither rebels nor reformers, but as embryonic bureaucrats and organization men. Having no quarrel with society, afraid of unconventional behavior and heretical ideas, they did not wish the universities to provide mental challenges or awaken their social passions. Instead, they wanted their teachers to furnish them with the practical skills that ensured success in the adult world. So writers blamed both the schools and the students for being not only apolitical but anti-intellectual.

No matter what the subject, every social critic has in mind some past golden age that he imagines was infinitely superior to the dismal present. Accordingly, when writers were not scolding collegians for lacking the political fervor of the 1930s, they mourned the loss of intellectual commitment that supposedly animated American education in the nineteenth century.

Once school had functioned "as the formal agency transmitting the classical-cultural heritage to succeeding generations of the young," recalled an essayist in *Commentary*. Despite the elitist

premises of this education, "the value of the search for knowledge and vision went unquestioned as a desirable thing in itself."
During those halcyon days, people admired "intellectuality" and
sought more of it in lyceums, public lectures, and reading clubs.
But with the onset of Progressivism, and the insistence on com-
pulsory classroom attendance for the children of the masses, the
schools began to stress citizenship, practicality, efficiency—turning education into a "replica of the factory" in a vain effort "to
do *something* with the majority of the students . . . who [had] no
initial curiosity."[31]

The effects of this democratization could be seen in the undergraduates of the 1950s. Revisiting Vassar, Mary McCarthy found
her successors competent, civil, deferential to those who appeared learned, but serenely aloof "from what is currently going
on in the world of arts and letters." They appeared unredeem-
ably "docile" when confronted with difficult ideas, and they had
no capacity for intellectual play. "The vivid and extraordinary
student, familiar to the old teachers and the alumnae, is, at least
temporarily, absent from the scene," McCarthy asserted. She
missed the "idea of excellence, the zest for adventure, the fastidi-
ousness of mind and humanistic breadth of feeling," not to mention an "amplitude of style, the mantle of a calling, a sense of
historical dignity," all of which were "so noticeable at Vassar" in
the not-too-distant past.[32] Other observers worried that the minority of students who were still "fired by the quest for understanding" would grow "defensive, doctrinaire, withdrawn, lacking in self-assurance, and socially unpredictable." Though these
wretches continued to believe in the traditional values of education, they might become "pariahs" because the modern university had "little if any place for them" in its pedagogy.[33]

No doubt the critics of the schools exaggerated both the anti-
intellectual predilections of the young and the thirst for culture
exhibited by previous generations. But the present mood on
campus seemed to writers an unwelcome expression of the very
tendencies they deplored in the rest of American life. Since they
perceived college as a mirror of middle-class aspirations, their
attack on contemporary attitudes toward education had reverberations for the larger society.

Hence, Mary McCarthy objected to the monumental impor-

tance of extracurricular organizations at Vassar because in a setting where "every hour is planned for and assigned to some
scheduled group activity," the virtues of "solitude and self-ques-
tioning" were "regulated out of existence."[34] Other writers decried the undergraduates' fixation with dress and personal appearance in order to differentiate themselves from the poorer
classes, their assumption that physical attractiveness was a "virtually infallible index to success in all lines of social competition,"
their attempts to "rate" and "belong" by dating the right people
and joining the right fraternities or sororities, and their hunger
for "a good time, social prestige, a mate, a job."[35] Education had
become in the eyes of McCarthy and her colleagues almost exclusively a "preparation for civic life and marriage," a placement
bureau and breeding ground for tomorrow's respectable suburbanites.[36]

To help students navigate this rite of passage, even the best
universities converted themselves into vocational schools.
Equipped with a specialty and a diploma, their graduates could
smoothly adapt to the norms of the corporation, the law firm, the
medical practice, or the government—none of whose requirements were very different from those of the modern university.
As Isaac Rosenfeld noted, college administrators and future employers desired the same product: "more or less healthy and
well-adjusted young men and women of rather inflexible mind,
who regard life not as an adventure but an investment," and who
were ambitious only for what another writer called the "safe
berth" and a "steady income."[37]

Worst of all, there seemed to be no alternatives to the utilitarian spirit that pervaded American campuses. Few people, Rosenfeld claimed, had any "adequate idea of what the cultural life in
and around a university should be."[38] Instead, the colleges simply expanded their enrollments and intensified their mission as
service centers for the economy, providing students with the
practical training necessary to maintain the nation's postwar
prosperity. By the close of the decade, educators themselves
began referring (not without pride) to the "multiversity"—a massive conglomerate where faculty members undertook subsidized
and sometimes secret research for the government or the mili-

tary, where administrators presided over complex and frequently omnipotent bureaucracies, where classrooms were transformed into auditoriums and teaching became a theatrical spectacle complete with audio-visual pyrotechnics designed to entertain the passive and faceless multitudes, where undergraduates often felt trapped in a maze of impersonal rules and computerized degree programs, where the students' struggle to manipulate or evade the system took precedence over learning a subject (though such experiences inadvertently gave them exactly the skills they needed to cope with the institutions of adulthood). The multiversity was a concoction of the 1950s, but it would bequeath its deficiencies to the 1960s when the mood on campus had substantially changed. Until then, the idea that schools should function as islands of dissent, rather than as bridges to society, sounded harmlessly naïve.

Nevertheless, some writers detected the rudiments of an adversary culture stirring beneath the placid surface of undergraduate life. Isaac Rosenfeld saw in the tastes and idioms of students at the University of Chicago—their preference for "dirty or neglected clothes," their penchant for "bop-talk," their fascination with the "folkways of jazz musicians" and black people, their fondness for the dropouts and street characters who lent a bohemian flavor to the neighborhoods surrounding the campus, their self-conscious efforts to be "cool" and "uncommitted"—an instinctive rejection of bourgeois standards and expectations.[39]

Yet these affectations appeared innocuous compared to the mounting instances of juvenile delinquency. The eruption of gang warfare in the urban slums, the palpable resentment in the eyes and mannerisms of those for whom education was not an avenue to wealth and status, seemed a disturbing sign of America's failure to nurture its young. The sullen gang member became the subject of innumerable movies, novels, and journalistic investigations, especially when adolescent violence threatened to spread from the inner city to the affluent suburb.[40] Soon the various images associated with the delinquent entered popular mythology: Marlon Brando's motorcycle and black leather jacket in *The Wild One,* Sal Mineo's moodiness and yearning for a "family" in *Rebel Without a Cause,* James Dean's inability to communicate with his father both in *Rebel* and in *East of Eden,* the blind hatred for all manifestations of cultural authority symbolized by the smashing of a teacher's cherished record collection in *The Blackboard Jungle,* the sexual explicitness of Elvis Presley's early performances (before he was tamed by television and the army).

In 1958, commenting on Meyer Levin's best-selling novel, *Compulsion,* Harvey Swados contended that readers now showed more interest in Leopold and Loeb—those youthful murderers of the 1920s—than in Sacco and Vanzetti. Because the former were apolitical, psychotic, mindlessly destructive, and the offspring of prosperous parents, they possessed precisely the qualities that defined the "lost teenagers" of the 1950s. Leopold and Loeb were an early omen of the "tormenting discontent" felt by contemporary adolescents for whom "everything is being done, to [whom] everything is being given . . . except a reason for living and for building a socially useful life."[41]

Like the Beats, hipsters, rock 'n' roll idols, and black founders of modern jazz, the juvenile delinquent was one of the "freaks" of the 1950s. Together with them, he stood as an authentic outsider, a personification of the youthful attraction to maladjustment and nonconformity, an inarticulate but vivid reproach to the comfortable reign of middle-class organization men. These attitudes in turn pointed to the formation of a nascent "counterculture" among the young, with a vernacular, a special consciousness, and a code of conduct separate from and antagonistic to the adult universe. While neither rock 'n' roll nor Hollywood's version of delinquency inspired the young to remake America (the ideologies of Elvis Presley and James Dean not being a conspicuous part of their appeal), the adolescent's sense of belonging however vicariously to a distinctive community, with its own language, perceptions, and values, foreshadowed the generational battles of the 1960s.

But at this juncture, adults were not entirely excluded from the darker realms of rebellion and alienation. Near the end of the 1950s, they obtained their own visa to the underworld in the form of a hit Broadway musical: Leonard Bernstein's *West Side Story*—the Jets and the Sharks inflating the problems of the delinquent into a neo-Shakespearean tragedy.

The most serious (and prophetic) analysis of America's difficulties with its children could be found in Paul Goodman's *Growing Up Absurd*. At first glance, Goodman did not seem to have any particular expertise about the present problems of the young. His early life was fairly typical of those intellectuals who came to prominence following World War II. Born in New York in 1911, he attended CCNY during the opening years of the Depression, and went on to earn a Ph.D. in humanities from the University of Chicago. But Goodman had neither the patience nor the instinct for specialization to be a full-time academic. Though he taught at Chicago, New York University, Black Mountain College, Sarah Lawrence, and the University of Wisconsin, his favorite lectern was the little magazine; his articles regularly appeared in *Partisan Review*, Dwight Macdonald's *Politics*, *Commentary*, *Dissent*, and *Kenyon Review*. At various intervals in his career, he was an eclectic champion of anarchism, Marx, Freud, Wilhelm Reich, progressive education, and decentralized regional communities. In addition to his works of social criticism, the most well-known of which was *Communitas* (1947), Goodman churned out novels, short stories, and poems. Indeed, he believed his diverse talents made him a modern Renaissance man; as Alfred Kazin remembered, Goodman "radiated authority in all branches of learning and in all departments of literature."[42] This trait, however, was virtually a prerequisite within the New York Jewish intelligentsia; one had to pretend omniscience simply to gain attention amid the clamor of competing essays, books, and letters to the editor.

Where Goodman differed from his peers was in his willingness to go beyond their customary concerns, and to identify personally (rather than romantically) with those who had dropped out or deviated from the middle-class scramble for success and respectability. He continued to think of himself as a "radical" during the 1950s. More important, he wrote about the gloomier corners of American life with greater sympathy and realism than most of his colleagues could usually muster.

He also adopted a more colloquial tone to fit his less exalted subjects, which sometimes made his prose seem banal, repetitious, and dreary. Norman Mailer later reflected sourly that "the literary experience of encountering Goodman's style . . . was not unrelated to the journeys one undertook in the company of a laundry bag."[43] But then Mailer disliked Goodman's fame as well as his ideas by the 1960s, since each man had once probed the same topic, with Goodman's *Growing Up Absurd* enjoying a more favorable reception than Mailer's "The White Negro."

Actually, until the publication of *Growing Up Absurd* in 1960, Goodman's stature among intellectuals had suffered a decade-long decline. Nineteen publishers rejected the manuscript during the late 1950s before Norman Podhoretz, the new editor of *Commentary,* enthusiastically serialized it in his magazine and helped Goodman extract a contract from Random House. Because of its themes—the portrait of American society as psychologically and culturally oppressive, the treatment of the young as disillusioned and incipiently rebellious, the notion that contemporary institutions did not serve human needs—*Growing Up Absurd* appeared at exactly the right time. Within a few years, it sold over 100,000 copies, and became what Podhoretz called "one of the campus bibles of the sixties." The book also restored Goodman's reputation as a radical activist who was speaking to and for a new generation of people marching in the streets, sitting in at the multiversities, assaulting the Pentagon.[44] Though *Growing Up Absurd* was a product of the 1950s, it influenced the politics and culture of the next decade more directly than any work save C. Wright Mills's *The Power Elite.*

Norman Mailer was right to consider Goodman an early rival for the identical intellectual turf. In the summer of 1957, Mailer had published "The White Negro" in *Dissent.* Characteristically, the essay was pugnacious, outrageous, and guaranteed to scandalize the decorous social democrats who subscribed to the journal.

The "hipster," Mailer announced at the outset, was an "American existentialist" and therefore the only true revolutionary at a time when the "stench of fear" oozed from every pore of national life. How could one recognize this new insurgent, this "psychic outlaw"? The hipster lived solely in the present, Mailer responded. He had no "memory or planned intention"; he took risks and gambled with his energy in order to pass daily tests and win "new kinds of perception"; he deliberately divorced himself from society in order to embark on an "uncharted journey with the rebellious imperatives of the self." The specific destination did not matter; what counted was the search, the style with which a man conducted his private explorations and confronted the presence of death. (Here Mailer's hipster—or perhaps just Mailer —sounded more like a protagonist in a Hemingway novel than a disciple of Sartre or Camus.) There was, however, one persistent objective in the quest: the gradual accumulation of those "isolated truths" the individual felt "at each instant of his existence." In this pursuit, the holiest of Holy Grails was the experience of an "orgasm more apocalyptic than the one which preceded it."[45]

If this proposition was not enough to offend the sexual sensibilities of his fellow intellectuals, Mailer offered some models for the hipster's behavior that seemed equally an affront to the political and moral rectitude of the Old Left. For example, he suggested that the brutality of the hoodlum (in such cases as the bludgeoning of a 50-year-old candy store owner by teen-age thugs during the course of a robbery) should not be despised. The criminal, after all, was violating private property, entering into "a new relation with the police," and "daring the unknown." But Mailer saw black people as the real archetypes for the bohemian and the juvenile delinquent. Blacks supplied the argot, the worship of "abstract states of feeling" (nourished by marijuana), and the knowledge of what it meant to live with perpetual danger. Insofar as the hipster had absorbed the "existentialist synapses" of the blacks, he was in effect a "white Negro." Moreover, his "intense view of existence" matched the experience of most adolescents, and reinforced their own "desire to rebel."[46]

In Mailer's eyes, the hipster, the blacks, the hoodlums, the Beats, and the juvenile delinquents were linked by their "emphasis upon courage at the moment of crisis." Ultimately, he submitted, the "isolated courage of isolated people" might provide a "glimpse of the necessity of life to become more than it has been," thereby "widening the arena of the possible" for everyone.[47]

Mailer's impulse to shock, combined with his longing to uncover some vestiges of political dissidence in the 1950s, led him
to glamorize groups that were more apt to destroy themselves
than to change society. "The White Negro" was a strained and
desperate (though clever) polemic, but the constituency in which
Mailer invested his hopes was too implausible to serve as the
vehicle for his arguments. Still, he had anticipated the emergence
of a new radicalism that would be both economic and sexual,
social and cultural, political and personal. When events caught
up with his ideas, as they did in *The Armies of the Night* and *Miami
and the Siege of Chicago,* his style grew more relaxed, funnier, less
portentous, more deeply felt (particularly in his descriptions of
the existential bravery of the antiwar marchers who spent the
night on the steps of the Pentagon, and the naked pacifists in
their freezing jail cells who offered penance for the sins of America). The demonstrators of the 1960s, unlike the hipsters of the
previous decade, were taking authentic risks, testing themselves
against the power of the state and the encrusted shibboleths of
the Cold War. In the 1950s, Mailer's speculations were prema-
ture, and his designated rebels scarcely deserved his benediction.
But the moment when his insights and American realities finally
coincided was not far off.

Paul Goodman shared Mailer's desire for a fundamental challenge to established attitudes and institutions, but the mood of
Growing Up Absurd was less splenetic and more skeptical than that
of "The White Negro." Like Mailer and other writers in the
1950s, Goodman did not believe that affluence eliminated discontent. Adolescents could hardly hope to lead fulfilling lives
in the future, he contended, because society presented so few
opportunities for personal growth and interesting work. When
the ideals of craftsmanship and "rational productivity," as well as
the importance of having a useful vocation, were in disrepute, the
majority of people had no incentive to care about their jobs or
their employers. Bored, thwarted, cynical, they spent their adult
years doing what they knew was "no good." So if parents lacked
a "calling" and a sense of "honor" in their daily affairs, Goodman
reasoned, why should they expect their offspring to value service,
truthfulness, and integrity?[48]

Echoing the judgment of his colleagues, Goodman foresaw no imminent transformations in American life. But where most intellectuals either praised or at least accepted the stability and benevolence of contemporary institutions, he described the society as a "closed room," at the center of which was an incessant "rat race." Dispensing with the classic concepts of unlimited progress and class struggle, Goodman complained that people could no longer conceive of any alternatives to the existing order. The network of organizations in America preempted the available techniques of social change, bought up "as much of the intelligence as it can," and muffled the "voices of dissent." Under these circumstances, Goodman recognized that it was "desperately hard" for an "average child to grow up to be a man," much less a revolutionary.[49]

Goodman understood the attractiveness of hipsters and juvenile delinquents as symbols of disaffection from the bourgeoisie. He himself admired the Beat generation for scorning the rat race and choosing instead to live in small impoverished communities on the fringes of society, fashioning a distinctive culture based on personal experience rather than on the stereotypes transmitted through the mass media.[50]

But unlike Mailer, Goodman refused to magnify the rebelliousness of the young (and their gurus), or to overlook their disdain for politics and abstract ideas. No one, he charged, really took the plight of the marginal man seriously; the adolescent street gangs and the bohemian wanderers were treated as symptoms of a "youth problem" or as harbingers of a radical movement. In actuality, the Beats and the juvenile delinquents wasted a "vast amount of time doing nothing." And without worthwhile work, they began to think of themselves as "worthless"—members of a surplus population as resigned to their impotence and as obsessed with their self-image as the poor devils in the closed room. To Goodman, the hipster and the teen-age hoodlum suffered the same frustrations and behaved in the same ways as the organization man. Far from being insurgents, they played roles, dutifully conformed to the opinions of their peers, and confused the "short cut" and the "empty sensation" with "honest effort and earnest goals." Lacking a satisfying trade or profession, they were no more "effective in changing the system" than those who had adapted to its demands.[51]

Goodman's assessment was more persuasive than Mailer's. The flaunting of unconventional clothes and patterns of speech could not by themselves alter America. Quite the contrary, such gestures imposed an equally constricting set of norms. Where the businessman or lawyer dressed in narrow ties and button-down-collar shirts, the bohemian indulged in peasant costumes. The middle class fueled itself with alcohol, and Goodman's dropouts experimented with drugs. Consumers were bombarded with the clichés of Madison Avenue, while Mailer's hipsters spouted the jargon of jazz and the black ghetto. When most Americans still had some faith in the Protestant ethic of hard work and getting ahead, Jack Kerouac's Beats followed the Zen Buddhist path of contemplation and passivity.

The larger society could easily tolerate these expressions of discontent. They threatened no institution; provoked no uprisings; disturbed no one in power. If anything, the rebels themselves often seemed on the brink of surrender. The agonies of James Dean were invariably those of adolescence, curable if only his parents showed more compassion. The characters in Kerouac's novels (as Goodman pointed out) constantly married and divorced, left school and returned, raised children and yearned for literary fame. The Beats appeared more apathetic toward, than angry at, their fellow citizens.[52] The delinquents and outlaws who captured the imagination of certain novelists, film makers, and journalists rarely engaged in any acts of overt insurrection beyond petty thievery. They might sometimes terrorize a neighborhood or a classroom, but there was always a Mr. Dadio waiting to show Sidney Poitier the way out of the blackboard jungle.

Yet despite his pessimism about the revolutionary instincts and capabilities of the young, Goodman continued to insist on the need for radical measures. Like Daniel Bell, he objected to the overemphasis (especially among social scientists) on harmony, adjustment, the smooth functioning of institutions. American society was "absurd," Goodman argued, because it did not provide outlets for those aspects of human nature—"grace, discrimination, intellect, feeling"—that he considered crucial in shaping a satisfactory life. The effort to fit people into the limited roles the social order presently offered, while ignoring their private emotions and hunger to perform useful tasks, seemed to him utterly insane. In this nuthouse, Goodman asserted, "fighting and dissenting," generational conflict and deviant behavior, should be regarded as "proper social functions." But eventually there had to be "changes in our society and its culture" in order to "meet the appetites and capacities" of human beings, and permit children as well as adults to grow up.[53]

The issues Goodman addressed throughout his book were both psychological and institutional, personal and economic. He agreed with other postwar intellectuals that such problems could only have arisen at a time of general prosperity. Hence the very sorts of questions Goodman asked—"how is it possible to have more meaning and honor in work? to put wealth to some real use? to have a high standard of living of whose quality we are not ashamed? to get social justice for those who have been . . . left out? to have a use of leisure that is not a dismaying waste of a hundred million adults?"—required more innovative answers than those normally given by liberal reformers.[54] To this extent, Goodman anticipated the concerns of the New Left in the 1960s.

But his own proposals reflected the distaste for ideological language common to the 1950s. Goodman rarely referred to social classes, trade unions, capitalism, or the state. Instead, he spoke repeatedly about the prerequisites for individual growth, the necessity of having "real opportunities for worthwhile experience," the nation's responsibility to provide "every youth with his right calling." In Goodman's ideal society, there would be an "organic integration of work, living, and play." Men would enjoy greater economic opportunities through the development of new small enterprises, rather than having to rely on the largess of huge corporations. Blue-collar laborers would be "technically educated" and gain "a say in management." Democracy would again begin in town meetings and "regional variety" would be encouraged. Popular culture would become "daring and passionate." Finally, each child would have "plenty of objective . . . activities" to "observe, fall in with, do, learn, improvise on his own."[55]

Who could quibble with Goodman's vision of paradise? His

recommendations sounded so sane, so constructive, so healthy. The trouble was that after listening to Goodman on the subject of children, one longed for W. C. Fields.

Goodman's dismissal of women, however, was far more exasperating than his single-minded solicitude for the plight of "young men and boys." The problems on which his book focused, he stated in the introduction,

> belong primarily, in our society, to the boys: how to be useful and make something of oneself. A girl does not *have* to . . . 'make something' of herself. Her career does not have to be self-justifying, for she will have children, which is absolutely self-justifying, like any other natural or creative act. With this background, it is less important . . . what job an average young woman works at till she is married. . . . Yet as every woman knows, these problems are intensely interesting to women, for if the boys do not grow up to be men, where shall the women find men?[56]

A reader might never guess from Goodman's pronouncements that 40 percent of all women over the age of sixteen held jobs by 1960, that the very ability of families to enter the middle class and participate in the postwar prosperity depended on the additional income of working wives and mothers, or that employment offered women their only chance to fashion an identity and a sense of independence outside the home. Nor did Goodman's assumptions take into account the actual difficulties women still faced in the 1950s: their continuing relegation to traditionally "female" occupations (nursing, schoolteaching, secretarial work, retail sales); the meager career opportunities open to them in the professions or politics; the lower pay scales and absence of institutional supports (maternity leaves, day-care centers, flexible hours); the exhaustion that resulted from having to raise children, arrange for baby-sitters, attend PTA meetings, manage a household, please the husband, entertain guests, pose as a gourmet cook and a sexual bombshell, and earn money all at the same time.[57] Given these oversights, it was hard to suppress the thought that Goodman's preoccupation with "manly" virtues said more about his own sexual prejudices than about the current and future predicaments of women or men.

But despite its eccentricities and indulgence in stereotypes, *Growing Up Absurd* did reflect the major concerns of many intellectuals in the 1950s. The notion that an affluent postindustrial society had special dilemmas of its own, the realization that material comfort was not sufficient to dispel the individual's feelings of anxiety and discontent, the lack of satisfaction on the job or in the suburbs, the failure of parents and schools to stimulate the young, and the search for new radical groups who might resist the conformist tendencies of the middle class were familiar themes by the end of the decade.

Yet paradoxically, these criticisms tended to obscure the impetus for change inherent in the conditions of postwar American life. In a period when powerful institutions shaped national policy, it was understandable that people should concentrate on the acquisition of merchandise and the uses of leisure time as a way of exercising some control over their private destinies. Similarly, the traumas of adolescence and the emergence of a youth culture (however inarticulate or shallow) could be seen as expressions of a real effort to develop a less orthodox and more personal moral style, as well as to question and reevaluate the goals prescribed by a business civilization. Indeed, the political passivity attributed to both students and adults, their indifference to social causes and withdrawal from ideological movements, their preference for staying "cool" and uncommitted, may have been less the stigmata of a "silent generation" than a covert rejection of conventional leaders, established organizations, and group pressures. From this perspective, apathy might be as much a sign of estrangement from and protest against the prevailing social order as a capitulation to bourgeois values.[58]

Still, none of these attitudes resulted in concrete programs to transform America. As defined by intellectuals and experienced by ordinary citizens, the problems of prosperity appeared intrinsic to human existence rather than the product of particular economic arrangements. Thus, it did not seem possible to alleviate the difficulties of modern living through political remedies.

Writers attacked the quality of American life in the 1950s, but they could imagine few structural alternatives. Although their heirs in the 1960s expanded the indictment, they eventually reached the same impasse. Without analyzing the relationship between cultural issues and political institutions, neither generation could hope to build a new society.

The Message of the Media

In 1968, Sidney Lumet directed a movie called *Bye Bye Braverman*, based on the 1964 novel *To an Early Grave* by Wallace Markfield. Both the novel and the film are about four New York Jewish intellectuals cruising the streets of darkest Brooklyn in a Volkswagen, searching for the funeral of their friend, Leslie Braverman—poet, critic, professor, unfortunately "between grants" at the time of his death, eulogized by his mourners as a "second-rate mind of the highest order." Having "made it" in Manhattan but irretrievably lost in the land of their childhood, the four pilgrims meditate on their lives, loves, ambitions, the Holocaust, the failure of socialism, and Chinese food. At one point, the driver adjusts his beret and announces proudly that in the fall he will be teaching a course on popular culture at Columbia. Immediately, he is pelted with questions by his envious colleagues. One asks him if this is truly his "métier." Another subjects him to a quiz on comic strip characters, nearly stumping him with the name of Danny Dimwit—though the driver objects that Danny was a latecomer who occupied "essentially a fringe position." Finally, as if to certify that mass culture is every intellectual's métier, all four erupt into a spirited rendition of the Fitch shampoo commercial.

This scene could have been played to perfection by any number of writers in the 1950s. Even a partial list of those who had something to say about the state of popular culture in America reads like a pollster's sample of prominent intellectuals: Dwight Macdonald, Clement Greenberg, Irving Howe, Daniel Bell, Seymour Lipset, Gilbert Seldes, Daniel Boorstin, Paul Goodman, Ernest van den Haag, Robert Warshow, Leslie Fiedler, William Phillips, Herbert Gans, Harold Rosenberg. They and others realized the enormous impact of the mass media on their society and on their own lives. They also understood that if one wanted to know what was distinctively "American" about the culture of the modern world, one had to examine radio, television, popular music, cartoons and comic strips, best-selling books, advertising, political imagery, the travel industry, motels, and of course the movies. No critique of contemporary America could possibly overlook the issue of how people spent their leisure time.

The concern with mass culture was not unique to American intellectuals. Nor did it originate in the postwar years. During the 1930s, a group of refugee writers from Europe formerly associated with what became known as the Frankfurt School (Max Horkheimer, Paul Lazarsfeld, Theodor Adorno, Leo Lowenthal, Walter Benjamin, Herbert Marcuse, and Erich Fromm) began to explore the interrelationship between popular culture and the emergence of modern mass societies. Profoundly disturbed by Hitler's manipulation of the media to attain and consolidate his power, they tried to explain the rise of totalitarianism by joining Marxist and Freudian ideas to an analysis of the new cultural techniques for controlling public opinion and human behavior. Their work continued after 1945, both in the United States and in Europe, and it influenced the perspective of many American intellectuals now attentive to the same problems.[59]

But even without the European contribution, Americans themselves had started in the 1930s to investigate the effects of mass communications on the nation's politics and psyche. Lewis Mumford's *Technics and Civilization* (1934), Hadley Cantril and Gordon Allport's *The Psychology of Radio* (1935), Harold Lasswell's *Politics: Who Gets What, When, How* (1936), Thurman Arnold's *The Folklore of Capitalism* (1937), Robert and Helen Lynd's *Middletown in Transition* (1937), and Lewis Jacobs's *The Rise of the American Film* (1939) each discussed in differing ways the role of the media in shaping political ideologies, social attitudes, and private fantasies. Toward the end of the decade Clement Greenberg and Dwight Macdonald mounted a major assault in *Partisan Review* on "kitsch," the esthetic banalities of the Popular Front, and the cultural nationalism they detected in the Soviet Union and the United States. The categories they employed to expose the mediocrity of popular culture, and to defend the achievements of modernism and the avant-garde, became an indispensable part of the intellectuals' vocabulary by the 1950s.[60]

Still, however much its roots could be traced to the 1930s, the criticism of mass culture did not emerge fully until the postwar era. At this juncture, certain social and economic trends in the United States were unmistakable. The liberal agenda of the early twentieth century had been completed: The work week had shrunk from sixty to forty hours; child labor had been curtailed; free universal education was a fact of American life; more people than ever before were enjoying prosperity and entering the middle class. Reformers and radicals had fought for these goals in the hope that, once freed from the fear of poverty and unemployment, Americans might use their newly acquired leisure to improve their minds. Instead, as Paul Lazarsfeld pointed out, the average citizen seemed increasingly hypnotized by radio and the movies; he passed his time "with the Columbia Broadcasting System rather than with Columbia University." The benefactor of the masses felt duped and disappointed; the media had somehow "cheated reformers of the fruits of their victories."[61]

Meanwhile, as intellectuals discarded the language of Marx and grew bored with politics of all kinds, they no longer assailed their traditional enemies—the capitalists, the political bosses, the labor barons, the military chieftains—with the old ideological fervor. But if they wished to preserve a little of the radical heritage, they could concentrate on popular tastes and values as the new opiates of their countrymen. Both Irving Howe and Daniel Bell agreed that "the criticism of mass culture" served "conveniently to replace the criticism of bourgeois society."[62] By castigating the media, writers might demonstrate their dislike for the quality of American life without having to challenge the nation's political or economic institutions as well.

Yet for all their professed commitment to high culture, for all their eagerness to instill in the American people an appreciation for the best books and the finest ideas, many intellectuals themselves carried around in their heads snatches of advertising jingles and movie dialogue, memories of announcers' voices and images of actors' faces, cherished moments from countless situation comedies and detective thrillers. Who among them could not confess to what Norman Podhoretz called "a thousand guilty secret loves" for the minutiae of popular culture?[63] Who had not, like Woody Allen, yearned furtively to deliver Humphrey Bogart's closing lines in *Casablanca*? In their essays and books, writers evaluated the offerings of the media with great theoretical sophistication, almost as if they relished this exercise far more than their somber discussions of Western art and political philosophy. Perhaps the intellectuals' willingness to devote their energies and talents to such primitive artifacts of the popular imagination revealed their own unquenchable fascination with mass culture. For them, no less than for the ordinary member of the audience (as Woody Allen again showed in *Stardust Memories*), it was often hard to figure out where the movies ended and one's life began.

In fact, not everyone was critical of the media. A few writers asserted that popular culture was no worse and no more dangerous today than it had been in the past. From their perspective, the common man of the nineteenth century was not a paragon of esthetic sensibility despite the current efforts to endow him with a superior education and discriminating tastes. He had flocked to circuses and wild-west shows, gorged himself on dime novels, treated politics as a spectacle, sought information that would confirm his opinions rather than shake his complacency, and succumbed to demagogues like Napoleon long before the birth of radio.[64]

But one could hardly expect to pacify the media's detractors by suggesting that, because popular culture was always shallow, intellectuals ought not feel alarmed by its present deficiencies. Seymour Lipset advanced a more plausible case when he claimed that in a democracy, where culture was available to everyone, not just to elites, the "market for good books, good paintings, and good music" actually expanded.[65] Similarly Clement Greenberg, though no admirer of the mass mind, admitted that the media did provide "some sort of enlightenment" for the average American, and could increase the opportunities for his cultural enrichment at a much lower cost than ever before.[66] Gilbert Seldes, a longtime advocate of mass communications, extended this argument by reminding the critics that their modernist heroes had given up trying to speak to an audience, whereas the "popular" artist acceded to the people's legitimate desire for comprehensible prose, recognizable paintings and melodies, romance, moral uplift, patriotic sentiments, and helpful solutions to the problems of daily life.[67] Finally, one contributor to *Dissent* speculated that mass culture might even have a radicalizing effect on its clientele. It expressed their "yearning for a different world" and a "different humanity"; its escapist content reflected "preconscious states of rebellion"; at the very least, it enlarged "the range of [their] experience" and the possibilities of social change.[68]

These propositions failed to convert the majority of commentators. While they acknowledged the existence of earlier forms of popular entertainment and the potential benefits accompanying the democratization of culture, they insisted that mass communications (like totalitarianism) was a genuinely new phenomenon in human history, and that it created unique dilemmas for every modern industrial society.

In the view of Dwight Macdonald, Clement Greenberg, Ernest van den Haag, and Daniel Boorstin, the rise of the media was associated with the decline of a traditional elite that once dominated the arts as well as the political and economic affairs of Western civilization through the monarchies, the church, and the universities. The disintegration of the upper class also coincided with the emergence in the nineteenth century of a large urban bourgeoisie that had its own conception of what constituted leisure and amusement. Above all, the industrial and technological revolutions made feasible the cheap production and distribution of books, magazines, phonographs, movies, radio and television sets, all in sufficient quantities to satisfy the "cultural demands of the newly awakened masses."[69] By the early twentieth century, the ancient class barriers between the aristocracy and the common people had completely eroded, an event that was in Macdonald's estimation "desirable politically" but brought "unfortunate results culturally." It led to the development of mass societies where the individual felt no connection to a group or community, and no real sense of rapport even with his own family; instead he depended on the media as his sole source of emotional stimulation and social contact. Eventually, the "mass man" stood at both ends of the assembly line, grinding out and consuming a steady flow of cultural junk.[70]

There seemed no reprieve from this gloomy historical verdict. Indeed, the cultural consequences appeared more deplorable than a reader might initially suppose. Both Greenberg and S. I. Hayakawa (then a semanticist and later a Republican senator from California) regretted the ways in which the clichés of the media had "diluted" the "unsentimental and realistic" vigor of folk art.[71] Greenberg and Macdonald, however, were much more distressed by the corruption of high culture in its losing battle with the tastes of the "mob." The inability of the avant-garde to withstand the temptations of the marketplace, now controlled by an affluent middle class that had no "ingrained" familiarity with difficult novels or paintings and no real respect for "standards," meant that the discoveries of modernism would be absorbed and "vulgarized," while the quality of the artist's work would inevitably descend to the level of "commercialized formulae."[72]

To Paul Goodman and Daniel Boorstin, the most unsettling result of this cultural deterioration was the diminished significance of the written word. Literature had been reduced to a "minor art" in the twentieth century, they sighed. The novel presently mattered less to mass and elite audiences than the movie adaptation, radio and television programs, photography, architecture, and recorded music. Theatergoers cared more about "the stars, the spectacle, . . . and the production" than about the play. Worst of all, the mastery of argument and ideas, the appreciation for the "subtle and learned explanation," the attempt to arrive at truth through "cogent reasoning" and "poetic expression" had given way to a fascination with images, slogans, trademarks, and public relations stratagems. It was especially ironic to hear Boorstin, the historian who had applauded America's indifference to political theory and doctrinal controversy, grumble that corporate policy underwent a "change of heart" less often than a "change of face," that a debate over national issues frequently dissolved into a competition for the most compelling myths and aphorisms, that intellectuals themselves now regarded an "explicit statement of ideals" as "corny" and naïve.[73] In a nation whose "genius" allegedly sprang from its lack of ideology, what else did Boorstin expect? Still, when it came to the preservation of philosophy, literature, and the arts, no writer—not even Boorstin—preferred pragmatic compromise to a defense of eternal principles.

Yet the main objection to mass culture centered not on its social origins and evolution, nor on its damage to traditional prose and cognitive skills, but on its current manifestations and the human needs it unquestionably served. As Clement Greenberg and Ernest van den Haag conceded, the media existed primarily to provide rest and recuperation from the "monotony of work." People intentionally sought distractions in their leisure time; they longed for the excitement, the spontaneity, and the "immediate satisfactions" they missed on the job. But the "meaningless drain" on their energies during working hours drove them naturally to forms of recreation that required only a "minimum of mental exertion."[74]

The media's power therefore flowed from its capacity to meet these demands. The distinctive feature of mass culture in the opinion of many intellectuals, the element that guaranteed its success with the public, was its reliance on the techniques of industrial production. Where the classical artist had spoken in his own voice, Paul Goodman and Dwight Macdonald recalled, where his vision and feelings were "idiosyncratic," his successors now functioned as members of a team—especially if they toiled for Hollywood, the television networks, or the major publishing houses. The film director was merely a specialist on the conveyor belt. The best-selling author "manufactured" rather than "composed" his books, assembling each chapter as mechanically as the stylists who designed the "latest atrocity from Detroit," deliberately suppressing any "personal note" in order to attract the widest possible audience. Edgar Allan Poe, for example, wrote mystery stories as a means of self-expression and a release from private anxieties; it was inconceivable to Macdonald that Erle Stanley Gardner, the Henry Ford of recent detective fiction, could be "afflicted with anything as individual as a neurosis."[75]

The emphasis on collective creation resulted in a standardized product, Macdonald and Greenberg insisted. The chorus of every popular song contained the "same number of bars." Hollywood studios edited each of their films at a "uniformly rapid tempo." Consequently, audiences knew exactly what to expect; they would never be surprised by a "fresh experience."[76] These impersonal methods, according to van den Haag and Herbert Gans, further penalized "individual taste" and esthetic originality in favor of a blatant appeal to the "lowest common denominator" of "group acceptance." When consumers were "treated as a crowd," they were neither stimulated nor antagonized, but simply soothed.[77]

At least one writer refused to exempt his own peers from this indictment. In an article for *Commentary* called "The Herd of Independent Minds" (the essay surely deserved some sort of award for having the best title in the entire postwar era), Harold Rosenberg suggested that intellectuals exhibited the same mental traits as the lords of the media. The audience for the works of the avant-garde and the subscription lists for highbrow journals might be minuscule, he admitted. But the tendency of writers to translate their hypotheses into "formulas of common experience," to assume that every intellectual had identical notions about modern history and art, to talk grandiloquently about "our" generation or "our time," was no different a type of myth making than one found in the fabrications of mass culture. The intelligentsia, Rosenberg charged, could be equally conformist, equally oblivious to individual perspectives and personal peculiarities, as hostile to independent thought as the Hollywood mogul or network president.[78]

Whether or not intellectuals huddled together in a herd of their own, they did agree on two points. First, the pervasiveness of mass culture in the twentieth century destroyed any sense of what was shoddy in contemporary literature and education; it blurred the distinctions between the "genuine and the spurious," and it elevated "frivolous" entertainment over "serious" works of art.[79] Second, the media gave people just what they wanted: leisure activities that were "easy to assimilate," that promised diversion and relaxation but not "disturbance" or "insight."[80] Hence the very breadth and accessibility of mass culture, its democratic disregard for formal excellence and refined nuance, strengthened its magnetism for a populace that wanted a respite from both the strains of work and the complications of modern life.

Even when the middle class aspired to a more respectable use of its leisure time, some writers remained unimpressed. From the 1930s on, Clement Greenberg and Dwight Macdonald conducted an unceasing campaign against the "middlebrow" mentality—by which they meant the bourgeois hunger for self-improvement, the consumer's conscientious effort to "keep up" with whatever "large, new theories" seemed to be "in the air," the ostentatious display of cultural interests (often in the form of coffee-table books) that transcended mere entertainment.[81]

The media eagerly serviced this market with an endless supply of kitsch. Among the ponderous icons of middlebrow culture, Macdonald took special pleasure in deflating the Book of the Month Club, Thorton Wilder's *Our Town* and Archibald Mac-Leish's *J.B.* (both Pulitzer prize–winning plays), Ernest Hemingway's *The Old Man and the Sea* ("appropriately" published in *Life*), James Gould Cozzens's *By Love Possessed* (a best seller and extravagantly praised by the critics despite or because of its "portentousness"), magazines like *Harper's* and the *Saturday Review of Literature* (edited with a "genteel slickness" that was more irritating than the "simple vulgarity" of the tabloid press), the Revised Standard Version of the Bible (with its mutation of the King James Version's "incantatory" language and "poetic intensity" into a "tepid expository prose" that instantly let the reader know "What's It All About"), and the transition from Rodgers and Hart to Rodgers and Hammerstein (the "gay tough lyrics" of *Pal Joey* yielding to the "folk-fakery" of *Oklahoma!* and the "orotund sentimentalities" of *South Pacific*). Macdonald found most middlebrow works insufferable because they were so well-intentioned; the artist studiously tackled "some big central issue" and took himself "very seriously." However meretricious the result, readers and critics alike felt obliged to congratulate the author on a "jolly good try."[82] For his part, Macdonald could tolerate honest trash more readily than the cultural pretentions of the middle class.

But no matter what shapes mass culture assumed, its unforgiv-

able sin in the eyes of many intellectuals was its encouragement
of fantasy and escapism. The media declined to deal with "real
problems," Ernest van den Haag and S. I. Hayakawa complained;
people invariably received "false or misleading" conceptions
about the world, and were therefore ill equipped to cope with the
predicaments of their own lives. Worse, the individual's addiction to mass culture impaired his capacity for direct, personal
experience. In place of spontaneous emotional and moral reactions to events, Robert Warshow argued, the media substituted
a "system of conventionalized 'responses'" that protected people from the "shock" of living, but also concealed their "helplessness."[83]

None of these writers advocated a return to the "social realism" of the 1930s. On the contrary, Warshow believed that the
political platitudes of the Popular Front had interfered with private knowledge and feeling, a constraint under which Americans
still labored. Thus, the intellectuals attacked the media not so
much because it presented distorted pictures of society, but because it robbed the individual of chances for self-development.

In *The Image,* a book whose critical tone was antithetical to the
celebratory spirit of *The Genius of American Politics,* Daniel Boorstin
made the alienating effects of mass communications his central
theme. He also broadened the definition of popular culture to
include almost every facet of American life: the revolution in
graphics and design, the increasingly sophisticated techniques
for transmitting information through the instruments of sight
and sound rather than print, the impact of advertising on political
rhetoric and policy, the metamorphosis of the traveler into a
tourist, the machinery of fame, the public performance as "pseudo-event."

As Boorstin described it, everything about the lives of his fellow citizens seemed secondhand, vicarious, contrived. No one
had to leave home; the world, or at least its representation, was
brought to the living room through radio, television, newspapers, magazines, encyclopedias, slides, telephones, advertisements, travel brochures, political leaflets, and junk mail. Eminent
personages and faraway places appeared familiar, though such

intimacies were clearly deceptive. Ultimately these images and sensations, no matter how fraudulent, became more important than reality.

When the individual did decide to venture forth, Boorstin noted, he went as a spectator. Where the old-style traveler was "active," searching for different people and new knowledge, the modern tourist was "passive": He expected "interesting things to happen to him." The guided tour guaranteed excitement without risk. One never encountered the natives, just one's fellow passengers. Normally, the tourist was "isolated from the landscape he traverses." The hypnotic super highways that bypassed any sign of human life except at rest areas with their diners and motels of "uniform design," the Disneylands that offered pallid imitations of nature and history, the airplanes that showed the same films and stocked the same magazines, the stewardesses with their "homogenized blandness," the international hotel chains with their identical interiors differentiated only by an "inoffensive bit of 'local atmosphere,'" the air-conditioned "sightseeing" buses, the excursions to museums that had become warehouses where the specimens of a formerly "living culture" were now "collected and embalmed," the carefully rehearsed festivals and ceremonies with their "earnest picturesqueness" and "papier-mâché" rituals, the obsession with taking pictures and buying postcards, all conspired to transform the external world into a movie set, and travel itself into a montage of illusions. After a while, Boorstin concluded, each place seemed indistinguishable from the next. The tourist no longer knew or cared where he was. The fuzzy, generalized impression supplanted the sharp, singular insight.[84]

Whether the individual traveled or stayed at home, he was surrounded by the unreal. In Boorstin's view, the political and cultural life of the United States could be understood as a series of staged happenings arranged by and for the media, and scheduled for the convenience of the audience. These "pseudo-events" were infinitely more dramatic, more intelligible, and more reassuring than any natural occurrence.[85]

As examples of the political pseudo-event, Boorstin cited the televised interview or press conference with a public figure, which had become the standard device for "making news," the close attention paid to a politician's performance in following a "prepared script" while appearing to debate the issues (with reporters serving as theater critics), the interest in "how a particular speech was put together" rather than a concern for "what it said," the evaluation of a candidate's potential as a "star" instead of as a spokesman for a coherent legislative program.[86] Such pseudo-events prevented "the man or woman of great deeds" from ever becoming a model for society, Boorstin declared. Instead, the contemporary "hero" had a press agent who kept his client in the news. Fame degenerated into mere "notoriety"; the authentic genius vanished in a haze of publicity and gossip. In the long run, truth mattered less than "credibility." As the real world receded before the camera eye, as facts melted into imagery, the spectator found himself even more at the mercy of the media. For Boorstin, the most dangerous consequence of mass culture was its success in inventing situations where anything could be believed.[87]

Such awesome power had obvious political and social implications. To many intellectuals, the media was insidious because it allowed leaders to "manipulate the ideas, opinions and emotions of vast audiences." The resort to "mass persuasion," the use of subtle forms of mind control, seemed much more effective than the conventional tactics of economic exploitation and physical force. In the somewhat overheated estimation of Theodor Adorno and Hortense Powdermaker (who described the movie industry as a "dream factory"), television's appeal to the "smugness" and "gullibility" of its viewers, and Hollywood's rationale that it gave the people what they wanted, sounded suspiciously similar to the creed of totalitarianism.[88] Less melodramatically, Paul Lazarsfeld argued that the media exposed the individual to a flood of mostly superficial information, making him think that "*knowing* about [the] problems of the day" was the same as "*doing* something about them," thereby reinforcing his passivity. For this reason, popular culture was a "respectable and efficient" narcotic, promoting social apathy if not necessarily preparing the masses for dictatorship.[89]

Adorno, Lazarsfeld, Boorstin, van den Haag, and Irving Howe all agreed that the media seriously weakened the individual's will to resist both the state and the prescribed rules of social behavior. Its message—subsidized by the large corporations—not only affirmed the status quo, but failed to "raise essential questions about the structure of society." Hence in their judgment, mass culture helped suppress the individual's sense of his own identity, fostered "conformity" to the "accepted style of life" in America, restrained the "cogent development of a genuinely critical outlook," and inhibited any impulse toward change.[90]

In view of the media's innumerable sins, were there no possibilities for its redemption? Few writers had much hope of raising the quality of popular culture either in the United States or in the rest of the world. At best, most commentators thought that a new set of attitudes must precede any improvements in mass communications. Thus Clement Greenberg, like Daniel Bell and Paul Goodman, insisted that only when work and leisure were reintegrated could culture become an important part of, rather than a flight from, daily life.[91] In Daniel Boorstin's opinion, the primary mechanism for transforming the media was not institutional but personal. Somehow the individual had to extricate himself from the "thicket of unreality" that stood between him and the "facts of life." He needed to recognize the signs of his own "disease," cease his "collaboration" with the media, become literally disenchanted with its messages and stereotypes, stop "sleepwalking" and start discovering the world as it actually was.[92] Boorstin did not tell his readers how they might accomplish this private emancipation; apparently, each citizen could awaken to a higher level of consciousness through an act of will.

Barring such miracles, the more pressing question for intellectuals was whether *high* culture could survive in the middle of the twentieth century. Throughout their analyses, they had always contrasted the media's wares with true works of art. Where popular culture remained "safe" and one dimensional, the modernist novel or painting demanded "effort" as well as a "creative response from the audience," Irving Howe and Dwight Macdonald pointed out. Joyce and Picasso were intentionally difficult; they made no compromises or concessions; yet it was precisely their ability to appeal on "so many planes" that permitted the reader or viewer to reach new "heights of sensibility."[93] Furthermore,

Harold Rosenberg observed, high culture was not mass produced; instead it represented a communication from the individual artist to the individual member of the audience, both of whom were engaged in a struggle for "self-knowledge." The result of this interchange, Ernest van den Haag, Rosenberg, and Macdonald all believed, was a greater awareness of the essential realities underlying people's dreams and fantasies. Hence the finest works of modernism were not escapist, formulaic, or reassuring; just the opposite, they undermined "generally accepted ideas" and customary moral and esthetic assumptions in order to bring forth a "fresh vision" of life.[94]

Given these distinctions, the central issue for Greenberg and Macdonald was how to preserve an avant-garde that would continue to fight for "high standards," maintain its distance from the mass audience, and avoid any pandering to popular tastes and commercial success. To them, the alienation of the artist was a virtue and a necessity. But he need not feel totally isolated. Even in America, Macdonald realized, one stumbled across "a number of smaller, more specialized audiences" for good writing, classical music, experimental drama, foreign films, philosophy, abstract painting and sculpture. On this foundation, Macdonald hoped to erect new barriers between the "intellectual elite" and the mob. Typically, his solution to the problems posed by the media was the most forthright of his generation. Macdonald wished to keep the two cultures—"one for the masses and the other for the classes"—permanently separated. This required the reemergence of a self-conscious intelligentsia dedicated to supporting the values of high culture without slipping back into the "agreeable ooze" of the middlebrow "swamp," a community of artists and critics "joyously" and "implacably" set off from their fellow citizens who could provide direction and discipline for one another, an unabashed "cognoscenti" carrying on both the traditions and the innovations of the avant-garde.[95]

Macdonald's response to the menace of popular culture was certainly ingenious. If one couldn't defeat the hordes, why not ignore them? Most writers, however, were not prepared to follow his reasoning to its logical conclusion. They remained suspended between two equally uncomfortable positions. On the one hand, they urged the media to uplift the average American by offering more news and information, more political debates and documentaries, more "serious" music and drama. So they became disillusioned whenever the movies and television failed to properly instruct the masses. On the other hand, when they granted the conservative thesis that high culture could flourish only in a society of class divisions, where an elite sponsored the arts while the common man wallowed in trivia, this offended what was left of their socialist or democratic instincts.

Whichever stance they adopted, the intellectuals assumed that there was only one way to enlighten the populace, only one path to the world of culture and ideas. That road was clearly marked with the signposts of painting, sculpture, novels, poetry, classical music, and philosophy. Despite their recognition that in radio, television, and films they were confronting radically new forms of technology and communication, they continued to judge the success or failure of the media by traditional artistic and literary standards. According to these criteria, the escapist fare on the airwaves and silver screen could never be educational, stimulating, or creative. And writers were not content to let the media merely divert or amuse the people.

Yet the kinds of entertainment an audience chooses can indicate more than just a longing for fantasies, illusions, and flight. It can reveal real needs, as well as dissatisfactions. Oddly, for all their sensitivity to the historical and social effects of mass culture, few commentators bothered to examine what the media actually presented. Apart from several notable film critics (James Agee, Manny Farber, Robert Warshow, the young Pauline Kael, and by the 1960s Dwight Macdonald), most writers rarely analyzed particular films, much less radio and television programs, to see whether these had the dire influence with which they were charged. It might not have been entirely irrelevant for someone to ask why *Suspense Theater* and *Inner Sanctum* seemed so enthralling on the radio, what *Father Knows Best* and *I Love Lucy* said to and about the 1950s, how Sid Caesar and Ernie Kovacs took advantage of the mechanics of television to become authentically innovative satirists, why the *Sergeant Bilko Show* and *Maverick* flourished in the age of Curtis LeMay and John Wayne, what significance lay in the emergence of Marlon Brando and James Dean as culture heroes for a population that supposedly admired only Dwight Eisenhower and the man in the gray flannel suit.

One suspects that the situation comedies and variety shows, the action series and Westerns, the live dramas on radio and television, as well as a considerable number of Hollywood movies in the postwar years, might have been more imaginative, more irreverent, more provocative, and therefore more liberating than the intellectuals were willing to admit. In fact, the true education of the masses may have come at exactly those moments when they stubbornly listened to and watched what a generation of media theorists told them to turn off.

This is not to suggest that intellectuals should have abandoned their mission as critics in order to revel in pap. But to comprehend the nature and impact of popular culture, they did need new definitions of what constituted art and knowledge after the twentieth century revolution in communications. Perhaps then they might have been less bewildered or angered by the counterculture of the 1960s—especially its use of music, movies, and the media to challenge existing political institutions and social attitudes. There was a clear line of descent from the elitist critics of mass culture in the 1950s to the neoconservative intellectuals of the 1970s and 1980s, which involved a shared hostility not only to the politics of the New Left but also to its presumed dislike for traditional learning, the written word, and the role of authority figures in government and in the classroom. In effect, Macdonald's "two cultures" became a reality by the 1960s, though not with the results he intended.

The rupture between the generations over cultural and political values was probably inevitable, but the consequent bitterness on both sides might have been reduced had the intellectuals of the 1950s recalled that they were consumers as well as critics of the media. Like their alter egos in *Bye Bye Braverman,* they too could sing the Fitch shampoo commercial—or at least whistle the theme from *Playhouse 90.*

Additionally, they ought to have remembered that improving the quality of American culture would not by itself force the ordinary citizen to read and to think, nor would it alter society.

The problem rested, as it always had, with institutions and individuals rather than with images. Intellectuals were right to demand more of the media, but each member of the audience was
ultimately responsible for what he made of its message. That was
where the movies ended and one's life began.

From Adjustment to Autonomy: William Whyte
and David Riesman

Eventually, most intellectuals who tried to maintain their critical perspective faced a frustrating dilemma. Since they assumed
that prosperity was a permanent feature of American life, and
that pragmatic reforms were preferable to ideological strife, they
doubted the likelihood of and necessity for a radical transformation of the nation's political and economic institutions. But they
could not ignore the psychological and cultural costs of middle-
class affluence, or the moral compromises involved in the individual's readiness to embrace the attitudes and expectations of his
peers. So while they accepted the basic structure of society, they
believed that the private citizen must somehow resist the entice-
ments of material comfort and the pressures to conform.

Two writers, William Whyte and David Riesman, were especially alert to the tension between the American's desire to fit in
and his occasional impulse to rebel. Hoping to resolve this conflict, they sought to revive neither the individualism of the nineteenth century nor the collectivism of the 1930s. Instead, they
explored the possibilities of personal freedom *within* the existing
social order. Because of the questions they raised, the answers
they offered, and the phrases they introduced into the national
lexicon, Whyte's *The Organization Man* (1956) and Riesman's *The
Lonely Crowd* (1950) emerged as the decade's classic critiques of
American society.

William Whyte was not a typical member of the postwar intellectual community. Although he grew up during the Depression,
he graduated from Princeton—a few miles away yet a world apart
from the doctrinal clashes that kept the young revolutionaries at
CCNY in tumult. After the war, Whyte found a home not with the
little magazines or in the universities, but at *Fortune* magazine.
While a number of other writers labored at various times for

Henry Luce (Dwight Macdonald, James Agee, John Hersey, John Kenneth Galbraith, Daniel Bell), they looked upon their journalistic interludes as incidental to their main pursuits. Whyte remained a correspondent and an editor for most of his career. *The Organization Man* began as a series of articles for *Fortune*, and its success derived as much from its reportorial style and wit as from its sociological insights. Whyte skillfully blended interviews anecdotes, autobiographical vignettes, generalizations about American history and culture, and personal commentary. In these respects, *The Organization Man* was a precursor of the next decade's "new journalism."

Whyte also differed from his contemporaries in forswearing any radical or satiric intent. Where many intellectuals represented themselves as critics of American life, even when they sprinkled their works with plaudits for the political and economic system, Whyte denied that his book was a "plea for nonconformity" or a "censure of the fact of organization society." The reader would be spared the usual "strictures against ranch wagons, or television sets, or gray flannel suits." Nor did Whyte have in mind a "paradise lost," an "idyllic eighteenth century" in contrast with a "dehumanized twentieth."[96] Actually, he thought there was much to be said in favor of social cooperation, shared responsibilities and the benevolence of modern institutions—particularly when compared to the exploitation and poverty of the past.

Despite these disclaimers, Whyte's discussion of the large corporations, the governmental bureaucracies, the multiversities, and suburbia was about as nonjudgmental as Thorstein Veblen's insistence that "conspicuous consumption" should be taken as a neutral term with no invidious connotations. Whyte did refrain from denouncing the political and economic implications of concentrated power, but this freed him to focus on what he regarded as an equally important issue: "the personal impact that organization life has had on the individuals within it."[97] It was exactly this preoccupation with the psychological effects of organizational values on the middle class that made Whyte's portrait so unflattering—and therefore so central to the critical outlook of the 1950s.

Perhaps the element in Whyte's book that seemed most characteristic of the postwar mood was his barely concealed antagonism to the collectivist sentiments of the 1930s. From the opening pages, he complained about America's recent conversion from the Protestant ethic to a "social ethic": the "belief in the group as the source of creativity"; the notion that "belongingness" was the "ultimate need of the individual"; the conviction that each person could feel worthwhile only when he restrained his ego and collaborated with his peers in some common enterprise. According to this credo, public agreement, psychological adjustment, and a sense of "total integration" with others were the goals toward which everyone thought they must strive; disorganization, conflict, tension, fluidity, "solitary and selfish contemplation," were the "evils from which man should be insulated." Ideally, no fundamental disputes between the citizen and society ought ever arise, merely "misunderstandings" or "breakdowns in communication." In the end, as Whyte described it, the group was supposed to bring out the best in the individual; when people worked together, they could produce a "combustion of ideas" and a consensus on the proper "lines of action" beyond the capabilities of anyone thinking or struggling alone.[98] This philosophy first sprouted in the Depression years as a radical alternative to the capitalist emphasis on competition and personal gain. But to its postwar proponents—bureaucrats, business executives, personnel experts, senior partners of law firms, university administrators, consultants to foundations—the social ethic had become in Whyte's opinion a rationale for conformity and conservatism.

The social ethic also furnished the ideological impetus for the emergence of organization men as the "dominant members of our society." These were not ordinary white-collar employees who toiled sullenly in offices and department stores, Whyte cautioned, but middle-class professionals who identified completely with the purposes of the government agency, the corporation, the bank, the hospital or private clinic, the Wall Street law factory, the aerospace contractor, the military, the trade union, the church hierarchy. In short, they were the bulwarks of "our great self-perpetuating institutions"; it was their values that now shaped the "American temper."[99]

Whyte's depiction of the organization man's mentality, though couched in dispassionate prose, could hardly have been more biting. The new functionaries, he charged, cared less about their own creativity than about supervising the work of their subordinates. Concentrating almost exclusively on the "personality relationships within the group," they preferred cooperation to open rivalry, managerial efficiency to disruptive debate, the "practical team-player" to the eccentric genius, getting along with others to getting ahead. On all occasions, company loyalty mattered more than displays of imagination, curiosity, or independence. In Whyte's view, the supreme objective of the well-rounded organization man was not to rise to the top but to remain in the middle —to be "obtrusive in no particular, excessive in no zeal." And at the end of the day, unwinding on the commuter train or navigating the freeway to suburbia, the organization man dreamed not about wealth but about job security and the "good life." Nevertheless, it was the firm, rather than the suburb, that gave him a stable home and a feeling of having "roots" in a nation where everyone seemed on the move.[100]

At times, Whyte abandoned his impartial pose and attacked both the premises and the consequences of the social ethic. Deriding the "wishful vision of total harmony now being touted," he argued that a "conflict of allegiances" between one's private aspirations and the "demands of the system" was natural and essential. In fact, the current hostility within the organization to strong, assertive personalities, the suspicion of "anyone who has ideas of his own or who differs with others on basic policy," the reliance on staffs and committees to cobble together compromise proposals, all appeared "more repressive" to creative thinking and personal freedom than the decrees of an authoritarian chairman of the board. The individual soon discovered that it was his "moral duty" to participate in joint activities, however much he might feel "imprisoned in brotherhood." On balance, Whyte began to appreciate the old-fashioned boss: "What he wanted primarily from you was your sweat" whereas the organization asked for "your soul."[101]

These compulsions were enormously difficult to combat. The organization, after all, was not malign or nakedly coercive. On the contrary, Whyte pointed out, its "very beneficence," the "democratic atmosphere" it cultivated, the comfort it offered in moments of personal distress, made the individual less able to "justify *to himself* a departure from its norm." The average citizen submitted voluntarily to the group; he internalized its attitudes; his tyranny was "self-imposed."[102] Still, this form of intimidation seemed to Whyte and his contemporaries the most ominous result of the postwar affluence, and a forerunner of the totalitarian state of mind. As George Orwell had warned, when people deferred gratefully to their leaders, when they longed to be relieved of the burdens of choice, when they finally learned to love Big Brother, there was no hope for rebellion.

Whyte did not believe that the organization had yet evolved into an animal farm. But like most writers in the 1950s, he could imagine no movements or programs to challenge the established social arrangements. The modern organization, with all its pressures and constraints, was a necessary component of every advanced technological society, and was obviously here to stay. So for Whyte the crucial problem lay not in America's institutions but in people's blind "worship" of organizational values—particularly the elevation of the social ethic into a religion of human behavior. Since the fault rested with attitudes rather than structures, Whyte concluded that the individual would have to reassess his own commitments to the organization before any other changes could occur.[103]

Given his pessimism about the chances of altering the procedures or spirit of the organization, Whyte limited himself to analyzing the ways in which the individual might broaden his freedom within the perimeters of collective work. One need not be entirely subservient to the group. The key to personal liberation, Whyte declared, was to *understand* rather than to deify the organization. The individual must recognize the existence of options, and demonstrate his independence whenever feasible. He also had to grasp the differences between altruism and conformity, agreement and capitulation. Once he attained this higher consciousness, he could fight his peers without sounding stupid or self-destructive. In extreme situations, Whyte noted, the individual's capacity to "champion the unpopular view" depended psychologically on his willingness to move from one firm to another. But absolute freedom was an illusion. Most of the time, others would determine the contours of one's life. In Whyte's estimation, each person could control his destiny only to the extent that he realized when to cooperate with and when to resist whatever organization he presently served.[104]

This was hardly an expansive conception of human liberty, much less a call to arms. Whyte pictured the successful American (typically a chief executive rather than a middle-level manager) as resourceful, moderately ambitious, sensitive to the disparity between his inner drives and the requirements of the organization, aloof from his peers and indifferent to their code of good-fellowship yet adept at office politics, inclined to take only those risks whose consequences he had calculated in advance, fully capable of manipulating the system to his own advantage but always careful to play by the rules of the game. Rarely faced with a genuine crisis of integrity, Whyte's hero knew how to survive and prosper inside the narrow boundaries of his bureaucratic world.

Whyte clearly implied that it was all right for the individual to deceive his colleagues so long as he remained true to himself. Assuming that the essential framework of the modern organization remained intact, the conduct Whyte urged might seem morally ambiguous but it was certainly realistic. The more troubling dilemma was whether Whyte's recommendations really aided the individual at all, or only the institutions for which he worked.

Sometimes Whyte suggested that, the issue of personal freedom aside, organizations themselves would improve if they adopted his advice. The primary defect of the social ethic, he observed, was its refusal to see that the individual's isolation from and disagreements with the group might "eventually discharge the greater service" to society. The nonconformist actually helped the community remember its nobler ideals; he was the devil's advocate, infuriating his fellow citizens for their own good. Similarly, the executive's readiness to resign from his current post not only increased his leverage over his peers, but also ensured that corporate policy would never become too "static" or complacent. Whyte's disparagement of business schools followed the same logic. The interests of the organization could be more effectively promoted if universities did not give their students a specialty or practical instruction in how to handle other people, but instead provided better training in the "fundamental disciplines." This in turn would guarantee a steady flow of graduates who valued basic research, original ideas, and unorthodox opinions, rather than companionship, conferences, and team-work.[105] In the long run, Whyte hinted, everyone would benefit: The individual could fulfill his potential while the organization grew more productive.

Still, despite the ambivalence of his arguments, Whyte wanted to strengthen the individual's ability to question the organizational mystique. If people were aware of and utilized their opportunities for dissent, they might at times transcend both the organization and the social ethic. Beyond this, Whyte would not go. For him, and for other intellectuals in the 1950s, outright rebellion was pointless. The best one could do was bend (though not surrender) to the demands of a managerial society, hoping to preserve some small areas of privacy and self-respect in the bargain.

David Riesman's approach to the problem of conformity was less descriptive and more theoretical than Whyte's. In *The Lonely Crowd* and *Individualism Reconsidered*, a collection of articles he had written for numerous academic and popular journals between 1947 and 1953, Riesman juggled trends in a variety of disciplines with spectacular dexterity. He drew on every available source: his early career as a law professor; the ideas of his colleagues in sociology at the University of Chicago, Yale, and Harvard; his collaboration with Nathan Glazer and Reuel Denney in the research for and writing of *The Lonely Crowd;* the work of neo-Freudian psychoanalysts, especially Erich Fromm, with whom Riesman once trained; Max Weber's reliance on ideal types to explain the contrasts in social and intellectual development between different periods and civilizations; the discussion of bureaucratic power and managerial elites in the books of Harold Lasswell and C. Wright Mills; the emphasis among anthropologists like Margaret Mead, Ruth Benedict, and Clyde Kluckhohn on the relationship between culture and personality; the studies of local communities conducted by Lloyd Warner and John Dollard; the growing interest in public opinion surveys to measure the nation's attitudes and perceptions; recent data on demographic shifts and what if anything they revealed about changing values; the postwar liberals' aversion to mass movements and ideological fanaticism; the economic arguments of Thorstein Veblen and John Kenneth Galbraith; contemporary indictments of education, the media, and the misuse of leisure time; the renewed fascination with the insights of Alexis de Tocqueville and the current effort by historians to identify the special qualities of the "American character."

Riesman's achievement was to weave these disparate influences into a coherent critique of the way the middle class presently lived. Together with *The Organization Man, The Lonely Crowd* and *Individualism Reconsidered* offered a more imaginative response to the issues of the 1950s than one usually found in the works of other commentators. But like *The Organization Man, The Lonely Crowd* also illustrated the limits of intellectual discourse and social vision that hampered most writers throughout the postwar era.

Riesman was as ambivalent toward modern America as any of his fellow intellectuals. On the one hand, he too thought that the United States was a model of political democracy and social stability, that the government knew how to banish poverty and unemployment, and that prosperity eliminated the need for revolutionary programs or movements. On the other hand, he agreed with John Kenneth Galbraith, Dwight Macdonald, and Paul Goodman that affluence itself introduced a new set of questions, which could not be answered merely by adding a few more items to the agenda of liberal reform. Thus Riesman, like so many writers of the period, felt optimistic about the continuing health of America's institutions and had no wish to revive the radical panaceas of the 1930s. But he shared as well their misgivings about the quality of American life, and their belief that the problems of culture and psychology now took precedence over political and economic affairs.

In 1960, Riesman acknowledged in the preface to a new edition of *The Lonely Crowd* the divergent impulses behind the original volume. The book "grew out of a critical view" of American society, he recalled, yet it had seemed archaic "to interpret what was wrong" by a "Marxist class-analysis."[106] This might explain why Riesman chose to substitute such terms as tradition-directed, inner-directed, and other-directed for the conventional Marxist categories of feudalism, industrial capitalism, and socialism. Riesman's classifications accurately indicated where his true interests lay. Moving beyond the Marxist preoccupations with wealth, poverty, and control over the means of production, he proposed to study those issues that appeared more important in the postwar climate: the effects of leisure and mass consumption on social values, the process of child-rearing and character-formation, changing styles of personal behavior, relationships at work, the belief that status and material possessions were the principal signs of a successful life.

In the same vein, Riesman no longer considered it essential to deal with the predicaments of the workers or the poor. As larger numbers of Americans became economically comfortable, he could turn his attention to the "upper social strata," particularly to the "new middle class of salaried professionals and managers" whose concerns were sure to govern the future of the country. Riesman therefore made no apologies for concentrating on the "malaise of the privileged."[107]

Like William Whyte, Riesman assumed that the philosophy of nineteenth century laissez-faire and the collectivist rhetoric of the 1930s were equally antiquated; neither would resolve the contemporary conflict between conformity and alienation. But Riesman also sounded similar to Whyte in his special antipathy for the communitarian ideal. Where prewar radicals had railed against the selfishness and competition underlying the structure of capitalism, Riesman was far more worried about the intrusions on one's privacy, the increasing stress on patriotism and national unity, the totalitarian implications of a mass society. These apprehensions led him to assert that the "problem for people in America today" was not the "material environment" but "other people"—a statement which (together with Whyte's complaint about being "imprisoned in brotherhood") would have been inconceivable in the Depression years.[108] Since Riesman was convinced that "no ideology, however noble, can justify the sacrifice of an individual to the needs of the group," he pledged himself to "speak for" the freedom of the solitary person; others could defend the prerogatives of society.[109] Hence it was scarcely surprising that he doubted the efficacy of political cures. These would only intensify the pressure on the individual to accept the superior wisdom of everyone else.

Riesman's unmistakable distaste for collectivism influenced the format and arguments of *The Lonely Crowd.* His historical models were designed less to describe actual economic and technological developments than to suggest a "metaphorical background" with which the present could be (often unfavorably) compared.[110] As dramatic tools, if not as precise interpretations of social change, they were extremely effective.

A tradition-directed society, in Riesman's account, corresponded loosely to the feudal epoch. Here, each person was a member of a particular family, clan, or caste. The patterns of agrarian life were controlled by rituals and routines, by religion and rigid codes of social etiquette, by precedents and customs that had persisted for centuries and were transmitted orally from one generation to the next through folk tales, songs, legends, and myths. Parents taught their children to "succeed *them,* rather than to 'succeed' by rising in the social system." One did not fantasize about "personal lifelong goals" or a destiny apart from the village. The tradition-directed peasant hardly thought of himself as an individual, Riesman remarked. He wanted simply to follow and obey; any fleeting desire to deviate from the behavior sanctioned by society was stifled by the "fear of being *shamed.*"[111]

In contrast, Riesman's inner-directed man emerged at a time of increased social mobility, the rapid accumulation of capital, constant industrial expansion, and sharp divisions of labor. By the nineteenth century, Western nations had begun to value personal choice and initiative, individual responsibility and self-sufficiency, competition and long-term planning instead of a reliance on inherited habits, science and rationality rather than a faith in ceremonies and magic. The inner-directed child was no longer instructed to emulate, but to be different from and better than his parents. His education came through the solitary experience of reading books, especially those that showed how to move upward and triumph in business. What counted now was intellectual drive and economic achievement, not communal loyalties. Ultimately, the individual spent more of his time struggling endlessly for wealth and power; he no longer venerated the past or worried about being happy in the present. Life might be a ruthless race to the top, and one might suffer guilt as the penalty for failure, but Riesman could not help admiring the relative freedom that accompanied the age of inner-direction.[112]

But Riesman's main intention in *The Lonely Crowd* and in his essays was to scrutinize the attitudes and conduct of the other-directed man, a species that evidently thrived in postwar America. Here the natural environment was perfect for the creation of a new psyche. The economy had permanently shifted from production to consumption, from scarcity to abundance, from the compulsions of work to the rewards of leisure as promoted by the mass media. Consequently, the classic other-directed type could be found in the largest cities, engaged in some administrative or managerial occupation. His greatest talent, Riesman observed, lay not in manufacturing a commodity or exercising his professional skills, but in marketing his personality. Goals and results were less significant than the ability to maintain cordial relationships with one's peers on and off the job. Social "gregariousness" therefore mattered more than "technological competence." Just as the other-directed child learned to treasure popularity over intellectual passion, a sensitivity to the opinions and preferences of his "play group" over the satisfaction of his inner needs, so the adult tried harder to win the approval of his fellow workers than to acquire money or fame. For Riesman as for Whyte, success in America depended not on what the individual did or thought, but on how well he could "package" himself and manipulate the perceptions of others.[113]

This emphasis on cooperation and the willingness to perform as a "member of a team," together with the horror of "offending anyone" and the repression of all "knobby or idiosyncratic qualities and vices," did not in Riesman's estimation extinguish private ambition. Instead, the other-directed man carefully veiled his competitive instincts behind a mask of amiability.

Meanwhile, where his historical predecessors had been haunted either by shame at not adhering to ancestral traditions, or by guilt for having failed to rise, the modern American felt a "diffuse *anxiety*" about the prospect of losing the affection of his contemporaries if he excelled. But as long as he continued to "surrender any claim to independence of judgment and taste," as long as he looked to others "for cues as to what in life is worthwhile," Riesman feared that the current demands for the individual's "submission to the group" would grow even stronger.[114]

Despite Riesman's diatribe against the affable and conformist impulses of the other-directed man, there were other traits he could commend. He revealed his mixed feelings about other-direction most vividly in his contradictory appraisal of political behavior in the United States.

In part, Riesman echoed writers like Arthur Schlesinger, Oscar Handlin, Daniel Bell, and Seymour Lipset in his praise for American pluralism. The nation no longer had a visible ruling class, he declared. An other-directed politics rested on the dispersal of power among veto groups, voluntary associations, and ad hoc coalitions. Under these "amorphous" circumstances, one could barely distinguish the leaders from the led. So captivated did Riesman seem with this idyllic picture of democracy that at one point in *The Lonely Crowd* he listed all those people who controlled America's future: "small business and professional men . . . such as realtors, lawyers, car salesmen, undertakers"; legislators; the military brass; "big business managers"; labor leaders; southern whites; Poles, Italians, Jews, and Irishmen; newspaper editors; farmers and ranchers; even the Russians, because they determined "much of our agenda of attention"—in other words, practically everyone. Moreover, since Riesman was more concerned with the way psychological perceptions rather than economic institutions shaped human conduct, the possession of power was for him largely a question of "interpersonal expectations and attitudes," emotions and self-images. Hence, "if businessmen feel weak and dependent, they do in actuality become weaker and more dependent, no matter what material resources may be ascribed to them."[115]

No wonder Riesman found it difficult to locate who was in charge. America apparently kept running on its own internal momentum.

Yet Riesman differed from his fellow pluralists in contending that their much-praised voluntary associations were "not voluntary enough"; they intensified "the pressure on the individual to *join*, to submerge himself in the group—any group—and to lower still further not only his feeling that he can, but that he has a right, to stand on his own." The sole relief from these political and social obligations was the widely deplored escape into "apathy," though Riesman considered this the means by which the individual could "protect the remnants of his privacy." In the end, he decided that other-direction did not really enhance democracy. Rather, the disappearance of old-fashioned leaders fostered a sense of "helplessness" among ordinary citizens, and prompted them to withdraw from "affairs that had become unmanageable and incomprehensible."[116] Thus Riesman was almost alone among postwar intellectuals in translating the doctrine of pluralism—the alleged source of America's democratic ideals and pragmatic temperament—into an explanation of modern political passivity.

In his view, however, the worst form of powerlessness did not involve politics or class relationships at all, but the degree to which the individual had become psychologically dependent on and incapable of opposing his peers. The other-directed man incorporated the authority of the group "into his very character" because he dreaded "aloneness" more than anything else. But this in turn transformed him into a "succession of roles and encounters," all of which prevented him from learning "who he is or where he is going." For Riesman, the individual's loss of identity was much more dangerous than his unwillingness to participate in social movements or public causes. People should therefore be encouraged not to become better citizens but to "develop their private selves," to flee from "groupism," to "find their own way," if necessary to "go it alone."[117]

Riesman denied that he meant by these exhortations a resurrection of nineteenth century individualism. The inner-directed man was "no less a conformist to others" than his other-directed

the central preoccupations. If people were occasionally able to withstand the pressures of conformity, if they recognized that certain conflicts between the citizen and the state were irreconcilable, if they could gain some measure of solitude within the confines of a mass society, they might achieve "autonomy" without a fundamental transformation of the political and economic order. In this way, the majority of writers hoped to enrich the quality of life as much as possible while leaving contemporary institutions intact.

The most unsatisfying feature of *The Lonely Crowd* and *The Organization Man* was how sketchily each author resolved the problems his book raised. Aside from a phrase here, a metaphor there, an afterthought somewhere else, neither Riesman nor Whyte devoted much space to outlining in any detail the strategies by which conformity could be overcome. But they were not alone in this respect; the same haste in suggesting alternatives to the present social arrangements was evident in the work of Richard Hofstadter, Louis Hartz, Dwight Macdonald, Daniel Bell, Daniel Boorstin, and Paul Goodman. Having discarded the "smelly orthodoxies" of the 1930s, suspicious even of the search for certitude, many intellectuals in the 1950s were more interested in posing questions, pursuing new fields of inquiry, and offering tentative hypotheses than in describing with ideological assurance or theoretical clarity what a different America might look like in the future.

These predilections underscored the dramatic reversal of those ideas associated with the Depression years. Reading Whyte or Riesman, one sensed a profound shift in language, or in the connotations assigned to the same words. What the writers of the 1930s called "community," the postwar intelligentsia labeled "conformity." Cooperation now became "other-direction"; social consciousness had turned into "groupism"; solidarity with others implied an invasion of privacy; "collectivism" ushered in a "mass society"; ideology translated into imagery; economic exploitation yielded to bureaucratic manipulation; the radical activist was just another organization man.

The change in vocabulary indicated a change in orientation as well. The intellectuals of the 1950s had transferred their attention from the substance of politics to styles of behavior, from the sharecropper to the suburbanite, from labor to leisure, from "conditions" to consciousness, from revolution to resistance.

Behind this new rhetoric and outlook lay a new set of values. The planned, orderly, equitable nation envisioned by the Old Left gave way to an admiration for any signs of marginality, eccentricity, self-expression, and private indifference to public life. Alienation was no longer a problem to be surmounted, but a virtue to be nourished. The individual had to free himself, not from the chains of capitalism, but from the smothering embrace of "other people."

It is easy to see the limitations of this perspective. By minimizing the need for alterations in America's political and economic institutions, by insisting that the country's most serious predicaments were cultural and psychological, by focusing almost exclusively on the possibilities of inner rejuvenation in an otherwise stable society, the majority of postwar intellectuals had obscured the links between the social order and personal discontent. One seldom encountered in their books and essays the suggestion that the psyche of the organization man could not be remodeled without restructuring the organization itself, that the number of "autonomous" individuals might multiply only when they could affect the policies of those in power, that true freedom consisted not merely in making choices but also in the choices made.

Yet whatever the weaknesses in their analyses, writers like Whyte and Riesman were neither conservative nor complacent. Their attack on conformity contained radical implications from which they drew back because the one alternative theory they could imagine—socialism—seemed responsible for the very collectivist attitudes they condemned. But in their willingness to raise questions without supplying answers, in their critique of the quality of middle-class life, in their efforts to encourage self-awareness and higher forms of consciousness, and in their appreciation for individual resistance and dissent, Whyte and Riesman (as well as Macdonald and Goodman, Bell and Boorstin, Hartz and Galbraith) were challenging the official tenets of the 1950s and articulating many of the issues that would galvanize the young in the following decade.

C. Wright Mills: The Culture of Power and the Power of Culture

Of all the postwar writers, no one seemed more alienated, more at odds with the political orthodoxies of his time, and more sweeping in his indictment of modern America than C. Wright Mills. Certainly no one had a more direct impact on the rhetoric of the New Left in the 1960s. The "Port Huron Statement," the manifesto that first brought the Students for a Democratic Society to public attention in 1962, read like a gloss on *The Power Elite*. Thereafter, Mills's most prominent concerns—the triumvirate of presidential advisers, corporate executives, and military warlords who ruled America, the ways in which they managed the nation's cultural institutions to disseminate information and manipulate the opinions of the populace, the inability of ordinary citizens to influence the decisions that affected their lives—became familiar refrains. Such phrases as "participatory democracy" and "community control" arose out of a Millsian perspective, even if they did not always coincide with what he actually intended. Above all, after his death in 1962, Mills loomed increasingly as a legendary figure, a heroic misfit, a voice in the intellectual wilderness of the 1950s who aroused the wrath of his otherwise complacent contemporaries, a lonely prophet despised and dishonored but ultimately vindicated by the members of the "movement" in the 1960s who truly were his children.

In the midst of this canonization, Mills's essential ideas were compressed into slogans and truisms. That Mills was not quite the pariah his posthumous image implied, that he sometimes collaborated in the making of his own myth, that he embellished his credentials as the ultimate dissenter while sharing many of the premises of his peers, does no discredit to the complexity of his mind or the brilliance of his work. If anything, his importance stemmed from his capacity to draw on and move beyond the arguments of other writers. The problems he discussed were often those they also explored. But more than anyone else, he disclosed the radical consequences lurking in this common body of criticism.

Hence Mills deserves to be remembered not so much as the patron saint of the New Left, but as one of the few intellectuals in the 1950s who emphasized the connections between culture and politics, between the individual's private discontent and the society in which he lived. In keeping with the preoccupations of the decade's writers, Mills examined the moral and psychological price of affluence, the anxieties of the middle class, the impact of mass communications, the pressures to conform, and the pervasive sense of alienation and ennui in postwar America. He insisted, however, that these problems were inextricably linked to the structure of the economy, the nature and uses of power, and the issue of war and peace. Further, he believed that the intellectual had to challenge the men in command, that the world of knowledge should be independent from but relevant to the world of public affairs. To Mills, a renascent radicalism would emerge not in the form of ideological absolutes, but as a fusion of cultural criticism, political analysis, and programmatic alternatives to the status quo.

Mills tried to exemplify these values in his own career. Trained in philosophy and sociology at the universities of Texas and Wisconsin, he taught briefly at Maryland before moving in 1945 to Columbia where he remained for the rest of his life. He wrote prolifically for both scholarly and popular journals, but he had neither the disposition nor the tolerance for "respectable" academic research, much less for the rituals of academic collegiality. Instead, he persistently taunted the majority of social scientists for the narrow focus of their work, while devoting himself to the larger subjects they supposedly neglected. These accusations hardly endeared him to his fellow sociologists, and they normally dismissed his books as too journalistic or polemical to be taken seriously. Nevertheless, Mills found an audience in other disciplines and outside the university. In 1948, he published *The New Men of Power,* a study of labor leaders, but his reputation as an intellectual in the mold of Thorstein Veblen was ensured with the appearance of *White Collar* (1951), *The Power Elite* (1956), and *The Sociological Imagination* (1959).

In his books and articles, Mills displayed a breadth of vision and a talent for generalization unmatched by any other writer except Hannah Arendt. At first glance, the "radical" American and the "conservative" European may seem oddly paired. Yet Mills's most cherished political ideas were the same as Arendt's. *The Power Elite* and *The Origins of Totalitarianism* approached the modern world with a deeply felt allegiance to certain democratic principles, temporarily lost but potentially retrievable. To understand how Mills could be both a part and ahead of his era, one had to appreciate the conservative roots of his radical ideas.

Mills continually sought to reconcile these conflicting tendencies, though he frequently left the reader with a set of paradoxes rather than a sense of synthesis. Still, he could not talk about a particular trend in American life without stressing its relationship to other phenomena. What mattered to him were the points of contact between individuals and institutions, personal perceptions and social position, intellectual freedom and economic organization, traditional assumptions and modern realities.

The cast of his mind was best revealed in his serpentine conception of power. Mills argued that neither Marxists nor liberals offered an adequate explanation for contemporary political behavior because they restricted their vision to single factors which once were pivotal but had since become incidental to the type of society now in existence in the United States. The Marxist fixation with economic class obscured the equally important role of the state and the military establishment. The liberal faith in rational debate and citizen participation ignored the deterioration of open political contests into a series of "administrative routines" presided over by a bureaucratic hierarchy that made policy without having to take parties, pressure groups, or the voters into account. For Mills, as for Dwight Macdonald, the failure of Marxism and liberalism to serve as useful guides for political action was symbolized by the impersonal violence of the Nazi concentration camps, the inexorable development of nuclear weapons, and the efficient planning for World War III—none of which had been halted on the barricades or at the polls.[123]

Given the enlargement and centralization of administrative authority, Mills contended that the powerful no longer simply owned the means of production or exercised influence over political movements. The key criterion for inclusion in the elite was one's access to the basic mechanisms of decision making on issues that had national or international significance. There was, he declared, a small but "overlapping" circle of men who occupied the crucial posts in the major institutions, through which they shaped the country's destiny at home and abroad. The chairmen and managers of the "two or three hundred giant corporations," the president and his intimate associates, and the members of the Joint Chiefs of Staff were not mere bureaucrats according to Mills. Rather, they ran the government agencies, dominated the business community, and directed the military departments. Within their own domains, they were supreme. Yet they no longer inhabited separate realms, as in the nineteenth century. Instead, they had to deal with one another as equals; they were bound together like feudal barons in an intricate partnership, sharing and allocating power for the advantage of all. The corporate executive was dependent on but exerted leverage over the policies of the state. The general or admiral had turned into a geopolitician; his notions of military necessity now prevailed among his colleagues in business and government. The White House and the National Security Council became for Mills the arenas where the "interlocking" interests of the power elite were clarified and translated into a unified strategy. This merger of economic, military, and political institutions was a product of World War II and the exigencies of the Cold War. But what impressed Mills at this juncture was the *combined* power of the modern elite, an unprecedented development in human history. By their decisions or their inability to decide, he asserted, they determined the fluctuations of domestic prosperity and recession, as well as world-wide questions of war or peace. In their secluded chambers, they controlled the fate of millions who could not act but only adapt.[124]

Mills denied that he was representing the history of America since World War II as a "secret plot" or a "great and co-ordinated conspiracy" on the part of the elite. On the other hand, he did not imagine that the consolidation of authority was purely the result of what Marxists liked to call "objective conditions"— the grim unfolding of political and economic forces beyond the capacity of humans to influence or alter. Mills spent many pages in his books and essays describing the evolution and present structure of power in the United States, but he also thought it was equally important to know about the kinds of men who composed the elite. Typically, he concentrated on the interconnections between the "character or will or intelligence" of certain individuals and the institutional positions they held. He explored their psychological traits, family backgrounds, educational pedigrees, marital ties, private clubs, vacation preferences, career patterns, and lifelong professional contacts because these were all vital in forming the proper personnel for America's hierarchies. Indeed, the very willingness of the nation's leaders to cooperate sprang from their similar cultural experiences, their ability to accept and understand one another's point of view, their predisposition "to work and to think if not together at least alike." And just as they pursued political and economic objectives that were mutually beneficial, so they exchanged institutional roles, moving easily from the armed forces to the corporate boardrooms to the Cabinet or even the White House. Along the road, they acquired self-confidence in their own wisdom, as well as the conviction that they should naturally be "The Ones Who Decide." For Mills, such social affinities and shared attitudes gave the elite the "internal discipline" and emotional unity it needed to rule. Hence he constantly tried to maintain a double vision in depicting the centralization of power in America. In his judgment, the government, the corporations, and the military selected precisely those individuals who were best able to capitalize on the power with which they were invested. But the relationship was always reciprocal: The problems of modern society provided the impetus for the rise of a new set of potentates, who in turn remodeled society to suit their common assumptions and values.[125]

The most disturbing consequence of these developments for Mills was the way in which decisions now got made. Contemporary leaders seemed to Mills deliberately remote, impersonal, inaccessible, anonymous. They conducted their affairs in private; they rarely engaged in "public or even Congressional debate"; they relied neither on force nor "reasonable discussion" but on the techniques of psychological manipulation (and when all else failed, the allusion to the "official secret") to pacify the electorate. Thus their policies could not be effectively opposed; there were now no explicit "targets for revolt." Here Mills was not merely weighing the difficulties of defying the organization or the peer group. Where William Whyte and David Riesman had treated the problem of resistance primarily as a personal and moral question, Mills wanted to point out its political ramifications. When power was "hidden" and actions were taken "behind men's backs," when people's lives were transformed without their knowledge or consent, the choice between other-direction and autonomy hardly mattered. Democracy itself had become a hoax.[126]

This line of argument clearly contradicted the idea set forth by writers like Seymour Lipset, Daniel Bell, Arthur Schlesinger, and Oscar Handlin that America was a pluralistic society, with political parties and voluntary associations joining in a delicate balance of power. In Mills's view, the liberal commentators presupposed that power was distributed more or less equally among a variety of "independent" organizations, that there was no concentration of authority at the top to which everyone ultimately deferred. The liberal felt relatively assured that the United States was genuinely democratic, with none of the oligarchical tendencies which beset the rest of the world. For his part, Mills objected to the "folklore" of pluralism because it focused exclusively on the "middle levels" of political activity, thereby distracting attention from the issue of who made the "big decisions."[127]

Since Mills believed that power in America was structured vertically, he insisted that none of the institutions or pressure groups on which liberals relied to implement their democratic theories actually had a real influence on national and international affairs. Congressmen, professional diplomats, the civil servants who staffed the government agencies, state and city officials, labor leaders, farm spokesmen, members of local chambers of commerce, and the representatives of religious and educational organizations were all preoccupied with the aspirations of their particular constituencies. They furnished information to the higher-ups, lobbied for pet projects, jockeyed for position and status. So their vision remained "parochial," their impact was "fragmented," and their competing programs usually floundered in a legislative stalemate. They never functioned as a "countervailing" force. Consequently, they did not offer the individual a medium for political participation or a means of affecting those at the "summit" of power. Between the state and the solitary citizen, there were no "intermediate associations" through which a person could regain control over his own life.[128]

Mills criticized the pluralists not because he disliked their political ideas, but because their version of democracy no longer obtained in the United States. And he was not optimistic about a possible restoration of democratic institutions. Instead, he feared that America had already traveled half the distance to totalitarianism.

Nowhere were Mills's nightmares about the future better revealed than in his discussion of powerlessness. At the bottom of his political pyramid lay the phlegmatic inhabitants of the mass society. In *White Collar*, he presented as doleful an account of middle-class life as could be found in the works of his contemporaries. Up to a point, Mills sounded indistinguishable from Dwight Macdonald, Clement Greenberg, Daniel Boorstin, Mary McCarthy, Paul Goodman, Daniel Bell, David Riesman, or William Whyte. His white-collar man was riddled with the same afflictions they had diagnosed. "Bored at work and restless at play," stuck in the middle of someone else's organization without the opportunity to rise or the incentive to protest, chained to "routinized tasks" and lacking any pride in craftsmanship, sacrificing his identity in order to get along with his customers and fellow employees, entirely dependent on the media for his tastes and diversions, he was a faceless, insignificant cog in a bureaucratic machine. He therefore suffered, not surprisingly, from status anxieties, emotional insecurity, and free-floating alienation.[129]

But Mills was not content simply to delineate the cultural and psychological frustrations of the bourgeoisie. The average American's sense of political helplessness seemed much more alarming to Mills than the problem of conformity. The modern citizen had become a "small creature," far removed from the "centers of power." Rarely heard or consulted, "driven by forces" he could "neither understand nor govern," he languished as a spectator in his own country. To make matters

worse, he remained ideologically passive and politically unorgan-
ized. Thus for Mills the notorious apathy of middle-class Americans was not just the mask they wore to protect their privacy, as
David Riesman had speculated. It was also an understandable
"response to a condition of powerlessness." People lost the "will
for decision," he noted, when they did not "possess the instruments for decision," and when they saw no way to achieve their
political aims.[130]

These were exactly the circumstances that Mills most dreaded.
Echoing Hannah Arendt, he deplored America's decline from a
"community of publics" (with a set of "autonomous" institutions
enabling people to engage in intelligent political debate, respond
directly to the policies of their government, and depose those in
authority when necessary) to a "mass society" where the majority
could not "answer back immediately" to the official "definitions
of reality" they received from the media, where there were no
other institutional mechanisms through which to acquire divergent information or advocate unconventional ideas, where no
one except the elite could comprehend or act upon the larger
"structural" issues that shaped the life of the nation. Once having
abandoned its nineteenth century democratic heritage, the
United States was embarked on a perilous journey that Mills
thought would end inevitably in the erection of a totalitarian
state.[131]

By the 1950s, was there still time for the country to turn back?
Given the impotence of most Americans, and the ineffectiveness
of those in the middle ranges of Mills's hierarchy, who could
bring about such a reversal?

Mills was no more sanguine than any of his contemporaries
about the capacity of the trade unions to provide political leadership in the future. Nor did he place as much hope as John
Kenneth Galbraith in the rise of a "new class" of highly educated
professionals and technicians. The only people he felt had the
faintest chance of arresting the drift toward totalitarianism were
the intellectuals, and he considered their recent performance
fairly dismal.[132]

Because Mills attached such importance to the role of America's writers and scholars, he criticized their values and conduct

more bitterly than those of any other group. Since the end of
World War II, he declared, intellectuals had refused to raise the
most fundamental questions about the nature and direction of
American life. Some seemed satisfied to serve as experts and
counselors to the men in charge, subtly recasting their own ideas
to suit the needs of their employers, permitting their research
interests to be defined by the state or the corporations or the
military or the foundations, limiting themselves to "safe" and
often "microscopic fields of inquiry" rather than studying "man
and society as a whole," cultivating the "fetish of objectivity"
while declining to interpret or analyze the facts they had labori-
ously collected, exhibiting the "discretion" and "good judgment" required of "academic gentlemen" even if this led to a
form of "voluntary censorship." Others, attracted to the posture
of alienation, retreated from politics altogether and immersed
themselves in cultural matters—a tactic that left the dominant
institutions intact but at least gave the powerless writer a "fashionable" excuse for "being overwhelmed." Whichever stance
they adopted, Mills argued, they had ceased to dissent from or
oppose the decisions of the elite.[133]

Paradoxically, it was just because Mills equated power with
decision making, rather than with entrenched wealth or class
privilege, that he envisioned the possibility of writers having a
political impact on both the elite and the larger society. Like
others in the 1950s, Mills had no specific ideological scenario to
propose. He was less interested in the resuscitation of radical
doctrines and movements than in the revival of radical thinking
among intellectuals themselves. But in this enterprise, he too
stressed the primacy of consciousness, the need for writers to be
acutely aware of their ambiguous entanglements with existing
institutions. Only then could they begin to "unmask" and "resist" the distortions of the media and the assumptions of those
at the top.[134]

Beyond these initial precepts, Mills contended that writers
alone possessed the skill and insight (if not yet the motivation)
to illuminate the connections between the individual's inner anxieties and the deeper problems of American life. As the last of the
"craftsmen" in an industrial epoch, they could still "decide what

they will or will not do" in their work. They were "strategically placed" to offer an analysis that was "at once political and cultural."[135]

The average man might have a vague sense of his own moral and psychic malaise, Mills suggested, but he rarely recognized that his uneasiness was shared by others. It was the special responsibility of the intellectual to translate these "personal troubles into social issues," to point out the public "meaning and source" of private discontent. Thus, writers ought to explain why the solitary citizen felt powerless to prevent a nuclear war or cope with capitalism's instability, why neither the good intentions nor the technical ingenuity of the city dweller were enough to eradicate the blight of the "overdeveloped megalopolis and the overdeveloped automobile," why the American family as an economic and social entity turned "women into darling little slaves and men into their chief providers and unweaned dependents." The willingness of writers to link the personal and the political, to infuse their cultural critiques with a sensitivity to the "*structure* of institutions" and the "*foundations* of policies," and finally to formulate a set of "demands and programs" on the basis of this synthesis, was in Mills's judgment a prerequisite for the rebirth of a radical intelligentsia.[136]

Mills's prescriptions for his fellow writers seemed remarkably similar to what David Riesman meant by "autonomy." Because intellectuals could choose whether to resist or conform, they might again be the masters of their own activities and ideas. Presumably, the Millsian journalist would not accept the obfuscations of the White House or the state department; the atomic physicist would never bow to the military machine; the social scientist would shun trivial subjects; the university professor would ignore the pressures of careerism. Mills's ideal intellectual served always as the "moral conscience" of his country. He did not pretend to be a consultant or an administrator or a proletarian revolutionary. Neither was he satisfied merely to contemplate his own alienation. Instead, he used his information, his knowledge, and his sense of estrangement to challenge the reign of the elite. He published and spoke through the media, but always on his own terms and for his own purposes. He waged political and cultural battles as an independent thinker, not as a propagandist in the Cold War. He remained "detached from *any* enclosure of mind or nationalist celebration" in order to conduct a "continuing, uncompromising criticism" of all official creeds and established regimes. He tried to understand and to transform the social order by communicating his discoveries as coherently and truthfully as possible to the "right people, at the right time, and in the right way." By these means, Mills believed, the intellectual could be both a free and an effective man, both a rebel against and a participant in American society.[137]

Mills realized, however, that the "autonomous" intellectual could not stay forever "independent of power but powerfully related to it" unless there also existed a "free and knowledgeable public" to whom he could address his arguments and to whom the leaders of the nation were "truly responsible." Hence Mills hoped for the emergence of a new constituency that, sufficiently organized and no longer passive, might convert the theories and recommendations of the intelligentsia into concrete political action. In describing the composition of this constituency, Mills most nearly resembled Hannah Arendt. He was calling not for a mass upheaval with socialism as its ultimate aim, nor for the anarchistic repudiation of all institutions that sometimes characterized the activism of the 1960s. Rather, he was urging a return to those democratic procedures and ideals more commonly associated with the nineteenth century: political parties that debated "openly and clearly" the issues before America and the world; a "neutral" but socially "relevant" civil service that functioned as a "depository of brainpower and executive skill"; interest groups that really did mediate between "families and smaller communities . . . on the one hand, and the state, the military, the corporation on the other."[138] The loose and contractual bond between knowledge and power, intellectuals and society, enlightened citizens and their leaders that Mills favored did not presently prevail in the United States. In fact, such conservative notions seemed almost radical in the context of modern life. Yet these were the only remedies Mills could conceive to cure the political and cultural ills of postwar America.

Mills frequently sounded as pessimistic as other writers about the prospects for social change. The singular mission he entrusted to the intelligentsia—like John Kenneth Galbraith's faith in education to overcome the "cultural lag" between economic dogma and social realities, or Louis Hartz's reliance on America's encounters with the rest of the world as the sole means of surmounting an archaic liberalism, or Dwight Macdonald's search for an avant-garde to resist the banalities of mass culture, or David Riesman's and William Whyte's emphasis on the individual's reassertion of freedom and identity *within* the framework of society's organizations—reflected a general suspicion among intellectuals that the nation's institutions were now too stable and too imposing to be altered by ordinary people acting through conventional parties or movements. As a consequence, many writers including Mills may have exaggerated the strength of the social order and underestimated the number of institutional conflicts that could easily arise.

Mills, for example, assumed that all white-collar workers were politically passive and impervious to unionization. Yet in the next few years the labor movement gained its most militant converts among teachers and government employees, who in turn became increasingly active in politics at all levels of American life. Just as important, the emergence of the "new journalism" in the 1960s, the popularity of investigative reporting, and television's critical treatment of the Vietnam war and the "credibility gap" in the Johnson presidency undermined his thesis that the media was totally controlled by the elite. If anything, the networks and the major newspapers seemed more and more the adversaries of those in command. At the same time, the collapse of the Hollywood studio system and the growing significance of independent producing companies meant that the movies would expose their audiences to a far more discordant view of America than either Mills or the media theorists thought possible. Finally, Congress —the embodiment for Mills of "middle-level" parochialism and political paralysis—together with the courts, an institution he rarely mentioned, demonstrated their own independence and power when they dismantled an entire administration in the aftermath of Watergate.

But however much Mills shared the attitudes of his fellow intellectuals in the 1950s, he also anticipated the themes of the following decade. His recognition that people had power only when they could make free decisions about their own lives, his quest for alternative constituencies to resist the manipulative rule of the government-corporate-military alliance, and his insistence that a rejuvenated radicalism must involve the creation of a new politics as well as a new culture helped inspire the "students and young professors and writers" whom in 1960 he identified as the likeliest "agencies of historic change."[139] That the next generation failed to fulfill Mills's expectations, or even move beyond his insights, does not diminish his stature as the one intellectual in the postwar era who came closest to unifying and transcending the disparate ideas of his age.

5
✿

Are You Now, Have You Ever Been, and Will You Give Us the Names of Those Who Were?

As it happened, the idea that individuals must resist the power of the state and the demands of society was not a purely theoretical proposition. From the late 1940s to the mid-1950s, the willingness and capacity to withstand organized pressure became a measure of one's moral strength and personal integrity. The question of when and how much to cooperate, when and how much to dissent, had to be answered privately as well as publicly. Intellectuals, scientists, professors, university administrators, government officials, lawyers, clergymen, actors, playwrights, movie and television directors were forced to decide—on their own and by themselves—how they should behave in their daily work, at hearings, toward friends. They faced a human as much as a political and social predicament that no book or abstract thesis could easily resolve. For a time, their postwar values were crystallized into an elementary test of conscience and character.

Joseph McCarthy gave the period its name, but "McCarthyism" began well before his rise to prominence and outlasted his political demise. Indeed, what made the years between 1947 and 1955 so fearsome was precisely that the climate of repression did not originate with or depend on the ravings of a single demagogue.

McCarthyism coincided with the most traumatic episodes of the Cold War: the Stalinization of eastern Europe, the Berlin blockade, Russia's explosion of its own atomic bomb, the "fall" of China to the Communists, and the military stalemate in Korea. These calamities abroad triggered a series of investigations at home to which many people and institutions across the political spectrum contributed. McCarthyism took a variety of forms: the security checks, loyalty oaths, and attorney general's list of subversive organizations initiated by the Truman administration; the trials of Alger Hiss, Communist party leaders, and the Rosenbergs conducted by Truman's department of justice from evidence assembled by the FBI; the labor movement's expulsion of its Communist-dominated unions; the presidential campaign of 1948 in which liberals accused Henry Wallace of being a spokesman for Moscow, followed by the campaign of 1952 in which conservatives charged Democrats with being "soft on Communism"; the congressional exposés of Communist infiltration in Hollywood, television, newspapers, churches, universities, and public schools; the efforts by intellectuals and legal scholars to narrow the limits of academic freedom and civil liberties in an era of espionage, sabotage, and conspiracy.

Amid this uproar, it seemed not to matter that the estimated membership of the Communist party had declined from 80,000 in 1944 to 40,000 in 1950, or that the *Daily Worker* claimed a circulation of only 23,400 in 1949.[1] Actual numbers were less important than potential influence. The Party itself was disintegrating, but traces of its poison might still linger in the minds of ex-Communists, fellow travelers, dupes, one-worlders, neutralists, Popular Front sentimentalists, political innocents, and "liberals who haven't learned."[2] Thus the impulse persisted through the mid-1950s to investigate, maintain lists, scrutinize the activities of leftish organizations, distinguish between acceptable and intolerable ideas, promise redemption to the properly penitent and banish those who were insufficiently contrite about their past sins.

The victims of McCarthyism—particularly in the entertainment world, the state department, and the scientific community—are by now well known.[3] One reason there were so many victims is because they had so few defenders. A person confronted with the option of either complying with or rebuffing a congressional committee or the FBI, with salvaging his career or languishing on a blacklist, had to make that choice alone. No institutions, guilds, support groups, or role models offered assistance and encouragement if he wished not to submit. Each individual was thrown back on whatever inner courage or simple sense of honor he could summon from his previous experiences and present inclinations.

Given these lonely circumstances, the "friendly" witness should not be too facilely judged or condemned. We all like to think that we would behave well in a similar situation, that we would stand up to pressure and hurl Woody Allen's closing lines in *The Front* at our own grand inquisitors: "Look, fellows, you don't have any right to ask me these questions. You can all go fuck yourselves." But the truth is that no one knows in advance exactly how he will act when his work, his family, his future are at stake. Until we ourselves have passed the test more nobly than our predecessors, we ought to have compassion for both the informers and the victims. We do know, however, that the conclusion of *The Front* is largely a fantasy. Very few people before a committee or in print uttered the equivalent of the film's climactic words.

Why did so many face their fate in solitude? Why were they normally advised to give in, testify, provide information, name names? One might have expected intellectuals—those most alert to totalitarian infringements on civil liberties and cultural freedom—to attack the investigators, challenge the premises of McCarthyism, urge defiance, cheer any display of independence and "autonomy" in the midst of conformity.

But the majority of writers during the 1940s and 1950s preached a different sermon. In one form or another, and with varying degrees of sophistication, they counseled or practiced collaboration—not as a matter of expediency, not so as to save their own or anyone else's career, but on principle. They argued, rationally and sincerely, that citizens should help the government purge America of the last vestiges of Stalinism. They insisted that the Cold War required extraordinary legislation to extinguish domestic subversion. They disliked McCarthyism, yet they reinforced its assumptions and helped refine its methods because they detested Communism even more. In the end, by justifying its persecutions and by distorting their commitment to personal freedom in the interest of a "higher" ideal, they too were victimized by McCarthyism. Only, unlike the terrified and now apolitical inhabitants of Hollywood, the intellectuals who adopted this stance were politically knowledgeable and philosophically resourceful. They should have known better.

There were some who did not believe in cooperation, who did know better. In their books and essays they resisted not simply the tactics of but the rationale for McCarthyism. And when it sometimes became necessary, they refused in person to serve the state. They were not especially ideological or heroic. Maybe they were just instinctively recalcitrant, as if they found the mixture of orthodoxy and vindictiveness in their fellow writers physically distasteful. But regardless of their motivations or their disagreements on other political and cultural issues, they thought and acted like genuinely free intellectuals when it counted most. So the members of this small band among the intelligentsia— Dwight Macdonald, Henry Steele Commager, I. F. Stone, Mary McCarthy, Lillian Hellman, Arthur Miller, Michael Harrington— deserve more than praise or respect. They deserve our thanks.

The Rise of McCarthyism: Radical Guilt and Liberal Innocence

For all the publicity generated by the House Un-American Activities Committee's myriad investigations of Hollywood, and Joseph McCarthy's allegations about Communist influence in the state department and the army, the most systematic and wideranging pursuit of subversives was undertaken by the Truman administration. Partly to deflect the suspicion that Democrats were secretly sympathetic to Communism, and partly as a reaction to the unrelieved tensions of the Cold War, Truman's government launched or assumed control over the campaign to purge America of spies and security risks. While Congress indulged in more bombast, the administration—through its loyalty programs, its prosecution of Alger Hiss and the Rosenbergs, and its success in dismantling the leadership of the Communist party under the Smith Act—established the tenets and perfected the techniques of what became known as McCarthyism.

Because the president could not be ridiculed as a fanatic or a political Neanderthal, because he himself denounced the atmosphere of fright in America, and because his actions seemed judicious in comparison with the sensational innuendos of HUAC and McCarthy, the antisubversive policies of his administration touched off a serious debate among intellectuals over the dangers of Communism within the United States, as well as about the degree to which their own radical pasts had contributed to the nation's vulnerability in the Cold War. Which, after all, was worse: to be guilty of once having harbored Marxist illusions, or to be still innocent of the evils of Stalinism? And in either case, what measures should writers now accept to rid themselves and their country of any remaining totalitarian predilections? The way intellectuals answered these questions, and the way they criticized or supported the Truman administration's security apparatus, conditioned their overall response to McCarthyism.

In March 1947, ten days after the proclamation of the Truman doctrine, the president issued an executive order authorizing the FBI to assess the loyalty of all current and prospective federal employees. These probes, culminating with each official's signature of an oath pledging his fidelity to the Constitution and the government, were justified by the need to guard America's national security in an increasingly perilous time.

Soon the methods of inquiry followed a prescribed format. The FBI gathered information on an individual from his family, friends, neighbors, teachers, professional acquaintances, former employers—anyone who claimed to know something about a man's past or present political allegiances and ideas. The sources remained anonymous; the person under investigation could seldom learn the identity of those who were questioned or the substance of what they had said. Without the right to cross-examine informants, the individual found it almost impossible to rebut any damaging testimony in his dossier. Indeed, he was often presumed guilty in the eyes of his investigators until he could prove his innocence; any indications of doubt about his loyalty became sufficient reason to deny him a security clearance. The FBI did not have to produce evidence of illegal or even radical acts. Membership in or "sympathetic association" with an organization designated as subversive on the attorney general's list was enough to bar one from government service.[4] The administration's security checks spawned loyalty tests at all levels of American life. A number of state legislatures passed laws requiring their employees (particularly teachers in public schools and universities) to sign affidavits certifying that they were not members of the Communist party or affiliated with any of its fronts. To ordinary citizens, the definition of disloyalty began to seem far more inclusive: It could mean giving money to or attending meetings of any "radical" group. Thus, instead of calming the nation, Truman's policies intensified the fear that subversives might be lurking everywhere.

At the outset, some commentators objected to the loyalty program because of its dubious constitutionality and its potentially counterproductive effects. Henry Wallace complained that the machinery for guaranteeing America's impregnability provided no opportunities for open hearings, "no trial by jury, or review or appeal to the existing higher courts." Its procedures were "bound to injure many innocent victims," while inhibiting the "free flow of thought and interchange of ideas" the country needed in coping with a "changing world." Yet the supreme irony to Wallace was that the hunt for subversives would only drive the Communists "underground," thereby making them an even greater threat to the United States.[5]

Dwight Macdonald was more disturbed by the Orwellian implications of Truman's executive order. "This is a proposal to fight a totalitarian group—the American Communist Party—with its own methods," he asserted. Punishment based on "anonymous denunciations for unspecified crimes is the essence of Nazi–Stalinist jurisprudence." What kind of democracy, Macdonald and Wallace both wondered, would survive when its putative saviors relied on the "use of terror and secret police?"[6]

Most intellectuals, however, concluded in the next few years that Truman's security measures had been unfortunate but necessary. To Leslie Fiedler, Sidney Hook, Arthur Schlesinger, Daniel Bell, Richard Rovere (a regular contributor to *The New Yorker* and later a biographer of Senator McCarthy), Robert Bendiner (a liberal journalist and associate editor of the *Nation*), and Irving Kristol (by the early 1950s the managing editor of *Commentary*), the Communists were not simply a "legitimate dissenting group" or a radical political party entitled to the customary protections of the Bill of Rights. Rather, they functioned as virtual "agents of a foreign power" (Hook); they used Marxist ideas solely as "strategems" to further the "national interests of the Soviet Union" (Kristol, Bendiner, Fiedler); they were participants in a treasonous "conspiracy to end forever the whole conception of a society based on free discussion" (Schlesinger); their intrigues constituted a "clear and present danger" to democracy (Bell). Therefore America had to shield itself against this menace. The government must "draw the line" somewhere if it wished to preserve the nation's "inner moral strength" (Schlesinger), which at a minimum meant keeping the Communists "out of places where they can do harm" (Hook). Since the Communist party played "an important role in Soviet espionage," it was "perfectly reasonable" for certain agencies—the state and defense departments, the White House, the Atomic Energy Commission—to "screen" present and future employees, even to invoke the criteria of "guilt by association in determining security risks," though such tests "should be soberly applied" (Schlesinger, Rovere). The right to work for the government was "not clearly a part of the civil liberties of a citizen"; on the contrary, the "failure to discharge suspicious persons" could do more to "imperil national security" than any restrictions on the expression of heretical opinion (Schlesinger). These arguments not only reinforced the assumptions behind the loyalty program, they also blurred whatever distinctions still persisted between Russian spies and legal Party members.[7]

Several writers shared Henry Wallace's fear that the careers of innocent people could be destroyed in the quest for traitors. Arthur Schlesinger worried that the current "anti-Communist feeling" in America would "boil over into a vicious and unconstitutional attack on nonconformists in general," while Robert Bendiner warned that a "repressive spirit in high places . . . can all too easily get out of hand."[8]

Worse, the FBI might not appreciate the differences between

Stalinists and liberals. "Where every progressive is painted red," Bendiner observed, "who is to know the real Communist from the New Dealer, the totalitarian from the democrat?" But Bendiner blamed his fellow liberals, not government investigators, for this confusion of identities. The liberals had "allowed their institutions to be infiltrated . . . by those of a completely alien political faith," he declared in language indistinguishable from a HUAC memorandum. Hence he urged liberals to cleanse themselves of any pro-Soviet taint, and stop thinking they were "somehow joined" with the Communists in a common crusade for civil liberties.[9]

Yet such attempts at political purification would not entirely solve the problem of bureaucratic excesses. The "critical question" for Alan Westin, a lawyer and professor of government first at Harvard and later at Columbia, was how to "detect as many disloyal persons as possible before they can commit security violations . . . without setting up a process that works against the unorthodox or the dissenter."[10] This conundrum led Schlesinger, Rovere, and Bendiner to demand that the administration rely scrupulously on "constitutional methods"—public "debate, identification and exposure" when feasible; adherence to the principle that the individual rather than the security agency be given the "benefit of the doubt"; prompt hearings with the opportunity for those under suspicion to confront their accusers; an unbiased evaluation of evidence; "fair" mechanisms for dismissal "hedged around with firm procedural safeguards."[11] Paul Kecskemeti, a philosopher and social scientist who often wrote for *Commentary,* desired more laws that stipulated which activities were in fact "subversive" so that "repression" could "take the form of legal penalties" instead of administrative blacklists.[12] In effect, these writers were willing to grant the justifications for the security apparatus, but they wanted its operation to be democratic, juridical, and above all accurate in differentiating between hardened conspirators and mere free-thinkers.

Still, the contention that Communism was nothing more than a plot to infiltrate and undermine the American government did not spring exclusively from the overheated imagination of anti-Stalinist intellectuals. By the late 1940s, the loyalty program seemed warranted because of the mounting evidence that there had been real spies both in Washington and in the wartime atomic bomb project. These disclosures appeared to confirm the most preposterous insinuations of conservatives in Congress, while forcing writers to examine their own unwitting complicity in the "crimes" of the Left.

The psychodrama of mystery and revelation, imputations of guilt and protestations of innocence, began in 1948—the year of the coup in Czechoslovakia, the crisis over Berlin, the rise and fall of Henry Wallace's Progressive party, and Harry Truman's re-election campaign as a domestic reformer and indomitable Cold Warrior. In July, before the House Un-American Activities Committee, Elizabeth Bentley repeated the story she previously told the FBI and a federal grand jury of having transmitted information from several officials in Washington to Soviet intelligence operatives in New York during World War II. Among her government contacts, she identified William Remington (who worked for the commerce department) and Harry Dexter White (assistant secretary of the treasury under Henry Morgenthau, a principal designer of the World Bank, and after 1946 the director of the International Monetary Fund). Her testimony helped persuade the grand jury to indict twelve leaders of the Communist party for violating the Smith Act. It also led to the firing of eleven state department employees. Remington and White denied Bentley's allegations, but the damage inflicted on them was brutal. White, suffering from heart disease, died a few days after testifying to HUAC. Remington, convicted twice of perjury in 1951 and 1953 for lying about his past association with the Communist party and his role as a conduit to Bentley, was murdered in jail by another inmate.

But no one revealed the connections between Soviet espionage and American Communists more vividly than Whittaker Chambers. Formerly a courier in the Communist underground in the 1930s, later a senior editor of *Time* magazine, Chambers appeared before HUAC in August 1948 to relate the details of how subversives had penetrated the New Deal. He implicated eight secret Communists, the most well-known of whom was Alger Hiss.

There was good reason for the public to recognize the name. Hiss had been a protégé of Oliver Wendell Holmes and Felix Frankfurter, and he counted among his friends or patrons such luminaries as Eleanor Roosevelt, Adlai Stevenson, Dean Acheson, and John Foster Dulles. Hiss entered the New Deal as a lawyer for the Agricultural Adjustment Administration, but he eventually moved on to loftier positions. In addition to a career in the state department, he became an architect of the Dumbarton Oaks Conference, one of Franklin Roosevelt's advisers at Yalta, and the organizer and temporary chairman of the United Nations' first meetings in San Francisco in 1945. He left the government in 1947 to become president of the Carnegie Endowment for International Peace. Obviously, if a man with such an illustrious vita could have been a Communist, not to mention a spy, then nothing the government did was safe from Soviet eyes.

Hiss professed his innocence to HUAC under oath, and sued for libel when Chambers reiterated his charges on *Meet the Press*. During the hearings in August, Hiss equivocated about whether, under what circumstances, and how long he knew Chambers in the 1930s. But he continued to insist throughout the fall that he had never joined or sympathized with the Communist party.

In November, replying to the libel suit, Chambers declared that Hiss had not only been a Communist, but had engaged in espionage. To corroborate his claim, Chambers produced sensational documentation: sixty-five pages of state department material (some of which were allegedly recopied on a typewriter owned by Hiss), three memoranda in Hiss's handwriting, and five rolls of microfilm which Chambers said he received from Hiss and other conspirators in 1937 and 1938. In December, the same New York grand jury that heard the evidence against the Communist party leaders indicted Hiss on two counts of perjury. Because the statute of limitations on espionage had elapsed, Hiss could be tried only for lying when he testified that he never saw Chambers after 1936 or gave him state department papers to pass on to the Russians. Hiss's first trial in 1949 ended in a hung jury, but he was convicted at a second trial in 1950 and sentenced to five years in jail.[13]

The conviction of Alger Hiss, even more than the cases against William Remington and Harry Dexter White, lent credence to the theory that all Communists should be regarded as potential foreign agents. For many intellectuals, the saga of Chambers and Hiss also implied that the radicalism of the Depression years had been corrupted, liberals had been naïve, and ex-Communists who were now witnesses on behalf of the state must at least be respected for exposing the truth. Few felt comfortable with the idea that on this occasion HUAC served as an effective forum for the detection of subversives. But Hiss's failure to explain away Chambers's evidence convinced writers like Arthur Schlesinger, Richard Rovere, James Wechsler, Robert Bendiner, Bruce Bliven, Leslie Fiedler, Murray Kempton, Philip Rahv, and Harold Rosenberg that Hiss was guilty.[14]

Moreover, Chambers seemed credible to certain anti-Stalinist intellectuals with whom he had maintained a friendship of sorts in the 1930s: Lionel and Diana Trilling, Meyer Schapiro, Sidney Hook. He kept them generally advised of his adventures underground, indicated to them his own growing disillusion with Stalinism, and pleaded for their assistance when he decided to defect in 1938. In his prophetic novel, *The Middle of the Journey* (1947), Lionel Trilling drew on his memories of Chambers to create the character of Gifford Maxim, the self-flagellating former Communist who converts to a gloomy Augustinian pessimism, thereby horrifying those liberals still addicted to the Soviet myth. In 1948, Chambers went so far as to display his incriminating microfilm to Meyer Schapiro before turning it over to the justice department. Thus these particular writers had some personal as well as political reasons for believing Chambers (though no one exhibited as much assurance as Sidney Hook when he recommended to *Life* magazine in 1957 that Chambers of all people review Hiss's apologia, *In the Court of Public Opinion*, to get an authoritative appraisal of the author's recollections).[15] But whatever their motives or involvements, a number of intellectuals were eager to explore the meaning of Hiss's treachery, and to establish new, more prudent standards for liberal behavior.

Diana Trilling, writing just after Hiss's conviction, urged her anti-Communist colleagues to separate themselves both from

Hiss's admirers on the left who continued to proclaim his innocence, and from right-wing witch hunters who thought every liberal was un-American. One must maintain "a very delicate position which neither supports a McCarthy nor automatically defends anyone whom a McCarthy attacks." The most odious reactionary might again "turn up someone who is as guilty as Hiss," she warned. Therefore, the wise observer did not succumb to hysteria, rush to embrace the victims of McCarthyism, or assume the purity of either the accusers or the accused. He awaited the "proper legal evidence" before making up his mind.[16] For Trilling, the once-burned liberal should henceforth pay attention to the facts of a case, rather than to the imagery of competing political camps.

Her counsel went mostly unheeded. By the early 1950s, Hiss was no longer treated as a unique individual who may or may not have committed specific felonies. Instead, he came to symbolize much that was wrong with both the Old Left and postwar America. In fact, there seemed to be a variety of Hisses, each standing for some trait writers deplored in middle-class culture, liberal politics, and occasionally in themselves.

Although Hiss had presumably acted in the interests of an ideology, his conduct could not be interpreted in Marxist terms. For most analysts, only a quasi-psychological approach would remove his many masks, and invest his life with the appropriate moral lessons.

Several writers cast Hiss as the embodiment not only of Communist perfidy, but also as a classic 1950s-style conformist—a double bind from which he could never extricate himself no matter what he said or did. In this view, Hiss represented the radical as organization man, clad not in proletarian overalls but in government-issue pinstripes. The trajectory of his life revealed what happened when the Left exchanged revolution for respectability during the days of the Popular Front and World War II.

Thus Harold Rosenberg accused Hiss and other fellow-traveling bureaucrats of being in reality "middle-class careerists," a "sodden group of Philistines" whose culture and politics were as implacably smug as any social climber with an eye on the "Good Spot in the government, the university, Hollywood, publishing."[17] Murray Kempton, poking through the ruins of the 1930s in *Part of Our Time* (1955), was a bit less scornful. He too argued that many radicals had never been rebels at all but merely men "desperate to conform," to belong to a movement, to be a part of history. They fled from the "fact of solitude to a myth of community." Yet they were divided souls; hence the peculiarly symbiotic relationship between Chambers and Hiss, as if each reflected the other's hidden yearnings. "Could Chambers have seen in Hiss the image of absolute security, absolute breeding, and absolute normality?" Kempton conjectured. "Could Hiss have seen in Chambers the image of absolute revolt and the breaking of the bands?" Kempton did not pursue the inquiry. A genuine revolutionary, he concluded, behaved like David Riesman's autonomous hero: He knew how to be alone, how to act on his own convictions, how to maintain his independence despite the pressures of politics and society.[18]

Leslie Fiedler also depicted Hiss's duplicity as emblematic of the radical's ambivalence toward the very bourgeois values he hoped eventually to overturn. Indeed Chambers, for all his bizarre mannerisms and baroque self-dramatization, appeared to Fiedler a more authentic prototype of the "open rebel, the poet-bum chanting songs of protest" than the suave Hiss with his "pressed suit" and "clean-cut look." Reading Fiedler, one was almost persuaded to salute Chambers as the quintessential outsider, an exotic misfit forever at odds with convention and rectitude, a forerunner of those marginal men of the 1950s, the delinquents and hipsters who haunted the middle-class imagination. On the other hand, Chambers might have more plausibly resembled a Method actor mumbling about Communism, religion, alienation, and other large thoughts. But if Chambers was an enigma, Hiss emerged on Fiedler's canvas as the ultimate hypocrite, a congenital square trapped for most of his working life in the American rat race, donating his off-hours to the Soviet Union as a signal that he had not totally " 'sold out' to the bourgeois world in which he was making a splendid career," rationalizing to himself that each step up the ladder of success provided additional "opportunities . . . for infiltration." Only, this "double allegiance" molded Hiss into a Machiavellian rather than a revolutionary, according to Fiedler. Worst of all, in "profiting immensely" from the society he pretended to want to "destroy," Hiss ended by deceiving himself as well as everyone else.[19] Yet the Hiss case served as more than a metaphor for the compromises and complacency intellectuals detested in the radicals of the 1930s and the suburbanites of the 1950s. Hiss's refusal to confess, to acknowledge his true identity and affiliations, or to stoutly defend his deeds in the name of revolutionary idealism were all symptoms not just of socialism betrayed but of a perpetually whining adolescence. The "qualifying act of moral adulthood," Fiedler announced, "is precisely this admission of responsibility for the past and its consequences." Hiss, it seemed, had not yet grown up, accepted his fraudulence as the first sign of maturity. Besides, on a more mundane level, Fiedler reminded his readers that Hiss was tried not for treason but for perjury. All he had to do was tell the truth, and "he need not even have gone to prison." Why, Fiedler asked with a certain disingenuousness of his own, "did he lie?"[20]

There were, of course, several conceivable answers to Fiedler's question, none of which he had any intention of contemplating seriously. Hiss might really have been innocent of the charges against him, and so had nothing to confess. Or he might not have considered his actions a crime, and therefore felt no "guilt." Or perhaps he was protecting other possible conspirators, notably his wife. Or, as was likely, he cared more about salvaging his tattered reputation than about engaging in public repentance.

Fiedler's explication, however, was relentlessly psychiatric. Hiss's neurotic demeanor reflected the "Popular Front mind at bay": specifically, a hunger to "pose as The Victim" and indulge in the "pathos of the persecuted" while simultaneously preserving one's "aura of unblemished respectability." Such a person was temperamentally "incapable of honesty even when there is no hope in anything else."[21]

And what did this cautionary tale signify for the rest of us? To Fiedler and Philip Rahv, a generation of romantic liberals, ex-New Dealers, and muddled radicals, all still nostalgic for the platitudes of the 1930s, stood in the dock with Hiss. They were culpable, Fiedler submitted, not "for having struggled toward a better world, but for having substituted sentimentality for intelligence in that struggle." They did not want to "confront the facts of political life," Rahv found. They flayed Chambers and fought to exonerate Hiss "in order to safeguard [their] own illusions and to escape the knowledge of [their] gullibility and chronic refusal of reality." This "half-deliberate blindness of so many decent people," Fiedler sensed, would be lifted only when they too held themselves accountable for their entanglement in villainy. To speed their recovery, Fiedler took their burden as his own. "We have desired good, and we have done some," he conceded, "but we have also done great evil." With this revelation, Fiedler and Rahv consigned the tortured past to the grave. The "age of innocence," like the age of ideology, was "dead."[22]

Apart from the spectacle of Jewish intellectuals impersonating Catholic priests, this rhetorical fervor for confession and absolution turned the complexities of history into a parable of Everyman's wickedness. Harold Rosenberg, ever on the alert for signs of formulaic thinking and facile myth making among the intelligentsia, searched his own memory and discovered he had nothing for which to atone. Whether or not "they" or "we" were sinners, he declined to march in the procession. "I never shared anything with Mr. Hiss, including automobiles or apartments; certainly not illusions," Rosenberg divulged. If some people felt "contaminated" by their particular pasts, they could not soothe their bad consciences by falsifying the experience of the Left in America. To correct the impression that all intellectuals should be on symbolic trial before the state, Rosenberg recalled that neither old-fashioned liberals nor anti-Stalinist radicals were in any way "responsible for Communist vileness," that the "reality" of the 1930s (at least in Rosenberg's version of the decade) "lay in its battles" between the devious politics and middle-brow tastes of the Popular Front on the one side and the partisans of modernism and independent socialism on the other. Now the doctrine of collective guilt, so dear to the totalitarian mind, had slipped into postwar America in the guise of the witness begging forgiveness for "our" transgressions, with the amateur psychoanalyst and lay preacher assuming the "function of the secret police." To Rosenberg, those writers who preferred Chambers's eccentricity to Hiss's propriety were playing a "hoax" on themselves. Still thirsting for "solidarity" despite his nonconformist posture, the "distracted dissident" used the therapist's couch and the confession booth as devices to rejoin society. "No longer alone," endowed with a positive role, the anti-Communist intellectual of the 1950s seemed as spurious a rebel to Rosenberg as his Stalinist counterpart in the 1930s. Both saw in their respective allegiances a "chance for uniformity."[23]

Rosenberg had cleverly reversed the values of Kempton, Fiedler, and Rahv, implying that deep down they too were intellectuals on the make, while only he remained an intransigent revolutionary. But he evaded their basic argument, which was not that everyone should renounce innocence and show remorse for his guilty past. Rather, Communism was simply the most extreme example for them of the general principle (favored by many writers in the 1950s) that all political movements threatened to rob the individual of his distinctive identity.

This proposition emerged most clearly not in the assessments of Alger Hiss, but in the obituaries on Julius and Ethel Rosenberg. The FBI arrested the Rosenbergs in 1950, accusing them of having organized an espionage ring during World War II to transmit details of the atomic bomb's construction to the Soviet Union. As with Hiss, the main evidence against them was supplied by a coconspirator-turned-informer—in this instance David Greenglass, whose testimony appeared much more credible than that of Whittaker Chambers because he was Ethel's brother, and surely would not have lied about her in order to save his own neck (or so it seemed to the jury). The Rosenbergs, like Hiss, vehemently denied any involvement with the Communist party or its couriers and spies. Nonetheless, they were convicted in 1951.

In imposing the death sentence, the presiding judge attributed to the Rosenbergs an even more heinous crime than wartime espionage. They were indirectly responsible for 50,000 American casualties in Korea, he deduced, because their activities hastened the development of a Russian atomic bomb, the possession of which emboldened Moscow to unleash its North Korean proxies on the forces of the free world—a heavy load of guilt for a former inspector of electronic products and his earnestly left-wing wife to bear. For the next two years, they persisted in protesting their innocence, refusing to recant despite the possibilities of clemency. So on June 19, 1953, the Rosenbergs were electrocuted.[24]

In the fall of 1953, Robert Warshow and Leslie Fiedler each presented a post-mortem on the Rosenbergs. Their appraisals were strikingly similar. Both essays revealed more about the attitudes of intellectuals toward contemporary culture and politics than about what the Rosenbergs were supposed to have done. Indeed, Warshow and Fiedler were not interested in evaluating the legal and ideological issues raised by the trial and execution. The evidence against the Rosenbergs was "overwhelming," Fiedler shrugged; the government had an "open-and-shut" case. Only those who longed to elevate the Rosenbergs into legendary "victims of the class struggle and the Cold War," who fancied them as reincarnations of Sacco and Vanzetti, who needed newer "martyrs" to replace the worn-out symbols of lynched Negroes and Spanish Loyalists and inmates of the Nazi concentration camps, could ignore their "palpable guilt".[25] Thus Warshow and Fiedler were more concerned with stereotypes, language, insights into the Rosenbergs' minds, the lives of this obscure couple as a text for literary and moral instruction.[26]

The letters Julius and Ethel wrote to each other in prison, published shortly before their deaths, proved to Warshow and Fiedler that leftist ideas could no longer be treated seriously. For them, the Rosenbergs were purer specimens of the Popular Front mentality than Alger Hiss. Hiss had spent too much time cultivating his aristocratic disdain to be caught eulogizing the Brooklyn Dodgers for their contributions to racial harmony. Nor was he likely to take middle-brow comfort in his jail cell by humming snatches of every musical treasure from Beethoven's Ninth to the Tennessee Waltz. In their letters, the Rosenbergs sounded so very petit bourgeois, so socially conscious, so filled with Jewish vibrations that they might have been invented by Clifford Odets.

That was the trouble. The Rosenbergs were inauthentic. They willfully converted themselves into puppets in an agitprop melodrama; they were forever editorializing on current events, ransacking history for any pertinent analogies to their fate, striking a blow for humanity, struggling on behalf of millions everywhere.

To Warshow, their letters seemed stilted, banal, crude, empty—
a perfect blend of Communist histrionics and middle-class vulgarity.[27]

But the Rosenbergs were not being castigated simply for their
stylistic gaffes or their abysmal tastes. Their chief offense was to
have submerged their personalities in their social role. They
exemplified to Fiedler the inevitable "conflict between the
human and the political." Awaiting death, that most private of
agonies, they maintained a "stubborn silence" about their deepest beliefs and affiliations; they resorted to "hints and evasions,"
whispers and allusions, instead of affirming aloud their commitments; they were "quite incapable of saying . . . just what it was
for which they thought they were dying." The Rosenbergs, like
Hiss, would not confess, so in their lack of candor they had been
mainly untrue to themselves. By declining to speak in their own
voices, to acknowledge their deeds however shabby, to retrieve
their individuality from the rubble of left-wing slogans and catch
phrases, they had sacrificed any "internal sense" of who they
were. Cluttering their lives with "second-hand" emotions, having
"almost nothing [that] really belonged to them, not even their
own experience," they turned their "final intimacies" into "official clichés." For Warshow and Fiedler, the failure of the Rosenbergs to "think of themselves as real people," their determination to externalize even their deaths, was the ultimate
"betrayal."[28]

Apparently, it did not occur to Warshow and Fiedler that they
too had translated the Rosenbergs into an object lesson. They
wished, of course, to use the case to make a different point: that
a person's privacy should not be violated to serve a social cause,
that the quality of one's life and thought offered a better hope of
salvation than all the belief systems devised by reformers and
revolutionaries. But the Rosenbergs seemed no more human in
these essays than in their prison letters to one another. After their
execution, they remained cartoon figures, all-purpose illustra-
tions for whatever message anyone wanted to send.

Many intellectuals found the Hiss and Rosenberg cases rich in
symbolism because of the public posture adopted by the defendants, because of their unwillingness to clear up the mystery of

what they had done or why, and because they consistently rejected the allegation that they were either Communists or agents
of the Soviet Union. Consequently, it appeared that all the participants could best be understood not as individuals ensnared in
a legal or historical predicament, but as characters in a novel or
play. In the end, the themes of guilt and innocence, social roles
and private authenticity, ideological commitment and moral ac-
countability inspired in writers an analysis that owed more to art
than to politics.

No one saw any such metaphorical overtones in the government's prosecution of the Communist party leaders in the late
1940s and early 1950s. Here, the defendants were neither myste-
rious nor silent about their political ties (though they did contest
the justice department's portrait of them as dangerous revolutionaries). The principal question was not ethical but constitutional: Could the state deprive Communists of the protections
afforded by the First Amendment?

The Smith Act, originally passed in 1940, made it illegal for
anyone to advocate or teach the overthrow of the government by
force or violence. In July 1948, a federal grand jury in New York
indicted twelve members of the Party's national board, not for
any concrete acts of espionage, but for conspiring after April
1945 to organize a group (the reconstituted Communist party of
the United States) that advocated the violent overthrow of the
American government, and that actually taught this doctrine in
its books, journals, schools, and meetings. The justice department contended that all of these activities were violations of the
Smith Act.

In October 1949, after a trial lasting nine months, the Communists were convicted and sentenced to prison terms of from three
to five years. Throughout the proceedings, the Party leaders
denied that they intended to forcibly dismantle the government;
rather, they said they hoped eventually to bring socialism to
America through peaceful means. Nevertheless, the Supreme
Court upheld their convictions in 1951 on the grounds that the
First Amendment's guarantees of freedom of speech and political
assembly could not extend to conspirators or foreign agents
seeking the violent destruction of the American constitutional

system, especially when the tensions of the Cold War increased the probability of domestic subversion. With the Court's decision, membership in the Communist party was virtually forbidden since to be a Communist now automatically implied one's participation in a conspiratorial movement whose ideology encouraged people to engage in sabotage and violence against the state. In effect, the Court provided the legal foundations for what most intellectuals and ordinary citizens already presumed.

As the justice department brought lower-echelon officials to trial in the early 1950s, the average functionary drifted away or vanished "underground." By 1957, the number of Party members in America had shrunk to 10,000. Perhaps only J. Edgar Hoover knew how many of these were really Bolshevik plotters, and how many were FBI informants still making the country safe for democracy.[29]

From 1948 on, the arrests and prosecutions of Communists under the Smith Act forced writers to clarify their ideas about what was permissible radical behavior in the United States. The loyalty program, and the cases of Alger Hiss and the Rosenbergs, focused only on the existence of subversives in government and in secret military projects. The issue in these instances was whether particular people in "sensitive" positions could be trusted with classified information, and whether those accused of spying for the Soviet Union were in fact guilty as charged. But the Smith Act trials introduced the broader notion that Communists should be excluded from all areas of American political life, not because of their specific deeds but because of their general beliefs. The extent to which intellectuals embraced this concept indicated how deeply they had been affected by the Cold War, and how susceptible they were to the premises of McCarthyism.

Some observers criticized the legal ramifications of the Smith Act prosecutions. Roger Baldwin, the long-time director of the American Civil Liberties Union, argued that the Communist party was not a secret cabal, nor had the government cited any examples of overt criminal activity. The justice department rested its case solely on the Party's speeches and books. "No language, publication or propaganda should be punished," Baldwin submitted, "unless it constitutes . . . a clear and present danger of unlawful acts." Unable to demonstrate that the Communists were explicitly exhorting their followers to use force, the government was trying to prohibit certain unpleasant "utterances . . . dealing with public questions." But Baldwin was prepared to tolerate the suppression of the Party if the prosecution could show some direct and immediate connection between Communist rhetoric and a genuinely threatening assault on the state.[30] Like those who did not want to judge Hiss or the Rosenbergs until they had all the facts, Baldwin objected not so much to the assumptions behind the Smith Act trials, as to the government's current lack of evidence to prove its case.

The *New Republic* opposed the prosecutions for more pragmatic reasons. It was an "unwise public policy" to ban the Communists merely for espousing their philosophy, the editors cautioned. A "political trial" conducted in such an atmosphere of "hysteria" could become grist for the propaganda mill of the enemy. The Communists, the journal predicted, "will be delighted to be made martyrs," while America would seem increasingly similar to the Soviet Union in the eyes of the rest of the world.[31] Thus the *New Republic* urged that Communists be tolerated not on principle but in order for America to score a tactical advantage in the Cold War.

It was left to Mary McCarthy to point out the ironic change that had taken place in American attitudes toward freedom during the past thirty years. In the 1920s, she recollected, censorship meant that "a book was prosecuted in court while the author remained relatively undisturbed." Now ideas were allowed to circulate in bookstores, libraries, newspapers, and magazines, but "the individual holding them may be jailed."[32] Whether or not this represented an advance for the cause of liberty, she didn't say.

Most commentators, however, had little sympathy for the image of Communists as victims of censorship. If anything, they berated the Party officials for repudiating their insurrectionary heritage when faced with imprisonment. Murray Kempton complained that the Communists on trial disguised themselves as democrats; they belonged to the "only political party in our history with a great body of members consistently embarrassed to admit their allegiance."[33] It was bad enough that Hiss and the

Rosenbergs refused to confess, Leslie Fiedler mused, but one might at least have expected the "avowed and open leaders of the movement . . . to cry out their faith proudly before the tribunal" instead of pleading "in the teeth of the evidence of their own early writings that they had never advocated revolution."[34]

Mary McCarthy granted that in the present circumstances Communists could hardly express their convictions publicly without risking further harassments from the state. Yet she too felt that a man should "acknowledge kinship with his own ideas and deeds, even those that are now unpopular." The Communists, it turned out, accepted the new ground rules of repression. They "would rather go to jail than proclaim" their beliefs, she noted, where in the past "a liberal or social revolutionary would rather go to jail than *not* proclaim" what he stood for.[35]

These attacks on the deceptions of the Smith Act defendants overlooked the differences between the mood of an earlier era, one less inclined to link rebellion with conspiracies engineered by foreign powers, and the Cold War dictum that Communism was not a radical program or movement but an instrument of Soviet imperialism. Previous political outcasts—anarchists, pacifists, socialists, Wobblies, opponents of World War I—could normally count on the support of more than a few liberals, intellectuals, artists, labor leaders, academics, lawyers, journalists, and students. After 1948, the Communists were almost completely isolated from these constituencies. No one marched for them as they and others had once marched to liberate Tom Mooney, Sacco and Vanzetti, the Scottsboro boys. If the Party spokesmen did not follow the example of Max Eastman, militantly and eloquently justifying their fidelity to socialism as he had done at the *Masses* trial in 1918, this may have been in part because their only audience was the jury and the judge.

In fact, a number of writers devoted more energy to defending the position of the state than to upholding the freedom or rights of those in the dock. Like Karl Marx but with a different purpose in mind, Diana Trilling dismissed the artificial distinctions between theory and practice. "Ideas are not to be separated from the acts to which they might lead," she asserted. Whether or not an ideology actually led to specific actions was in her opinion "irrelevant." Because what the Party leaders said could and often did influence the behavior of their followers, "the Communist idea must be judged as a Communist act." She therefore suggested that, since the Communists sought both to articulate the ideas of totalitarianism and to take power through conspiracy and subversion, liberals should not only endorse the prosecution of the Party chieftains but also question their "right to hold office in a democracy."[36] This view, in its most extreme form, carried the implication that Communists should not be allowed to either publicize their philosophy or engage in political activity. Though Trilling stopped short of such a conclusion, her analysis indicated how diminished were the conceptions of freedom among those intellectuals who spoke most fervently in its name.

Sidney Hook had fewer qualms about curtailing the liberties of Communists. He admitted that the Smith Act dealt not primarily with "overt actions" but with advocacy, incitement, speech, writing, thoughts. Nevertheless, the crucial issue for Hook, as for Diana Trilling, was the way in which the Communists' beliefs necessarily shaped their political conduct. That American Communists represented a "clear, present, flourishing, and extremely powerful" menace to the country's "national survival" seemed to him "undeniable." They were dangerous not because of their ideas, their numbers, or their political strength (none of which was very impressive), but because of their "organizational ties" to the Kremlin. They served "literally" as a "paramilitary fifth column" of the "Red Army"; they were composed of "some tens of thousands of disciplined conspirators, absolutely controlled by a declared enemy" that already dominated the "human and natural resources of one-third of the globe"; they were "obligated to strike whenever their foreign masters give the word." The aim of the Smith Act was to "paralyze" the domestic allies of Moscow before they could come close to achieving their goals. The Smith Act did not restrict the constitutional principles of free speech and political assembly, Hook insisted; merely the doctrines and activities of those who functioned as incipient quislings of a foreign power.[37]

Hook then issued a warning to anyone who still doubted the wisdom of such legislation. To repeal the Smith Act at this perilous juncture in the Cold War "would give new life" to the "illusion" that the Communists were a "political party like any other on the American scene and therefore entitled to the same rights and privileges as all other American political parties."[38] Only the most naïve soul could subscribe any longer to that archaic proposition.

Hook's arguments in favor of the Smith Act differed in detail from those of other intellectuals, just as they in turn had disagreed among themselves about the precise reasons for supporting Truman's loyalty program, or about the disparate meanings to be found in the trials and convictions of Alger Hiss and the Rosenbergs. But despite their varying reservations about specific policies or episodes, writers like Hook, Arthur Schlesinger, Diana Trilling, Robert Bendiner, Richard Rovere, Murray Kempton, Leslie Fiedler, Robert Warshow, and Philip Rahv all contributed to the forging of a common outlook on the problem of domestic subversion. Together they concurred on the continuing danger of traitors and spies in high places, the necessity of security checks and legislative restraints to safeguard democracy, the tendency of Communists on trial to dissemble and deceive, the definition of Communism itself as a foreign conspiracy, and the need for intellectuals to acknowledge their moral guilt and cast off their political innocence. These perceptions made it exceedingly difficult for them to battle against McCarthyism. Quite the contrary, it led some to sanction even more repressive measures in the early 1950s.

The Boundaries of Freedom

American intellectuals did not confine their discussion of McCarthyism solely to its most dramatic manifestations. The eruption of loyalty oaths, congressional inquisitions, and spy trials provoked a more general debate among writers about whether they themselves ought to accept certain constraints on academic freedom and civil liberties in the interests of national security. The very existence of this controversy revealed how easy it was for intellectuals to internalize the assumptions of the Right even as they strove to moderate its worst abuses.

To those suspected or accused of subversion and disloyalty—
the partisans of Henry Wallace, labor leaders identified as Communist sympathizers, past or present members of organizations
on the attorney general's list, supporters of Alger Hiss and the
Rosenbergs, violators of the Smith Act, teachers and entertainers
under investigation for their political ideas and activities—the
postwar red scare seemed a sinister omen of America's susceptibility to fascism. These anxieties reverberated in the fiction of the
period as well. Robert Penn Warren's *All the King's Men* offered
its readers the prototype of a fascist demagogue in Willy Stark,
while Norman Mailer and James Jones interrupted their narra-
tives in *The Naked and the Dead* and *From Here to Eternity* for ponderous speculations about the possibility of right-wing army
officers seizing on the anti-Communist crusade to transform their
own hunger for order and discipline into a bid for national
power. In the meantime many Europeans, watching the trial of
Alger Hiss, the execution of the Rosenbergs, and the havoc
wrought by Joseph McCarthy, seemed convinced that fascism had
migrated to the New World.

In reply, several writers took pains to point out that McCarthy
was not a replica of Hitler, and that the HUAC investigations of
Hollywood—however humiliating to the informers and injurious
to the victims—were not quite the same as setting up the concentration camps. Robert Bendiner, for example, did not wish to
minimize the "inroads being made by the McCarthys on the
constitutional liberties of Americans." But he rejected the insinu-
ation that the United States was in the "grip of panic," that "no
man dares speak his mind," or that liberals had "surrendered to
the forces of militarism and repression." In his view, the suggestion that "dissenting opinion" had been silenced, that "Americans look over their shoulders when they talk," that political
conversation went on "only behind closed doors," and that "a
whole apparatus of informers, secret police, and terrorism [had]
been imposed on the country" was to "conjure up a picture so
far from reality that it either constitutes willful deception or borders on the psychopathic." And even if one could find an element
of truth in this nightmarish vision, the fault lay not with America
but with Russia. McCarthyism was to Bendiner an ugly reflection

of the "very real fears" that had been "forced upon" Americans by Soviet aggression.[39] Europeans should therefore blame the red scare on the Reds.

Furthermore, writers described the style of repression in America as qualitatively different from the totalitarian brand. "A democracy moves slowly and reluctantly towards the abridgment of personal rights," Sidney Hook assured the readers of *Commentary,* and then only in response to a "genuine crisis." Regimes like those of Stalin and Hitler, in contrast, turned "immediately, brutally, and arbitrarily towards suppression."[40] Nor was this merely a matter of how quickly or in what context a government reduced the liberties of its citizens. Despite the "apparent parallelisms" between the tactics of a police state and "certain anti-Communist practices and policies in America," Paul Kecskemeti observed, totalitarians "outlawed and banished" entire social or racial groups. Democrats, motivated strictly by "self-defense," directed their intolerance only against a particular political party or subversive organization.[41] Thus there were no real grounds for anyone to equate McCarthyism with its Communist adversary.

Still, a number of writers were troubled by the evident similarities between McCarthyites and Stalinists. Robert Bendiner, like Diana Trilling, felt that liberal intellectuals had an obligation to "fight the enemies of liberty on both the right and the left," to oppose the Communists "no matter how much aid and comfort that might give the McCarthys," while simultaneously "combating the McCarthys themselves [in] their crass attempts to exploit" anti-Communism "for their own political purposes."[42] In theory, this was an admirable stance. In actuality, and on specific issues, many found such a balance impossible to sustain, largely because they continued to despise the Left more than they feared the Right.

Ironically, the severest test of the intellectuals' capacity to withstand the onslaught of McCarthyism occurred on their own turf. Confronted with the question of whether Communists or fellow travelers should be allowed to teach in America's universities and public schools, few performed with distinction.

The efforts to redraw the boundaries of academic freedom in the late 1940s and early 1950s might not have exactly resembled a reign of terror, but the effects were chilling enough. By 1949, as David Caute has shown, twenty-two states required their teachers to sign loyalty oaths as a condition of employment, twenty-one forbade "seditious" classroom instruction, and thirty-one considered membership in subversive organizations as defined by the justice department a sufficient cause for dismissal. New York adopted the Feinberg Law, which ordered principals to file reports on the loyalty of their teachers and clerical staff with the superintendent of schools; the principals themselves were to be "cleared" by assistant superintendents. Twenty-eight public and private colleges in California, including Stanford and Berkeley, agreed to install security officers (usually former FBI agents) who compiled information on the political beliefs and affiliations of professors for use by state officials engaged in purging education of all un-American (or at least un-Californian) impulses. Meanwhile, both HUAC and the Senate Internal Security Subcommittee conducted their own investigations of various university faculties in 1952 and 1953.[43]

Just as the Hollywood studios and professional guilds withdrew their support from those in the film industry who fell under suspicion, leaving each individual to save his career as best he could, so the institutions and authority figures of the academic world tended to desert the teacher who declined to cooperate with a congressional committee, a state agency, or the FBI. The American Association of University Professors did officially oppose the idea that teachers should be automatically fired if they pleaded the Fifth Amendment. But the Association of American Universities (which represented the administrators of thirty-seven major colleges), many university presidents and governing boards, and the American Federation of Teachers announced in differing ways that they would not defend a person's right to teach or remain employed if he was a member of the Communist party or refused to testify about his political allegiances.[44]

Caute has calculated that as a consequence of these laws, loyalty oaths, and institutional pressures, more than six hundred public school teachers and professors lost their jobs. Three hundred eighty were either fired or forced to resign in New York City alone. But the victims could be found everywhere: at Harvard, where President Nathan Pusey and Dean of Arts and Sciences McGeorge Bundy publicly resisted McCarthy's attempts to inspect the university's personnel files while privately threatening untenured instructors with termination if they did not supply information to the FBI about their own political pasts and the names of those with whom they had once associated; at MIT, where Dirk Struik, a mathematician and coeditor of the Marxist journal *Science and Society,* was suspended from teaching for five years (though he continued to receive his full salary) while he remained under a state indictment for conspiring to advocate and incite the violent overthrow of both the Commonwealth of Massachusetts and the federal government; at Columbia, NYU, Rutgers, Ohio State, the University of Vermont, Temple, Boston University, Michigan, and Fisk, where administrators ousted professors who invoked the Fifth Amendment before HUAC or the Senate Internal Security Subcommittee; at the universities of Washington and Colorado, each of which discharged teachers who had been identified as present or former members of the Communist party by state investigating committees or FBI agents; throughout the University of California system, where the Board of Regents imposed a loyalty oath on the faculty in 1949 that resulted by 1951 in the dismissal of twenty-six professors who refused to sign the affidavit, thirty-seven additional resignations in protest, forty-seven instances in which scholars at other institutions turned down offers of appointment in California and elected to remain where they were, and the elimination of fifty-five courses from the university's curriculum.[45] In the aftermath of this carnage, one could never know how many teachers chose to temper their political and intellectual enthusiasms, to protect their careers by refraining from controversial statements and activities both in and out of school.

Administrators and trustees were not the only representatives of the educational establishment who shared with congressional committees and state governments the belief that Communists and suspected fellow travelers should be barred from classrooms. A number of prominent professors and free-lance intellectuals contended that Communists had no place in America's schools. Although they regarded themselves as guardians of academic freedom, their arguments helped justify precisely the restrictive policies they said they most abhorred. In the end they contributed, however unintentionally, to the further isolation of those teachers already under attack for their political convictions —which in turn meant that the ability of the nation's public schools and universities to maintain their independence from social and ideological pressures grew even weaker.

The intellectuals' rationale for expelling Communists from academic positions took several forms. Arthur Schlesinger and Richard Rovere assumed that addicts of the Party line were by definition dishonest and shallow. "A genuinely Communistic textbook would be unacceptable for its distortions of fact," Schlesinger asserted, and a Communist professor who "imported" his dogmas into the classroom "would be an incompetent teacher." Rovere found it "very hard to conceive of a Communist writing a good book," though he still had a right to teach until he proved his ineptitude, as in the natural course of time he must.[46]

As always, Sidney Hook was less concerned with what Communists wrote or thought than with their subservience to a world movement bent on sabotaging the true aims of education. "It is not because of his *ideas* that a Communist party member is unfit to teach," Hook submitted, "but because of his *professional misconduct* in joining a conspiratorial organization, one of whose declared purposes is corruption of the teaching process for political purposes."[47] To Hook, Norman Thomas (the veteran Socialist party leader), and Paul Hays (an activist in New York's Liberal party and professor of law at Columbia), a commitment to Communism necessarily forced a teacher to abandon what Thomas called the "quest for truth." Unlike social democrats, liberals, and conservatives, all of whom were presumably nonpartisan and unbiased in their classroom presentations, the Communist instructor in Hook's opinion was "not free" to pursue ideas wherever they led. Nor could he adhere to the "scientific method of inquiry" or "verify evidence" and reach conclusions objectively. Instead, by his continuing membership in the Party, he "signified his willingness to teach *according to directives received*" from the Kremlin. In addition, he was "under instruction" at all times to "build cells" and "capture departments" on his particular campus. In short, Hook and Hays insisted, Communist professors were compelled to subordinate their "intellectual integrity" to the goal of "bringing about the destruction of the United States and the success of the Soviet Union."[48]

Yet for Hook the principal menace to American education was not the faithful Party member but the professorial fellow travelers—that "little army of 'progressive' intellectuals" who "invariably" lent their names and prestige to front groups, who always championed Russian foreign policy and defended their Communist colleagues "against even the mildest and most justified of administrative measures." Hook conceded the fellow traveler's right to remain in the academic community, but he implored the rest of the faculty on any given campus to combat the influence of these "ideological 'typhus Marys' " at every opportunity. A teacher who persistently apologized for Soviet brutality, who refused to "protest outrages against civil liberties" in Russia and eastern Europe while complaining about repression in America, "should be exposed as a political hypocrite" and "have his credentials to competent scholarship openly questioned by his peers." At the same time, Hook urged that courses on the "theory and practice of official Communism" be required at all colleges. If these were taught "properly" (i.e., by non-fellow-traveling professors), students would learn that the "communist parties in all countries" functioned exclusively as "tools of the Soviet regime." Such instruction could thereby make undergraduates less vulnerable to indoctrination by Stalin's agents in the schools.[49]

Behind the campaign to discredit fellow travelers lay the fear that if universities did not cleanse themselves of Communist sympathizers, more primitive forces would surely intervene. Hook, Alan Westin, and Robert Bendiner all opposed the intrusion of congressional committees, boards of regents, and administrators into educational affairs. But they did so on the grounds that academic freedom could best be safeguarded by teachers willing to undertake their own investigations of a colleague's political ideas and associations. Westin recommended that faculty committees be given the responsibility to examine the career and evaluate the testimony of any professor who took the Fifth Amendment. They could hold hearings in which the offending instructor was offered a chance to explain his reasons for declining to answer questions, and to "clarify his present status as regards Communist Party membership." Then his peers could decide whether he should be retained or dismissed. Otherwise, an "angry Congress" or an unstable demagogue "aware of the public's dissatisfaction with the counsels of inaction" might deprive universities of the power to set their own criteria for whom they could hire and fire.[50]

These proposals were clearly designed to ward off a right-wing witch hunt in the public schools and colleges, and to allow teachers to exercise as much control as possible over their own domain. Yet the preservation of a university's autonomy seemed to depend on its readiness to sacrifice the substance (though not the rituals) of academic freedom. Essentially, writers like Schlesinger, Rovere, Hook, Hays, Westin, and Bendiner were suggesting that faculties themselves should do the dirty work of the administrators, the trustees, and the government—even if this meant investigating and punishing suspicious colleagues before outsiders got around to it. But what was the point of having teachers determine the limits of permissible academic behavior if their mission was mostly to anticipate and carry out the wishes of the university bureaucracy and the larger society? The alternatives Westin and others favored made the "democratic" professor as much the servant of a political creed as his Communist rival. Neither would be free to challenge the tactics, programs, or values of their respective superiors, whether these were deans or commissars.

It was difficult in any case to resist external pressures when one agreed with the Right that pro-Communist sentiments had to be eliminated from the nation's campuses. Many intellectuals and academics were not trying to sound merely pragmatic when they advised universities to police themselves. They genuinely believed that any teacher who joined the Communist party must accept its dictates, that he had to obey its orders to infiltrate the faculty and seduce his students with propaganda, that his political obligations were incompatible with a commitment to free

thought and open discussion. Few asked whether Party membership really did convert the teacher into a mouthpiece for Soviet
ideology, or make him a disciplined functionary in the Stalinist
apparatus. The intellectuals' ability and desire to defy the
McCarthyite invasion of the classroom was thus undermined by
their acceptance of its general outlook and objectives. The majority of writers promised only to be fairer and more judicious in
achieving the same results.

Not everyone thought the defense of academic freedom required an accommodation to the prevailing political climate in
America. The historian Henry Steele Commager considered the
crusade against Communists in the schools both a tactical mistake and a betrayal of intellectual principles. Writing in the *New
Republic* in 1949, he contended that the imposition of loyalty
oaths on teachers and the threat of automatic dismissal for Party
membership would simply put a "premium on concealment,"
thereby forcing not only Communists but others with a radical
past to disguise their allegiances as the price of professional
survival. Besides, Commager saw no hard evidence that Communists inevitably engaged in "bad teaching" and "worthless scholarship," or "actually did harm to students" and to "scientific
truth." Indeed, the prophecy that a Communist would "fatally
mislead" innocent undergraduates was "based on the quite
unexplored assumption that college students are such nincom-
poops that they are unable to distinguish between truth and
falsehood, between impartial teaching and propaganda, and on
the further misconception that they invariably believe all that
their teachers tell them."[51] Hence for Commager the Communists presented no real peril to unformed young minds, particularly since those minds were far more skeptical about (or indifferent to) all political doctrines than their overly protective mentors
cared to admit.

But Commager was apprehensive about the consequences for
democracy and intellectual life if Americans insisted on "tracking down and driving out a few 'subversives' in colleges and
universities." Would professors, he asked, feel "free in the future . . . to explore dangerous ideas, to embark upon original
research, to associate with non-conformists? Will students be as

free . . . to discuss whatever interests them, to join whatever organizations appeal to them, to test their intellectual muscles on controversial issues?" These were all prescient questions at the dawn of the 1950s. "Surely," Commager observed optimistically, "those who are confident of the superiority of their own way of life should not fear competition, in the realm of ideas, from other systems or philosophies."[52] Yet if the campuses became as torpid as critics later in the decade claimed, if students and professors alike preferred discretion to discord, this may have been in part because both the university and society were more inclined to surrender to McCarthyism than to welcome the political and intellectual competition Commager took for granted.

By 1952, Mary McCarthy was less sanguine than Commager about America's tolerance for cultural diversity and academic freedom. "The student today," she charged, "far from being in danger of [indoctrination] by Communism, is in danger of being stupified by the complacent propaganda for democracy." She especially disliked the "pious, priggish, groupy" tone in which democratic traditions were self-righteously reaffirmed. But she objected even more to what these homilies revealed about the current state of mind in the United States. The "fear and hatred of Communism," she felt, did not reflect "just a revulsion from the crimes of Stalin." It also represented a wealthy country's tenacious hostility to the "original ideals of Communism" and revolution. Americans were exhibiting "the psychology of rich people"; they were "afraid of poverty, of 'agitators,' of any jarring notes in the national harmony." Beneath the affluent façade there lurked a "guilty fear of criticism," a "sense of being surrounded by an unappreciative world," which in turn led to intensified demands for the "loyalty" of every citizen.[53]

Given this unease, McCarthy went on, adult Americans had good reason to be sensitive about their schools. They worried that their children, having a "natural lack of bias" and a "detached and innocent faculty of observation," would all too quickly "prick up their ears if they hear our society criticized." Pupils might listen more closely to a teacher than to a parent because "they have already noticed the injustices of our society and want to know the why of it." This was not the sort of education society expected or desired, but then, as McCarthy pointed out, "people with bad consciences always fear the judgment of children."[54]

Thus the typical American, McCarthy argued, yearned to inoculate students against the "contagion" of Communist ideas because he suspected that Marxism had a "more evident correspondence with the realities of social inequity" than did his own democratic ideals. In her estimation, the crusaders against subversion and fellow traveling were secretly terrified that Communist ideas "may be catching," that they contained "a 'germ' of truth." This "phobia" would linger, she predicted, "as long as we . . . try to sell the white lie of democracy abroad, to the starving nations who in fact are the 'children'—the ignorant and uneducated—whose allegiance we question, rightly, and whose judgment of us we, rightly, dread."[55]

Neither Henry Steele Commager nor Mary McCarthy were advocating that liberals suspend their opposition to the Soviet Union. But their refusal to ratify the purge of Communist teachers, their old-fashioned conviction that a public school or university ought to function as an open and independent marketplace of competing ideas, was refreshing at a time when most Americans (including too many intellectuals) seemed more interested in making sure the academic world was patriotic rather than free.

The controversy over whether Communists and fellow travelers should keep their teaching posts underscored the larger issue of when and how much a democracy should abridge the civil liberties of its own citizens as well as those of its ideological foes. This was an especially painful dilemma for the liberal intellectual who liked to think of himself as the preeminent custodian of freedom in an era of dictators on the left and demagogues on the right. His task, therefore, was not just to redefine the rights of teachers, but to reassess the conditions under which everyone's liberty might survive.

The liberal's predicament was additionally complicated because he himself had enemies in Washington. As Diana Trilling and Robert Bendiner realized, the liberal cause would not be served if in fighting Stalinism one was trampled by McCarthyism.

Yet it was hard for some writers in the 1950s to elude this danger since, however ardently they had repudiated their past ties to the Left, they continued to feel vulnerable to recriminations from the Right.

A few tried to demonstrate their contrition by reluctantly admitting that the yahoos in Congress weren't all fools. Leslie Fiedler rebuked liberals for their intellectual arrogance in supposing they were immune to "political error," when in fact they had been "wrong, drastically wrong" about Communism. Accordingly, Fiedler was prepared to accept the "unpalatable truth" that the "buffoons and bullies, those who *knew* really nothing about the Soviet Union at all, were right—stupidly right, . . . accidentally right, right for the wrong reasons, but damnably right." The liberals had handed McCarthy and his entourage a moral victory they could not "fritter away" no matter how many future blunders they made or "downright lies" they told.[56]

Irving Kristol, somewhat less grudgingly, concurred. In what has become an almost legendary screed, Kristol informed the readers of *Commentary* in 1952 that liberal intellectuals and politicians deserved the suspicion of their countrymen. "For there is one thing that the American people know about Senator McCarthy," Kristol declared: "he, like them, is unequivocally anti-Communist. About the spokesmen for American liberalism, they feel they know no such thing. *And with some justification.*" The reason liberals merited distrust, Kristol explained, was because "a generation of earnest reformers who helped give this country a New Deal" also permitted themselves to be "stained with the guilt of having lent aid and comfort to Stalinist tyranny." Like Fiedler, Kristol had discovered a "truth" that "might as well be owned up to." And if liberals were not willing "to discriminate between [their] achievements and [their] sins," he warned, they would never be able to battle McCarthyism.[57]

Since the Right could happily endorse Kristol's appraisal of the New Deal's derelictions, one wondered what was left for contemporary liberals to fight with McCarthy about. For his part, Kristol replied that liberals might protect their values from right-wing hooligans only if they discarded the notion that the freedom of Communists must also be upheld. Should a liberal wish to sup-

port the civil liberties of Stalinists and fellow travelers, he had
first to show that he was entering "the court of American opinion
with clean hands and a clear mind." He needed to "bluntly acknowledge" that Communists threatened the "consensus on
which civil society and its liberties are based" before he could
suggest that it was tactically prudent in "particular circumstances" to let subversives continue to speak.[58]

The docility with which Fiedler and Kristol assented to the
allegations of the Right, not to mention their unerring instinct for
the inflammatory phrase, outraged even those intellectuals who
felt a similar repugnance toward Communism. Richard Rovere
criticized Kristol for adopting a "double standard": He blithely
ignored the vicious effects of McCarthy's "demagogy" while
chastizing New Dealers for having overlooked the evidence of
Stalin's iniquities. Furthermore, Rovere did not believe a person
had to become politically immaculate in the eyes of reactionaries
before he could defend the ideals of democracy. Liberals seemed
to him perfectly capable of grappling with Communism without
the assistance or blessings of the McCarthyites.[59]

Alan Westin was more disturbed by Kristol's meager rationale
for granting civil liberties to the Communists and their sympathizers. Westin wanted to base his defense of liberalism on
broader grounds than those of pragmatism and expediency. In
his view, any effort to deprive the Communists of their constitutional rights could lead to a "loss of liberty" for every citizen who
might need the same protections at some future date.[60] Thus the
maintenance of freedom should be a matter of principle, not just
a wise policy in certain situations.

Yet Westin's other reasons for safeguarding civil liberties were
as practical as Kristol's. America ought to refrain from witch
hunts, he believed, because "we want to keep our science devel-
oping at maximum efficiency, our foreign service ably staffed and
advised, and our universities free of the tensions of an oath
campaign." But above all, one had to take into account the ever
present international conflict, the potential damage to America's
global posture if other countries perceived the United States as
blindly repressive. For Westin, the "civil libertarian's position"
ultimately rested on the recognition that the nation must sustain

its "moral leadership in the world as the arsenal of freedom."[61] Paradoxically, Westin was arguing that the demands of the Cold War provided the best incentive for preserving liberty at home —though the Right had come to exactly the opposite conclusion.

The trouble with Westin's position was that it too linked the protection of constitutional rights to an evaluation of current political crises. Rational men could therefore disagree about when some movement represented a "clear and present danger" in a particular time and place. Westin, Rovere, and even Kristol happened to feel that America could still afford to be relatively tolerant toward the Communists in its midst. But others, analyzing the tensions of the Cold War differently, might just as easily decide that Trotskyists, social democrats, and liberals excessively concerned with peace or overly cordial to revolutions in other parts of the world, constituted an imminent peril to the internal security of the United States. Then the dispute would be resolved solely on the basis of who held power in Washington—which in the 1950s hardly promised an outcome pleasing to liberal intellectuals.

Moreover, the discussion of academic freedom and civil liberties was continually cast in negative terms. Most writers quarreled about whether and to what extent the rights of certain citizens *should be curbed,* not about how constitutional guarantees could be strengthened and expanded. They rarely portrayed freedom as a positive virtue. Rather, it seemed to them at best a tentative concession—something society permitted but could always withdraw—and at worst a slogan to be used in the propaganda war between the United States and the Soviet Union.

Mary McCarthy was again one of the handful who tried to transcend this perspective, and at the same time to challenge the assumptions of her contemporaries. She suspected that the public as well as the nation's leading intellectuals regarded liberty as a "gift or trust bestowed on the individual by the state pending *good behavior.*" But if freedom appeared to be a mere privilege, a license (like the ones allowing people to drive, hunt, or carry firearms) that was "subject to all sorts of restrictions and limitations," then the government could at any moment revoke its use by groups it deemed unreliable, unpatriotic, or simply unnerving. "Once the state is looked upon as the *source* of rights, rather than their bound protector," she pointed out, "freedom becomes conditional on the pleasure of the state."[62]

Yet the deeper problem, in McCarthy's judgment, involved not privileges or rights but power. Those who found it possible to approve Truman's loyalty program, the Smith Act trials, and the exclusion of Communists from the academic or entertainment worlds usually proclaimed that "nobody has a right to perform on television or the radio, nobody has a right to a government job, nobody has a right to a passport, nobody has a right to teach in a public school, nobody has a right to conspire against the government." In the same breath, however, they supported the "right" of Hollywood producers, television executives, local boards of education, university presidents, the FBI, Congress, and the government to investigate an employee's political attachments and discharge whomever they chose. What these arguments really implied, she asserted, was that "nobody has the *power* to keep the government from denying a passport or to keep an employer from firing a Communist," while conversely no teacher or entertainer or civil servant "has . . . the power to retain his job."[63]

To rectify this imbalance, McCarthy proposed that civil liberties be construed not as an instrument of power or as a reward for respectable political conduct, but as a set of "inherent rights" to which the citizens of a democracy were naturally entitled. Further, she suggested that if Americans began to conceive of liberty "not only as a right but as a good, we would be more hesitant to deprive people of it than we are when we think of it as a privilege or license within the bestowal of the state." Finally, if people did accept the theory that freedom was a "primary, axiomatic good," they might also conclude that "the more [one] had of it, the better." Then "even in situations of danger" they could concentrate on "maximums rather than minimums," asking themselves "how much liberty our free society ought to extend, if it is to live up to its name, rather than how much liberty was owing to this or that individual."[64]

In 1952, neither the country nor the majority of its intellectuals were prepared to consider, much less act upon, Mary McCarthy's hypotheses. To most Americans, the defense of liberty required more than ever a firm opposition to Communism abroad and an increased vigilance against potential subversives at home. Given the tenets of the Cold War, it was hard for anyone to embrace the idea that a citizen had an intrinsic right to pursue his career whatever his political beliefs or affiliations, that indeed the entire society might be stronger and safer if it thought more about how to broaden the boundaries of freedom for everyone than about how to restrain the influence of its reputed enemies. Unfortunately, the national inability to grasp just such notions left the way open for an unprecedented assault on the liberties and livelihoods of countless individuals—an assault from which the intellectuals themselves were by no means exempt.

Rites of Passage

Almost every writer at one point or another had misgivings about particular aspects of the loyalty program, the wisdom of the Smith Act prosecutions, the methods used to bar Communists from the nation's classrooms, and the political and legal implications of restricting civil liberties. But no matter what stand they took on these issues, they agreed that Communism could no longer be considered a "radical" doctrine, that the Party had no legitimate role to play on the American left, and that individual Communists were not dissenters or nonconformists or even revolutionaries but only participants in an organized conspiracy to cripple democratic institutions. The traumas of the Cold War, the analyses of totalitarianism, the evidence of Stalin's crimes which had been accumulating since the late 1930s, and the disclosure of espionage rings in the Hiss and Rosenberg cases all seemed to corroborate the view that the American Communist party was nothing more than a tightly disciplined and treacherous clique dedicated to carrying out Moscow's commands. Many intellectuals therefore limited themselves to the question of which policy would cause the United States more harm: permitting Communists to exercise their constitutional rights regardless of the possible risks to national security, or driving them from public life despite the chance that this might endanger the civil liberties of everyone else as well.

Yet the intellectuals' assumptions about the nature of American Communism were always dubious. Had the typical Party member or sympathizer really spent his time conspiring to overthrow the government, passing classified documents to Soviet agents, indoctrinating students, and serving as a propagandist for totalitarianism? Or did he join the Party or become a fellow traveler because he believed in socialism and wanted to support the labor movement, aid the Spanish Loyalists, defeat the Nazis, avert a nuclear holocaust? He may well have been naïve, but should he now be held personally accountable because the Soviet Union had tarnished his dreams? Must he betray the ideals of his past to hold on to his present job? Leaving history, politics, the Cold War, and legal controversies aside, at what point was it necessary—as a matter of elementary honor and self-respect—for the individual to resist the efforts of the state or his employer to examine his politics and force him to recant? When should one finally say I will not go along with this for no other reason than because it is wrong?

Eventually, most writers had to confront these questions because they were central to the hearings and investigations of the McCarthy era. The answers they gave could not be purely philosophical. The average defendants in the political inquisitions of the postwar years were not elite government officials accused of perjury, or obscure functionaries accused of espionage, or veteran Communist leaders accused of advocating violence against the state. Instead, they were professors, screenwriters, film directors, actors and actresses, clerics, scientists, journalists—and they were being asked not to confess to a crime but to repudiate their youthful commitments and reveal the names of their former associates.

Hence an observer had to decide not only what he thought about the morality of these inquiries, but how he would act if he himself were called to testify. For many intellectuals—whether they simply wrote about the on-going interrogations of their fellow writers, artists, and teachers, or found themselves momentarily on trial—the experience came as a rite of passage, a test of one's character as much as a defense of one's public principles.

Despite the notoriety Joseph McCarthy acquired when he embarked on his rampages in 1950, the House Un-American Activities Committee actually developed and perfected the techniques of intimidation. HUAC remained the principal source of Cold War hysteria from the late 1940s to the mid-1950s; it could claim credit not only for exposing Alger Hiss, but also for launching and sustaining the probes of government agencies, the universities and public schools, the churches, and the entertainment world. Perhaps its most distinctive contribution was to provide the forum in which an individual could choose either to absolve himself of all radical heresies and thereby resume his career, or suffer banishment to an indefinite blacklist.

HUAC had been invented at the end of the 1930s, though it did not emerge as a major force in American political and cultural life until the early years of the Cold War. Its first and most illustrious victim was not Alger Hiss but Hollywood. Thereafter, the media remained HUAC's favorite quarry.

The hunt began in earnest in 1947 when HUAC issued subpoenas to nineteen members of Hollywood's radical community, each of whom was rumored to be a member of or have close ties to the Communist party. The ostensible purpose of the hearings, which opened on October 20, was to investigate subversion in the film industry, particularly the attempt by Communists to influence the content of America's movies.

The proceedings ended before eight of the nineteen testified. Those who were not called included four writers (Richard Collins, Gordon Kahn, Irving Pichel, and Waldo Salt), two directors (Lewis Milestone and Robert Rossen), one producer (Howard Koch), and one actor (Larry Parks).

The rest of what came to be known as the "Unfriendly Nineteen" took the stand. Ten invoked the First Amendment in refusing to answer any questions about their political pasts. They also tried to deliver statements denouncing HUAC's very existence and its right to hold such hearings, but the chairman usually had them dragged from the room before they finished while a member of the committee's staff read aloud the identification number on each of their Communist party cards. All ten were cited for contempt of Congress on the grounds that the First Amendment did not permit them to avoid responding when asked by a congressional committee if they now were or ever had been Communists. Of these, seven were writers (Alvah Bessie, Lester Cole,

Ring Lardner, Jr., John Howard Lawson, Albert Maltz, Samuel Ornitz, and Dalton Trumbo); two were directors (Herbert Biberman and Edward Dmytryk); and one was a writer-producer (Adrian Scott).

The eleventh and best-known witness really could be called "un-American" since he was the German playwright Bertolt Brecht. A refugee from Nazism temporarily living in Hollywood, Brecht parried the committee's questions, denied that he was a Communist, and (probably because he had no desire to watch the rise of yet another group of Brownshirts) promptly departed the United States for East Germany (where, unfortunately, a new set of Brownshirts was already in power).[65]

None of those who received subpoenas from HUAC considered themselves "intellectuals" in any precise sense, but they *were* artists and writers, and they had been charged with manipulating the opinions of the American people through the mass media. Thus other writers could not ignore the plight of the Hollywood Ten because similar accusations might some day be directed against them. The hearings raised questions about the relationship between culture and politics, as well as about what it meant to have been both an artist or an intellectual and a Communist.

Looking back on the HUAC investigations of 1947 from the perspective of the 1950s, Murray Kempton derided the radicalism of the Hollywood Ten in much the same way that Leslie Fiedler and Robert Warshow had satirized the style and tastes of the Rosenbergs. To Kempton, the Communists in movieland were harmless because they had no talent. Not even their worst enemies could prove "that they had left any permanent impress upon the screen." Far from injecting socialist ideas into their films, or forming independent production companies to make movies about current problems, they quickly adapted to the "cultural pattern" of the major studios and "fit easily into the demands of the B picture." The years they spent absorbing the habits of Hollywood had "reduced their prose to the muddier depths of a Nash-Kelvinator ad." Like the Rosenbergs, Kempton moralized, the Ten failed to be "true to themselves"; they were mostly guilty of "sitting up too long with their own press releases."[66]

Kempton's judgment was too harsh. Several of the original

nineteen had made some memorable films, and would create even better ones later on when given the chance. Ring Lardner, Jr., shared an Academy Award for the screenplay of *Woman of the Year* (1942) and, once off the blacklist, wrote the script for *M*A*S*H* (1969). Adrian Scott and Edward Dmytryk collaborated on *Crossfire* (1947). Howard Koch coauthored the screenplay for *Casablanca* (1942). Lewis Milestone had directed *All Quiet on the Western Front* (1930), *The Front Page* (1931), and *A Walk in the Sun* (1946). Robert Rossen directed *Body and Soul* (1947) and *All the King's Men* (1949), though his finest movie was to be *The Hustler* (1961). Waldo Salt returned to films with the screenplay for *Midnight Cowboy* (1968). Dalton Trumbo was the highest-paid scenarist in Hollywood until the HUAC hearings; he won an Academy Award under a pseudonym for *The Brave One* (1956), and became the first blacklisted writer to again receive credit when in 1960 his name appeared on the screen as the writer of *Exodus* and *Spartacus*. Bertolt Brecht's abilities were never in dispute.

But the question of whether any of these men had been genuinely radical artists or merely skilled technicians was irrelevant to their predicament in 1947. Most of the Hollywood Communists found themselves in trouble not because of the movies they worked on, but because of their political activities within and outside the film industry. They had helped organize the screenwriters', actors', and directors' guilds; they raised money for Spain and other causes; they wrote for the Communist press and recruited members for the Party; they participated in strikes against the studios in the mid-1940s; at the time of the hearings, they were lending their names and prestige to Henry Wallace's embryonic presidential campaign.[67]

These may have been left-wing enterprises, but they hardly seemed subversive. Nevertheless, the Hollywood Ten were now facing the prospect of losing their jobs because they had once been or presently were Communists. Whatever Kempton and other intellectuals might say about their artistic accomplishments or political commitments, this was presently the most important issue—not just for the Ten but for everyone who could be similarly stigmatized in the future.

This point became unmistakably clear on November 24, 1947

—the day Congress voted contempt citations against the Ten—when fifty studio executives met in New York's Waldorf-Astoria Hotel to plan their course of action. Under the imprimatur of the Association of Motion Picture Producers, they issued a statement claiming that the behavior of the Ten before HUAC constituted a "disservice to their employers" and "impaired their usefulness to the industry." Consequently, the producers pledged that they would "forthwith discharge or suspend without compensation" all of the Ten, and would not rehire any of them until each "purged himself of contempt" and, more importantly, declared "under oath that he is not a Communist." Then the executives added a warning for the rest of the Hollywood community: "We will not knowingly employ a Communist or a member of any party or group which advocates the overthrow of the Government of the United States by force or by illegal or unconstitutional methods." Acknowledging that such a policy could hurt "innocent people" and create an "atmosphere of fear," the producers invited the "Hollywood talent guilds to work with us to eliminate any subversives" and to exculpate those who had done nothing wrong.[68] With this manifesto, the rationale for the blacklist and the mechanisms for clearance were formally introduced into American life. Though in 1947 the studio chiefs were speaking only for Hollywood, their actions served as a model for the subsequent expulsion of Communists, fellow travelers, alleged subversives, radicals, and even liberals from other institutions as well.

Some observers instantly grasped the broader implications of these events for American culture. HUAC, one writer asserted in the *New Republic,* had deprived the Hollywood Ten of "their good names" while the producers were stripping them of "their livelihoods."[69] Robert Bendiner insisted that no congressional committee had the right to "question citizens publicly about their politics" solely in order to "bring about [their] dismissal from private employment."[70] Martha Gellhorn, who had survived the sectarian battles of the 1930s, the Spanish Civil War, and a term as Ernest Hemingway's wife, remarked sardonically that the current furor contained the hint of only "a little terror, calculated to frighten little people." But "it works"; under such pressure, "a man can be well and truly destroyed." Henceforth, she prophesied, someone "with a family will think many times before speaking his mind fearlessly and critically when there lies ahead the threat of an Un-Americans' investigation, a publicized branding, and his job gone." For if the state and its accomplices could extinguish the careers of the Hollywood Ten, "pretty soon you can ruin a painter and a teacher and a writer and a lawyer and an actor and a scientist; and presently you have made a silent place."[71]

In fact, the Ten lost more than their jobs. They were convicted of contempt of Congress and, after the courts rejected their appeals, they entered prison in 1950 with sentences ranging from six months to one year. Upon their release, all except Edward Dmytryk (who reappeared before HUAC to renounce his earlier position and identify those in Hollywood he knew to be Communists) were blacklisted, some for the rest of their lives.[72]

As Dalton Trumbo later pointed out, the Ten did not foresee when they took the stand in 1947 what might happen to them. They supposed that the courts would uphold their use of the First Amendment, with its provisions for free speech and political assembly, as a constitutional justification for refusing to answer questions. They also imagined that the studios would keep them employed. Now everyone in Hollywood realized that neither of these assumptions was valid. In the future, a person who received a HUAC subpoena had three equally unpleasant choices: He could invoke the First Amendment and challenge the committee's authority to inquire about his political ideas and associations, thereby risking a possible prison sentence for contempt of Congress; he could decline to testify about himself or others by claiming the Fifth Amendment's protection against self-incrimination, thereby avoiding jail but casting himself as uncooperative, probably guilty, and automatically unemployable; or he could submit to interrogation, give the committee the information it craved, accept its power to subject him to humiliation, and continue to work at his chosen profession.[73]

By 1951, when HUAC resumed its hearings on Hollywood, economic considerations had become a potent stimulus for the spread of the blacklist throughout the entertainment world. The profits of the film industry were steadily declining due to higher production and labor costs, the Supreme Court's ruling in 1948 that the studios must relinquish their ownership of theater chains (a monopoly which previously enabled Hollywood to count on a guaranteed flow of box office receipts), and the growing competition from television for the attentions of the mass audience. Meanwhile, self-appointed vigilantes appeared, threatening to organize boycotts against any studio that did not faithfully observe the blacklist, and against any advertiser who did not request the radio and television networks to remove from a program he sponsored all suspicious writers, directors, and performers. These guardians of national security included the American Legion and the Catholic War Veterans, the magazines *Red Channels* and *Counterattack*, and certain gossip columnists (especially Walter Winchell, Hedda Hopper, Westbrook Pegler, Victor Riesel, George Sokolsky, and Jack O'Brian). Their joint mission was to publicize the names of "subversives" still at work in the media, so that they could be ejected more easily. Among those *Red Channels* designated as dangerous were Lillian Hellman, Arthur Miller, Dorothy Parker, Irwin Shaw, William L. Shirer, Louis Untermeyer, Leonard Bernstein, Aaron Copland, Orson Welles, Fredric March, Judy Holliday, Zero Mostel, Lee J. Cobb, Edward G. Robinson, José Ferrer, and John Garfield.[74]

Given Hollywood's shrinking earnings and the economic leverage the vigilantes promised to exert, both the film industry and the broadcasters were willing to dispense with purported troublemakers. Every studio and network had a clearance officer who inspected the political loyalties of company personnel; CBS forced its employees to sign an oath certifying that they harbored no pro-Communist sentiments. Only Broadway seemed immune to these anxieties, largely because its audiences were regarded as more liberal than those for movies and television programs, and because its plays were financed by individuals rather than by the corporations that bankrolled movies or advertised on the air waves and thus feared the power of interest groups to spurn their products. So, despite the contention of many postwar intellectuals that capitalism offered more crevices for artistic diversity and freedom than did a totalitarian regime, most of the people who ran the media in America capitulated to a congressional committee and commercial pressure as speedily as the cultural commissars in the Soviet Union complied with the ukases of Stalin.[75]

A number of writers criticized HUAC's investigations and the proliferation of private blacklisters, but usually on the grounds of pragmatism rather than principle. As early as 1948, the *New Republic* complained that HUAC's flamboyance, its penchant for publicity, and its inexhaustible list of alleged subversives actually hindered the work of traditional government agencies. "Spy hunting," the editors argued, "is properly the function of the Department of Justice in collaboration with the military establishment and the F.B.I." Indeed, in the journal's estimation, HUAC's hearings had the unfortunate result of allowing the Communists to "assume a martyred pose as the champions of civil liberties," which made it even more difficult to expose their intrigues and reduce their influence in the United States.[76] From this reasoning one might conclude that the problem with the committee was not so much its objectives as its ineffectiveness.

By the 1950s, the tendency to deplore the specific tactics of HUAC and the blacklisters while agreeing with their general aims grew more pronounced. In *Partisan Review,* James Burnham charged that Communists really had infiltrated American culture, often with the unwitting assistance of the nation's businessmen, no less. "Funds from the great foundations are dispensed to communist-line writers, artists, teachers," Burnham contended, and the "endowments of great Universities, supervised by businessmen trustees, maintain in the comfort to which they are accustomed notorious apologists for communist causes." Pamphlets, books, speeches, and reports "pleasing to the Kremlin" were routinely published by the Foreign Policy Association and the Institute of Pacific Relations, both subsidized by "suicidal" industrialists. Nor had the financiers of the film studios and the commercial theater used all their clout to purify popular culture. "How strange," Burnham mused, "that Hollywood and Broadway, which so readily . . . ground out pro-Soviet movies and plays during the War and immediate post-War period, seem so inhibited in their output of anti-communist productions."[77]

Similarly, Louis Berg (the film and television editor of *This Week*) told the readers of *Commentary* that although he wasn't sure a blacklist truly existed, there might well be a need for one. "In the past decade," he recalled, "the temper, the atmosphere, the prevailing mode in entertainment circles was to an alarming extent pro-Communist." This state of affairs seemed particularly ominous to Berg because during the Cold War "the question of who commands a public forum looms no less large than the possession of air bases and planes in Korea." It was therefore proper that citizens should be "troubled" and "angered" by Communist penetration of America's "schools and universities," its "newspapers, magazines, [and] publishing houses," not to mention the media. The people also had cause to resent the "so-called civil libertarians, whose record is one of hampering inquiry" into Communist cultural activities. A "free society," Berg conceded, "may have to tolerate its enemies," but it did not have to "reward" them with a career in mass communications. According to Berg, a performer with obvious Communist sympathies should expect public retaliation, even the loss of his job.[78]

Still, Berg did not approve of free-lance blacklisters because they were customarily indiscriminate; as the Waldorf statement predicted, they too often injured the innocent along with the guilty. What Berg favored was an "impartial board of inquiry" that would "give people who may be unjustly accused an opportunity to be heard, to be cleared, to be returned to a 'non-controversial' status." Once such a board got the "good" and "innocuous" artists "off the hook," it could then "take up the question of what to do with the bad."[79]

Hence Berg, like the editors of the *New Republic,* wanted more equitable and careful investigations. Neither asked whether in fact there was anything to investigate because both presumed that Communists and fellow travelers naturally used their artistic talents to undermine democracy. Moreover, the sincere concern Berg and the *New Republic* showed for the damage inflicted on innocent people, and their desire for some impeccable procedure to "clear" those who were mistakenly tainted, inadvertently confirmed the premises of the blacklist. For the effort to distinguish the "good" American from the "un-American" reinforced the notion that some individuals did deserve to be barred from their professions, if only they could be correctly identified. What the nation needed, in this view, was more accurate lists rather than no lists at all.[80]

Fair or not, the blacklist in the entertainment world achieved its purpose. The horror stories are now familiar: Charles Chaplin's *Monsieur Verdoux* withdrawn from circulation after being picketed by the American Legion; movie and television actors and actresses unemployed for years; at least one suicide (Philip Loeb) and several early deaths (J. Edward Bromberg, John Garfield, Canada Lee); writers submitting scripts under pseudonyms or "fronts" and paid a fraction of their former fees. David Caute has estimated that nearly 350 performers, screenwriters, and directors lost their jobs in Hollywood; the *New York Times* reported that the number affected in radio and television by 1954 reached 1500.[81] Within a short time, the blacklist had turned into a casualty list.

Despite these developments, the paramount issue for some other intellectuals was not whether to criticize and improve the methods of HUAC and the blacklisters, but whether witnesses at hearings should remain silent as a remonstrance against the investigators or testify about what they knew. Several writers (Alan Westin, Sidney Hook, James Burnham, Paul Hays) advised the latter course in the interest of candor and as an act of courage, rather than merely as a strategy to salvage one's livelihood.

Westin was the most sensitive to a prospective witness's ambivalent emotions in deciding how to behave at a hearing. "What sort of person," he wondered, "would feel any conflict of alternatives if he should be called before an investigating committee?" Who would be "tempted" not to answer questions? Some ex-Communists and all current fellow travelers, Westin replied, could be expected to choose "silence" as a form of "political protest and self-protection." But the liberal without any Communist affiliations might also take the Fifth Amendment, though he ran no risk of self-incrimination, because he perceived the investigations "as threatening *his* ideas and *his* values," because he wished to "safeguard lawful but unpopular political activities," and because he yearned to register his own opposition to McCarthyism. And even if he were not asked to testify, a liberal with such attitudes would normally tend to "approve the silence of other witnesses."[82]

Yet in the opinion of Westin, Hays, and Hook, all these motives were either questionable or counterproductive. Hays objected to the increasingly fashionable sentiment that invoking the Fifth Amendment was morally obligatory: A witness had the "legal *right* to protect himself by taking refuge in technical defenses," but "to suggest that there is some *duty* to do so appears unwarranted."[83] Worse, Westin pointed out, the decision not to testify only aided the Communists who wanted all witnesses "to choose silence in order to camouflage the activities of . . . party members."[84] Besides, the refusal to cooperate with a congressional committee or government agency (whether this meant declining to sign a loyalty oath, reveal whether or not one was ever a Communist, or name names) invariably left the impression that the individual had something to hide. Both Hook and Westin argued that pleading the Fifth Amendment "creates an inference or presumption of guilt." Unless this suspicion was quickly dispelled, the silent witness could anticipate "official and unofficial reprisals," which in fact were justified—especially the denial of "employment to someone in a position of trust."[85] So in the end, Westin asserted, the Fifth Amendment was an impractical and dangerous option for those who were innocent of any wrongdoing. Its use summoned up in the "mind of most well-intentioned people simply the image of one more Communist . . . cloaking his activities in the disguise of an appeal to civil liberties" while preventing the authentic liberal from communicating his true convictions to congressmen, school authorities, or the public.[86]

The problem, then, was how to indicate to an investigative committee an antipathy for Stalinism, a distrust of witch hunts, and a regard for liberal principles, all at the same time. Obviously, silence would achieve none of these goals. Burnham, Westin, and Hays therefore recommended that witnesses be as forthcoming as possible.

Actually, Burnham cared more about the service an ex-Communist witness could render to the state than about the excesses of McCarthyism or the preservation of civil liberties. Communism, he insisted, "must be experienced, lived through, in order to be fully understood." Those who had never been infected by and "successfully cured" of Communism could only oppose its programs on the basis of "prejudice and ignorance." In contrast, the former Communist's struggle against Stalinism sprang from "knowledge and inner torment." Hence he could play a "prominent and even leading part in the conduct of the fight," Burnham believed, by furnishing authoritative information about the strengths and weaknesses of the Communist enemy.[87] Burnham did not doubt that the ex-Communist, now turned anti-Communist, would perform admirably when called to the stand.

Hays and Westin were equally convinced that former Communists and fellow travelers could make an important contribution by testifying, though they seemed more interested in how this would benefit the liberal cause than in blocking Soviet ambitions. "Is it really so shocking an invasion of civil liberties," Hays inquired, "to ask those who have participated in and supported the [Communist] conspiracy, however innocently, to tell what they know about it?"[88] Clearly, he thought not. "Witnesses should answer the questions about their organizational memberships or actions," Westin advised, as a preliminary but indispensable step in defending "their current political positions before the committee and thus before public opinion." Only by "open speech" could they demonstrate that they were "dissenters," partisans of intellectual and academic freedom, true liberals, "not conspirators."[89]

Westin recognized that the central difficulty with a policy of "complete responsiveness" was that "it would probably require former Communists . . . to answer questions as to their associates." Indeed, this was the heart of the dilemma for most witnesses. The Supreme Court ruled in 1951 that once a witness testified about his prior Party ties (thereby waiving the Fifth Amendment and incriminating himself), he could not then refuse to answer questions about other people with whom he had been involved. Consequently, witnesses before HUAC who might have been willing to talk about their own pasts but who did not wish to identify others claimed the Fifth Amendment from the outset of a hearing, thus avoiding the role of informer while condemning themselves to the blacklist.[90]

Westin, however, was less concerned with the individual's moral predicament than with the necessity of exposing subversion and affirming one's commitment to democracy. The former Communist, he declared, did not have the right to make an entirely private decision about how to act at a hearing because his ex-comrades might still be "dangerous" to America. He "must weigh a personal code of honor against the need for full disclosure in a free society under attack." To underline this point, Westin quoted Robert Gorham Davis (a Marxist literary critic in the 1930s but by 1953 a professor of English at Smith College who had recently recounted to HUAC the activities of several Communists at Harvard during the Depression): "The price of speaking out is being willing to name others. No decent person likes to give such testimony, but some of the information obtained this way is essential and can be obtained in no other way." Following this logic, both Westin and Hays urged their liberal readers to respect and support those witnesses who declined to claim the Fifth Amendment, who upheld civil liberties by "telling what they know or knew of the Communist Party," who refused to shroud its machinations in secrecy and silence.[91]

Notwithstanding the idealism in which Hook, Burnham, Hays, and Westin couched their arguments for total candor, there were several problems with their position. First, most witnesses (including the archetype of the breed, Whittaker Chambers) rarely came forward voluntarily with information; they usually testified only in response to a subpoena or because they felt under pressure from their employers to "clear" their records. The understandable desire to elude the blacklist, for example, provided at least as much incentive for "full disclosure" as did high-minded anti-Communism.[92]

Second, a HUAC hearing, an FBI interrogation, or an in-house security check hardly seemed the most auspicious occasion on which to defend civil liberties, cultural freedom, and democratic institutions. One might decide to cooperate with the investigators for all sorts of reasons, like self-preservation or the weight of family responsibilities or political agreement, but it was hard to imagine how assisting the McCarthyites also helped vindicate liberalism.

Third, and most troubling, Westin, Hays, and Davis assumed that the naming of names really did supply "essential" information America needed to protect itself against Communist malevolence. Yet was the witness being asked to divulge the whole truth about himself and his associates, or to engage in a charade that had an altogether different purpose from the one the hearings were officially designed to serve? If a writer, an actor, a director, a teacher, or any other citizen was confronted not with a legitimate quest for knowledge but with a rigidly choreographed rite, then his moral stance, his conduct, his "personal code of honor" became the only issue that mattered. Seen in this light, the choice between speech and silence was less important than the conflict between the demands of the state and one's private integrity.

From 1947 on, HUAC seemed engrossed with particular aspects of an individual's past experience. The committee was as inquisitive about a man's acquaintances as about any specific acts he may have committed. The congressmen and staff lawyers continually asked witnesses not only to describe their organizational connections, but to recall who else had been a member, signed a petition, attended a meeting, endorsed a fund raiser, entertained at a benefit. By the early 1950s, the Senate Internal Security Subcommittee and Joseph McCarthy's own Subcommittee on Investigations shared these preoccupations.

Yet after a few years, the investigators added very little new material to their files. Nor did this appear to be the intent of the questioning, as several writers realized at the time. Commenting on Arthur Miller's encounter with HUAC in 1956, Mary McCarthy stressed a point the intellectuals who counseled candor too often evaded. "Everything that emerged from the testimony," she noted, "was previously known to the Committee and to the public as well. . . . No fresh information was gained from the hearing." The congressmen wanted Miller "to repeat, under interrogation, facts they already knew." They didn't even require him to provide additional details; they simply wished him "to agree that two persons, whom they themselves named for him, had been present" at certain meetings.[93] Moreover, since HUAC normally rehearsed "friendly" witnesses in executive session before they took the stand, thereby acquiring all the desired data in advance, the public testimony seemed redundant and unnecessary.[94]

What, then, were the real objectives of these inquiries? Initially, in Mary McCarthy's view, HUAC was "trying to find out whether Mr. Miller [or any other witness] was going to be 'cooperative.' "[95] As a committee member admitted in 1951, HUAC measured an individual's character, sincerity, and "credibility" by his sheer readiness to aid the investigation. To pass such an examination, one had to demonstrate that he was willing to give "full details as to not only the place of activities, but also the names of those who participated with him in the activities of the Communist Party."[96] It made no difference that HUAC might already possess this knowledge; the question was whether the witness would perform on cue. A person whose loyalty was in doubt could verify his Americanism only by following the committee's prescribed script, both behind the scenes and on stage.

Beyond their theatrical overtones, the proceedings had a quasi-religious function. A HUAC hearing, Murray Kempton observed, was "less a search for the guilty than a confessional for the repentant. The committee was especially proud of its record of conversion and regeneration."[97] Accordingly, a witness showed that he was worthy of salvation by publicly apologizing for his sordid past, denouncing his former colleagues, and throwing himself on the committee's mercy.

HUAC, however, reserved the right to be the final judge of a sinner's rebirth. Its "litmus test" for determining "what kind of man" had come before its tribunal, Mary McCarthy asserted, turned on the answer to a single query: "Was the witness willing to name others or not?"[98] This issue was vital in part because, as the *New Republic*'s editor Michael Straight contended, the committee thirsted to "bring as many names under suspicion as possible."[99] But who these enemies of the people actually were seemed irrelevant. What HUAC demanded above all was evidence of contrition, which the witness could offer only at the instant he began to recite his litany of names. "For the Committee's purpose," Mary McCarthy recognized, "it was not necessary that Mr. Miller *be* an informer; he was merely being asked to *act* like one."[100] As long as the individual played his assigned role and served as a model for the next penitent witness, he could identify someone who had died or been blacklisted for years.

In the end, the committee was seeking neither to understand the Communist mentality nor to combat subversion. It was applying its own "loyalty test," Mary McCarthy declared. By requesting witnesses not so much to furnish information about specific people as to participate in the ceremony of naming names, HUAC proposed that Americans accept "the *principle* of betrayal as a norm of good citizenship." If the compliant witness set the proper example of "civic obedience," the committee would acknowledge both his penance and his patriotism. He could then rejoin society and resume his career.[101]

Most of those who testified before HUAC or the Senate committees were as aware as Murray Kempton and Mary McCarthy that these hearings had a primarily ritualistic aim. They knew the choice before them was either to consent to the social codes as defined by their inquisitors, or become symbolic pariahs. After all the legalistic and political meditations about how a witness should behave, a number of writers had to determine in the most personal way whether this was the moment to conform or resist.

For several intellectuals, the ultimate test came in 1953. By this time, the decision to make public one's past relationship to the Communist party, chronicle its activities, and identify others had become a familiar if not entirely respectable feature of American political and cultural life. During the late 1940s, the evidence of Communist infiltration and espionage had been supplied largely by informers (though the government preferred the word "informants," probably because it had a more neutral, less treacherous connotation). The testimony of Whittaker Chambers against Alger Hiss, David Greenglass against the Rosenbergs, and disillusioned Party members or undercover FBI agents against the Smith Act defendants all legitimized the notion that the namer of names was helping to expose a criminal conspiracy. As a result, even when the goal of most investigations in the early 1950s was no longer to unearth illegal acts but to trace the influence of pro-Soviet ideas, it seemed acceptable, necessary, and patriotic for witnesses to assist the state—especially if this represented their only path to redemption in the public mind.[102]

Individuals might still waver for weeks or years before choosing to inform, but eventually many stepped forward. From 1951 through 1953, the entertainment world provided the most voluble experts on Communism. Those who answered the questions of HUAC or the Senate Internal Security Subcommittee included writers (Budd Schulberg, Clifford Odets, Abe Burrows), directors (Edward Dmytryk, Elia Kazan, Jerome Robbins, Robert Rossen), and performers (Larry Parks, Sterling Hayden, José Ferrer, Edward G. Robinson, Lee J. Cobb, Judy Holliday, Sam Levenson, Burl Ives).[103] In 1955, Norman Mailer dramatized their surrender in *The Deer Park*, particularly in the character appropriately named Charles Eitel—the film director who (like Dmytryk and Rossen) first refuses to collaborate, then endures the obligatory banishment from Hollywood as well as persistent invitations to recant, and finally succumbs to personal and career pressures, whereupon he returns to work.

Thus when the congressional investigators summoned certain professors and journalists in 1953, the precedents, justifications, and rituals for cooperation had been firmly established. In February, HUAC began to examine Communist attempts to penetrate university faculties and indoctrinate students. The hearings focused on a Communist "cell" at Harvard during the late 1930s in the hope of revealing how the Party imposed the same form of "thought control" on its academic followers as on its Hollywood clientele.[104]

Three witnesses—Robert Gorham Davis, Daniel Boorstin, and Granville Hicks—had been instructors at Harvard in 1938 and 1939. Each testified in executive session before taking the stand to tell the committee and the nation about his past membership, experiences, and associates in the Communist party. They all sounded ambivalent and reluctant, but in the end they gave the committee the information it required.

Robert Gorham Davis expressed his "extreme concern over the necessity of naming names" not only because he feared the impact of "loose charges" on teachers who were merely "speaking their honest convictions," but also because he thought "the American people generally dislike informers." Nevertheless, he considered it essential "to fight the influence of the Communist Party in those areas where I could be most effective," even if this meant accepting the "unpleasant duty" of testifying before

HUAC. Davis therefore described the Party's ambitions to conquer the academic world, and he identified nine people who participated in the Communist invasion of Harvard. At the close of his testimony, he acknowledged that he was "glad to use this opportunity to clear the record and say what I believed."[105]

Daniel Boorstin confessed that he had belonged to the Communist party for a year, withdrawing in "disgust" in September 1939 after the announcement of the Nazi–Soviet Pact. In his view, the Party had not tried to "affect what one said in the classroom" or to recruit students. Rather, it simply conducted a Marxist "study group" among young faculty and sought to influence "the policies and the leadership of the Harvard Teachers' Union." Yet he now affirmed that "a member of the Communist party should not be employed by a university" because such an affiliation was "virtually conclusive evidence that a person was not intellectually free." During the course of the proceedings, Boorstin named three of his colleagues at Harvard as having been fellow Communists. When asked to give examples of his current anti-Communist stance, he cited his "activities in the Hillel Foundation" at the University of Chicago (since religion was a "bulwark against Communism"), and his efforts as a historian "to discover and explain to students, in my teaching and in my writing, the unique virtues of American democracy." Hence the committee learned that Boorstin intended *The Lost World of Thomas Jefferson* and *The Genius of American Politics* to be read in part as contributions to the cultural Cold War.[106]

Granville Hicks, the Party's premier literary critic in the 1930s, echoed the doubts raised by Davis and Boorstin about the usefulness of the hearings. He suggested that a "mood of irrational apprehension has been encouraged . . . by legislative investigating committees," which was dangerous because "innocent people will be hurt." In addition, he believed that there were "situations in which it would be better to let a Communist keep his job than to disrupt the whole fabric of academic freedom." But Hicks also felt that "every member of the Communist Party is an actual or a potential agent of the Soviet Union," and he too offered the committee the names of four individuals who regularly attended the meetings of the Harvard cell.[107]

A year later, Hicks admitted his regret over his testimony. In *Where We Came Out* (1954), he noted that "no conspiracy was exposed; no spies or saboteurs were apprehended. No record of current Communist activity of any sort was brought to light." But he did "know of one innocent person . . . who was hurt by me" when Hicks inadvertently characterized him as a possible Communist. "Subsequently subpoenaed by the committee," Hicks related, "this man hired counsel, had photostats made of articles he had written, and went to Washington for a private hearing. . . . If he had not been able to produce rather impressive evidence" of his guiltlessness, "his career might have been blasted."[108]

Given the devastating injury to an individual's reputation and livelihood if he were so much as mentioned in a hearing, was there any excuse for yielding to the investigators' incessant demands for names? James Wechsler wrestled with this question and his conscience when he appeared before Joseph McCarthy's committee in April 1953.

Wechsler had been a member of the Young Communist League until 1937. He then broke with the Party. After World War II, he resigned from *PM* because of its sympathies for the Soviet Union, and he fought against the Communists in the American Newspaper Guild. He was presently an editor of the liberal New York *Post* which, while staunchly anti-Communist, had recently published a series of articles castigating McCarthy. Wechsler looked upon his subpoena as a challenge to the freedom of the press and he was prepared, even eager, to strike back at the devil himself.[109]

But Wechsler's combativeness was undercut by the assumptions he brought with him to the hearings. He had resolved that "silence was suicidal in dealing with McCarthy." Wechsler suspected the senator wanted him to "refuse to testify so that he could use my silence to charge that I had something to hide." For his part, Wechsler "was determined not to walk into [McCarthy's] trap." On the contrary, he shared his fellow liberals' conviction that "muteness" was rarely "equated with valor," and that an individual should be ready "to state his case in any public place at any time."[110]

Furthermore, Wechsler saw himself as a battler against the "totalitarians of the Left as well as of the Right." He yearned to "establish beyond dispute that an American might be as resolutely anti-communist as anti-McCarthy, and that being anti-McCarthy did not involve any sentimentality about communists or communism." Consequently, Wechsler could not let himself be portrayed as a "silent witness" because then he might never clarify his liberal precepts. Instead, he would simply become a symbol of the very Communist conspiracy he detested.[111]

As it turned out, Wechsler's own logic led him into another kind of trap. Early in the proceedings, McCarthy asked Wechsler for the names of any present or former members of the Young Communist League now working for the New York *Post*. Wechsler indicated his "protest" at the question, but identified four ex-Communists (among them, Robert Bendiner and Murray Kempton) on the staff of the newspaper. Later McCarthy ordered Wechsler to compile a list for the committee of all "Young Communist Leaguers" he had once known. Here Wechsler hesitated. "The notion of placing any names" in McCarthy's hands was "repugnant"; such an act could "hurt helpless people" while serving "no conceivable national purpose." Yet though Wechsler realized "it was wrong to expose others to McCarthy's wickedness," he considered it "equally wrong" to "embrace the principle that a former communist should tell nothing to anyone." Wechsler had "chosen to talk"; he "could not balk now" lest he be ridiculed as a Fifth Amendment Communist. So he elected to give McCarthy the list, but to fight for its "non-publication" in order to protect the persons he named, and to "preserve the anonymity which may surround them in the communities where they live." To this end, he thoughtfully recommended to the committee that the "proper disposal of this list would be its transmission to the FBI."[112]

McCarthy's reaction to the list was predictable in view of the rite through which Wechsler had just passed. "There are no names on here," the senator snorted, "except names of those who have been publicly known as communists."[113] Though Wechsler heatedly denied McCarthy's claim, it did seem anticlimactic—or possibly pathetic—that after struggling with a painful personal and moral dilemma, he found himself accused of having supplied no new information to his antagonist. Like other witnesses, Wechsler was reduced to a cameo performance in McCarthy's long-running play.

In retrospect, Wechsler argued that his pugnacious behavior before McCarthy's committee compensated for his decision to satisfy its hunger for names. He had been a "responsive but not friendly witness."[114] Yet his acquiescence, however grudging, helped sustain the idea that the government could scrutinize the political experiences and associations of any individual in any manner it pleased. Like Davis, Boorstin, and Hicks, Wechsler had chosen to submit not out of fear but out of a distorted idealism. They all recognized the harm they could cause to the people they identified; they all regarded their testimony as pointless. Nevertheless, their hatred of Stalinism, their abhorrence of pleading the Fifth Amendment, and their assumption that liberal values could only be defended by those who were willing to publicly renounce their radical pasts persuaded them at the most crucial moment to conform to, rather than challenge, the ground rules of their interrogators.

Since so many of the cooperative witnesses were prominent artists, writers, teachers, and entertainers, the impression persists that the vast majority of those who received subpoenas named names. Yet among the Hollywood contingent alone, two thirds of the people called decided not to divert suspicion from themselves by implicating others.[115] And there were a number of academics, intellectuals, scientists, clerics, and ex-government officials who chose the same course. Their reasons varied. Some may have been Communists with little to lose; others may have been named so often they could not escape a blacklist no matter what they said at a hearing. But the most well-known of the unfriendly witnesses refused to enlist in the witch hunt either because they didn't believe in the existence of witches (i.e., widespread Communist infiltration of American culture and politics), or because they viscerally recoiled at playing the role of informer.

Perhaps I. F. Stone spoke for all of them when in 1951 he condemned the national "tendency to turn a whole generation of Americans into stool-pigeons." The government was not investi-

gating ordinary crimes, Stone contended; it was prosecuting political philosophies. One might despise another person's ideas or
allegiances, he granted. Still, a "true libertarian" would always
"fear the greater danger in allowing the state to police men's
thoughts. To inform under such circumstances is as much a viola-
tion of conscience and moral obligation as it once was to return
an escaped slave to his master. The task of tracking radicals is for
dogs, not men."[116]

It was, of course, one thing to write these militant words in a
column, and quite another to act on them before a congressional
committee. Once on the stand, witnesses pledged to resistance
could only hope their conduct would not betray their principles.

Lillian Hellman felt precisely these anxieties when she was
summoned by HUAC in 1952. A year earlier her friend and lover,
Dashiell Hammett, had gone to jail rather than disclose to the
government the names of the contributors to the bail bond fund
of the Civil Rights Congress, a fund for which he was an honorary
trustee despite (or maybe because of) the fact that the department of justice had placed the organization on its subversive list.
In addition to the prison sentence, Hammett's most famous
fictional creations, Sam Spade and the Thin Man, were banned
for a time from the radio. In fact, Hellman recalled, Hammett
"did not know the name of a single contributor." But he would
not admit his lack of information in court since this meant
conceding that the state had a right to ask such questions in the
first place. Hammett might offer his life for democracy, he declared to Hellman, but "I don't let cops or judges tell me what
I think democracy is."[117] Now Hellman faced a similar quandary:
Should she risk a contempt citation and a term in jail by invoking
the First Amendment, resign herself to a life on the blacklist by
declining to testify on the grounds of the Fifth Amendment, or
continue to write screenplays in Hollywood by answering
HUAC's questions?

In *Scoundrel Time* (1976), her memoir of the episode, Hellman
reflected on the ways she and others in Hollywood and the intellectual community arrived at their differing conclusions about
how to behave. An individual may think he knows what he's going
to do, she observed, "but you can't be sure what will happen to
you under pressure." Indeed, "under special circumstances, tor-

ture, for example, people will and should break." But HUAC's lash was "mental," not physical; its intimidations were hardly equivalent to the "broken arms and burned tongues" suffered by the captured members of the European resistance movements during World War II. Besides, Hellman found it impossible to imagine that "a grown man, intelligent, doesn't have some sense of how he will act" when being bullied. "It's all been decided so long ago, when you are very young, all mixed up with your childhood's definition of pride or dignity."[118]

Thus in Hellman's case, what counted was not a carefully crafted political position, but the capacity to be true to one's deepest instincts. After having heard all the sophisticated analyses of how witnesses could combat McCarthyism by confessing, speaking out, hiding nothing, revealing names if necessary, her "belief in liberalism was mostly gone." In place of its corrupted ideals, Hellman had "substituted . . . something private called . . . decency." Also self-respect. "Just make sure," she told herself, "you come out unashamed. That will be enough."[119]

So on the issue of informing, Hellman tried to abide by an elementary code. According to her "thin morality book," it was "plain not cricket to clear yourself by jumping on people who are themselves in trouble." Instead, she wrote a memorable letter to the committee. She was prepared to "waive the privilege against self-incrimination" and testify about her own opinions and actions, regardless of the personal consequences. She would, however, be "forced to plead . . . the Fifth Amendment" from the beginning if HUAC insisted that she name others. The legal technicalities aside, Hellman reemphasized her conviction that "to hurt innocent people whom I knew many years ago in order to save myself is, to me, inhuman and indecent and dishonorable."[120]

The committee rejected her petition but permitted the letter to be read aloud, thereby making it an official and public part of the proceedings.[121] For the first time, a "silent witness" had managed to explain in a hearing some of the reasons for refusing to answer questions.

Hellman herself was dissatisfied with her testimony. She had "really wanted to say" to HUAC that "there is no Communist menace in this country and you know it. You have made cowards

into liars, an ugly business, and you made me write a letter in
which I acknowledged your power. I should have gone into your
Committee room, given my name and address, and walked out."
But this was a fantasy of courage after the event, the "bravery of
the staircase."[122] In reality, she had avoided the twin dilemmas
of cooperation or prosecution, though she would now be exiled
to the blacklist. Still, she had not shamed herself or her principles. In a rite of passage, this truly was enough.

Four years later, another famous playwright confronted an
identical ordeal. By 1956, when he was subpoenaed by HUAC,
Arthur Miller had already been blacklisted from films, radio, and
television. His plays continued to appear on Broadway and in
Europe, though he could not attend any of the productions overseas because the state department had refused since 1954 to issue
him a passport. Among his many heresies, Miller had signed a
statement circulated by the Civil Rights Congress attacking both
the wave of anti-Communist legislation and the HUAC investigations.[123]

Miller's legal stance differed from Hellman's, but he was
equally obstinate on the subject of informing. Miller did not take
refuge in the Fifth Amendment; just the opposite, he testified
loquaciously about his own political past. Yet when asked to
identify the participants at a meeting of Communist party writers
in 1947, he demurred. "I understand the philosophy behind this
question," Miller replied to the committee, "and I want you to
understand mine. . . . I am not protecting the Communists or the
Communist Party. I am trying to . . . *protect my sense of myself.* I
could not use the name of another person and bring trouble on
him." After being threatened with citation for contempt, Miller
repeated that his conscience would not permit him to talk about
anyone else.[124]

Theoretically, Miller's reliance on the First Amendment promised him no more shelter than it had for the Hollywood Ten. He
was duly arraigned and convicted for contempt of Congress,
fined five hundred dollars, and reprimanded with a suspended
sentence of thirty days in jail. In 1958, the court of appeals
overturned his conviction on the grounds that HUAC had not
sufficiently explained to him the legal jeopardies in declining to

answer questions about others—a ruling which at least spared America from the spectacle of having officially sentenced to prison one of its leading artists, thereby tarnishing its global image as a bastion of cultural freedom in contrast to the Soviet Union.[125]

When faced with the inevitable request to name names, Miller must have wondered whether his life was about to imitate his art. In 1953, *The Crucible*—Miller's finest play after *Death of a Salesman* —opened on Broadway. At the time, not every critic seemed enamored with the obvious analogy between McCarthyism and the seventeenth century witch hunts in Salem, Massachusetts. Robert Warshow objected to the parallel because those charged with witchcraft had been "totally innocent, accused of a crime that does not even exist, the arbitrary victims of a fantastic error" perpetrated by an "insanely mistaken community"—whereas Alger Hiss, the Rosenbergs, and the Communist party chieftains tried under the Smith Act were entitled to no such sympathy since "of course" their claims of innocence would never "stand up." Warshow complained that Miller's pseudohistorical drama enabled contemporary liberal audiences to shout "Bravo!" without having to think about what they were so enthusiastically applauding, probably because they, like Miller, supposed the "guilt" of the Communists was "not important."[126]

Warshow had a point. Much of the opposition to McCarthyism was based on the argument that its victims were in fact innocent of any crime, that the Communist "conspiracy" was a myth, that there were no traitors or subversives in the government or the schools or the media, any more than there had been witches in Salem. But the hidden corollary to this thesis was that if and when the state could actually prove the existence of Communist knavery, then it would be acceptable to blacklist these modern witches, even send them to jail. Few defended the right of an individual to belong to the Communist party and still work at his craft; it was easier (and usually more accurate) simply to maintain that liberals and radicals were being unfairly maligned for beliefs they no longer held.

And yet *The Crucible* remains a powerful and moving play because, in the end, it is not really about Communism or witchcraft, guilt or innocence. What fascinated Miller, as it did Hellman, were the shifting motivations, values, and behavior patterns of people undergoing a test of character. In such a personal crisis, ideology mattered less to Miller than integrity—a lesson many other intellectuals consistently reiterated in the 1950s but promptly forgot whenever they sought to parade their anti-Communist credentials before the McCarthyites.

These, then, were the similarities between colonial Salem and Cold War America that preoccupied Miller throughout the play. In his introduction to act one, Miller stressed the extent to which public policy lent respectability to private vendettas. He interpreted the witch hunts, and by implication the McCarthy era, as an opportunity for some members of society to act out their ancient resentments and frustrations toward others. "Long-held hatreds of neighbors could now be openly expressed, and vengeance taken," he observed. The "land-lust" formerly reflected in "constant bickering over boundaries and deeds, could now be elevated to the arena of morality. . . . Old scores could be settled on a plane of heavenly combat between Lucifer and the Lord."[127]

Into this inferno strides the professional ideologue and expert witness to other people's delusions and transgressions: the Reverend Hale, "a tight-skinned, eager-eyed intellectual" on a "beloved errand," feeling the "pride of the specialist whose unique knowledge has at last been publicly called for." After Hale has established the premises of the inquisition, he is succeeded by the less metaphysical, more resolute spokesman for the state, Deputy Governor Danforth, who knows there can be no neutrality in a cosmic crusade. "A person," he announces, "is either with this court or he must be counted against it, there be no road between."[128]

The state demands confessions and repentance in order to validate its presumption that certain people have engaged in an evil conspiracy to indoctrinate the unwitting and erode their respect for the prevailing institutions. Confessions are easy to extract from the citizenry when the penalty for intransigence is one's life. The urge for salvation, whether from a blacklist or a noose, does not surprise Miller's blunt hero, John Proctor. "There are them that will swear to anything before they'll hang," he reminds Hale, once the apostle of certitude, now assailed by doubt. "Have you never thought of that?"[129]

Yet Proctor too wants his life. Those who "stand mute" will surely be arrested "for contempt of this court" and condemned. All Proctor must do to save himself from the gallows and return to society is agree with his interrogators that he has "seen some person with the Devil." It doesn't matter whom he names; indeed the state would even prefer that he identify a person previously indicted, the better to reconfirm the justice of its trials. The perplexed Danforth cannot understand why a name he suggests is rejected: "Mr. Proctor, a score of people have already testified they saw this woman with the Devil." "Then it is proved," Proctor responds. "Why must I say it?"[130]

The answer, of course, is that the state does not care about accumulating more evidence of someone else's subversive thoughts or actions. "Your soul alone is the issue here," Danforth thunders, "and you will prove its whiteness or you cannot live in a Christian country." Proctor, like his successors in the 1950s, is being asked to demonstrate his purity by impersonating an informer. This, however, is the one role he is morally incapable of performing. "I like not to spoil their names," he cries. "I speak my own sins; I cannot judge another. I have no tongue for it."[131]

Reluctantly, Danforth lets Proctor confess his personal misdeeds but insists on Proctor's signature to a public statement so that it can be posted for everyone in the village to see. Proctor's name, after all, is "weighty" in the community; it will serve as a model, encouraging others to submit. Driven to the edge, Proctor defends what is ultimately at stake for him. It is not just his friends whose names he will "blacken . . . when this is nailed to the church the very day they hang for silence!" Danforth can invent any tale he wishes about Proctor's surrender, but he cannot "use" Proctor's name. When the deputy governor asks why Proctor will not sign what he has admitted, Proctor (realizing his stubbornness now sounds "insane") shrieks: "Because it is my name! Because I cannot have another in my life! . . . How may I live without my name? I have given you my soul; leave me my name!"[132] For this desperate gesture of defiance, he will hang with the rest of the unregenerate.

Proctor, like his author three years later, is protecting his last but most precious possession: his private honor, his sense of himself. "Names" are a constant refrain in *The Crucible* as well as in Miller's next play, *A View from the Bridge* (1955). It is his "name" that the informer Eddie Carbone longs to retrieve, and it is his *own* name that Proctor finally will not give. This intense, almost obsessive commitment to one's identity, the half-deranged, half-suicidal refusal to be used by society and the state, the intuition that in naming others one betrayed oneself, was perhaps all that resistance could mean in the age of McCarthy. Yet John Proctor is blood brother to Augie March, Robert E. Lee Prewitt, Holden Caulfield, the Invisible Man. And also to Dashiell Hammett, Lillian Hellman, and Arthur Miller. Each might be seen as an exemplar of autonomy at a time when most intellectuals—who were supposed to be the custodians of America's conscience—too often talked and acted like the very organization men they otherwise reviled.

The Roots of Reaction

By the mid-1950s, after nearly a decade of spectacular trials and hearings, the more oppressive forms of domestic anti-Communism began slowly to fade from American life. The congressional committees appeared to be running out of individuals and institutions to harass. Meanwhile, the Senate officially condemned Joseph McCarthy in November 1954 because of his dubious financial arrangements and his persistent vilification of fellow senators.[133] But the political and cultural sources of McCarthyism still seemed deeply ingrained in the national psyche.

At this juncture, several writers tried to assess the larger significance of the red scare for American history and society. All of them detested McCarthyism, but they were less concerned with formulating strategies to resist its pressures than with understanding its origins and contemporary manifestations. Some participated jointly in the inquest. Seymour Lipset, Richard Hofstadter, David Riesman, Nathan Glazer, Peter Viereck, and

Talcott Parsons each contributed essays to a book edited by Daniel Bell entitled *The New American Right* (1955). Others, like Leslie Fiedler and Dwight Macdonald, pursued their own analyses of McCarthy's character and symbolic role. Separately or together, these writers offered the most incisive critiques of the right-wing mentality that could be found in the 1950s. Yet the very factors they chose to emphasize, as well as those they either minimized or ignored, unintentionally illuminated the strength and deficiencies of the intellectuals' response to McCarthyism.

Nearly everyone agreed that the phenomenon of McCarthyism was closely linked to the postwar prosperity, as attention to the nation's economic problems gave way to a preoccupation with international affairs. This shift especially distressed an opponent of ideology like Daniel Bell, since it magnified America's habitual predilection for messianic language in coping with the rest of the world. While domestic issues had always been discussed "in hard-headed, practical terms," he noted, the problems of foreign policy were usually framed in "moral rather than pragmatic discourse." Hence in the 1950s any reasonable debate over American diplomacy was cut short by the simplistic "equation of communism with sin."[134] Nor could this feverish rhetoric naturally subside, Seymour Lipset added, when the United States was enduring so many fiascos abroad. The "loss" of eastern Europe and China, the impasse in Korea and Indo-China, the inability to escape the nuclear balance of terror all "required an explanation." It was obviously more "palatable" to "hunt for the internal conspirators" responsible for these defeats than to admit the "possibility that the Communists have stronger political assets than we do." Extremists capitalized on America's "doubts and fears," Lipset pointed out, but the perpetual crises overseas were basically to blame for the failure of the "political moderate" to calm the hysteria at home.[135]

In the meantime, Leslie Fiedler observed, no one was better at ferreting out the requisite scapegoats than Joe McCarthy. Yet ironically, McCarthy seemed in Fiedler's portrait to be as dehumanized as his victims. Emulating Alger Hiss and the Rosenbergs, McCarthy sacrificed his individuality to enrich "his own legend"; one could "almost feel pity for the man who has become as vividly unreal as a political slogan."[136] For Fiedler, it was again the nature of mass movements, whether of the Right or the Left, to rob even their leaders of any distinctive personality.

Dwight Macdonald felt no pity for the man, but he was equally impressed by McCarthy's skill at manipulating America's cultural idiosyncrasies. "The puzzling thing about McCarthy," Macdonald mused, "was that he had no ideology, no program, not even any prejudices." Unlike previous demagogues, in both the United States and Europe, McCarthy sounded neither racist nor anti-Semitic; he baited no ethnic groups, inflamed no national phobias, incited no one to violence. But he did exploit the country's fetish for concrete details. His rise to power "represented a melancholy Triumph of the Fact"—any fact that helped promote the fantasy that Americans still lived in a "small, neat, understandable world" where complex political shadings dissolved into "melodramatic black and white," where the newspaper reader could quickly grasp the issues and "see Results." McCarthy, in Macdonald's opinion, was a throwback to an earlier era: "half confidence man, half ward politician"; a "village gossip" whose "daily revelations" had to be interesting rather than true; a small-town district attorney whose briefcase bulged with documents, affidavits, names, and numbers. McCarthy's reign also coincided with what Macdonald considered the peculiar way Americans approached Communism. The domestic Cold War was not a "confrontation of principles" but instead a "legalistic haggling" over discrete events and deeds—whether Alger Hiss really did transmit state department papers to Whittaker Chambers, whether the Rosenbergs actually passed on sketches of the atomic bomb's triggering device to Soviet agents, whether the Communist leaders literally plotted to overthrow the government—the sorts of questions that might yield specific answers and lead to the punishment of specific miscreants.[137] Thus for Macdonald, McCarthy's ostentatious references to the secret data in his possession provided symbolic reassurances to an agitated population in an uncertain time.

But not every citizen required an old-fashioned faith healer to help him adjust to the postwar world. What intrigued the contributors to *The New American Right* were the particular social groups to whom McCarthyism most appealed. Their efforts to delineate the special characteristics of the McCarthyite constituency, to fathom the social and psychological motivations behind the popular lurch to the right, to indicate both the historical antecedents of and possible bulwarks against American extremism, all revealed as much about their own values as about the subjects they set out to explore.

To Bell and Lipset, the partisans of McCarthyism were a remarkably heterogeneous lot. They included traditional isolationists; various ethnic groups such as the Irish and Italian Catholics who were theologically antagonistic to Communism, or the descendants of eastern European immigrants who fretted about their acceptance in American society as well as about the Soviets' control over their ancestral homelands; "insecure" small businessmen dwelling in "provincial communities" who were excluded "from 'cosmopolitan' culture" and felt increasingly "constrained" by the power of Washington, the large corporations, and the labor unions; "soured patricians" who retained an emotional stake in Teddy Roosevelt's "muscular" nationalism; the "new rich" who needed the psychological confirmation "that they, like their forebears, had earned their own wealth, rather than (as in fact) through government aid," who feared that taxes would shrink their millions, and who therefore subsidized any movement or politician endorsing "extreme conservative doctrines in economic matters"; and finally a tiny band of intellectuals, "some of them cankered ex-Communists," who seized upon the red scare to "attack . . . liberalism in general."[138]

The reactionary predisposition of most of these groups seemed predictable, but there was one segment of the population whose susceptibility to McCarthyism startled the diagnosticians of the American Right. They had long recognized the tendency of the lower middle class, the workers, and the poor—the cornerstones of the New Deal coalition—to prefer short-term reforms to the utopian schemes of social revolutionaries. Indeed, writers like Bell and Lipset thought it was precisely this devotion to higher wages, graduated income taxes, and welfare legislation that gave the have-nots an investment in existing institutions and so strengthened their trust in the techniques of pragmatism and compromise.

Now it turned out that the masses were not noticeably tolerant or democratic, particularly on noneconomic issues. The "lower a person is in socio-economic status or educational attainment," Lipset declared, "the more likely he is to support McCarthy, favor restrictions on civil liberties, and back a 'get tough' policy with the Communist states." Conversely, the "well-to-do" appeared more liberal and more sophisticated in their attitudes toward political and cultural diversity. In Lipset's eyes, the propensity of the working class to march behind "authoritarian" politicians— not only in the United States but also in Mussolini's Italy, Hitler's Germany, and Perón's Argentina—"posed a tragic dilemma for those intellectuals of the democratic left who once believed the proletariat necessarily to be a force for liberty, racial equality, and social progress."[139]

Richard Hofstadter reacted to these developments more in anger than in sorrow. Drawing on the studies of Theodor Adorno and others, Hofstadter explained the conservatism of the lower classes as the paradoxical expression of an "enormous hostility to authority, which cannot be admitted to consciousness," so that it emerged instead in the form of a "massive overcompensation" reflected in their "extravagant submissiveness to strong power." Unable to "criticize justly and in moderation the failings of parents," profoundly uncomfortable in the presence of "ambiguities of thought and feeling," alternating in their human relationships between the urge for "complete domination" and total obedience, the authoritarians among the common people regarded government, elite administrators, and conventional political parties as little more than cabals designed to "manipulate and deprive" them throughout their lives. Hence they enjoyed "seeing outstanding generals, distinguished secretaries of state, and prominent scholars browbeaten and humiliated" by upstart demagogues who promised psychic gratifications in return for the masses' loyalty.[140]

David Riesman and Nathan Glazer were more sympathetic to the grievances of workers and second-generation immigrants than either Lipset or Hofstadter. They saw the class animosities in postwar America as the product of real differences in expectations and ideals. "Having precariously won respectability in paycheck and consumption style," they argued, the newly arrived and upwardly mobile found their achievements scorned or menaced by "educated" liberals who constantly called for the lowering of barriers between nations, ideologies, ethnic groups, blacks and whites, men and women, parents and children. Consequently, the average man now had good reason to resent his presumptuous benefactors, and to search for charismatic heroes who would rout the "do-gooders and bleeding hearts."[141]

Nevertheless, whether one attributed the right-wing inclinations of the masses to their deep-seated neuroses or their justifiable discontent with the whole tenor of modern life, no contemporary leader save McCarthy effectively articulated their values or defended their outlook. He alone thrust their anxieties into the political arena, affording people the sense that their amorphous complaints were at least being listened to if not resolved.

For that matter, McCarthyism itself appeared to Hofstadter, Bell, Lipset, Riesman, and Glazer as the inevitable political response to an affluent age where the problems of society were more cultural and moral than economic or institutional. During the Depression, Hofstadter and Lipset remembered with just a trace of nostalgia, people had understandably focused on "material aims and needs": jobs, housing, prices, credit, the clash of group and class interests. Politics was therefore rational, "highly programmatic," concerned with "concrete" legislative reforms and immediate social improvements. By the 1950s, however, political controversies assumed what Hofstadter called an "emotional intensity" and a "dense . . . irrationality" he personally deplored. The typical McCarthyite cared little for expedience or tradition; he was in Hofstadter's mind a "pseudo-conservative" because he employed the vocabulary of conservatism to communicate his "serious and restless dissatisfaction" with the quality of life in the United States. Despite his economic gains, the pseudoconservative's troubles proliferated. He felt vaguely uneasy in the midst of prosperity, Riesman and Glazer observed; he had "reached the promised land" but still he suffered though he scarcely knew why. He was preoccupied not with wealth or property or power, Bell, Lipset, and Hofstadter contended, but with his slippery status in the American race for success. Old families on the way down met new minorities on the way up; they were all "anxious" about their prestige, their "claims to . . . social position," their "rightful place" in the national hierarchy. Such evanescent worries suggested to Hofstadter that the pseudocon-servatives "do not know who they are or what they are or what they belong to or what belongs to them." Rootless, confused, envious, they lacked a stable sense of identity. Each of these writers believed that the projection of essentially psychological agonies into the public domain resulted in a politics of "grous-ing" and "vindictiveness," belligerent accusations of "conspiracy and betrayal," the chronic "search for scapegoats" and foreign villains who might be conveniently indicted for all that had changed or gone wrong in postwar America. And in the absence of "realistic proposals for positive action," the government could provide no "clear-cut solutions" that would ever subdue the McCarthyite's inner rage.[142]

The American Right was racked by another disease intellectu-als found especially virulent in the 1950s. According to Bell and Hofstadter, the pseudoconservatives continually sought to im-pose their values on everyone else. "The nonconformity of oth-ers" seemed to them "a frivolous challenge to the whole order of things." Thus their demand for uniformity in conduct and opinion was a means of "displaying [their] own soundness." This mania for orthodoxy was particularly evident among the ethnic groups, Hofstadter and Lipset submitted. "Tormented by a nag-ging doubt as to whether they are really and truly and fully American," they became "ultra-patriotic" and could not distin-guish between issues of "national security and the question of personal loyalty." Ultimately, they translated "Americanism" into the same kind of political creed as socialism, communism, or fascism. For them, as for their perennial enemies abroad, "ideo-logical conformity" was "one of the conditions for good citizen-ship."[143]

All of these compulsions were rooted in the past, although they had grown more frenzied by midcentury. Influenced by Hof-stadter's *The Age of Reform* and a seminal essay by Oscar Handlin published in *Commentary* in 1951 which located the beginnings of American anti-Semitism in the 1890s, Bell, Lipset, Fiedler, and Peter Viereck (a poet and historian of conservative ideas) saw in the demagogic rhetoric and acute anxieties of earlier movements like Populism and Progressivism the seeds of the current McCarthyite aversion to eastern breeding, urban complexity, and elitist credentials. Indeed, each writer purposely stressed the more sinister consequences of late nineteenth and early twentieth century liberalism. From their accounts, one learned that the Populists and Progressives exhibited strong symptoms of "generalized Xenophobia" and particularly blamed the Jews for their own political disappointments; that they regarded the "Big City," with its swarming immigrants, "international bankers," and greedy industrialists, as the supreme enemy; that they distrusted all forms of "expert knowledge"; that they hated "parliamentary or constitutional democracy" as well as the "concept of party"; and that they believed "only the people acting for themselves" could "take back 'their' government from the . . . Powers That Be." As if these notions were not sufficiently lunatic, Lipset reminded his readers that the "Ku Klux Klan of the 1920s was a latter-day expression of provincial Populism," while the native fascists of the 1930s (Huey Long and Father Coughlin) also attracted farmers, small merchants, and villagers by railing against Jews, financiers, democratic procedures, and the domination of America by its "metropolitan centers."[144]

McCarthyism, therefore, could be viewed as merely the latest specimen in this long and dishonorable tradition. In the opinion of Fiedler and Lipset, it had inherited the same bitter antipathy to Wall Street and the "upper class," to established political institutions and leaders, to alien-sounding organizations and programs. Most of all, Lipset asserted, McCarthyism, like Populism, mirrored the "insoluble frustrations of those who feel cut off from the main trends of modern society."[145]

Yet there were important and ominous differences between McCarthyism and its predecessors. Populism and Progressivism, after all, enlisted the support of philosophers, journalists, professors, social activists—the types of people with whom the essayists in *The New American Right* closely identified. Now these groups had become the principal objects of derision. To writers like Riesman, Glazer, Hofstadter, and Lipset, it was no less unsettling for the McCarthyites to have discarded overt racism and anti-Semitism in favor of "attacks on Harvard," on the "educated classes of the East, with their culture and refinement," on "liberals, critics, and nonconformists." Lipset grumbled that the "masses nowhere have real understanding of or sympathy for the problems of intellectual life, and they can be aroused against the intellectuals as part of their general resentment against the advantages of the more privileged and powerful."[146]

Worse, the intellectual community itself seemed increasingly indistinguishable from the corporate and diplomatic elite. Each embraced the welfare state at home and interventionism abroad, and each appeared unbearably supercilious and condescending to the plebeians on the right. No public figure more faithfully embodied this merger of styles than Harry Truman's secretary of state, Dean Acheson, and no one offered a more fitting target for McCarthy's vituperation. To Fiedler, Acheson was a "projection of all the hostilities of the Midwestern mind at bay: his waxed mustache, his mincing accent, his personal loyalty to a traitor [Alger Hiss] who also belonged to the Harvard Club" made him a perfect visual metaphor for the intellectual-as-aristocrat-as-subversive.[147] Similarly, the televised Army–McCarthy hearings provided another ideal setting in which to glimpse the collision of ethnic, religious, and class symbols. "Every member of McCarthy's staff," Lipset recalled, "was either Catholic, Jewish, or Greek Orthodox. . . . The nonmilitary spokesmen of the Eisenhower administration on the other hand were largely wealthy Anglo-Saxon Protestants."[148] In the presence of these transparent rivalries in manners and mores, it was easy for Viereck to conclude that McCarthyism was the "revenge of the noses" that "for twenty years of fancy parties were pressed against the outside window pane."[149]

Clearly, the new Right touched all the exposed nerves of the postwar intellectuals. Not only did the McCarthyites fail to show the proper respect for the best minds in America, but they also displayed the semi-totalitarian impulses writers had learned to dread: an indulgence in nationalistic bravado rather than a reliance on patient negotiations among career diplomats and heads of state, a glorification of the common folk rather than an appreciation for bureaucratic expertise, an appetite for mass action rather than for political bargaining and high-level decision making. Almost in self-defense, Riesman, Glazer, and the sociologist Talcott Parsons drew the appropriate lessons. If, as Riesman and Glazer claimed, "Wall Street was closer to the liberal intellectuals on the two domestic issues that were still alive—civil rights and civil liberties," if in addition the "great financiers and the giant corporations" agreed with the intellectuals' perceptions on foreign policy, and if industrialists demonstrated "a far greater cosmopolitanism and tolerance" for culture and ideas than did the workers or the "lower classes," then writers might more wisely "seek allies among the rich and well-born" instead of continuing to cater to those groups with whom they no longer shared a common social passion. Intellectuals would also do better to recognize that domestic freedoms were "protected, not by majority vote (which is overwhelmingly unsympathetic), but by traditional institutions, class prerogatives, and judicial life-tenure." In fact, to fend off the egalitarian menace of McCarthyism, Parsons believed that C. Wright Mills's "elite" must actually be "greatly strengthened."[150] In effect, each of these writers, with varying degrees of enthusiasm, was advising his fellow intellectuals to become authentically conservative in order to resist and survive the "pseudo-conservatism" of the McCarthyites.

The interpretation of McCarthyism that emerged in *The New American Right,* as well as in the essays of Macdonald and Fiedler, was so grandly inclusive as to be both contradictory and paralyzing. Nearly everything and everyone in American life, past and present, seemed somehow responsible for the postwar hysteria. McCarthyism paid homage to the country's nativist and isolationist sentiments, but simultaneously advocated a moralistic and missionary foreign policy against the Communists. It summoned up the memories and imagery of rural America, yet reflected the peculiar psychological tensions of the affluent 1950s. It was at once the product of an earlier version of liberalism now turned cranky, and the most recent manifestation of the ordinary citizen's exasperation with class distinctions and governmental arrogance. It exalted the masses and called for a revival of popular democracy, while sneering at political parties and elected officials. It remained suspicious of authority figures, yet attracted millions of authoritarian personalities. It adored the rebellious, vulgar, disorderly, deviant behavior of its own spokesmen— McCarthy himself acted as if he were the classic nonconformist, implacably refusing to defer to the elite—but it also yearned to wrap the entire nation in an ideological strait jacket.[151] Its supporters came from all levels of society: the new rich, old families dismayed at their loss of status, small businessmen, ambitious ethnics, blue-collar workers. Yet its ultimate concerns were more cosmic than social; it reflected the individual's alienation from modernity, his estrangement from any fixed community, his sense of living in an impersonal and uncontrollable universe. With all these disparate historical forces, group conflicts, and psychic strains at the core of McCarthyism, no wonder its inquisitions were so difficult to contest, much less to quell.

There was, however, one conspicuous omission from this analysis of the many factors that led to the recrudescence of the American Right. McCarthyism found its chief inspiration in the ideology of the Cold War—an ideology that was constructed not by Populists, Progressives, conservative Republicans, or people afflicted with status anxieties and other ephemeral discontents, but by liberal politicians and anti-Stalinist intellectuals who were responding to what they regarded as a genuine threat from the Soviet Union. Whatever the original merits of their geopolitical conceptions, they developed and refined the theories the Right then simplified for its own purposes.

In the context of a relentlessly anti-Communist era, the arguments of the McCarthyites had a certain logical (if also pathological) validity. Given the attitudes of the Cold War, the need to contain the spread of totalitarianism, the assumption that the United States should be the leader and policeman of the "free world," it seemed not unreasonable to ask who "lost" China, why so many concessions were granted to Stalin at Yalta, whether well-placed spies enabled Russia to build its atomic bomb more rapidly than America's scientists and military experts forecast, why the Korean War was stalemated, why the state department preferred to restrain rather than roll back the Communists, why the Roosevelt and Truman administrations tolerated appeasers and traitors in their inner circles. If one accepted the idea that

Moscow was masterminding a global conspiracy dedicated eventually to the overthrow of American democracy, if one defined Marxism as essentially a matter of espionage and subversion, if one thought of revolutions in other countries as a disguised form of Soviet aggression, if one insisted that every confrontation with Russia was not simply a strategic test over the world-wide balance of power but also a moral and cultural crusade, and if one felt that the incessant international crises required some abridgment of civil liberties at home—theses to which liberals as well as conservatives assented—then the exhortations of the Right to guard against treason in government and infiltration in the schools, investigate the media and jail or blacklist uncooperative witnesses, return the country to its traditional values and pursue a policy of total victory abroad, all had a perverse credibility.

What the contributors to *The New American Right* chose to overlook was that the postwar liberals had functioned as modern Dr. Frankensteins. Only after eight years of HUAC and four years of McCarthy did they begin to feel horrified by the monster they had created. McCarthyism was an extension, however distorted, of the liberals' own militant anti-Communism—a philosophy to which they still subscribed in the mid-1950s. The Right may have perfected the techniques of repression, but the liberal politicians and intellectuals who feared security risks more than loyalty oaths, who concurred in the expulsion of Communist teachers from the nation's classrooms and decried the cultural influence of fellow travelers were by no means blameless.

The essayists in *The New American Right* were doubtlessly correct about the schizoid antecedents and contemporary dangers of McCarthyism. But they could not effectively dispel the current red scare until they disavowed its ideological premises. This they were not yet ready or able to do.

Shock Waves and Reverberations

One of the ironic effects of McCarthyism was to make many intellectuals themselves more conservative and authoritarian. This trend could be seen not only in their disparagement of any ideas or organizations that seemed even remotely pro-Communist, but also in their wistful reliance on the elite to offset the masses' susceptibility to demagoguery. From World War II on, liberals especially had trusted the state to be the primary engine of social change and the sturdiest shield against reaction. Now more than ever they hoped the powerful would protect them from the powerless. In their view, the government should serve as the ultimate arbiter of political strife, with the right to define the permissible limits of dissent and coercion.

A few writers perceived the debilitating consequences of these notions. Since its inception in 1951, the American Committee for Cultural Freedom had operated as a pulpit from which the country's most prominent intellectuals delivered semiofficial sermons on the outstanding issues of the day: the Cold War, McCarthyism, "neutralism" in western Europe, the survival of free speech and free thought in a world threatened by totalitarianism. Yet as early as 1952, Mary McCarthy complained that these "so-called 'experts' " on the differences between liberty and Communism were inspired less by an appreciation of democratic values than by the "emergency mentality" characteristic of both their Stalinist and McCarthyite adversaries. Too many intellectuals, she charged, behaved as if "cultural freedom, in the sense of the genuine freedom of individuals, must be deferred until some future date when everybody will be in total agreement; on that date, it can be afforded" though it might no longer have any meaning.[152] Sharing the same assumptions, the witch hunters in Congress and the bureaucrats in the Kremlin could hardly quibble with the priorities or the state of mind of America's intellectual leaders.

In 1955, Michael Harrington—at this point a young writer and activist with ties to the Catholic Worker movement and the Socialist Party—offered an even more withering appraisal of the ACCF in *Dissent*. In his eyes, the recent election of Whittaker Chambers to its executive committee confirmed the ACCF's steady drift to the right. "Anti-Stalinism of the most indiscriminate kind" was now "the only essential requirement for membership." The ACCF consistently wept over the absence of liberty in the Soviet Union though it could do nothing to alter the situation there, while maintaining a studious silence about attacks on "cultural freedom in the United States," where it did have some leverage. In fact, far from upholding the ideal of intellectual independence, Harrington argued, the ACCF "enthusiastically laid itself open to the pressures and shaping influences of State Department policies and rationales," so that it had become less an organization defending democracy than a public relations bureau of the government, "an agency propagandizing the American party line." In its conformity to and apologies for the restrictive political atmosphere in the United States, the ACCF had helped bring about an "almost complete reversal" of the intellectual's classic role as the "focus of opposition toward the status quo." By collaborating with the new conservatism, Harrington concluded, the ACCF had abdicated its "critical function."[153]

To some extent, these portraits of the ACCF were too monochromatic. Insofar as the committee represented the opinions of many in the intellectual community, those opinions were themselves in flux. By 1953, for example, the editors of *Partisan Review* (particularly Philip Rahv) were beginning to sound increasingly apprehensive about the impact of McCarthyism, fearing that the anti-Stalinist crusade had perhaps gone too far. Accordingly, the editors asked James Burnham to resign from the magazine's advisory board because they considered his neutrality toward McCarthy's methods an impediment to their desire for a more forthright condemnation of McCarthyism in general.[154] But no episode so shocked the intellectuals in the ACCF, or forced them to acknowledge what a feeble guardian of their interests the government actually was, than when the domestic Cold War claimed its most illustrious victim—who also happened to be one of their own.

The rise and fall of J. Robert Oppenheimer was exemplary in several respects. Until the 1950s, Oppenheimer enjoyed a brilliant career as a physicist and intellectual. After a flirtation with radicalism in the 1930s, he made his peace with society and wound up occupying some of the most important posts the government could bestow in the 1940s. Yet he seemed perpetually ambivalent about his triumphs, uneasy with his accommodations. Indeed, the political and cultural contradictions in his life reflected in an exaggerated fashion the competing values to which many intellectuals had given their allegiance over the previous twenty years. Oppenheimer became both a servant of the state and a critic of its policies, an effective administrator and a tortured mystic, an organization man and an enigmatic misfit, an eminent professor who flourished at the very center of national power and a vulnerable ex-leftist who was eventually blacklisted as thoroughly as any minor Hollywood screenwriter or public school teacher with a suspicious past.

During the Depression, Oppenheimer taught theoretical physics at Berkeley and gravitated toward all the obligatory causes of the Popular Front period: He raised funds for the Spanish Loyalists, joined the local teachers' union, associated professionally and personally with Communists, gave money to the Party, and was by his own later admission a model fellow traveler. His life changed forever when in 1943, despite his youthful radical connections, he was selected to direct the laboratory at Los Alamos, which meant overseeing the construction of the atomic bomb. The spectacular success of this enterprise propelled Oppenheimer to even more prestigious positions following the war. In 1946, he coauthored the Acheson–Lilienthal report (the foundation of the Baruch plan) for international control of atomic weapons, a proposal the Soviet Union turned down. In 1947, President Truman appointed Oppenheimer to the General Advisory Committee of the Atomic Energy Commission, and he was soon elected its chairman. In addition, he became director of the Institute for Advanced Study at Princeton. At the close of the 1940s, few other scientists could match his influence in the highest circles of government.

Oppenheimer supposed he knew how to navigate the corridors of power in Washington, but like John Kenneth Galbraith he also had an abrasive personality, an arrogant scorn for less gifted antagonists, and several ideas that infuriated those with whom he had to work. For a time he opposed the development of the hydrogen bomb, and he persistently criticized the air force's infatuation with a strategy of massive retaliation based on the most destructive nuclear weapons it could acquire. Oppenheimer preferred a more varied and flexible arsenal, emphasizing early-warning systems and guided missiles, and he wanted the military to show a greater concern for the fate of American civilians in the event of an all-out nuclear war. As the 1950s dawned, therefore, his enemies included not only the Pentagon but former colleagues like Lewis Strauss (President Eisenhower's appointee as chairman of the AEC) and Edward Teller (the "father" and most vehement proponent of the hydrogen bomb).

Oppenheimer remained a consultant to the AEC, but by 1953 he was being subjected to a series of escalating humiliations. In the summer, Eisenhower denied Oppenheimer access to all classified scientific documents. In December, Oppenheimer's security clearance was suspended pending a hearing by the AEC's three-member Personnel Security Board. The allegations against him stemmed from his shadowy past: the front organizations to which he belonged in the 1930s; the beliefs he held and the political campaigns he endorsed; the Communist and fellow-traveling scientists he employed at the Berkeley Radiation Laboratory and on the atomic bomb project; his initial reluctance in 1943 to identify a friend who had approached him about cooperating more closely with and possibly giving scientific information to the Soviet Union. After three weeks of interrogation in 1954, during which Oppenheimer conceded his naïveté but not his disloyalty, the board decided by a vote of two to one that his previous associations and temperament made him an authentic security risk whose clearance should not be restored.[155]

Thereafter, Oppenheimer retained his directorship of the Institute at Princeton, not the most desolate locale to which a person might be exiled. Still, to take away a distinguished nuclear physicist's security clearance was the same as preventing an ordinary citizen on strictly political grounds from continuing to pursue his chosen career. In this sense, the Oppenheimer case seemed identical to that of the Hollywood Ten and other "unfriendly" witnesses. But there was one crucial difference. Most of the blacklistees were victims of reactionary congressmen, self-appointed vigilantes, university trustees, state boards of education, studio and network chiefs. Oppenheimer's banishment was instigated by the executive branch of the federal government—the very institution the intellectuals had fancied as their staunchest ally.

The disillusion was rapid and intense. Within the American

Committee for Cultural Freedom (of which Oppenheimer was a member), the consensus began to crumble on both the right and the left. James Burnham defected in 1954 over the committee's growing disapproval of McCarthyism. In 1955, Arthur Schlesinger upbraided the ACCF for its fanatical anti-Communism. By 1956, he had departed, along with James Wechsler, Richard Rovere, David Riesman, John Kenneth Galbraith, and Diana Trilling.[156] Each offered different explanations for resigning, but a major catalyst was clearly the persecution of Oppenheimer. If the government could turn against him regardless of his "innocence," his achievements, or his respectability, then no one was safe. For many intellectuals, the trials and hearings had finally come too close to home. It was time, they felt, to terminate the American inquisition.

Yet the repercussions of McCarthyism lingered even after the worst of the political terrorism subsided, and some of the victims began to be rehabilitated. From the mid-1950s on, the blacklist in the entertainment world lost its potency; the courts gradually reduced the scope and started to question the constitutionality of the loyalty oaths and the Smith Act prosecutions; scientists and teachers regained their jobs or found new ones; the state department eventually stopped using its authority to grant or refuse passports as a weapon to promote ideological conformity. But the basic assumptions of the Cold War, which had fueled the red scare, remained largely unchallenged.

In 1955, at a moment when one could detect the first signs of a relaxation in international and domestic tensions, Michael Harrington wrote another article for *Dissent* assessing the aftereffects of McCarthyism. Americans appeared to him still mystified by the "tremendous power of anti-capitalism and anti-imperialism" in the rest of the world, and still inclined to blame the nation's troubles on "plotters rather than social forces." Nor could they yet fully differentiate between Soviet espionage on the one hand, and radical ideas or activities on the other. Consequently, the United States continued to regard all left-wing organizations as invariably conspiratorial. As long as this belief persisted, Harrington predicted, certain institutions and practices would be indigenous to American life—especially the resort to "police methods" to suppress radical movements, open-ended political investigations that resembled the proceedings of a "star chamber," and the ritualistic reliance on informers to stigmatize those who had consorted with the Devil. These techniques persuaded Harrington that the assault on the freedom of dissident individuals was not merely an "administrative error" but a "logical, inevitable" result of the way Americans viewed the Cold War—a perspective they seemed so far unable to shed.[157]

McCarthyism had other reverberations as well. Throughout the 1950s there was intense pressure on government officials, particularly in the state department and the foreign service, to keep whatever unconventional ideas they might have to themselves, to exercise extreme caution in suggesting new strategies to cope with Russia and China, to understand that advances in one's career more often coincided with the willingness to carry out traditional programs phrased in traditional language. Thus the nation's leaders normally refrained from seeking fundamental alternatives to existing domestic and global policies in the interest of personal discretion and political survival.

The average citizen may also have embraced these attitudes, and for the same reasons. To the degree that millions of ordinary Americans seemed afraid to speak out, take risks, join movements, engage in controversial political activities, sign statements, associate with radicals, or do anything that might cause suspicion and possibly foreclose opportunities in the future, they had unconsciously internalized the values of McCarthyism. Self-censorship, after all, was a far more effective mechanism to guarantee social and intellectual uniformity than any external intimidations the state or the McCarthyites could devise.

But if the majority of Americans chose silence rather than dissent, they were simply putting off and exacerbating the problems they would have to confront in the following decade. By trying to inhibit men's thought as well as their conduct, McCarthyism contributed both to the political quiescence of the Eisenhower era, and also to the social explosions and international disasters of the 1960s. And in the waning years of the 1950s, more than a few writers began to suspect that such eruptions were not far off.

6

Endings and Beginnings:
The Mood of the Late 1950s

To visualize the postwar years as a single unit of time is mentally convenient but historically simplistic. It would be more accurate to speak of three relatively distinct periods, each with its own dominant themes, experiences, and concerns. Between 1945 and 1948, American politicians and intellectuals clashed over the future shape of the nation and the world before arriving at a general consensus on domestic and foreign policy. From 1948 until the mid-1950s, their preoccupation with the Cold War and the dangers of Communism made them less amenable to political and economic discord within the United States. Though writers started to explore the cultural and psychological dilemmas of affluence, a topic to which they returned throughout the 1950s, few attempted to connect the tensions in people's private lives to the nation's public institutions and social arrangements. After 1955, however, a more critical spirit slowly emerged not only in the intellectual community but also among certain groups in the population, which in turn affected the outlook of a new generation of aspirants to the White House. By the end of the decade, an increasing number of Americans were questioning, if not discarding, many of the assumptions and practices of the previous fifteen years.

The impetus for this third change in mood came initially from abroad, which was not unusual since America's intellectuals and government officials had sometimes seemed more absorbed with events in postwar Europe than with the predicaments of their own countrymen. Hence, the death of Stalin in 1953 and the Soviet Union's partial repudiation of Stalinism in 1956 compelled most writers to reexamine their earlier suppositions about the Cold War. Statesmen on both sides of the Iron Curtain were now tacitly accepting the permanence of spheres of influence in a bipolar world: The Kremlin repeatedly advertised the practical advantages of peaceful coexistence, while the Eisenhower administration confessed its helplessness to intervene as Russian tanks suppressed the Hungarian revolution. At the same time, the world-wide longing for relief from the recurring nightmare of a nuclear conflagration stimulated movements in the United States and Europe to ban the hydrogen bomb, or at least to prohibit the atmospheric testing of megaton weapons whose radioactive fallout was incalculable. Intellectuals themselves acknowledged their weariness with the messianic fervor and theological rhetoric that frequently served as a substitute for realistic diplomacy. Accordingly, they undertook to revise and modify their theories of totalitarian behavior, searching for ways to replace the rigid axioms of containment with a more flexible approach to negotiations. Eventually, of course, the focus of the Cold War merely shifted from Europe to the underdeveloped world where it would be waged covertly, in obscure jungles, by military juntas, intelligence operatives, local guerrillas, and other proxies for the two superpowers. But the reign of Dr. Strangelove was for a time postponed.

At home, there were already signs by the mid-1950s that America's material comfort and social serenity might not last forever. In 1954, the Supreme Court unanimously declared that segregation in the public schools was unconstitutional, a decision with wide ramifications for the whole structure of a racially divided society. A year later, blacks in Montgomery, Alabama, boycotted the city's bus system in protest against the requirement that they must sit only in the rear. Soon civil rights marches and demonstrations spread throughout the South, introducing new tactics and new turmoil to a country that imagined its most visible social conflicts had vanished with the Depression. In 1957, Russia's success in flinging a satellite into space intensified the decade-long suspicion that American education was emphasizing group conformity at the expense of intellectual (and especially scientific) achievement. Toward the close of the 1950s, the indications of cultural and political disaffection among the young multiplied with the publicity surrounding the Beats and the revival of student activism. Concurrently, some writers began to suggest that the apparently chronic problems of poverty, racism, urban decay, and powerlessness demanded a sympathetic reconsideration of democratic socialism. Finally, the decade ended with an unexpected and serious economic recession neither the Eisenhower administration nor a Congress controlled by Democrats seemed able to alleviate. At this point, Americans could no longer take even their prosperity, much less the sagacity of their traditional postwar leaders, for granted.

Yet these disturbances contained differing omens for the future. On the one hand, the ideas and upheavals that became so indelibly associated with the "radical" 1960s first gained national attention during the late 1950s. The social and cultural analyses of writers like C. Wright Mills, Paul Goodman, Dwight Macdonald, David Riesman, John Kenneth Galbraith, Irving Howe, and Michael Harrington were being translated into political action, particularly with the birth of a "New Left" and the growing reliance on a strategy of civil disobedience. On the other hand, the hostility of many intellectuals to the Beats, the cult of the young, and the images of adolescent rebellion in movies and rock 'n' roll, their annoyance at what they perceived to be a mounting indifference toward the values of high culture and articulate expression, and their discomfort with the amoral implications of peaceful coexistence, all foreshadowed the attitudes of "neoconservative" writers in the 1970s and 1980s. In effect, the intellectual skirmishes which took place between 1955 and 1960 were rehearsals for the full-dress battles that continued to convulse the nation long after the age of Stalin, Truman, and Eisenhower had given way to Vietnam, Watergate, and a renewed Cold War.

The Ambiguities of Coexistence

The frigid relationship between the United States and the Soviet Union in the late 1940s and early 1950s offered at least the consolation that everyone knew where they stood and what they thought. The language Americans used to describe the conflict dramatized the starkness of the choices presumably facing mankind: the "Iron Curtain," cultural freedom versus Communist tyranny, the Western democracies versus the "captive" nations of eastern Europe, no appeasement of dictatorships, the only thing the Russians understand is force. The Soviets, naturally, had their own verbal repertoire: imperialism, capitalist encirclement, the "progressive" forces, the "socialist" camp. Each nation's enemy was demonic and insatiable, but also familiar, predictable, an almost immutable fixture in an otherwise volatile world.

So it was disconcerting when, after Stalin's demise, the new leadership in the Kremlin started to extol the benefits of "peaceful coexistence" and the American government responded with calls for summit conferences, economic and cultural exchange programs, and negotiations to slow down the arms race. The austere imagery of the Cold War perceptibly softened. Instead of everlasting confrontation, one now read about Eisenhower's proposals for "open skies," the "spirit of Geneva and Camp David," Nikita Khrushchev's visit to Disneyland and his repartee with Iowa corn farmers. International crises began to resemble household quarrels; by 1959, the balance of terror had dissolved into a "kitchen debate" between Nixon and Khrushchev.

For some intellectuals who had grown accustomed to—perhaps even counted on—the certitudes of the Cold War, these developments were not always welcome. The old maxims suddenly seemed a bit too mechanical. The new diplomacy required fewer formulas, subtler reactions, more complex ideas, a heightened sense of ambiguity.

Such mental adjustments did not come smoothly or swiftly, especially to those writers who feared that the slogan of peaceful coexistence might have more sinister consequences for the West than the habitual menace of the Red Army and the clanking of Stalinist propaganda. Among American intellectuals, the editors of and contributors to *Commentary* displayed the greatest skepticism about Soviet intentions. While Eliot Cohen remained nominally in charge of the magazine, his increasing spells of depression meant that *Commentary*'s political stance was usually shaped by its various associate and assistant editors: Martin Greenberg,

Clement Greenberg, Sherry Abel, and Norman Podhoretz.[1] Yet Cohen's original notion that *Commentary* should help the Jewish community assimilate to and feel at ease in the United States persisted despite his frequent absences, thus reinforcing the journal's tendency to defend existing policies and institutions. In the middle and late 1950s, many of its articles pointed out the perilous realities beneath the lure of coexistence, and continued to insist on a principled opposition to Communism no matter how jovial Stalin's successors presently appeared. Throughout this period, *Commentary* was more wedded to the vocabulary of the Cold War and less willing to examine the problems of life in America than either of its closest competitors, *Partisan Review* and *Dissent.*

Typically, the essayists in *Commentary* argued that Russia had altered its tactics but not its basic aims. Sidney Hertzberg, a former foreign correspondent for the *New York Times,* warned in 1954 that the Soviet pleas for "détente" simply masked the Kremlin's attempts to "win by means other than overt aggression." A year later, Paul Kecskemeti maintained that a superficial relaxation of tensions did not erase the underlying issues of the Cold War; in fact, the Russians were using the bait of summit conferences to accelerate the "dismantling of the Western defensive alliance." As late as 1959, the political scientist Hans Morgenthau (normally a proponent of negotiations) informed *Commentary*'s readers that while Khrushchev might sound less revolutionary than Lenin and less bellicose than Stalin, his strategy was even more insidious than theirs. Khrushchev, according to Morgenthau, sought to conquer the earth by outstripping the United States in "technological and productive achievements," by expanding Soviet influence "through foreign aid and trade," by offering Russian Communism as a model for the underdeveloped and nonaligned nations to emulate, and by enhancing Moscow's prestige to the point where it appeared "invincible."[2] In this perspective, coexistence was a cunning device to anesthetize the free world before its eventual subjugation.

Worse, Khrushchev's hypnotic scheme could very well succeed. *Commentary* worried constantly that détente would make the democracies indolent and encourage the spread of neutralist sentiments in other parts of the world. Hertzberg, Morgenthau, and Martin Greenberg were all alarmed by the "weakening" of American "resistance to Soviet totalitarianism," the "general lowering" of Western "military, ideological, and emotional" resolve, the desperate longing of people everywhere to "believe the struggle is over" when it clearly was not. Stalin's ritualistic rattling of missiles, they noted nostalgically, had generated a spirit of "unity" among the non-Communist countries, as well as a recognition of the need for armed might. Now these writers saw only lassitude and "dissension" in the West, an indifference to a firm "posture of defense," an inordinate zeal to grant concessions to the Soviet Union while gaining nothing in return, and the "beginning of a softening-up process which, if it is not stopped, can only end in the surrender of the Western position."[3]

For his part, Hertzberg urged a renewed emphasis on "military security" as the "basis for survival." But he also called for a "moral" reinvigoration of the democratic faith, together with a reaffirmation of the "primacy" of the anti-Communist crusade, in order to combat the "natural yearning for comfort and normality" people felt whenever the most direct threats to their lives had momentarily abated. In Hertzberg's estimation, the West must persist in its efforts to "reach and discipline the heart, mind, and muscle of every person," and it had to prepare for a "grueling, prolonged war of physical, emotional, and mental attrition."[4]

From these articles one sensed not only an understandable apprehension about the future, but also a barely concealed resentment that the familiar adages of the Cold War had lost their power to terrorize the democracies. The world certainly seemed simpler when Stalin was alive. *Commentary* may have been right about the Kremlin's current objectives. Nonetheless, the journal chose to interpret détente not as an opportunity for the West to moderate Soviet ambitions and thereby give people time to deal with other matters, but as another example of Russian deviousness that required an even more tenacious commitment to the struggle against Communism. Moreover, *Commentary*'s reservations about a revival of "normality" in international affairs, and its regret that the prospect of a nuclear doomsday could no longer unify the West, revealed the difficulty many American intellectuals had in giving up their comfortable if dour conceptions of how anti-Communist diplomacy should properly be conducted.

Partisan Review had fewer qualms about coexistence than *Commentary*. It also regarded the thaw in American–Soviet relations as an occasion for writers to reassert their independence from Washington, to stop serving as unofficial propagandists in the Cold War and resume their traditional role as critics of national policy. Because Stalin's regime had been for Philip Rahv and William Phillips the principal cause of their disenchantment with Marxism, they hoped his death would prompt the Kremlin to return to the initial precepts of the Bolshevik revolution, and to permit experiments with democratic socialism in eastern Europe. Additionally, they were dismayed that their own brand of anti-Stalinism—once the credo of a few radical intellectuals in the late 1930s and early 1940s—had degenerated into a set of platitudes for the McCarthyites, the military, the mass media, and the middle class.[5] Unlike the editors of *Commentary,* Rahv and Phillips felt it was time for *Partisan Review* to disentangle itself from the current American orthodoxies.

Thus when Diana Trilling objected in *Commentary* to Philip Rahv's favorable review of Graham Greene's *The Quiet American* because Rahv had minimized Greene's "neutralism" and "anti-Americanism" (both of which she considered veiled forms of "pro-Communism"), Rahv replied that "we cannot put writers under the ban for criticizing, however sharply and even unfairly from our point of view, certain qualities of American life without doing ourselves a very great injury, morally, culturally, and even politically." Trilling, Rahv submitted, was insisting on an "American party line in literature." Because of his memories of Communist literary dogmas in the 1930s and his aversion to McCarthyism in the 1950s, Rahv believed the intellectual's task should be to "maintain a critical and independent viewpoint without yielding to the crisis psychology that contemporary politics all too readily enforces."[6]

In the same vein, *Partisan Review* published a lengthy essay by Irving Howe in 1954 entitled "This Age of Conformity," which excoriated the intelligentsia for accommodating itself to American institutions. In Howe's eyes, most writers were far too "tame" in their acceptance of capitalism and the "war economy," too eager to engage in the obligatory "Marx-baiting" expected by the academic journals, too willing to "surrender their freedom of expression" for a position in government, too inclined to "acquiesce in what [they] no longer [felt] able to change or modify." The exigencies of the Cold War and the dangers of Stalinism might have required intellectuals temporarily to support Washington's diplomacy, Howe conceded, but this did not mean they had to become "partisans of bourgeois society." Sounding much like Dwight Macdonald and C. Wright Mills, Howe urged his fellow writers to rejoin the avant-garde, move again into "opposition," resist absorption into the "monster bureaucracies" of the modern state, rediscover their sense of "intellectual vocation— the idea of a life dedicated to values that cannot possibly be realized by a commercial civilization." Howe had no more faith than his contemporaries that a particular program or a "formal ideology" could adequately solve the problems America and its intellectuals confronted in the 1950s. All he recommended at this point was that writers regain their "critical skepticism" and keep their "distance from state power, *any* state power."[7] On behalf of these tenets, Howe founded *Dissent*—a journal that in the next few years questioned the tactics and goals of American foreign policy even more extensively than *Partisan Review*.

Howe's diatribe was mostly accurate, though it underestimated the degree to which intellectuals had continued to criticize American culture and society throughout the postwar era, if not with the political and economic rigor he craved. But his essay also appeared at just the moment when more and more writers were beginning to redefine their attitudes toward and reduce their emotional investment in the Cold War.

The reaction to détente on the part of those intellectuals who wanted to move beyond the rigidities of the Truman–Stalin years ranged from a belief that America and Russia were simply accepting a military stalemate to the hope that both nations might eventually find a way to avoid World War III. The first sentiment, however, seemed more prevalent and more realistic than the second.

In *Partisan Review,* for example, G. L. Arnold (one of the magazine's regular analysts of foreign affairs) saw coexistence as a confirmation that "the world is irremediably split into two political halves and that this cleavage will continue in the foreseeable future." Similarly Henry Pachter, a member of *Dissent*'s editorial board, contended that the Cold War had been "fought to a standstill, with each side admitting that it cannot hope to 'liberate' populations in the other's orbit." Such an impasse involved the "tacit understanding that the two powers . . . will respect each other's sovereignty and will not use open, direct aggression in trying to change the territorial status quo." But this merely implied that the United States and the Soviet Union had decided to tolerate an uneasy truce in Europe. As Arnold and Irving Howe pointed out, détente would not prevent the outbreak of innumerable "small localized wars" in other regions of the world. Moreover, even if the Red Army no longer posed a threat to western Europe, the historian H. Stuart Hughes observed, Moscow and Washington were still locked in a feverish economic and cultural contest, with "trade missions, technical experts, and artists on tour" often functioning as "more persuasive weapons than shipments of tanks and planes." Still, in the absence of a global Armageddon, Howe like Hans Morgenthau concluded that the "decisive struggle" between the superpowers would be carried on in the "arena of politics."[8]

Despite these bleak estimates of the chances for a genuine peace, several writers criticized the American government for not being more innovative in its foreign policy, and more cordial to the sorts of compromises that might further decrease the pressures of the Cold War. Morgenthau himself argued that Washington had become too enthralled with the sheer use of "force," too dependent on the "instruments of power" and the establishment of far-flung military alliances, to the exclusion of conventional diplomatic initiatives. Instead of trying to police the planet, he felt, the United States should combine military strength with a readiness to negotiate on those matters that truly affected its national interest.[9]

Though this idea was hardly novel, it did suggest a more supple approach to the Soviet Union than the Truman doctrine. It also appeared more suitable in a time when Russian behavior was corresponding less and less to the totalitarian model of the late 1940s. After Stalin's death, even *Commentary* acknowledged that the Soviets might not be automatically or infinitely expansionist, that there were differences of opinion within the Kremlin hierarchy, that behind the monolithic façade of its Marxist ideology Russia was just as preoccupied with survival as was America.[10] Therefore, it seemed reasonable to surmise (as G. L. Arnold did) that the West could "reach a *modus vivendi*" with Moscow based on "some form of *Realpolitik.*" Both sides would then pursue "limited aims, coming to blows only for short periods and over restricted areas," while conducting themselves "with enough circumspection to leave the fabric of civilization intact."[11]

The intellectuals' eagerness for diplomatic bargaining, an impulse dormant since 1948, was now tinged with desperation. "Temporary agreements" between the superpowers were urgent in Irving Howe's view because they gave the "whole human race *a little more time* . . . to live, to grope for solutions."[12] Coexistence provided what Henry Pachter and Emanuel Geltman, another editor of *Dissent,* characterized as a "breathing spell" to devise alternatives to a nuclear holocaust. While this interlude promised no advances in "social justice" or a permanent peace, it might produce an accord between America and Russia to restrain the manufacture and atmospheric testing of ever more destructive hydrogen bombs.[13] H. Stuart Hughes even allowed himself to imagine that each nation could end its "scramble for propaganda advantage in outer space" and contemplate instead an agenda for "general disarmament."[14] None of these propositions were radical in any ideological sense, and they turned out to be excessively optimistic both in the 1950s and afterward. But they did capture the intellectuals' vision of détente as at once a necessity and an opportunity to cool some of the fears and enmities that had tormented everyone in the immediate postwar years.

In the meantime, writers transferred their attention to the Third World, where the American-Soviet rivalry was actually intensifying and the obstacles to coexistence seemed more formidable. Here, however, there was a broader consensus among the journals and within the intellectual community about the failure of American policy to cope with or even comprehend the needs of the emerging nations. Many of the essays on the dilemmas of underdevelopment in the 1950s forecast the very difficulties the United States encountered during the following decades in Latin America, the Middle East, and Southeast Asia. Indeed, it was precisely in their analysis of the disparities between the affluent and the impoverished countries that a number of writers were able—unlike the government—to reconsider and transcend the postulates of the Cold War.

Where the strategy of containment, the Truman doctrine, and NATO had managed at least to stabilize the postwar division of Europe, it was clear after the triumph of the Communists in China in 1949 that these tactics could not be easily transported to the rest of the world. "Asia is a much more complex problem," Sidney Hertzberg admitted in 1950, and he predicted "no quick victories . . . diplomatic, military, or economic." On the contrary, as Arthur Schlesinger and H. Stuart Hughes noted both at the beginning and end of the decade, the Third World was more vulnerable than Europe to the "expansion of Communist influence"; with the disintegration of the colonial empires, Russia could rapidly fill the vacuum, posing not as a "conqueror" but as a "liberator." Conversely, there was "no evidence of broad popular support . . . for a pro-Western orientation," Hertzberg asserted. In his judgment, the situation in the Far East provided "a perfect background for disaster."[15]

To make matters more bleak, the United States often had nothing, or the wrong things, to say to the world's poor. Thus, the economist Oscar Gass pointed out in 1958 that the United States had refrained throughout the postwar period from any "general, systematic participation in the improvement of the economic condition of the poorest peoples." America proposed no Marshall Plan, no long-term subsidies or loans, no regional development programs for the "backward areas." Instead, both Gass and Hughes argued, "we have done our giving and lending primarily to the . . . rich" while exhorting the ex-colonies to rely on the virtues of "free enterprise"—a dictum that only reawakened their memories of "exploitation, economic waste," and the West's historic "solidarity with native profiteers."[16] To Hughes and Irving

Howe, America's unprecedented "concentration of wealth and power" reinforced its status as a "rich, pampered country, hated and envied, isolated by [its] doctrinaire devotion to capitalism in a world of poverty and over-population in which single-party, more or less socialist states were rapidly becoming the norm."[17]

In contrast to America's opulence and its ideological parochialism, Russia appeared to embody values more attractive to the Third World. As Gass and Daniel Bell recognized, the underdeveloped nations were concerned less with implementing the liberal ideal of a "free society" than with mobilizing their resources for "economic growth." To accomplish this task, they naturally counted more heavily on "socialized or nationalized enterprises" than the United States thought desirable.[18] Hence the Soviet Union, H. Stuart Hughes submitted, was "in a much more favorable position" to proffer assistance and advice to Asia, Africa, and the Middle East. The Russians looked appropriately "Spartan"; they did not seem, like the average American, to be "wallowing in luxury." More important, the Soviet Union stood as a "visible demonstration . . . of how an agrarian economy can industrialize itself by its unaided efforts in a matter of two generations."[19] For these reasons, Moscow possessed an enormous advantage in the race to win the allegiance of the countries beyond the shores of Europe.

Given this dismal appraisal of America's image abroad, how could Washington prevent coexistence from becoming a prelude to defeat? To many writers, the only answer was for the United States to dispense with the postures and policies that had succeeded in Europe in the late 1940s but were increasingly inapplicable to the Third World in the 1950s. In particular, this required a repudiation of some of the classic assumptions of postwar diplomacy.

For Hughes, the government and the intellectual community might well begin by moderating their hostility to neutralism. After years of denouncing uncommitted writers and nonaligned nations, he suggested, America ought to realize that the refusal to choose sides was a "necessity" for the newly liberated countries. Their aspirations—modernization, the creation of overseas markets for their products, advances in literacy and hygiene—

had little in common with the geopolitical priorities of Moscow and Washington. "In respect to what most of the world's people care most about," Hughes observed, "the ideological and great power struggle between the Soviet Union and the United States is *supremely irrelevant.*"[20] And once writers granted Hughes's hypothesis that neutrality was a prerequisite for the economic development of the poorer nations, they might also conclude that, rather than engage in a potentially losing battle with Russia for more client states, it better served America's interests to encourage the spirit of independence in the Third World.

Not everyone was prepared to go this far, but a number of intellectuals did believe that the United States would have to alter its definition of what constituted stable and "friendly" governments in Asia, Africa, the Middle East, and Latin America. Instead of courting any despot who called himself an anti-Communist and then promptly begged for American arms to bolster his tottering regime, Washington needed to adapt its diplomacy to a different type of politician. As early as 1950, Sidney Hertzberg thought the United States should be wary about entering into military pacts with local strong men: Their hunger for weapons and their resort to repression indicated that they were already on the brink of collapse. After all, he reminded the readers of *Commentary,* "what America got for its trouble in China was Chiang Kai-shek and his friends and relatives; what we lost was the people."[21]

Ten years later, *Dissent* made the same argument about Cuba, charging that America's traditional preference for "property rights" over "human rights" led it to prop up the Batista dictatorship for decades. Predictably, this strategy not only prevented an indigenous "political democracy" from taking root in Cuba, but it also forced Fidel Castro to embrace Communism—with all *its* tyrannical paraphernalia—as an act of "self-defense" against the American effort to destroy his revolution.[22]

Whether one wrote for *Commentary,* the *New Republic,* or *Dissent,* the appropriate lessons to extract from these follies seemed obvious. In order to forestall additional Communist victories in the Third World, the United States had to reconcile itself at a minimum to the new generation of nationalist leaders. Henry Pachter was even willing to tolerate rulers who were no less autocratic than the old colonial proconsuls as long as they represented "not foreign interests but the interests of [their] country."[23]

Yet most intellectuals hoped the United States could find a more inspiring ideal with which to identify than mere nationalism. The real question facing both America and the emerging nations, Daniel Bell pointed out, was whether the "new societies can grow by building democratic institutions and allowing people to make choices—and sacrifices—voluntarily, or whether the new elites, heady with power, will impose totalitarian means to transform their countries."[24] In the estimation of writers as politically diverse as Seymour Lipset, Irving Howe, and Sidney Hertzberg, the chances for democracy rested with America's realization that its "allies in the underdeveloped countries must be radicals, probably socialists," certainly "anti-capitalist" in their economic philosophies, because only movements which promised to "improve the situation of the masses through widespread reform" could retain the support of the people and compete with the appeal of Communism.[25]

In the long run, the reorientations in foreign policy these writers advocated would appear credible only if the United States associated itself not just with allies more devoted to social change, but with the communitarian ideals the Third World normally espoused. Washington could never win the contest for the "mind" of Asia, Irving Howe asserted, unless it projected "an image of a radically different America."[26] For H. Stuart Hughes, this meant publicizing in greater detail the transformations that had occurred in American life over the past fifteen years: the disenchantment with "relentless acquisition," the acceptance of the welfare state, the creation of a mixed economy which was neither "completely planned" nor "ruthlessly competitive."[27]

But paradoxically, the United States also had to become more conservative in its approach to the underdeveloped countries, especially in its expectations of what it could accomplish. America, Hughes and Oscar Gass suggested, should cultivate an "attitude of benevolent detachment, always alert to help where help is needed *and asked for,* but never importunate or intruding," ready to assist those governments that assumed their own "responsibility for thinking, planning, and organization," careful to play a "supporting role" in providing resources and technical expertise while drawing back from ideological prescriptions and moralistic pronouncements about the right way to proceed.[28] In sum, the United States must somehow exhibit more social compassion and less political ambition.

Throughout these years, the intellectuals' criticisms of American diplomacy were still framed in the vernacular of anti-Communism. Invariably, each writer presented his particular recommendation as a more effective tactic in pursuing the Cold War. But considered as a whole, their analyses anticipated the characteristic preoccupations, strains, and contradictions in the nation's foreign policy over the next several decades.

Although the majority of writers in the late 1950s regarded détente with varying degrees of suspicion, they acknowledged the necessity of negotiations with the Soviet Union, particularly to control the proliferation of nuclear weapons—a discordant set of emotions that continue to plague American politicians, diplomats, and intellectuals up to the present time. Simultaneously, their growing sensitivity to the importance of the underdeveloped countries prefigured Washington's almost obsessive involvement in Latin America, the Middle East, and Southeast Asia in the 1980s. Unfortunately, the White House, the National Security Council, and the state department never came to share the intellectuals' budding sympathy for neutralism (especially not in Europe) or for nationalist revolutions in other parts of the globe. More tragically, the idea that a democratic Left might emerge as the guiding political force in the Third World remained a fantasy both in the 1950s and afterward. Nor was such a movement ever likely to flourish as long as the United States favored "authoritarian" regimes in places like El Salvador, Chile, Brazil, Argentina, Saudi Arabia, Iran, and Vietnam.

There was, however one additional implication in the intellectuals' response to the ambiguous meanings of coexistence and the complexities of underdevelopment. Gradually, they were recognizing that America could not solve all the world's problems no matter how much Washington reshaped its diplomacy, that the nation's power was inherently limited, that it must learn to live on a diverse and disputatious planet without trying to impose its own principles or institutions on others. The United States might not yet be able to transcend its inherited ideology despite its encounters with the rest of the world, as Louis Hartz had hoped. It might still indulge in sporadic displays of arrogance even after the calamity of Vietnam. It might periodically revive the harsher rhetoric of the Cold War. Nevertheless, th' intellectuals' new-found but old-fashioned appreciation in th(late 1950s for what the country could *not* do in international affairs had the potential to serve as an indispensable constraint on America's adventures overseas, both then and in the future.

Europe After Stalin

Any reconsideration of American foreign policy required at the same time an evaluation of de-Stalinization in both the Soviet Union and eastern Europe. The diminution of the Cold War depended not only on summit conferences, trade, cultural exchanges, and treaties to end the atmospheric testing of thermonuclear bombs, but also on Western perceptions of the Kremlin's conduct after Stalin's death and on whether the internal transformations in Russia were substantive or superficial.

During the middle and late 1950s, American intellectuals sounded as uncertain about the consequences of de-Stalinization as they did about détente. On the one hand, they applauded every sign that the Soviet hierarchy was becoming more "liberal" in its posture toward the satellite countries. On the other hand, they doubted Moscow's willingness to tolerate reforms that moved too rapidly or went too far. The Kremlin may have officially repudiated Stalin's savagery, but it could be just as brutal in crushing the uprisings in East Germany, Poland, and Hungary. Hence, most writers had difficulty answering the question Irving Howe posed in 1956: "Which shall one stress—the extent to which important changes have occurred or the extent to which Russian society under Khrushchev remains continuous with that under Stalin?"[29] Since the evidence proved whatever one wished, the same intellectual could argue at different moments with equal facility that the glass was half full or half empty.

Much of the effort to ascertain the impact of de-Stalinization on Russia and eastern Europe took place in the pages of *Dissent* and *Partisan Review,* though similar discussions could be found, albeit less frequently, in *Encounter* and *Commentary.* Because many of the contributors to these magazines regarded themselves as social democrats, with a residual interest in Marxism and revolution, their ambivalence about the upheavals in the Soviet Union was particularly acute. Their articles were filled with a mixture of buoyancy and skepticism, an astonishment at the assault upon Stalin's reign and a fear that the totalitarian system was still intact.

The majority of writers confessed that their image of the Soviet Union—developed and solidified in the years of the Moscow trials, the purges, the labor camps, and the early Cold War—did not prepare them for what was now happening. "The Great Thaw has taken me by surprise," Dwight Macdonald exclaimed. "I never expected to hear the top Soviet leaders denounce Stalin in the same terms we Trotskyists used in the thirties."[30] Lewis Coser admitted that the "Manichean world view" in which "Russia represented absolute and immutable evil" might have led "radical and socialist" intellectuals to overlook the "possibilities of change" in the Soviet Union—changes that even so militant an anti-Communist as Sidney Hook thought could enlarge some of the "areas of freedom" in eastern Europe.[31] From the perspective of the post-Stalin era, G. L. Arnold ruminated, there appeared to be "no inherent reason" why the "Oriental despotism" of the past "should harden into permanence." Russia was presently stable enough so that the "totalitarian apparatus of terror and enslavement may at last be showing signs of breaking up."[32]

No one was disposed to minimize the contrasts between Khrushchev's relatively benign stewardship and Stalin's tyranny. The "full dress attack on the Stalin myth," Macdonald and Coser asserted, was not a "mere strategic retreat" nor a "public relations device," but a genuinely new phenomenon in the annals of Communism.[33] According to Coser and Isaac Deutscher, a historian of the Bolshevik revolution and a biographer of its leaders who had always been more charitable to Stalin than most American writers, the rejection of Stalinism was reflected in "every aspect of Soviet activity and thought": in the attempt to establish "regular procedures" in domestic politics and foreign policy; in the reduced jurisdiction of the secret police and the "striving for government by consent" or at least by "committee"; in the encouragement of a "diversity of outlook" in science and philosophy that promised eventually to alter the "whole atmosphere" of Russian life.[34]

Indeed, the intellectuals' positive appraisal of de-Stalinization was prompted as much by their hopes for more sweeping changes in the future as by their estimations of its current benefits. When the totalitarian chains were fully removed, Dwight Macdonald predicted, "human nature" should naturally spring back "to its normal shape."[35] Irving Howe and G. L. Arnold assumed that the inclination of the Soviet authorities to relax their grip and offer "concessions" to the people would inevitably stimulate further demands and greater resistance from below.[36] Lewis Coser foresaw a flood of consumer goods that would not only raise the living standards of ordinary Russians, but also whet the national appetite for cultural experimentation and more personal freedom.[37] Isaac Deutscher's scenario was the most utopian of all: He felt sure that the new "moral and political climate of Communism" could ultimately produce an authentic "socialist democracy" in the Soviet Union.[38]

A major reason for this optimism was the conviction that Marxism, however much it had been distorted and corrupted by the Stalinists, retained its power to challenge the ruling class—if not in the West, then in the Communist world. Sidney Hook and Irving Howe each recognized the irony that Marxism could best be used to counter the policies of those leaders who spoke most fervently in its behalf. The original ideals and vocabulary of socialism—the antipathy for every form of political and economic exploitation, the vision of a "workers' democracy," the call for a "permanent revolution"—were ideological weapons that presumably could shatter what was left of the "autocratic regimes" in Russia and eastern Europe.[39]

Not only did these writers believe the language of Marxism was still pertinent, they also suspected that the conception of Russia as a classic totalitarian society might have to be revised. To Coser and Howe, the model of totalitarianism as set forth by Hannah Arendt and George Orwell exaggerated the "static" qualities of Soviet behavior while underestimating the political conflicts, the subterranean but no less important social antagonisms, the masses' longing for "habits of life that we generally associate with the bourgeoisie," and the rulers' own sheer exhaustion with terrorism.[40] The transformations in Russia since the death of Stalin therefore seemed both an augury of additional liberalization and a confirmation that the premises of the Cold War were now growing obsolete.

Or were they? For all the speculations about the future, writers could hardly ignore the limits of de-Stalinization in the present. It did not, for example, escape Isaac Deutscher's notice that in Russia the chief proponents of the new political flexibility were "the former guardians of Stalinist orthodoxy." As accomplices in the erection of the totalitarian state, they could undertake the task of dismantling its institutions only "half-heartedly and hypo-critically." Deutscher grieved that so far the Russian people were merely an audience to a carefully circumscribed set of reforms bestowed "from above."[41]

Others realized that the Stalinists remained stubbornly in charge. Howe and Coser ascribed the more moderate style of the Khrushchev government to a *"nouveau riche"* desire on the part of the bureaucratic elite to savor its privileges and pursue its ambitions without worrying about doctrinal purity, the need for an automatic compliance with the whims of the Great Leader, or a sudden banishment to Siberia. In effect, an "inner circle" of managers and functionaries had been granted "some freedom of discussion concerning the techniques if not the nature of the regime," yet this scarcely heralded the imminent arrival of "democracy" in the Soviet Union. At most, Howe, Coser, Arnold, and Deutscher believed they were witnessing the attempt of the Kremlin to dissociate itself from Stalin's butchery, and to consolidate and legitimize the "authority of the dominant strata of the Communist Party." Once the Soviets no longer had to "defend or justify what was peculiarly barbarous, murderous and pathological about one man's personal rule," they could "restore a certain rationality" to the dictates of the Kremlin. But the "mental habits" of the past continued to influence policy; the autocracy endured; the world was being offered the spectacle of "Stalinism without Stalin."[42]

These judgments were reinforced by the persistence of Stalinist tactics in eastern Europe, manifested especially in the speed with which Moscow extinguished the Hungarian revolution. Thereafter, the restrictions the Kremlin imposed on all types of reform seemed unmistakable. Despite the Politburo's talk of many roads to socialism and the prophecy that the Soviet bloc would in time become less monolithic, the satellite governments were clearly buffeted by conflicting impulses and pressures. In Irving Howe's view, the Communist leaders in eastern Europe appeared "eager to wrench free from the Russians yet keep firm control at home." They sought not liberation for their people, but simply permission to "rule in their own way." However remarkable the amount of change in Poland, for instance, the workers did not possess the right to strike or to organize independent trade unions; the "indispensable freedoms of speech, press and assembly" were "far from being secure or complete"; there was no "decisive break with an oppressive *social system.*" Furthermore, Howe submitted, the eastern European regimes were trapped in a paradox. They could gain the "enthusiastic support" of the masses only by expanding the process of "democratization," which in turn meant that the rulers risked the loss of their power either because the reforms might "get out of hand" or because of the intervention of Russian troops.[43] Sidney Hook underscored this grim dilemma by pointing out that any "popular revolt" in eastern Europe would "achieve heroism [and] martyrdom, but not victory. In the modern technological age, a practically unarmed [people] cannot . . . stand against the massed might of tanks and other armor."[44] Howe and Hook had identified the ingredients of a perpetually tragic situation. Their awareness of the conflict between relaxation and repression in eastern Europe was applicable not only to Hungary in 1956, but also to Czechoslovakia in 1968 and Poland in 1981.

Thus whatever the political improvements in the Communist sphere, writers like Coser, Howe, Macdonald, and Arnold reluctantly concluded that on balance de-Stalinization had not greatly advanced the prospects for democratic socialism. They saw no indications that the Kremlin would tolerate the introduction of liberal values, the participation of the masses in decision making, the abolition of state censorship over the arts, or an end to the Party's "ideological monopoly" over public debate. In its essentials, they agreed, the Soviet Union remained a "totalitarian society."[45]

Yet regardless of its totalitarian appurtenances, had Khrushchev's reign departed sufficiently from Stalinism for American intellectuals to alter their stance toward Russia and eastern Europe? Could the tentative liberalization be somehow encouraged as well as criticized for its shortcomings? Was it possible to accept a more complex interpretation of Communism, keeping in mind its historic rigidity while appreciating its capacity for modification?

Irving Howe pondered these issues more deeply than most writers during the late 1950s, though the approach he eventually recommended was far from unique. In fact, many other intellectuals came to adopt his position—whether as social democrats at the close of the decade, or as neoconservatives in the 1970s and 1980s.

Howe urged his contemporaries to support "every step toward a loosening of the dictatorship" in both Russia and the satellite states. He considered it particularly important for Western intellectuals to affirm their solidarity with the dissidents of eastern Europe—to widen the lines of communication with Marxist revisionists, Polish philosophers, banned novelists, student activists, young technicians, anyone who wanted to emulate Tito's "national" Communism or experiment with a mixed economy. But this did not mean that the West should temper its "fundamental opposition" to the existing Communist regimes, no matter how conciliatory their recent behavior toward workers or factory managers. While political "arrangements may have to be made" with the Soviet Union in order to preserve the peace, Howe argued, the West ought not consent to a "moral coexistence" with totalitarianism.[46]

Howe's sensitivity to the polarities in Russian and eastern

European politics, his desire to empathize with and assist the liberal forces after de-Stalinization combined with his steadfast hostility to Communism in general, proved too contradictory a set of attitudes for most people in the West to sustain. Over the next several decades, it seemed easier and more consistent either to disregard the totalitarian features of Soviet life in the interest of avoiding a nuclear war, or to view all attempts to bargain with Moscow as evidence of the democracies' progressive moral decay.

Nevertheless, the ability of certain intellectuals at the end of the Eisenhower era to look at Russia with a double vision, to cheer some developments while condemning others, to understand that negotiations with the Kremlin did not imply an approval of its dictatorship, was a considerable improvement on the dogmatism of the early Cold War. Indeed, few American writers or politicians since have managed to propose a shrewder or more effective strategy for dealing with the Communist world.

Neobohemians and Neoconservatives

The feeling in the late 1950s that the United States might be on the verge of some momentous transformation sprang not just from the well-publicized shifts in Soviet and American foreign policy. The lull in the Cold War was accompanied by a growing restlessness at home, a sense of impending crisis, an intuition that the placid tone of American life—from President Eisenhower's avuncular assurances of peace and prosperity to Perry Como's half-comatose visage on television—was always deceptive, if not entirely fraudulent. A society whose politics had been defined as much by Joseph McCarthy as by Adlai Stevenson and Dwight Eisenhower, whose popular music was influenced as much by Chuck Berry and Elvis Presley as by Pat Boone and Frank Sinatra, whose comic sensibility was molded as much by Tom Lehrer and Mort Sahl and Lenny Bruce as by Ozzie and Harriet, whose movie heroes included James Dean and Marlon Brando as well as Rock Hudson and Tab Hunter, may never have preferred tranquility to turmoil. Beneath the ordinary American's complacent exterior, there apparently lurked a hunger for

corrosive wit, jangling sounds, disruptive behavior, defiant gestures, a revival of passion and intensity.

Near the end of the decade, some writers perceived the symptoms of discontent, though they did not usually relish the forms
it took. In their diagnosis of such fads as the Beat movement, they
revealed their own mixed emotions—their thirst for new social
clashes and more cultural ferment together with the fear of mindless disorder, rampant anti-intellectualism, a disrespect for authority and tradition. The "bohemians" of the late 1950s—
spaced-out jazz musicians, itinerant novelists and poets, aspiring
folk singers, tongue-tied Method actors, the coterie of young
people who flocked to concerts and coffee houses and foreign
films costumed exclusively in black—all made the contributors to
magazines like *Partisan Review* and *Commentary* uneasy, even enraged. If these phenomena betokened a resurgence of radicalism,
the intellectuals wanted it to be serious, learned, articulate, mature. They also assumed they would help shape its course. But in
their response to the latest expressions of cultural nonconformity, they often sounded like stereotypical conservatives who dis-
dained what they could not comprehend or control.

It was not that writers had no sympathy for the bohemian
impulse. They too loathed the respectable world of middle-class
adults, the political prejudices and esthetic tastes of the squares.
A youthful Norman Podhoretz warned the Jewish clientele of
Commentary that they should worry if they admired or identified
with Herman Wouk's *Marjorie Morningstar*. Wouk's fable of a Jew-
ish-American princess who eventually trades in her ambitions to
be an actress for a ranch house in suburbia was really an attack
upon the values associated with the young, Podhoretz charged,
"if by youth we mean recklessness, an appetite for diverse areas
of experience, an unwillingness to settle into the common routines, a refusal to surrender one's demands on the world without
a fight." Marjorie was a model for all those readers who, like her,
had resigned themselves to the limitations of middle age, who
had "flirted with the life of risk and given it up for submission to
law," who had "felt the lure of promiscuity and yet chosen chas-
tity," who had "seen Montmartre and settled in Mamaroneck."[47]
Commentary's subscribers, one imagined, would be better off with

The Adventures of Augie March on their coffee tables.

Dwight Macdonald found another of Wouk's best sellers, *The Caine Mutiny,* just as exasperating. Here, insurrection was first justified and then denounced. The lunacy of Captain Queeg is excused because he defended his country during its most perilous hours in World War II. Thus the military, no matter how psychotic, emerges as morally superior to those who dare to question rank and procedure—even if, as in this case, their mutiny prevents disaster. To Macdonald, Wouk's biases were "typically American": The responsible adult should "realize how awful the System is" and still bow to its conventions; growing up meant replacing the desire for "wholesale revolt" with a spirit of "wholesale acceptance"; there could be nothing in between.[48]

The director and drama critic Robert Brustein objected for similar reasons to the contemporary theater in America. In his view, the "psychodrama" of the 1950s, having eclipsed the "leftist melodrama" of the 1930s and the "liberal message play" of the 1940s, focused obsessively on the protagonist's "domestic problems" while neglecting the "world beyond the home." Whereas earlier playwrights like Clifford Odets or Arthur Miller wished their characters (and presumably their audiences) to cast aside familial expectations and pursue an "independent life in opposition to the prevailing social system," psychodramatists like William Inge and Paddy Chayefsky documented their "hero's hangdog return to the hearth." The climaxes of most current plays, Brustein complained, normally occurred when the central character, "seeking safety rather than danger," adjusted himself to the "compromises and complexities" of family living.[49]

The popularity of novels and plays that exhorted people to acquiesce in bourgeois domesticity suggested to Alfred Kazin and Norman Podhoretz that Americans were afflicted by a malaise more profound than mere conformity. "The human catastrophes visited upon our generation by totalitarianism," Kazin suspected, were "too great to understand, to describe, to cope with. History has become meaningless." Partly, it seemed, the intellectuals themselves were to blame for this absence of meaning in public and private life. The most "energetic" of the postwar social critics, Podhoretz recalled, had insisted that the "main enemy, both in culture and politics, was the 'true believer,' the fanatic of whatever complexion, the prisoner of ideology." Consequently, writers regarded the "loss of values" as a "positive" reflection of man's "liberation from rigid systems of belief "; they commended to individuals and to nations the merits of a "skeptical empiricist temperament." But "in losing [their] taste for ideology," Podhoretz lamented, people also found themselves without the "powerful convictions" that once set their "feelings on fire."[50]

Meanwhile, the frantic "air of militancy and rebelliousness" exhibited by younger novelists, playwrights, and poets in England and America (John Osborne, Norman Mailer, Jack Kerouac, Allen Ginsberg), their "appearance of radicalism" and ostentatious displays of "intense spirituality," struck Kazin and Podhoretz as unconscious testimonials to their lack of authentic emotions and ideas. These writers seemed more incensed at their own "inability to feel anger" than at some specific injustice. Closer in disposition to Albert Camus's "stranger" than to his "rebel," they relied heavily on psychoanalytic symbols because they were preoccupied with the assertion of identity, not with the quest for freedom. Yet what they and their readers really needed, according to Kazin and Podhoretz, was a "world they [could] believe in again," coupled with a sense of engagement that was "extreme, fervent, affirmative, and sweeping."[51]

Macdonald, Brustein, Podhoretz, and Kazin were not exactly advocating a return to the mood, much less the politics, of the 1930s, though their rhetoric in these articles was occasionally reminiscent of *Awake and Sing.* Still, they suffered from the same ennui and felt the same longings they attributed to the general populace, the Beats, and the Angry Young Men. After a decade of negativity—of dissociating themselves from Communists and McCarthyites, of railing against barbecue pits and television sets, of griping about organization men and their other-directed offspring—they yearned for a cause, a commitment, something to stir the brain and the blood. Only, the adversary culture of the late 1950s was not quite what they had in mind.

The changes that were increasingly evident in the theater and the movies furnished a set of metaphors for the intellectuals' displeasure with the new bohemians. Robert Brustein may have chafed at the tone of resignation in modern plays, but he was even more irritated by those performers whose mannerisms seemed at odds with the script's ostensible message. Not only did the dramatists of the 1930s show greater concern for social issues, he noted; they also created characters who were distinguished by their "extreme verbosity," who could "never stop talking" about the problems of their world. In contrast, the heroes of many plays and movies in the 1950s had lost both their political convictions and their "power of speech." They stammered, paused, stared into the middle distance. Worse, their incoherence had spread beyond the stage and screen. Popular music was no longer intelligible, Brustein declared; "beginning by ignoring language, rock and roll is now dispensing with melodic content and offering only animal sounds and repetitive rhythms." Elvis Presley was thus the "musical counterpart" of Stanley Kowalski.[52]

The prominence of the "inarticulate" hero was due in Brustein's judgment to the impact of Stanislavsky's famous method on a new generation of actors—especially Marlon Brando, James Dean, Montgomery Clift, Paul Newman, and Rod Steiger (Brustein, writing in 1958, could not have foreseen the continuing effects of this training on the acting styles of Warren Beatty, Al Pacino, and Robert De Niro). What Brustein believed these performers had in common was an ability to suggest an "inner life of unspecified anguish and torment" without the necessity of having to translate such sensations into words or ideas.[53] Unlike the British school of Shakespearean-bred actors who subordinated their personalities to whatever roles they were playing, or the classic American film stars who rarely appeared to be acting at all but instead treated a script as a vehicle to polish their familiar screen images, the disciples of the Method were taught to improvise, to rely on their prior experiences, to transcend the playwright's text, to communicate feelings rather than lines. Hence the play became less important than the performance, another illustration to Brustein of the mounting scorn for literacy and thought.

Yet Brustein recognized that the Method produced actors who

were not only "mute" but also unconventional. Their appeal rested on their capacity to demonstrate sensitivity and "profundity," as well as surliness and dissatisfaction, through the way they dressed, slouched, shrugged, and scratched. Typecast in roles that were always sexual and frequently violent, they at least offered symbolic alternatives to the bourgeois drive for wealth and social approval. In a nation of law-abiding conformists, their characters personified eccentricity, alienation, and the whiff of rebellion.[54]

Nevertheless, whispers and mutterings did not launch or sustain revolutions. Besides, no matter how repressive and imprisoning life seemed to be in the middle class, the characters the Method actors played were forever trying to adapt and assimilate. Although the hero started out on the "wrong side," Brustein observed, he was invariably "converted to righteousness before the end," usually by his girl friend who, in addition to being maternal and dutiful, could also speak "coherently and interminably" about rules, conscience, principles, and familial obligations. This reduced the rebel to a little boy, or at most an adolescent; the antagonism he felt "toward society, convention, law and order" became "merely an extension of [his] hostility toward his father." Caught in a "classic juvenile dilemma," denied the "social and political outlets" that might have led to a real revolt, the hero was forced to convert insurgency into a "Freudian protest." Thus his inarticulateness, Brustein contended, was not an omen of his challenge to existing institutions. Rather, it simply represented a "misunderstanding" between father and son, a "failure in communication" which could be rectified through expressions of paternal love and adolescent reconciliation, as in the final reels of *Rebel Without a Cause* and *East of Eden*.[55]

The trouble with these allegedly happy endings, in Brustein's opinion, was that the audience never saw the hero engaged in a "mature action." He had come home but he had not grown up. Nor had he learned to talk or think for himself. To remain speechless was, for Brustein, to prolong the infatuation with "anarchy," to "find consolation in raw feeling, in mindlessness, and in self-indulgence." As a way of offsetting this dangerous narcissism, Brustein wanted the nonconformists and the neobohemians to develop some respect for "language, tradition, education, and art," and to accept the "discipline" of "intelligence."[56]

Brustein's analysis of the Method actors and the characters they invented was not unpersuasive. Certainly, the tendency to identify rebellion with the ordeals of adolescence was reinforced by watching Montgomery Clift, James Dean, and Warren Beatty depict restive and perplexed juveniles in *Red River, East of Eden,* and *Splendor in the Grass.* Conversely, it helped to have the mature authority figures played by robust, forceful, self-assured, domineering actors like John Wayne in *Red River,* Lee J. Cobb in *On the Waterfront,* Burt Lancaster in *From Here to Eternity,* Raymond Massey in *East of Eden,* and George C. Scott in *The Hustler.* More important, when one was contemplating the prerequisites for an effective radical movement, a knowledge of art and history as well as an ability to speak and write intelligently were clearly preferable to mumbles, grunts, and childish fury.

Yet for all his insights, Brustein did not explain why the Method should have been so compelling a style in the 1950s, why it not only transformed acting but also created culture heroes who looked and sounded very different from all those nice sober men in their gray flannel suits. Neither did he fully capture the qualities that made Marlon Brando the embodiment of both the Method and nonconformity. Clift, Dean, and Beatty might have seemed haunted and tortured on screen, but Brando's performances were downright disturbing. Their characters might have silently longed to adjust to society, but his were instinctively antisocial and likely never to know shelter or security. Theirs might stop thinking by the end of the movie about whether or not they were happy, but his often got killed. Brando provided more than variations on the theme of youthful wrath and adult practicality; he was, after all, the only actor of his era to portray a genuine grown-up revolutionary in *Viva Zapata.*

In most of his movies, however, Brando appeared more alone and more isolated than his fellow actors, more detached from family, class, regional, and ethnic ties. Even in *A Streetcar Named Desire, Viva Zapata, On the Waterfront,* and *The Fugitive Kind,* where he played roles rooted in concrete social settings or historical periods, Brando's singular magnetism lay in the solitude and estrangement he projected beyond the special situations of time or place. In the midst of motorcyclists, dockworkers, or Mexican peasants, he seemed aloof and nearly unapproachable (perhaps of his successors, only Robert De Niro conveys the same sense of loneliness and mystery). The archetypal "wild one," Brando raised the image of the outcast to the level of myth. His characters were indeed powerful commentaries on and correctives to the reigning middle-class ideals. Yet they also suggested something else. In a decade with no visible social causes but plenty of moral crises, Brando's screen personality and demeanor hinted at the radical possibilities implicit in private, idiosyncratic dissent.

And he left a legacy. The attraction to drifters, lawbreakers, marginal people without conventional bonds and dependent only on themselves or on one another was enlarged in the 1960s and 1970s to the point where whole films, rather than single characters, became testaments to the legend of the rebellious outsider. *Bonnie and Clyde, The Wild Bunch, Alice's Restaurant, Easy Rider, Midnight Cowboy, Scarecrow, McCabe and Mrs. Miller* all reflected Brando's influence as an actor and as a political and cultural symbol. So it was appropriate that in *Last Tango in Paris* Brando himself should play the alienated bum at middle age, Stanley Kowalski or Terry Malloy twenty years older but still protecting his integrity, his right to be somebody, the perpetual contender searching for the moment when he can announce to the world—as Brando announces to Maria Schneider in the movie's closing scene—that this at last is the "title shot, baby. We're going all the way."

But where Stanley howled only for Stella, Allen Ginsberg and his friends howled for America, for the "best minds" of their generation "destroyed by madness," for that miraculous time when the country would be "worthy" of its "million Trotsky-ites."[57] The Beats were Method poets and novelists: They testified to the same frustrations, paid homage to the same cult of sensuality and experience, showed the same discourtesy to their elders, and appeared in the eyes of their critics equally illiterate and unintelligible—not only bohemians but barbarians snarling at the civilized decorum of both the bourgeoisie and the intellectual elite.

Like the Method actors, the Beats were often treated less as a group of artists with their own particular goals, triumphs, and failures, than as an emblem of whatever tendencies in American life the intellectuals currently disliked. Of course, the Beats themselves yearned to be more than a literary movement, and they conspired with newspapers and mass circulation magazines to promote their image as buffoons, free spirits, charlatans, hobos, latter-day Dadaists, and trend setters for the young. Their argot, their lofts, their bizarre attire, their pronouncements about drugs and sex, their transcontinental journeys, and their addiction to jazz and arcane Oriental trances all received wider publicity than their novels or poems. In fact, the titles of their two best-known works, Allen Ginsberg's *Howl* and Jack Kerouac's *On the Road*, both sounded sufficiently illustrative of the authors' intentions and outlook that one wondered how many people proceeded to the texts. It was not surprising, therefore, that intellectuals attuned to the same gossip should discuss the Beats as barometers of America's cultural disarray, instead of as individual writers with something distinctive to say.

Occasionally, a commentator could rise above caricature and listen to the words. In 1959, Allen Ginsberg, accompanied by Gregory Corso and Peter Orlovsky, gave a poetry reading at Columbia University. For Ginsberg this was a homecoming of sorts, since he had been an undergraduate at Columbia in the late 1940s, a student of no less an eminence than Lionel Trilling. Diana Trilling decided with some trepidation to attend the reading, leaving Lionel at home to preside at one of those "pleasant professional" gatherings where every man was "dressed in a proper suit" (except in this instance W. H. Auden, who regardless of his "battered old brown leather jacket" could not imagine how Diana might find the Beats interesting or newsworthy).[58] She herself was not entirely sure why she wanted to go, but the expedition did yield an article for *Partisan Review* that was at once satiric, self-mocking, and ultimately poignant.

With two other faculty wives, Ms. Trilling strode into the auditorium expecting the worst. Rumors had earlier spread of "vast barbarian hordes" converging on Columbia "from all the dark recesses of the city, howling for their leader." And here she sat, a trenchant literary and cultural critic in her own right, well connected to the academic world and the salons of the New York intellectuals, waiting to hear the pied piper of a protest movement which, characteristically for the 1950s, had assumed the "wholly non-political form of a bunch of panic-stricken kids in blue jeans, many of them publicly homosexual, talking about or taking drugs, assuring us that they [were] out of their minds, not responsible." As she scanned the hall, the audience looked more ominous, or maybe just more depressing, than the Visigoths about to seize the stage: She had to confront again the "always-new shock of so many young girls, so few of them pretty, and so many dreadful black stockings; so many young men, so few of them—despite the many black beards—with any promise of masculinity."[59] The clash of styles between her genteel companions and the pubescent throng that filled the hall portended a far greater collision of the generations. It required some getting used to—not only the assault on literary standards and the hierarchy of moral values, but also the collapse of old-fashioned clearly defined sexual preferences.

Yet Ms. Trilling needn't have worried. She was relieved to discover that the crowd, for all its slovenly appearance, did not "smell bad." Quite the contrary, "the audience was clean and Ginsberg was clean and Corso was clean and Orlovsky was clean." Besides, she told herself, "there's nothing dirty about a checked shirt or a lumberjacket and blue jeans, they're standard uniform in the best nursery schools." Moreover, the Academy imposed its own ancient etiquette on the invaders, affording them a "dignity" and respectability they otherwise lacked. The chairman for the evening was F. W. Dupee, a duly certified professor in the department of English and a founding editor of *Partisan Review*. He introduced Ginsberg by reminding the audience—with no trace of irony in his voice—that the last poet to read his work from this "same Columbia platform" was none other than T. S. Eliot. Dupee thereby "transformed a circus into a classroom." To Ms. Trilling's astonishment, Ginsberg himself in these surroundings acted more like an Oxford don than an oracle of looting and pillage. He was "very earnest about wanting his poetry to be understood"; he and his cohorts claimed the "right to be heard in the university" by demonstrating their "studious devotion to their art"; in the question-and-answer period, Ginsberg even appeared upset when he uttered an involuntary obscenity.[60]

Most of all, as Ginsberg read his verse aloud, he seemed to Ms. Trilling an unconscious traditionalist, giving the poems a natural "iambic beat." And no matter the "zany path" of his life, he tackled all the customary poetic subjects—"mourning and mothers and such." Ginsberg, it turned out, was not just part of a "sociological phenomenon"; he was a real person with parents, mentors, artistic ambitions, a man capable of acknowledging intellectual debts, as when he dedicated one of his poems to . . . Lionel Trilling.[61]

On returning home, Diana Trilling informed the gentlemen conversing politely in her "comfortable living-room" that she had been deeply moved (a sentiment for which Auden thought she should be "ashamed"). But she was not embarrassed. Instead she had one more disconcerting detail to add. "Allen Ginsberg read a love-poem to you, Lionel," she related; "I liked it very much." Later she supposed this remark might have been "a strange thing to say in the circumstances, perhaps even a little foolish. But I'm sure that Ginsberg's old teacher knew what I was saying, and why I was impelled to say it."[62]

Diana Trilling hardly evolved into a patron of the Beats after the bacchanal at Columbia. In order for her to approve their work at all, she had to emphasize their underlying conventionality and their links to the literary past. But however prim she made herself sound as an emissary from the educated classes reporting on her transactions with the sans-culottes, she did regard Ginsberg as a diligent, knowledgeable, and surprisingly decent poet.

Norman Podhoretz was not about to let himself be seduced by the Beats' pretensions to art. One could read his tirade against these "know-nothing" hooligans, published in *Partisan Review* in 1958, as a preview of the way many postwar intellectuals would respond to the New Left and the counterculture of the 1960s.

To Podhoretz, the Beats were harbingers of an apocalypse, not the legitimate heirs to any cultural tradition—least of all modernism. The American expatriates of the 1920s, he recollected, had rebelled against Gopher Prairie "in the name of civilization."

They consecrated themselves to the ideals of "intelligence, cultivation, spiritual refinement"; that was why they fled to Europe. Similarly, at their best the radicals of the 1930s exhibited a "deep intellectual seriousness." But the bohemianism of the 1950s, Podhoretz asserted, was "hostile to civilization"; it worshiped "primitivism, instinct, energy," and "emotion rather than cerebration." Like Robert Brustein's Method actors, Podhoretz's Beats looked upon the English language as "enemy territory"; their distinguishing trait was the "simple inability to express anything in words." In his view, shared also by Irving Howe, the Beat movement's immersion in "mystical doctrines" and "irrationalist philosophies," together with its "contempt for coherent . . . discourse," were all signs of its ferocious "anti-intellectualism."[63]

When in the twentieth century had these attitudes been previously trumpeted? The Beats, according to Podhoretz, did have a political if not a cultural ancestry: They were descendants of the Nazis. Theirs was yet another "revolt of the spiritually underprivileged and the crippled of soul." Despite their public amiability and the celebration of tolerance and peaceful meditation in their novels and poems, Podhoretz was not misled. He recognized the lust for "brutality" implicit in their works (as well as their "enormous" anxiety about their sexual performances); he detected in their statements the rancor of "young men who can't think straight and so hate anyone who can"; he sensed their barely suppressed desire to "kill the intellectuals" and all those other "incomprehensible characters who are capable of getting seriously involved with a woman, a job, a cause."[64]

Such latent malevolence must be repulsed, Podhoretz warned, before it erupted into a full-scale social war. As those most immediately imperiled, the intellectuals had to take a forthright stand against the Beat movement by "denying that incoherence [was] superior to precision; that ignorance [was] superior to knowledge"; that "carelessness" was a form of "spontaneity" and "inarticulateness" a form of "eloquence." In words that would have gratified Herman Wouk, Podhoretz implored his fellow writers to fight the "poisonous glorification of the adolescent in American popular culture," while supplying "authoritative standards to guide the young."[65] Only then could the nation feel safe from the newest savages.

Although Podhoretz was more strident than other critics in his denunciation of the Beats, both his irascibility and his stalwart defense of rationality, maturity, and high culture reflected the alarm of a generation of intellectuals that felt itself increasingly under siege. The "bohemians" offended those writers who had been reared on modernist literature, the Marxism of the Depression years, and the polemics of the Cold War, who loved to play with language and ideas, who thought of the intellectual life not only as a noble calling but also as fun. They had no ingrained fondness for and no wish to understand the Beat movement's fascination with vagabonds and peasants, its studied indifference to logic and erudition, its adoration of jazz and narcotics, its casual approach to sex, its lack of interest in politics or social theory. Yet the intellectuals' antagonism toward the Beats involved more than a conflict over values, styles, and preoccupations. What bothered the writers clustered around *Commentary* and *Partisan Review* was whether they would remain America's cultural arbiters in the future.

In the 1960s, this question loomed larger, and it made some intellectuals even more petulant. Looking back, the bohemians of the 1950s appeared tame in comparison with the New Left, just as Elvis Presley's songs sounded chaste next to those of the Rolling Stones. The Beats at least cared about literature, no matter how sloppy their prose; the devotees of the counterculture limited their esthetic affections almost exclusively to rock music and movies. Meanwhile, the younger radicals challenged the intellectuals on political grounds, putting out their own magazines and reiterating their own aphorisms, while trying to subvert the authority of administrators and professors in the universities. No wonder William Barrett, recalling the "disturbed" and "squalid" atmosphere of the 1960s from the neoconservative perspective of the 1980s, could grumble about the "excessively democratic" follies of that permissive decade, particularly the onslaughts against the "restraining barriers of taste." No wonder he had been glad to hurry past the first floor of the Museum of Modern Art, where the latest acquisitions seemed to him little more than "junk," and "escape upstairs to the permanent collection and the company of the Modern Masters."[66]

But the rift between the intelligentsia and the bohemians, in both the late 1950s and the 1960s, obscured what each group held in common. The Beats and the New Left shared the intellectuals' antipathy to suburbia, conformity, and mass culture. They all were sensitive to the monotony of modern work, the melancholy effects of affluence, the dangers in the centralization of power, and the terrors of nuclear annihilation. They believed equally in the importance of dissent, the need for independent thinking, the value of personal resistance.

And they were alike in one other way. The unwillingness of most intellectuals to acknowledge that the Beats, the partisans of the New Left, and the enthusiasts of the counterculture were their spiritual children was matched by the unwillingness of most of the neobohemians to acknowledge that the intellectuals were their spiritual parents. Thus the battle for cultural supremacy that began in the late 1950s and intensified in the 1960s was waged with all the hysteria one would expect to find in a typical family quarrel.

The Rebirth of the Left

One of the intellectuals' most unremitting complaints about the new bohemianism was that it failed to channel its sense of anger and discontent into constructive political programs. The Beats were scarcely alone in ignoring politics and other domestic issues during the 1950s, but in the middle of the decade a few writers began to point out that the Cold War, McCarthyism, suburbia, conformity, and mass culture were not the only quandaries with which Americans had to cope. Toward the end of the 1950s, this perception was corroborated by the emergence of the civil rights movement, the "rediscovery" of the poor, the crisis in education, and the evident strains in the economy. By 1960, after assuming for nearly fifteen years that the ideas of the Left were no longer applicable to a prosperous society, a growing number of intellectuals found themselves talking optimistically about a resurgence of reform and even of radicalism in the United States.

The origins of this revival could be traced to 1954. In that year, three significant events occurred: the Supreme Court's decision in Brown versus the Board of Education to order the desegregation of the nation's public schools; the Democrats' success in regaining control of Congress in the fall elections after having lost their majorities in the Eisenhower landslide of 1952; and the Senate's official condemnation of Joseph McCarthy.

At the same moment, a new journal appeared, appropriately named *Dissent,* that sought to rekindle the intellectuals' interest in democratic socialism. Its initial editorial board included Irving Howe, Lewis Coser, Meyer Schapiro, Erich Fromm, A. J. Muste, and Norman Mailer. Later in the decade, the quarterly added Michael Harrington, Norman Thomas, and Michael Walzer. Among its occasional contributors were Harold Rosenberg, C. Wright Mills, Harvey Swados, Richard Chase, Dwight Macdonald, and Paul Goodman. By 1957, it claimed a circulation of 4000—substantially below *Partisan Review, Commentary,* the *Nation,* or the *New Republic,* but large enough to exert an influence within the intellectual community.

The early articles in *Dissent* seemed at once pugnacious and defensive, as if the editors felt they first had to prove they weren't deranged to launch a magazine of the left in an age when many writers had drifted to the right. The opening editorial admitted that "no significant socialist movement" currently existed or was likely to arise any time soon. Nonetheless, the editors promised to attack the status quo as "independent radicals," discussing "freely and honestly what in the socialist tradition remains alive and what needs to be discarded or modified," and barring from their pages only "Stalinists" and those ex-leftists who had made their "peace" with society.[67]

Thereafter, the editors tried not to let their anti-Communism turn them into celebrants of America. To this end, they continually chided the liberals for having neglected the darker side of American affluence: the "crucial role" that "war production" played in maintaining the nation's prosperity; the government's "promotion of corporate power"; the "maldistribution of income"; inadequate medical care; the "haphazard" introduction of automation and its effect on blue-collar workers. Irving Howe was especially indignant about the presumption "that America consists exclusively of the middle class." Why, he wanted to know, did none of the rhapsodists of the "American character" think to investigate the "gradual decay of the New England textile towns or the social disruption of New York City under the pressure of Puerto Rican migration?" Why did no one trouble to find out whether the lives of the Southern sharecroppers had improved since the 1930s? Why did sociologists and journalists publish books like *The Lonely Crowd* and *The Organization Man,* and not also dream of "writing a sequel to James Agee's *Let Us Now Praise Famous Men?*"[68] A socialist America might be a fantasy at present, but a reexamination of such elementary matters as racism, poverty, industrial obsolescence, and urban disintegration seemed long overdue to Howe.

Yet *Dissent* itself often spent more time raising questions and enumerating problems than suggesting solutions or engaging in an extended analysis of American capitalism. This was chiefly because its editors could discern no radical constituency in the mid-1950s comparable to the labor movement of the 1930s. Initially, therefore, they conceived their task as one of keeping open the possibilities for socialism in the distant future. The journal, Lewis Coser submitted in 1956, should seek to "establish a link between radicals of an older generation and younger men and women who are untouched and even bored by the rhetoric of the thirties, yet repelled and frightened by the realities of the fifties." It should also exemplify to disaffected youths the "virtue of patience," the importance of simply being able to "endure." Finally, *Dissent* ought to foster "small enclaves" of "radical thought" where the values of criticism were esteemed and the contradictions between liberal ideals and "conformist behavior," between "democratic theory and bureaucratic practice," were exposed.[69]

These goals, however, were more in the nature of a holding action, analogous to what Irving Howe in another context described as the expatriates' effort "to find an honorable style of survival in a time of moral confusion."[70] One hesitates to think of Coser or Howe as reincarnations of Jake Barnes, but the editors of *Dissent* did see themselves as a tiny band of exiles (albeit in New York rather than Paris or Pamplona) whose continuing commitment to a socialist consciousness was as much a test of personal courage and resilience as an expression of political faith.

Apart from their doubts about the prospects for an early rebirth of radicalism in America, the editors were also reluctant to deluge their readers with "blueprints" and "elaborate schemes" because they shared the postwar aversion to utopias of every kind. Indeed, the editors sometimes appeared more eager to specify the preconditions for democracy than to sketch the outlines of a rehabilitated socialism. Drawing on the ideas of everyone from Daniel Bell and David Riesman to Dwight Macdonald and C. Wright Mills, Howe and Coser argued that any conception of an altered society must contain provisions for greater public participation in "decision-making," smaller units of industrial production over which the "non-expert" might exercise "real control," more guilds and cooperatives, and the strengthening of "pluralist" institutions to restrain the "concentration of authority" at the top. In addition, since the impact of the mass media, the threat to civil liberties, and the "general alienation of men in modern society" were as significant a set of problems as "economic injustice," the contemporary radical had to discover ways of allowing the individual "to be himself," to achieve a sense of "personal autonomy" in his daily relationships. But to be a socialist in the 1950s, Coser declared, meant above all to "refuse" one's "consent"; resistance almost for its own sake was a prerequisite "for any wider activity."[71]

Dissent's credo in the mid-1950s seemed more existential than Marxist, more a form of private protest than a rousing call for social change. Still, the editors succeeded in their main objective of providing a forum for the reassessment of socialist ideas. And as the nation's difficulties grew more transparent in the decade's waning years, *Dissent*'s very existence encouraged its competitors —some of whom had previously jeered at its self-righteousness —to broaden their own criticisms of American life.

Perhaps this shift in attitude was most noticeable at *Commentary*, though its adoption of a new outlook and format at the end of the 1950s came not just as a response to political and social events, but also as the result of a personal tragedy. In May 1959, after five years of severe psychiatric problems, Eliot Cohen committed suicide. The American Jewish Committee, the journal's publishers, eventually appointed Norman Podhoretz as the new editor beginning with the February 1960 issue.

Notwithstanding his contempt for the Beats and their entourage, Podhoretz had no intentions of being an apologist for America. He too was disturbed by certain trends in the late 1950s, several of which he identified in his introductory editorial: the possibility that "the prosperity of the Eisenhower Age [was] a deceptive sign of vigor and health"; the "boredom one senses on all sides, the torpor, the anxiety, the listlessness"; the fixation on the Cold War that prevented the nation from realizing its "future potentialities."[72] Podhoretz also had numerous objections to *Commentary*'s own posture during these years, as he later recalled. Having been impressed with the Soviet Union's capacity for reform after Khrushchev's denunciation of Stalin in 1956, he was bothered by the continuation of *Commentary*'s "hard anti-Communist position" as well as by its inclination to "place everything American in a favorable light," telling its readers "what was right" with their society far more frequently than "what was wrong." Hence, he hoped as editor to "take a fresh look at all the weary ideas and attitudes whose constant reiteration in the *Commentary* of the recent past . . . had made it so predictable."[73]

Additionally, Podhoretz—ever fascinated with the strategies by which one acquired cultural power in the United States—wanted to increase the magazine's prestige, get it "talked about once again in as many circles as possible," but especially among the "family" of New York intellectuals associated with *Partisan Review*. He embarked on a systematic campaign to attract as contributors those familial and by now familiar names: Lionel Trilling, Alfred Kazin, Dwight Macdonald, Hannah Arendt, Harold Rosenberg, William Barrett, Leslie Fiedler, Irving Howe. This was not, however, purely an exercise in editorial entrepreneurship. Podhoretz longed to convert *Commentary* into a "center for the revival of the long-dormant tradition of American social criticism." To help achieve this goal, the February 1960 issue featured the first installment of Paul Goodman's *Growing Up Absurd.* Ultimately, *Commentary*'s stature exceeded Podhoretz's original ambitions. Not only did it become more influential within the intellectual community because of its livelier approach to political and cultural affairs, but its general circulation climbed from 20,000 in 1960 to 60,000 by 1966.[74]

Yet *Commentary* was already changing even before Podhoretz took control. In 1958 and 1959, the journal started to publish a greater number of articles dealing with specific social and economic issues: the recession, unions, urban decay, juvenile delinquency, civil rights. One of the most dramatic examples of this tendency was the appearance in July 1959 of an essay by Michael Harrington on poverty in the United States which, along with a second article in August 1960, formed the basis of his classic book, *The Other America* (1962).

Harrington's interests were very different from those of most social critics in the 1950s. Where David Riesman, William Whyte, John Kenneth Galbraith, or C. Wright Mills concentrated on the mental habits and anxieties of the middle class, the dilemmas peculiar to affluence, and the structure of the national elite, assuming these to be the dominant concerns of a postindustrial society, Harrington returned the reader's attention to the "forgotten" Americans—the people whose situation was as wretched in the Eisenhower era as it had been in the age of Roosevelt. More than any other writer, he tried to deflate the "current myth" that the United States was a land of infinite economic promise, with its corollary that the poor were a "small, rapidly declining" sector of the population, "mostly non-whites and rural Southerners" whose numbers would shrink further as industrial productivity continued to rise, and who in any case had "achieved a substantial measure of protection as a result of the reforms of the New Deal." Countering these roseate notions, Harrington estimated that fifty million Americans—the same "third of the nation" FDR had memorialized—still lived below the "standards which we have been taught to regard as the decent minimums for food, housing, clothing, and health." In Harrington's portrait, the poor were "predominantly urban" and white.

They included the elderly who subsisted on fixed but inadequate pensions and who inhabited the most "blighted neighborhoods" of the cities, families trapped in regions of the country afflicted by industrial stagnation, the least skilled and lowest paid (janitors, maids and cleaning women, elevator operators, dishwashers, hospital orderlies, laundry attendants, migrant laborers), and certain minorities (blacks, Puerto Ricans, Mexican-Americans, Indians) shut away in ghettos or on reservations. These groups had not benefited from the welfare state; its "landmarks" —the right of collective bargaining, unemployment compensation, social security—largely aided the unionized workers and the middle class. Nor did the poor possess the necessary training to qualify for white-collar or highly technical jobs, which would have enabled them to share in the postwar prosperity. Basically, they survived according to Harrington on less than $4000 a year, and their plight was made more miserable by the present recession. Worst of all, Harrington denied that there was "any ground to hope for an easy, automatic amelioration" of America's mass, chronic poverty.[75]

A major reason for Harrington's pessimism was his sensitivity to the formidable problems of the poor. His essays did not simply disclose the statistics on poverty and identify the groups most cruelly oppressed. He cared equally about their cultural and psychological predicaments because these were as much a barrier to their escape from impoverishment as history and economics. In his view, the urban renewal schemes and public housing projects erected for the poor, the "concrete-and-steel warrens" so conspicuously lacking in cultural amenities and without any respect for ethnic or racial traditions, perpetuated both "ignorance" and a "slum psychology." They also intensified the feelings of failure, rootlessness, and alienation endemic to poverty. Imprisoned in the inner cities, devoid of aspiration, transmitting a mood of hopelessness and "passivity" from one generation to the next, more absorbed with immediate gratifications than with getting ahead or fulfilling the American Dream, the poor literally dwelt in "another nation."[76]

Given this grim diagnosis, Harrington thought the country could cure the disease of poverty only by committing itself to a "comprehensive" and specially designed regimen aimed at eradicating the "whole cultural and spiritual inheritance of the slum past." Specifically, he called on Washington to provide better health care and remedial education for adults as well as for children and adolescents, expand "social services of every kind," and experiment with small-scale low-rise housing "communities" integrated by race and income which would blend with the surrounding neighborhoods and permit the residents to make their own decisions about how to administer their environment.[77]

In the political climate of the late 1950s, Harrington's proposals sounded chimerical. Yet they helped inspire Lyndon Johnson's "war on poverty" in the 1960s, though because of another less benevolent war this particular battle never achieved the results Harrington envisioned. His principal contribution, however, was to make the poor visible again—indeed to make the persistence of poverty in the United States seem not only an economic scandal but a moral crime. In *The Other America*, Harrington wrote the book for which Irving Howe had yearned in 1955, a contemporary version of *Let Us Now Praise Famous Men* (and it was fitting, as the new decade dawned, that James Agee's own masterpiece should be reprinted in 1960).

Despite Harrington's assertion that the majority of the impoverished were whites, no discussion of their deprivation could be separated from the specter of racism. Just as magazines like *Dissent* and *Commentary* began to analyze the complexities of poverty near the end of the 1950s, so they had been devoting more of their pages to the spread of civil rights activity throughout the South. As early as 1956, Lewis Coser speculated on the vast implications of this new movement, guessing that the struggle against segregation might become "as meaningful a social act" as the "spectacular involvements" of the 1930s.[78] In 1957 and 1958, several articles by Samuel Lubell, Oscar Handlin, and C. Vann Woodward appeared in *Commentary* evaluating the dispatch of federal troops to Little Rock and the chances for congressional passage of civil rights legislation.[79] By 1960, a number of intellectuals—especially Michael Walzer, Dwight Macdonald, and David Riesman—were debating whether the tactic of nonviolent civil disobedience could serve as a political alternative both to conventional liberalism and to the moribund strategies of the Old Left.

For Walzer, the significance of the civil rights movement lay in its potential to transcend the two political dogmas most characteristic of the postwar years. The first of these followed from the rejection of Marxist ideology; it proclaimed that wholesale social change invariably brought purges, dictatorship, the "corruption of culture," and the "brutal manipulation of human beings." The second doctrine urged people to rely on "practical politics" and "gradual reform" as the only ways to avoid the nightmare of totalitarianism. In Walzer's judgment, there now existed a third course of action that was "radical and far-reaching" yet "entirely compatible with the moral repudiation of revolutionary terror."[80]

As it happened, the idea of resistance to which he referred was not novel even for the 1950s. On the contrary, as Walzer recalled, it had been a familiar weapon in the arsenal of American protest, though usually a last resort of the solitary individual whose "private conscience" moved him to oppose authority.[81] More recently, many writers—Dwight Macdonald, David Riesman, William Whyte, C. Wright Mills, Irving Howe, Lewis Coser, Philip Rahv, Lillian Hellman, Arthur Miller—had encouraged their readers to resist the centralization of power, the demands of the organization, the pressures of conformity, the intimidations of the McCarthyites, the diffusion of middle-brow tastes, and the deterioration of cultural standards. In fact, resistance became almost a catchword for intellectuals in the 1950s, the one device they could suggest to preserve some measure of personal freedom in a mass society.

What impressed Walzer was the extent to which black students and clerics were translating this essentially individualistic principle into a "collective activity," a new set of political instruments for the solution of "communal" problems. The current experiments with civil disobedience, he argued, did not offer occasions for a person simply to bear witness to social injustice, or to exhibit his "lonely courage" and capacity for martyrdom. Far from being "self-indulgent," the economic boycotts, marches, demonstrations, picketing, sit-ins at segregated lunch counters, and "freedom rides" to test discrimination in interstate transportation were all forms of "direct mass action" designed to mobilize blacks in the North and South as well as to win allies among white liberals.[82]

More important from Walzer's point of view, such techniques seemed superior to both old-fashioned "legalism" and revolutionary fanaticism. Reform, he observed, had always been a "governmental function," a "kind of philanthropy" dispensed from on high; revolution was typically the "task of professionals, requiring total commitment and life service." But the civil rights movement, as Walzer and Dwight Macdonald described it, appeared to be a miraculous blend of the differing values intellectuals had championed in the 1950s: It was decentralized and semi-anarchist in its dependence on "Gandhian" methods and face-to-face encounters; it seemed a product of "spontaneous" associations rooted in common local needs; it was receptive to new leaders who instinctively understood the advantages of popular participation; it represented a "politics for amateurs and citizens" who wanted once again to have some effect on decision making and some control over the "misuse of . . . power." Still, for all its radical connotations, the movement also displayed a conservative bent, another sign of its origins in the 1950s, which Walzer found equally appealing. Civil disobedience was really a tactic of moderation, not a prescription for endless upheaval, he submitted. It required "orderly and disciplined" preparation, together with a substantial degree of "self-control." And its intention was not to create a "utopia" but to achieve "concrete" and "limited" goals. Thus Walzer, Macdonald, and David Riesman each calculated that the civil rights movement could create a new constituency for even broader social changes, while at the same time retaining its pragmatic and democratic disposition.[83]

In retrospect, it is hard not to accuse these writers of wishful thinking. They had superimposed on the battle against segregation their own often conflicting sentiments. They longed for a movement that could demonstrate ideological restraint and a passion for radical innovation, that would remain small and personal yet alter the distribution of power on a national scale, that might link the individual to a "community" through the mechanism of resistance, though resistance itself—in spite of their efforts to invest it with fraternal meaning—was an idea which seemed fundamentally antithetical to all forms of social collaboration. Once more, as with the concept of "autonomy," the intellectuals were trying to find a theory and a cause that would allow them both to challenge the structure of American society and to continue to flourish within its institutional arrangements.

At the end of the 1950s, however, their aspirations for the civil rights movement sounded less contradictory than innocent. None of them could anticipate that the movement might eventually flounder, in part because its own strategies for restoring the voting rights of black people and integrating public facilities in the South were not adequate to construct the effective political coalition necessary to address the much more complicated issues of jobs, housing, and education. So one envies their sense of anticipation, their hopes for and enthusiasm about the tactics of civil disobedience, since such a moment may not soon come again.

There were a few writers in 1959 and 1960 who did feel somewhat less confident about where this resurgence of political activism might lead. Irving Howe, H. Stuart Hughes, Andrew Hacker (then a professor of government at Cornell), and Arthur Mitzman (a graduate student in European intellectual history at Brandeis with ties to the civil rights and antinuclear movements) were all intrigued with and generally pleased by the numerous signs of vitality on the left. Hughes exclaimed to the readers of *Partisan Review* that a new generation of radicals, many of them under the age of thirty, had "suddenly and surprisingly come to life after ten years of slumber." Notwithstanding the contentions of Daniel Bell, the attraction to "ideology and utopia" seemed "far from dead." Howe no longer considered himself and his colleagues at *Dissent* quite so alone; he now thought it possible that this "new American radicalism" could "push beyond the conventional liberal assumptions" without stumbling into the "corruptions and fantasies of the 1930s." In *Commentary,* Hacker focused on a small but influential group of graduate students in England and the United States who had grown "impatient with both the enlightened conservatism and the mild liberalism" of their senior professors; they were editing and writing for their own journals

—*New University Thought, Studies on the Left, New Left Review*—and their "radical outlook" was becoming more widespread. Mitzman predicted in *Dissent* that the Left would be guided in the 1960s and 1970s by precisely these students, "rather than by those who received their political training in the 1930s and 1940s."[84] From their articles, one gathered that C. Wright Mills's young intelligentsia was finally making its debut.

The new radicals also appeared to be adopting Mills's perspective and values. The issues they cared about, as reported by Hughes and Hacker, were certainly what Mills would have called the "big questions": segregation, the threat of nuclear war, the pernicious effects of mass culture on public opinion, the power of the military-industrial complex. Yet if the members of this generation were not consumed with trivia, neither were they rigidly doctrinaire. They saw themselves as "critics" rather than as "socialists"; they entertained "no illusions about Soviet Communism," nor were they devoted to the "abolition of private property" or the "establishing of human equality by political means." Their Marxism was pre-Bolshevik and undogmatic; it functioned as a "hypothesis" rather than as a "theory which effortlessly [furnished] ready answers to all social and historical questions." Like Mills, they said they hoped that "knowledge," not revolution, would ultimately change society.[85]

But there the resemblance ended. For despite the exhilaration with which these writers greeted the rebirth of radicalism, they were troubled by certain tendencies they could not overlook. Ironically it was Mitzman, himself a student, who offered the shrewdest insights about his generation. Though written in 1960, his article was eerily prophetic; many of his warnings could have been reproduced ten years later as explanations for why the New Left failed to fulfill its promise.

The young radicals, Mitzman pointed out, were cool toward "programs and *realpolitik*" since the "resolutions, machinations and polemics" of the Communists, socialists, and liberals, seemed "both futile and totally unnecessary for dealing with such clearcut questions as Strontium 90 and the right of a child to be decently educated." Having watched the older left-wing groups either insist on revolutionary purity or compromise their principles for an alliance with the Democratic party, Mitzman's generation had a justifiable "aversion to theory" and to bureaucratic organization. Yet in his opinion, these attitudes encouraged some less admirable traits: a prejudice against "rational thinking," an emphasis on a "direct emotional response" to issues, a preference for "moral" rather than political causes, an inclination to "chew over a few simple slogans and dicta," an indifference to "intellectual development." If anything, the New Leftists had learned too much from the mistakes of their elders, and they were overcompensating. To Mitzman, the radicals of the early 1960s seemed insufficiently "ideological"; like the Beats, they were essentially "rebels whose goals are so undefined and whose means are so undiscriminating that they can easily exhaust themselves in actions peripheral to their main purpose."[86]

Both Mitzman and Hacker believed these weaknesses could be overcome only if the young were able to create a "new radical theory" as well as provide "some concrete pictures" of a "better social order" for America. Even then, Hacker realized that in an affluent society, with neither a "class-conscious proletariat" nor any other obvious constituency for which to speak, it would be extraordinarily difficult for the new radicals to maintain their commitments over a lifetime.[87]

Regardless of their premonitions that the New Left might turn out to be as anti-intellectual and as capricious as the new bohemians, most of the contributors to *Dissent, Partisan Review,* and Norman Podhoretz's *Commentary* welcomed the transformations in American politics and social life at the close of the 1950s. Whatever the turmoil that could erupt in the future, the civil rights movement, the campaign to ban the bomb, the willingness of more and more people to engage in acts of resistance and civil disobedience, and the revival of interest in Marxist ideas all suggested that the United States was about to enter an epoch very different from the postwar years. It remained only for these trends to have some impact on the rhetoric and policies of the country's political leaders.

America After Eisenhower

Following Adlai Stevenson's defeat in 1952, the majority of intellectuals paid little attention to the internal squabbles and daily tribulations of the major parties. Perhaps this was because neither the Republicans nor the Democrats were doing anything exciting enough to talk about. Indeed, the dearth of fundamental conflicts between the two parties probably made the decade appear more quiescent than it actually was. The *New Republic* and the *Nation,* of course, continued their weekly coverage of political events. A few writers like Arthur Schlesinger and John Kennet⌐ Galbraith rejoined Stevenson in his doomed campaign of 195€ Other intellectuals, however, considered the truly interesting subjects to lie outside the political arena. They might discuss the institutional requirements for a stable and successful democracy; they might praise the nation's pragmatic temperament and the readiness of all groups to bargain and compromise; some might even examine the anatomy of the modern elite. Yet whatever aspects of the political system they chose to stress, they clearly did not want to spend their time scrutinizing the prosaic details of party strife. So their books and magazine articles were filled with sophisticated analyses of foreign affairs, social and economic problems, popular culture, the mentality of the middle class— while the programs and fortunes of America's leading politicians went largely ignored.

When on occasion they did survey the current political landscape, they could barely conceal their disaffection from and boredom with the Republicans and Democrats. In 1958, for example, William V. Shannon (then the Washington columnist for the New York *Post*) published a post-mortem on the Eisenhower administration in *Commentary* even though the president was only halfway through his second term. Undaunted, Shannon offered what became the standard appraisal of Eisenhower's reign until revisionist historians in the 1970s discovered virtues in the president's decisions and pronouncements that the intellectuals of the 1950s seemed unable to detect.

To Shannon, Eisenhower was at best a "transition figure." The president had not tried to shape the future, but neither had he repealed the past. Instead he was content to live off "the accumulated wisdom, the accumulated prestige, and the accumulated military strength of his predecessors," Franklin Roosevelt and Harry Truman. Meanwhile, he had "settled for" uneasy truces in Korea and Indo-China, a "minimum accommodation" with the Soviet Union in Europe, and a working arrangement with the Democrats in Congress that preserved the New Deal and the mixed economy. At the end of Eisenhower's tenure in office, Shannon forecast, the foreign and domestic policies of the "past generation" would still be intact, and the venerable "American Consensus" would remain "undisturbed."[88]

But in Shannon's gloomy opinion, the Eisenhower interregnum had also been "the time of the great postponement." No important "national problem, whether it be education, housing, urban revitalization, agriculture, or inflation" was any nearer to solution. Thus regardless of Eisenhower's affability and personal charm, his good intentions and his sense of moderation, he was leaving to his successors a "black heritage of time lost and opportunities wasted."[89]

If Eisenhower appeared to be in Shannon's account less a benign grandfather than a drowsy old man, Adlai Stevenson fared no better at the hands of Irving Howe. In fact, Howe was not concerned with Stevenson's positions or ideas, but with why he alone among contemporary politicians so captivated the intelligentsia. On domestic issues, Howe recalled, Harry Truman had been farther to the left. In contrast, Stevenson failed to arouse "much enthusiasm" in the working class, nor did he invoke the "plebeian sentiments" of the Roosevelt coalition. Yet he "completely captured the intellectuals," particularly those who were otherwise "disabused with the political life."[90] Since Stevenson was hardly a liberal, Howe concluded that his principal appeal lay in his style, in the subliminal messages he conveyed to his well-educated audiences, in how he spoke rather than what he said. The intellectuals saw in Stevenson the values they ascribed to themselves.

Stevenson's famous ambivalence about his status as a presidential candidate, Howe argued, perfectly mirrored the intellectuals' own "mixed feelings" about their participation in national affairs. On the one hand, they "admired and identified" with Stevenson "because he didn't seem really to *like* politics." Mysteriously, he gave the impression that his private emotions, his wit, his ironic approach to life were all divorced from the public role he was forced to play. On the other hand, both he and the intellectuals wanted to be "realists," even though this meant accepting the notion that every social group was simply jostling "for a little more of the contaminated swill." Stevenson's "soaring rhetoric" and his refusal to scramble after power permitted the intellectuals to suppose that they too could retain a bit of their idealism along with their new-found cynicism. In the end, Howe submitted, they could imagine that Stevenson was just like them (or at any rate how they wished to be). He was not a "mere politician" but a "statesman," a man of culture and learning who reluctantly assumed the burdens of leadership, a well-bred old-style intellectual whose courtly manners and genteel restraint led him to call "a spade an implement for the lifting of difficult objects."[91]

Howe's caricature resembled Mort Sahl's description of Stevenson as a typical Unitarian, the sort of man who believed in the "Ten Suggestions," and who would—if he were a member of the Ku Klux Klan—burn a question mark on your lawn. But in 1954, when Howe delivered his verdict, he was less amused than angry with both Stevenson and the intellectuals for the timidity of their response to McCarthyism. He may, however, have exaggerated their infatuation with Stevenson's style. Though Stevenson served as a prototype for the new breed of politicians emerging in the late 1950s, his charisma did not seem transferable. Whatever affection the intellectuals still felt for him, they were not nearly so enchanted with his clones.

By 1959, enough young liberal Democrats (John F. Kennedy, Edmund Muskie, Eugene McCarthy, Frank Church, Henry Jackson, William Proxmire, Philip Hart) and equally young, equally liberal Republicans (Nelson Rockefeller, Mark Hatfield, Clifford Case) had been elected as senators or governors to suggest that the American voter might at last be awakening from the somnolence of the Eisenhower era, might perhaps be longing for a return to the fervor and commotion of the Roosevelt–Truman years. Yet Lewis Coser and Karl Meyer, an editor of the Washington *Post* who also wrote for *Commentary,* did not rejoice in these developments. Quite the contrary, they feared that the passion of the New Deal was simply giving way to the geniality of the "Smooth Deal." In their eyes, the new politicians were "personable" and efficient, reasonably bright and aware of their limitations. But they also lacked a sense of purpose and a capacity for "indignation"; in place of Harry Truman's deep-rooted "partisanship" or even Henry Wallace's missionary zeal, they substituted prudence, "earnest sincerity," and a "bland smile." They advised no overhaul of the social system, only small repairs and adjustments. And though they regarded themselves as the political offspring of Adlai Stevenson, they had departed in one important respect from the Stevensonian tradition. According to Coser and Meyer, they looked and behaved less like patricians than suburbanites; their growing prominence foreshadowed not the ascendancy of the eggheads but the triumph of the "man in the middle."[92]

Given their caustic evaluations of all the current political leaders, it was scarcely surprising that many of the contributors to *Dissent* and *Commentary* expected little from Washington no matter who was in charge. Throughout the late 1950s, they regularly complained that both the Republicans and Democrats were "utterly without principle," that neither party was willing to confront the problems of modern American life. "Ikeism represents a sublime faith in the powers of drift," Irving Howe fumed; the present administration had convinced itself that the nation's affluence was "eternal and ordained," and so ignored "the great gaping holes in the fabric of . . . prosperity." But "Adlaism" was "fast becoming . . . Ikeism," only "with a touch of literacy and intelligence." In the meantime, "real differences of interest and opinion" got submerged in "compromise and rhetoric," while the substantive issues before the country were being systematically evaded.[93]

With neither liberals nor conservatives offering new ideas or programs, the question for some intellectuals on the eve of the 1960 presidential election was not which candidate to vote for but whether to vote at all. In the pages of *Commentary*, one could find articles by Norman Podhoretz, Dennis Wrong, and Dwight Macdonald asserting that Richard Nixon and John F. Kennedy were virtually indistinguishable in their domestic and foreign policies, indeed that each lacked the stature and magnetism of Adlai Stevenson or Nelson Rockefeller. Macdonald took the occasion to announce his intention to abstain. Since the 1930s, he had distrusted the liberals' quadrennial search for a political savior to vanquish whomever they considered an arch-villain, and he was presently unmoved by their frantic efforts to "Keep Nixon out of the White House." In his view, "national politics" was "mere busy-work to divert the civic-minded" from the "local, practical matters" over which they might have some genuine control. The alternative to Nixon, therefore, was not Kennedy but a form of "decentralization" which would "break up mass society into communities small enough so that the individual can make himself felt, can express and defend *his own special interests.*"[94]

Macdonald's vision, or at least his language, was later appropriated by radicals in the 1960s who talked about returning power to the people, and by conservatives in the 1970s who talked about returning power to the states. At the time, however, his argument failed to persuade many intellectuals, largely because the kinds of problems with which they and the nation had recently been struggling—desegregation, the recession, the persistence of poverty, urban decay, the ambiguous implications of détente, America's relationship to the Third World—could only be dealt with, if at all, by the federal government. Thus despite their disillusion with the major parties, most writers still thought it made some difference who ruled in Washington.

Moreover, the election of 1960 provided confirmation that a change had taken place in the country's political mood. The discontents of the late 1950s—whether reflected in the rise of the Beat generation, the civil rights demonstrations, the antinuclear movement, or the emergence of a New Left—were finally being addressed, no matter how vaguely, in the presidential campaign. This in turn caused several writers to speculate that the government might again be a source of innovation and reform. For all his skepticism about conventional politics, Irving Howe conceded even before the campaign began that a Democratic victory was likely because the public no longer trusted the "image of well-being and assurance" which had dominated American life for the past decade.[95] Immediately after the election, Michael Walzer noted that Kennedy's "central theme" had been "America's decline." Whatever this meant for future policies, it certainly marked "the end of the great celebration." Complacency, Walzer observed, was now "out of date" in Washington: "There is an openness to new ideas probably unlike anything since the thirties."[96]

To Amitai Etzioni, a sociologist at Columbia writing in *Commentary*, these trends were not unique to the United States. In western Europe as well as in America, he contended, ordinary people, political activists, and government officials were transferring their attention to a "new set of social problems." The primary concerns of the postwar years had been economic redevelopment and the steady increase of productivity. The issues of the 1960s would involve the proper allocation of private and public expenditures, the responsibility of the state to subsidize education and medical care, the implementation of a guaranteed annual wage, and the quest for improvements in the quality of life. In international affairs, Etzioni predicted, a growing number of Europeans and Americans would try to broaden the limited goals of peaceful coexistence to include a more general nuclear disarmament and the "termination of the cold war." For Etzioni as for Howe, all of these impulses attested to a revival of liberalism throughout the West.[97] On the basis of their prognoses, a reader might conclude that if the United States in particular was not quite ready to embrace the ideas of Dwight Macdonald, Paul Goodman, or C. Wright Mills, it had all but succumbed to the doctrines of John Kenneth Galbraith.

Yet while the majority of intellectuals were happy to leave the Eisenhower era behind, their hopes for the incoming administration were tempered with caution. Kennedy, after all, had been elected by a plurality of only 118,000 votes, the slimmest margin in seventy-two years. While winning the presidency, his party lost two seats in the Senate and twenty-two in the House of Representatives. Hence, his triumph seemed rather more personal than ideological. As Michael Walzer pointed out, Kennedy possessed no mandate to remake the country, nor in the course of the campaign did he endow the "new frontier" with any "programmatic substance." Instead, Kennedy skillfully articulated America's "restlessness" and "dissatisfaction" without creating a "liberal constituency" or specifying his positions on the major issues.

"Voting for Kennedy," Walzer declared, was essentially "an act of faith."[98]

Still, the very amorphousness of Kennedy's victory increased the chances for political and social experimentation. The implications of the 1960 election were exactly the opposite of those in 1948. Where Truman's triumph ratified a consensus that had already evolved on domestic and international affairs, thereby reinforcing the impression that there was nothing more to discuss, Kennedy's election could lead to an exploration of alternatives beyond those his administration might be willing to propose. But for intellectuals to make the most of this opportunity, they would have to remain the critics of their society, rather than become the counselors to Camelot.

From the perspective of 1960, the times could not have seemed more auspicious for writers to expand on the ideas they had developed in the 1940s and 1950s. Despite the difficulties of the past fifteen years—the pressures of the Cold War, the effects of McCarthyism, the problems of affluence, the heightening conflicts over culture and values—the country had remained socially and psychologically intact. It was thus possible for the intellectuals and their fellow citizens to believe that blacks and whites would continue to work together to eliminate racism, that poverty could be permanently abolished, that the nuclear arms race could be curtailed. It was also possible to believe that change could come in America without class and generational hatreds, riots, imperial presidencies, political repression, the televised carnage in Vietnam, or the murder of public men. No one, least of all the intellectuals, foresaw the shattering of these assumptions in the next two decades. For the moment, they felt little nostalgia for the past and much eagerness for whatever the future might bring.

Epilogue:
The Legacy of the Postwar Years

The image of postwar America as politically conservative and economically content was first introduced in the 1950s, mostly by intellectuals, novelists, poets, and journalists who could not stand the complacency of the middle class, the "silence" in the universities, and the miasma of conformity that infected every corner of national life. Then in the context of the turbulent 1960s, these stereotypes were dramatically reinforced. Not since the stock market crash obliterated the boom of the 1920s and ushered in the Great Depression had two adjoining decades seemed less alike. People in the 1950s were supposed to be sedate, blandly indifferent to social movements, exclusively concerned with their private predicaments. Their successors in the 1960s were perceived as shrill, intensely involved in public causes, in search of communal solutions to the problems of living in the modern world. Just as October 1929 marked the end of one era, so the election of John F. Kennedy presumably signaled the close of another phase in American history.

Yet in both instances, the ruptures may not have been as severe as they appeared at the time. The New Deal gave the country a new politics, a new collection of government agencies, and a new set of social and economic reforms. But the underlying values and assumptions of the average American in the 1930s did not seem so very different from those of the previous decade. Similarly, the youths who came of age in the 1960s might have had more in common with their older brothers and sisters who grew up in the 1950s (and with their parents whose formative experiences occurred in the midst of the Depression and World War II) than any of these generations cared to admit.

One way the essential continuities between the postwar years and the 1960s can best be seen is by exploring the ramifications of those ideas the intellectuals advanced to explain and criticize their society in the 1940s and 1950s. Though nearly every writer professed his disenchantment with the slogans and ideologies of the 1930s, though many believed that sweeping institutional changes in the United States were no longer necessary or desirable, though they feared mass movements and violent upheavals as the breeding grounds for totalitarianism, they did want to analyze the special and unprecedented dilemmas that now afflicted an affluent and stable America. All of these attitudes, however, contributed to the emergence of a rejuvenated radicalism in the 1960s.

Thus the intellectuals' scorn for the doctrines of the Old Left and their loss of faith in the revolutionary potential of the working class, which prompted some writers in the postwar period to celebrate the tactics of liberal reform, inspired a quest in the 1960s for new radical constituencies among students, blacks, and the poor. In this respect, the rise of a generation of dissidents based in the universities had its own antecedents in the youth culture of the 1950s—a link that was reflected not just in the earlier fascination with Beat poets and novelists, jazz musicians, rock 'n' roll singers, hipsters, delinquents, and movie portraits of adolescent insurrection, but also in the cool or apathetic masks young people might have worn to conceal their lack of enthusiasm for adult norms and bourgeois ideals.

At the same time, the postwar intellectuals' persistent dissatisfaction with the quality of American life, their conviction that the country's crucial problems were postindustrial, their disdain for suburbia and the mentality of the organization man, their disparagement of conformity, and their exasperation with the middle-class hunger for success and respectability encouraged an even greater preoccupation in the 1960s with the psychological consequences of materialism and mechanization, with the boredom and frustrations inherent in modern work, with the failure of capitalism to offer people opportunities for emotional gratification and a sense of personal fulfillment. Indeed, nothing better illustrates the intimate connections between the two decades than the extent to which the radicalism of the 1960s was primarily cultural rather than political or economic. The New Left always appeared less interested in transforming the nation's social structure than in altering the consciousness, values, and living arrangements of individuals. Such inclinations also moved the children of prosperous middle-class families to identify themselves *morally* with the plight of American blacks and Vietnamese peasants, as though Washington's unwillingness to extinguish racism and its obstinate commitment to the war were not so much the products of the country's domestic and foreign policies as symptoms of its ethical blindness.

Yet political issues were ultimately inescapable, no matter what the time period. Whether one was talking about the determination to drop the atomic bomb on Hiroshima and Nagasaki in 1945, the omnipotence of the military-industrial complex at the end of the 1950s, the government's escalations in Vietnam in 1965, or the implications of Watergate in 1973 and 1974, the question of who controlled America's destiny remained the same. Hence the sensitivity of writers in the postwar years to bureaucratic manipulation and centralized power led in the following decades to a desire for more popular participation in the decision-making process. Liberalism came under attack in the 1960s because it had grown administrative and managerial, because it had confused the role of intelligence with the authority of experts, because it had exchanged its historic trust in social criticism and moral rage for a dependence on technology and specialization. Still, the powerlessness of ordinary citizens to affect the actions of their government and their employers, and the need for people to regain some influence at least over the direction of their own lives, were ideas initially developed in the 1940s and 1950s. Only later did they become part of the New Left's verbal arsenal in its attempt to discredit the arrogant reign of the best and the brightest.

There were other similarities, some of them obscured by the

mutual animosity on both sides of the generation gap. In the 1950s a number of writers stoutly defended the virtues of high culture, modernism, and the avant-garde against the incursions of the mass media and the "anti-intellectualism" of younger novelists, poets, playwrights, and actors. But the counterculture of the late 1950s, the 1960s, and the early 1970s was not as simplistic, shallow, or mindless as these critics usually claimed. Nor was it merely a manifestation of youthful whimsy and rebellion before the inevitable acceptance of adult responsibility. At its best and conceived in its broadest sense, it was an adversary culture as antagonistic to middle-brow literature, education, journalism, movies, and music as were the intellectuals themselves. Moreover (and despite what neoconservative theorists might say), its roots lay deep in those very same bohemian communities formed by the European and American avant-garde that writers in the 1950s so cherished and sometimes romanticized. The counterculture reinvoked the spirit of Paris in the 1920s, Berlin at the summit of the Weimar Republic, New York's Greenwich Village, Rome after World War II. Its passions were archetypically modernist: an insistence on sexual and psychological experimentation, spontaneous and outrageous assaults on the authority of the old order, a love-hate relationship with science and technology, a worship of artistic improvisation and mental shock, a reliance on gesture and style. Its most characteristic works—Joseph Heller's *Catch-22* and Ken Kesey's *One Flew over the Cuckoo's Nest*, Tom Wolfe's *The Electric Kool-Aid Acid Test* and Norman Mailer's *The Armies of the Night*, Stanley Kubrick's *Dr. Strangelove* and Robert Altman's *Nashville*, Bob Dylan's solitary jeremiads and Sgt. Pepper's legendary marching band—were Dadaist, surreal, expressionist, mad farce and a glimpse of hell. In effect, the hippies and radicals of the 1960s, like the Beats and the intellectuals of the 1950s, were all children of Joyce and Hemingway, Beckett and Brecht, Ernst and Picasso, Chaplin and Fellini. Meanwhile, those who actually created the counterculture were drawing upon the masters of twentieth century fiction, drama, painting, and film to offer a vision not only of hell, but also of salvation.

Hell and salvation are religious words, but in a relentlessly secular decade like the 1960s they also had psychological connotations. They pointed to a concern with private principle, inner testing, personal integrity. Here too the partisans of the New Left and the counterculture owed a debt to their elders. The critiques of conformist behavior in the 1950s—and the resulting emphasis on self-awareness, the attraction to any signs of marginality and eccentricity, the efforts to define the meaning of autonomy, and the call for continuing acts of resistance—each helped to persuade young people in the 1960s that their feelings of alienation could be a positive force in reshaping American life. Only now the values of individual dissent and existential honesty, coupled with the still lively distrust of ideology and long-term planning, were translated into a yearning for direct moral confrontations over specific issues. Civil disobedience and public demonstrations thus became not merely political strategies, but a chance to assert one's identity, display one's authenticity, express one's *personal* commitment to a particular cause.

In fact, a major paradox of the 1960s is that for all the mass marches, rallies, community organizing campaigns, and rock music festivals, the most significant experiences and innovations were overwhelmingly personal. Individuals had to reconsider their assumptions, their ambitions, the way they wished to live. Parents were forced to reevaluate their relations with their children. Men and women were required to reassess their traditional roles. Professors felt compelled to reexamine what they taught their students and why. Simultaneously, with the collapse of the Hollywood studio system, American film directors began to emulate their European counterparts in offering private, idiosyncratic, semi-autobiographical portraits of American society. The troubadours of folk and rock music composed their own songs instead of performing someone else's; like the movie makers, they tried to be genuine *auteurs* rather than mechanics on a cultural assembly line. The "new journalists" (some of them old novelists) were no longer willing to hide their personalities behind gray columns of newspaper print and the customary pose of objectivity; they converted themselves into independent investigators and participants, writing about events from the "inside," reporting on their innermost feelings and attitudes as a means of better understanding the social conflicts of their age.

The 1960s was preeminently a time of personal experimentation, much of it disconcerting if not intolerable to those who
matured during the 1940s and 1950s. Parents who spent most of
their waking hours chasing the American Dream were often terrified and enraged by the counterculture's disregard for the old-
fashioned moralities of hard work and monogamous sex, especially when they discovered that their once nice and dutiful son
or daughter now smoked pot, signed petitions, occupied the
dean's office, got busted, lived with someone called a "friend,"
and preferred poverty to the Protestant ethic. Men (even the
angry young men of the New Left) felt uncomfortable with
women who weren't satisfied simply to cook, type, make love, and
breed children. Nevertheless, when women demanded to be
taken seriously, to share power rather than be treated as if they
were merely ornaments decorating the lives of their husbands or
lovers, they did so not because they hated men but because they
wanted to emancipate themselves from the expectations and
stereotypes that denied them their individuality. Similarly, when
students clamored for new curriculums, more "relevant"
courses, and less authoritarian teaching styles, it was not because
they were lazy or anti-intellectual or functionally illiterate, but
because they thought that books and ideas really mattered, that
culture could have a profound and immediate impact on how
they lived.

Ironically, these were precisely the values the postwar intellectuals had championed. They had longed for a society where the
arts were provocative, where students took risks and raised issues, where people could challenge the calcified policies of the
corporations and the government, where men and women would
think and act for themselves, where individuals might never stop
trying to change their own lives despite the pressures from parents and peers and presidents.

Of course, what actually happened in the 1960s did not exactly
correspond to the hopes of writers in the 1940s and 1950s. The
excesses are by now familiar: the naïveté and impatience of a New
Left that depended more on strident rhetoric than on carefully
constructed coalitions for political and economic reform; the
cultural revolution that was too often ignorant about and con-

temptuous of the past; the search for an alternative consciousness that too frequently turned into a hunt for more potent
drugs. But the origins of even these deficiencies could be traced
in part to the outlook of many intellectuals in the preceding two
decades. Their own hostility to formal theory, their aversion to
long-range blueprints for social change, and their admiration for
pragmatic and concrete remedies all tended to focus people's
attention on current ills rather than on comprehensive cures. If
radicals in the 1960s seemed more eager to stop some injustice
"now"—the war, racism, the depredations of urban slumlords,
the growth of the multiversity—than to offer systematic proposals for the future, they may only have been acting like good pupils
of their intellectual mentors. And if writers in the 1950s sounded
overly pessimistic about the possibilities of altering America's
institutions, if they stressed the degree to which life was tragic
and most human problems were insoluble, these notions too
were transmitted to the next generation, though they resulted
not in a heightened sense of realism but in the fury and despair
that devoured the New Left by the close of the 1960s.

Most of the writers I have discussed did not intend their ideas
to be used in these ways, and some seem never to have recovered
from the intemperance of the New Left and the counterculture.
Yet the national reaction to the turmoil of the 1960s, the "lessons" learned, also had their roots in the books and essays of the
postwar intelligentsia. In the 1970s and 1980s, Americans were
again reminded of the importance of leadership and expertise,
the necessity for order and intellectual discipline in the schools,
the advantages of bargaining among the elite representatives of
interest groups, the perils of mass movements, and the Soviet
Union's insatiable craving for world domination. Educators,
legislators, and parents praised the universities for returning to
standardized curriculums with regular examinations and grades.
Students, exhibiting a new sense of ambition and sober responsibility, earned the applause of ex-socialist, now neoconservative,
pundits who preferred competition between achievement-ori-
ented individuals to affirmative action programs for minorities
and women, and whose sympathy for the left-outs and have-nots
was less compelling than their solicitude for the freedom of the

marketplace and the revival of America's military strength. Politicians, whether Democrat or Republican, spoke ever more fervently about the benefits of political moderation and social stability, the strengths of the private sector in a mixed economy, the superiority of voluntary associations and activities, and the need to intensify the cultural and propaganda war against the Communists.

In the meantime, the preoccupations of middle-class adults and their offspring—once so savagely ridiculed by the postwar intellectuals—began to resemble those of their predecessors in the 1950s. Undergraduates flocked to courses of study that they hoped would guarantee them decent jobs and the prospect of a rising income, though the economy was no longer dependably affluent. They looked neater and worked harder, but they seemed to think and question less. The hippies and radicals who dropped out in the 1960s, presuming there would be infinite time in the future to launch careers and families, eventually tired of being poor, regretted the wasted years, and strove to catch up with their more prudent contemporaries. Upon graduation, and if lucky enough to find secure employment, the young (like their parents and older siblings) forswore large plans and utopian dreams. Retreating once more to those areas of life over which they might exercise some real control, people jogged, squabbled over zoning ordinances, crusaded on behalf of parks and lakes and bicycle paths, ate lots of yogurt and sprouts, took refuge in pseudo-religions and quack mind-cures, forgot where they stored their ash trays, and limited themselves to one glass of white wine. But then if they couldn't solve the problems of their society, they could at least watch their weight.

Under these circumstances, perhaps we should remember what the intellectuals of the 1940s and 1950s criticized. For the issues they wrote about have not gone away. We are still confronted by the spectacle of great cities teetering on the edge of disintegration, by inequalities of wealth and power, by simmering tensions between whites and blacks, by misunderstandings between anxious parents and sullen children, by questions about what education should be for, by the vacuousness of much of middle-class life, by an interminable Cold War and the permanent threat of a nuclear holocaust.

So, like the postwar intellectuals, we still find ourselves obliged to dissent from policies carried out in our names yet on which our opinions have not been heard or sought. And we still need to resist the efforts of the power elite, the organization men, and our own peers to tell us who we are, what we think, and how we should behave.

Following these precepts may not make us comfortable or well-liked or happy. But at least we won't spend the better part of our lives boasting about how healthy we are, while secretly regretting all the things we feared to do.

This the writers of the 1940s and 1950s also tried to teach us. But it remains a lesson we have still to learn.

Notes

1. The Intellectuals at War

1. For two brilliant portraits of World War I, both in reality and in literature, see Paul Fussell, *The Great War and Modern Memory* (New York, 1975); and Frederick Hoffman, *The Twenties* (New York, 1955), especially his chapter on "The War and the Postwar Temper."

2. The most celebrated dramatization of these ideas is, of course, Ernest Hemingway's *A Farewell to Arms.* They are central to all of Hemingway's fiction but they are also recurrent themes in the work of Ezra Pound, E. E. Cummings, John Dos Passos, Malcolm Cowley, and Gertrude Stein.

3. It is impossible to arrive at exact casualty figures for either World War I or II. All that can be said with much certainty is the mortality rate for the second war was approximately four times that of the first, and that the vast majority of deaths in World War II were civilian. For a discussion of the various myths and statistics on casualties emanating from both conflicts, see John Terraine, *The Smoke and the Fire* (London, 1980), 35–38.

4. There are several valuable studies of life on the American home front. Among the best are John Brooks, *The Great Leap* (New York, 1966); Richard Polenberg, *War and Society* (Philadelphia, 1972); Geoffrey Perrett, *Days of Sadness, Years of Triumph* (New York, 1973); and John Morton Blum, *V Was for Victory* (New York, 1976).

5. The story of the European intellectuals' impact on American art, science, and academic life during and after the war has been recounted in several books and memoirs, among which the most illuminating are Laura Fermi, *Illustrious Immigrants* (Chicago, 1968); Donald Fleming and Bernard Bailyn, eds., *The Intellectual Migration* (Cambridge, Mass., 1968); Martin Jay, *The Dialectical Imagination* (Boston, 1973); and H. Stuart Hughes, *The Sea Change* (New York, 1975).

6. For an acerbic account of the *New Republic* in the early years of the war, see Alfred Kazin, *New York Jew* (New York, 1978), 20–23.

7. These circulation and demographic statistics come from *"New Republic News,"* *New Republic,* CXV (September 9, 1946), 302; and Malcolm Cowley,

"Magazine Business: 1910–1946," *New Republic*, CXV (October 21, 1946), 522.

8. Arthur Schlesinger, Sr., "Do We Have National Unity?" *New Republic*, CVI (February 2, 1942), 142–143.

9. Malcolm Cowley, "Town Report: 1942," *New Republic*, CVII (November 23, 1942), 675–676.

10. Joseph Harrison, "Production Pageant," *New Republic*, CVI (June 29, 1942), 882–883.

11. "Grand Strategy in Washington," *New Republic*, CVI (January 5, 1942), 5.

12. Richard Lee Strout, "All Unquiet along the Potomac," *New Republic*, CVI (January 26, 1942), 113–114.

13. "The Opposition in War," *New Republic*, CVII (October 26, 1942), 530.

14. "A Time for Toughness," *New Republic*, CVII (September 14, 1942), 302.

15. T.R.B., "Washington Notes: National Unity," *New Republic*, CVI (June 29, 1942), 891. "T.R.B." was a pseudonym used by Kenneth Crawford until 1943, when the column was taken over by Richard Strout, who wrote it until the 1970s.

16. "Can Congress Run the War?" *New Republic*, CVIII (March 8, 1943), 303. See also "We Can Improve Congress," *New Republic*, CVI (February 23, 1942), 254–255.

17. "Congressional Meddling," *New Republic*, CVIII (March 29, 1943), 395; "Can Congress Run the War?" *loc. cit.*, 303.

18. "Do We Deserve Congress?" *New Republic*, CVI (February 16, 1942), 224.

19. Before the congressional election of 1942, the *New Republic* specifically advised its readers on how they should cast their votes. See "Make the Seventy-Eighth Good!" *New Republic*, CVI (May 18, 1942), 653–654; "Send Them Back," *New Republic*, CVI (May 18, 1942), 654–655; and "The Obstructionists," *New Republic*, CVI (May 18, 1942), 706–710.

20. "Can the Democracies Fight?" *New Republic*, CVI (February 23, 1942), 256.

21. "The Weak Spot in Our Armor," *New Republic*, CVI (January 12, 1942), 37–38.

22. "Deadwood at the Top," *New Republic*, CVI (March 2, 1942), 285; "Why the State Department Blunders," *New Republic*, CVI (January 5, 1942), 4.

23. "The Tragic Lag," *New Republic*, CVI (January 12, 1942), 39.

24. "FDR Gives Marching Orders," *New Republic*, CVI (January 19, 1942), 71.

25. See George West, "Mr. Roosevelt's Supreme Test," *New Republic*, CVIII (February 8, 1943), 170–172.

26. Max Lerner, "The Education of Wendell Willkie," *New Republic*, CVII (October 26, 1942), 536–538. For similar views on Willkie and other Republicans of whom the magazine approved, see T.R.B., "The Fight for Production," *New Republic*, CVI (January 19, 1942), 84, which called for Willkie's designation as "Minister of Supply"; Michael Straight, "Victory on the Fascist Front," *New Republic*, CVI (January 26, 1942), 105, which praised Donald Nelson's appointment as chairman of the War Production Board; and "The Opposition in War," *loc. cit.*, 531.

27. "Four Men Reshape the World," *New Republic,* CIX (December 13, 1943), 835–837.
28. Ernest Hauser, "T.V. for Victory," *New Republic,* CVI (January 26, 1942), 111–112.
29. Robert Lynd, "The Structure of Power," *New Republic,* CVII (November 9, 1942), 597–600.
30. Max Lerner, "Toward an Affirmative State," *New Republic,* CVI (June 8, 1942), 794–795.
31. Walton Hamilton, "The Smoldering Constitutional Crisis," *New Republic,* CVIII (January 18, 1943), 73–76.
32. C. Wright Mills, "The Political Gargoyles," *New Republic,* CVIII (April 12, 1943), 482–483.
33. Dwight Macdonald, "The (American) People's Century," *Partisan Review,* IX (July/August, 1942), 303–309.
34. Dwight Macdonald, "The British Genius," *Partisan Review,* IX (March/April, 1942), 167.
35. Dwight Macdonald, "Political Notes," *Partisan Review,* IX (November/-December, 1942), 477.
36. Sidney Hook, "The Failure of the Left," *Partisan Review,* X (March/April, 1943), 166–168, 170, 172–175.
37. *Ibid.,* 171, 175–176.
38. "A Statement by the Editors," *Partisan Review,* IX (January/February, 1942), 2.
39. Dwight Macdonald, "Letters," *Partisan Review,* X (July/August, 1943), 382.
40. Dwight Macdonald, *Politics Past* (New York, 1970, c. 1957), 25–26. Hereafter, a publication date given in this fashion means "copyright 1957," but that the pagination and quotations are from the 1970 edition.
41. Bruce Bliven, "The Hang-Back Boys," *New Republic,* CX (March 6, 1944), 305–307.
42. See "Mr. Hicks and the Liberals," *New Republic,* CXII (April 23, 1945), 544.
43. Bruce Bliven, "Where Do We Go From Here?" *New Republic,* CVII (December 21, 1942), 815.
44. George Soule, "Full Employment After the War," *New Republic,* CVII (August 10, 1942), 107. See also George Soule, "Farmers, Labor and Prices," *New Republic,* XVIII (March 1, 1943), 273–276.
45. Milo Perkins, "The Future We Fight For," *New Republic,* CVI (June 15, 1942), 820.
46. George Soule, "Techniques for a Postwar World," *New Republic,* CVIII (January 18, 1943), 80. For an earlier version of this argument, see George Soule, "The Lessons of the Last Time," *New Republic,* CVI (February 2, 1942), 163–183.
47. "Prosperity," *New Republic,* CXI (November 27, 1944), 724. See also "Demobilization Blues," *New Republic,* CVI (February 9, 1942), 190.
48. These goals are best elaborated in the following essays: Max Lerner, "Charter for a New America," *New Republic,* CVIII (March 22, 1943), 369–372;

Bruce Bliven, "When We Rebuild America," *New Republic,* CVIII (April 12, 1943), 473–474; Bruce Bliven, Max Lerner, and George Soule, "Charter for America," *New Republic,* CVIII (April 19, 1943), 523–542; and "A Congress to Win the War and the Peace," *New Republic,* CX (May 8, 1944), 643–658.

49. See Lerner, "Charter for a New America," *loc. cit.,* 370–371; Bliven, Lerner, and Soule, "Charter for America, *loc. cit.,* 526, 528, 535, 538–540; and "A Congress to Win the War and the Peace," *loc. cit.,* 645–646.

50. T.R.B., "Washington Notes: Is This Just Another War?" *New Republic,* CVIII (June 21, 1943), 828.

51. "Wallace for Vice President," *New Republic,* CXI (July 10, 1944), 30.

52. "Mr. Wallace Walks the Plank," *New Republic,* CIX (July 26, 1943), 95.

53. George Soule, "Roosevelt in 1943," *New Republic,* CIX (September 6, 1943), 327.

54. *Ibid.*

55. Bruce Bliven, "The Liberals After Chicago," *New Republic,* CXI (August 7, 1944), 152–153. For a similar rationale, see Helen Fuller, "Throwing Wallace to the Wolves," *New Republic,* CXI (July 31, 1944), 122.

56. "Democrats Face the Future," *New Republic,* CXI (July 31, 1944), 117–118.

57. Bliven, "The Liberals After Chicago," *loc. cit.,* 153–154. After Roosevelt's reelection, the journal remained exuberant. See "It's Roosevelt Again," *New Republic,* CXI (November 13, 1944), 613.

58. I have written at length on the intellectuals' changing assessments of the Soviet Union during the 1930s in *Radical Visions and American Dreams* (New York, 1973). See especially pages 61–69, 304–309, 346–356, 362–363.

59. "Good Sense from Sir Stafford," *New Republic,* CVI (February 16, 1942), 220.

60. Max Lerner, "The Pilgrimage of Winston Churchill," *New Republic,* CVI (January 5, 1942), 10.

61. J. F. Brown, "Morale for the American Dream," *New Republic,* CVI (May 4, 1942), 600.

62. Henry Wallace, "Beyond the Atlantic Charter," *New Republic,* CVII (November 23, 1942), 667.

63. Michael Straight, "United Nations: Tasks Ahead," *New Republic,* CVIII (January 11, 1943), 42.

64. "Three Speeches," *New Republic,* CVI (May 11, 1942), 622–623. For a similar sentiment, see "Stalingrad Expendables," *New Republic,* CVII (October 5, 1942), 395.

65. James Agee, *Agee on Film: Reviews and Comments* (Boston, 1964), 37. The review from which this quotation is taken originally appeared in the *Nation* (May 22, 1943).

66. "Russia and European Federation," *New Republic,* CIX (September 16, 1943), 320.

67. "Hitler's Appeasement Offensive," *New Republic,* CVIII (February 15, 1943), 200. See also "No Cause for Alarmism," *New Republic,* CVIII (February 22, 1943), 236.

68. "Russia in the Alliance," *New Republic*, CVI (June 22, 1942), 844.
69. George Soule, "Russia, Germany and the Peace," *New Republic*, CVIII (March 22, 1943), 374.
70. Max Lerner, "After the Comintern," *New Republic*, CVIII (June 17, 1943), 754.
71. Jerome Davis, "Russia's Postwar Claims," *New Republic*, CXI (September 4, 1944), 276–277. For other expressions of the same opinion, see "What Russia Wants," *New Republic*, CIX (October 11, 1943), 474–475; and "The Soviet–Czech Treaty," *New Republic*, CIX (December 27, 1943), 900.
72. "The Moscow Conference," *New Republic*, CIX (November 1, 1943), 603.
73. "Russia's Western Claims," *New Republic*, CX (January 17, 1944), 72. See also "The Great Pravda Mystery," *New Republic*, CX (January 31, 1944), 135–136.
74. Frederick Schuman, "The Polish Frontiers," *New Republic*, CX (January 31, 1944), 138–141. The editors agreed with Schuman. See "Russia's Sphere of Influence," *New Republic*, CX (February 21, 1944), 230–231.
75. Heinz Eulau, "Russia's Political Offensive," *New Republic*, CIX (October 18, 1943), 509–511.
76. Heinz Eulau, "Russia and the Balkans," *New Republic*, CX (April 3, 1944), 462–463.
77. "The Crimean Conference," *New Republic*, CXII (February 19, 1945), 243.
78. "The Crimean Charter," *New Republic*, CXII (February 26, 1945), 278.
79. Heinz Eulau, "As the Big Three Meet," *New Republic*, CXII (February 5, 1945), 168–170.
80. The full story of Varian Fry's efforts on behalf of European émigrés is told in Fermi, *Illustrious Immigrants*, 84–92.
81. Varian Fry, "The Massacre of the Jews," *New Republic*, CVII (December 21, 1942), 816–818.
82. "The Jews of Europe," *New Republic*, CIX (August 30, 1943), 304–305, 310–315. For additional suggestions on how the Allies might intervene, see "Help the Jews," *New Republic*, CIX (September 6, 1943), 319.
83. "The Jews of Europe," *loc. cit.*, 301.
84. *Ibid.*, 308–309.
85. "Robot Bombs," *New Republic*, CXI (July 10, 1944), 27.
86. Dwight Macdonald, "Horrors—Ours and Theirs," in *Politics Past*, 159. This essay originally appeared in *Politics* (May 1945).
87. Macdonald, *Politics Past*, 96. The essay from which this quotation is taken originally appeared in *Politics* (August 1945).
88. Kai Erikson, "A Final Accounting of Death and Destruction," *New York Times Book Review* (August 9, 1981), 24.
89. Bruce Bliven, "The Bomb and the Future," *New Republic*, CXIII (August 20, 1945), 210–212. Over the next several months, the *New Republic* continued to call for the international control of atomic power. See "Internationalize Atomic Energy," *New Republic*, CXIII (October 29, 1945), 555–556; and "The World Must Choose," *New Republic*, CXIII (November 19, 1945), 659–660.

90. T.R.B., "Washington Notes: Atomic Anxieties," *New Republic,* CXIII (August 20, 1945), 222.
91. Macdonald, *Politics Past,* 169, 171–173, 175. The essays from which these quotations are taken originally appeared in *Politics* (August and September, 1945). Italics his.
92. *Ibid.,* 171, 178–179.
93. Mary McCarthy, "A Letter to the Editor of *Politics,*" in *On the Contrary* (New York, 1962), 3–4. This letter originally appeared in *Politics* (November 1946).
94. Macdonald, *Politics Past,* 180. The essay from which these quotations are taken originally appeared in *Politics* (October 1946).
95. Alfred Kazin, *Starting Out in the Thirties* (Boston, 1965), 166.
96. Hannah Arendt, "Approaches to the 'German Problem,'" *Partisan Review,* XII (Winter 1945), 93–106.
97. Hannah Arendt, "Parties, Movements, and Classes," *Partisan Review,* XII (Fall 1945), 504–513.
98. George Orwell, "London Letter," *Partisan Review,* XII (Winter 1945), 78, 80. Italics his.
99. Dwight Macdonald, "The Prospects for Revolution," in *Politics Past,* 129. Italics his. This essay originally appeared in *Politics* (July 1944).
100. Dwight Macdonald, "The Future of Democratic Values," *Partisan Review,* X (July/August, 1943), 324–325. Italics his.
101. T.R.B., "Washington Notes: The New President," *New Republic,* CXII (April 23, 1945), 554.
102. Bruce Bliven, "Franklin D. Roosevelt," *New Republic,* CXII (April 23, 1945), 548. For a similar sentiment, see "President Truman's Task," *New Republic,* CXII (April 23, 1945), 539–541.
103. Dwight Macdonald, "The Death of F.D.R.," in *Politics Past,* 285–286. This essay originally appeared in *Politics* (May 1945).

2. The Shattered Peace

1. William Barrett, *The Truants* (New York, 1982), 20, 31. For an excellent summary of the intellectuals' political and economic assumptions in 1945, see Alonzo Hamby, *Beyond the New Deal* (New York, 1973), xvi–xviii.
2. Ronald Steel, "Two Cheers for Ike," *New York Review of Books,* XXVIII (September 24, 1981), 54.
3. In the first half of his book, Hamby persistently berates liberals for concentrating on Truman's personality while overlooking the wisdom of his policies. See *Beyond the New Deal,* 48, 53–54, 85, 141, 208, 274.
4. T.R.B., "Washington Notes: The World Moves to Washington," *New Republic,* CXIII (December 10, 1945), 797.
5. T.R.B., "Washington Notes: Capital Housecleaning," *New Republic,* CXIII (July 16, 1945), 77.
6. I. F. Stone, *The Truman Era* (New York, 1973, c. 1953), xxi.

7. T.R.B., "Washington Wire: Potomac Dog Days," *New Republic*, CXV (August 26, 1946), 216.

8. For an example of these demands, see "Elections: 1946," *New Republic*, CXIV (February 11, 1946), 230.

9. "Truman's Blunder," *New Republic*, CXIV (June 3, 1946), 787.

10. *Ibid.*, 787–788. For similar estimates, see Helen Fuller, "Has Truman Lost Labor?" *New Republic*, CXIV (June 10, 1946), 826–828; and "Liberals and the Labor Crisis," *New Republic*, CXIV (June 10, 1946), 830–831.

11. "After the Debacle," *New Republic*, CXV (November 18, 1946), 643. See also T.R.B., "Washington Wire: Voting at Home," *New Republic*, CXV (November 25, 1946), 680.

12. "Rift in the Big Three," *New Republic*, CXII (June 4, 1945), 772.

13. "Our European Policy," *New Republic*, CXII (May 21, 1945), 692. See also "Towards a New Europe," *New Republic*, CXIII (September 3, 1945), 272.

14. "Solution in Poland," *New Republic*, CXIII (July 2, 1945), 7. For a similar sentiment, see "The Potsdam Decisions," *New Republic*, CXIII (August 13, 1945), 173.

15. "What Does Mr. Truman Mean?" *New Republic*, CXIII (November 5, 1945), 589.

16. "Conflict in London," *New Republic*, CXIII (October 1, 1945), 423.

17. "The Greatest of All Our Hopes," *New Republic*, CXIV (March 18, 1946), 363.

18. "Hope and Peril at UN," *New Republic*, CXIV (June 10, 1946), 819.

19. For a summary of Henry Wallace's views before 1947, see Hamby, *Beyond the New Deal*, 122, 127, 129–130. For an example of the liberals' sympathy for his positions, see "An Honest Chance for Peace," *New Republic*, CXV (October 7, 1946), 427.

20. "Henry A. Wallace to Edit *New Republic*," *New Republic*, CXV (October 21, 1946), 499.

21. Henry Wallace, "The Fight for Peace Begins," *New Republic*, CXVI (March 24, 1947), 12–13. See also Henry Wallace, "The Way to Help Greece," *New Republic*, CXVI (March 17, 1947), 12–13; and Hamby, *Beyond the New Deal*, 175–176.

22. Henry Wallace, "The Constructive Alternative," *New Republic*, CXVI (May 19, 1947), 11–12.

23. "A New Deal with Russia: III," *New Republic*, CXVI (January 27, 1947), 26–31.

24. T.R.B., "Washington Wire: Home to Roost," *New Republic*, CXVI (April 28, 1947), 11.

25. "Marshallism Gains," *New Republic*, CXVI (June 30, 1947), 5.

26. Henry Wallace, "Bevin Muddies the Waters," *New Republic*, CXVI (June 30, 1947), 11–12.

27. Henry Wallace, "Too Little, Too Late," *New Republic*, CXVII (October 6, 1947), 11–12. For a more extended evaluation of the Marshall Plan as an

escalation of the Cold War, see Victor Perlo and David Ramsey, "Europe and American Aid," *New Republic*, CXVIII (January 12, 1948), 15–16, 18–20.

28. Henry Wallace, "Unity for Progress," *New Republic*, CXVI (January 20, 1947), 3, 46. See also Hamby, *Beyond the New Deal*, 159–160, 202.
29. Henry Wallace, "Report from the Middle West," *New Republic*, CXVI (May 26, 1947), 11.
30. Henry Wallace, "Report from the Southwest," *New Republic*, CXVI (June 2, 1947), 11, 35; Henry Wallace, "Report from California," *New Republic*, CXVI (June 9, 1947), 11, 13.
31. Henry Wallace, "Stand Up and Be Counted," *New Republic*, CXVIII (January 5, 1948), 5–10; Henry Wallace, "Farewell and Hail!" *New Republic*, CXIX (July 19, 1948), 14–18.
32. Dwight Macdonald, "The Truth About the UN," in *Politics Past* (New York, 1970, c. 1957), 297. This essay originally appeared in *Politics* (November 1946).
33. The history of *Partisan Review* in the 1930s is fully described in James Gilbert, *Writers and Partisans* (New York, 1968). The final chapter deals with the journal in the postwar years. I have elsewhere recounted *Partisan Review*'s disenchantment with Marxist ideas at the end of the Depression. See *Radical Visions and American Dreams* (New York, 1973), 334–346.
34. Eliot Cohen, "An Act of Affirmation," *Commentary*, I (November 1945), 1–2. For a hilarious and extremely perceptive account of *Commentary* in the 1940s and 1950s, see Norman Podhoretz, *Making It* (New York, 1967).
35. I do not mean to suggest that only Jews wrote for *Partisan Review* and *Commentary*, while only non-Jews contributed to the liberal journals. Edmund Wilson, Dwight Macdonald, James Burnham, Ralph Ellison, James Baldwin, Arthur Schlesinger, and Mary McCarthy were not Jewish, but their essays frequently appeared in *Partisan Review*. Max Lerner, Manny Farber, I. F. Stone, and Alfred Kazin were Jewish, yet each served at various times as an editor or columnist for the *New Republic*, the *Nation*, or *PM*. Nevertheless, there were obvious ethnic divisions. The *Nation* and the *New Republic* began in the nineteenth or early twentieth centuries as vehicles for the ideas of middle-class Protestant reformers, and these magazines continued to reflect their origins even in the postwar era. *Partisan Review* and *Commentary* were considered then and since as publications written by and aimed at a predominantly Jewish intellectual constituency; indeed, their increasing influence coincided with the rise to prominence of Jewish writers after World War II.
36. The backgrounds of the following writers illustrate these points: Sidney Hook (born 1902 in New York; educated at CCNY and Columbia; taught at NYU); Lionel Trilling (born 1905 in New York; educated and taught at Columbia); Harold Rosenberg (born 1906 in New York; educated at CCNY and Brooklyn Law School); Clement Greenberg (born 1909 in New York); Delmore Schwartz (born 1913 in Brooklyn; educated at NYU); Bernard Malamud (born 1914 in Brooklyn; educated at CCNY and Columbia); Alfred

Kazin (born 1915 in Brooklyn; educated at CCNY and Columbia); James Wechsler (born 1915 in New York; educated at Columbia); Robert Warshow (born 1917 in New York); Leslie Fiedler (born 1917 in Newark; educated at NYU); Daniel Bell (born 1919; educated at CCNY and Columbia); Irving Kristol (born 1920 in New York; educated at CCNY); Irving Howe (born 1920; educated at CCNY); Robert Lekachman (born 1920 in New York; educated at Columbia); Nathan Glazer (born 1923; educated at CCNY); James Baldwin (born 1924 in Harlem); Robert Brustein (born 1927 in Brooklyn; educated at Columbia); Norman Podhoretz (born 1930 in Brooklyn; educated at Columbia).

37. Alfred Kazin, *New York Jew* (New York, 1978), 152.
38. Irving Howe, "The New York Intellectuals," in *Decline of the New* (New York, 1970), 218. Italics his. This is a brilliant essay, to which my paragraph is much indebted.
39. *Ibid.*, 220.
40. John Diggins has perceptively evaluated Burnham's political and intellectual odyssey in *Up from Communism* (New York, 1977, c. 1975), 160–198, 303–337.
41. James Burnham, "Lenin's Heir," *Partisan Review*, XII (Winter 1945), 63–66, 69.
42. *Ibid.*, 66.
43. *Ibid.*, 70–72. Burnham was by no means alone in reaching these conclusions. For similar judgments, see Albert Parry, "Trotsky's Stalin," *New Republic*, CXIV (May 13, 1946), 701–702; Franz Borkenau, "Prophecy in the Light of History," *Commentary*, VII (May 1949), 430–436; and Harold Rosenberg, "The Communist," *Commentary*, VIII (July 1949), 1–9.
44. See Diggins, *Up from Communism*, 319–323.
45. Dwight Macdonald, "Beat Me Daddy," *Partisan Review*, XII (Spring 1945), 182, 184–186.
46. James Burnham, "Politics for the Nursery Set," *Partisan Review*, XII (Spring 1945), 188–189; William Phillips, "The Lions and the Foxes," *Partisan Review*, XII (Spring 1945), 194.
47. Phillips, "The Lions and the Foxes," *loc. cit.*, 191–193, 196–198.
48. Philip Rahv, "Versions of Bolshevism," *Partisan Review*, XIII (Summer 1946), 370, 372–374.
49. Philip Rahv, "The Unfuture of Utopia," *Partisan Review*, XVI (July 1949), 744, 746–747.
50. For an affectionate and perceptive description of Hannah Arendt and the effect she had on her American friends, see, Kazin, *New York Jew*, 195–203, 215–218. The full story of her life can be found in Elisabeth Young-Bruehl, *Hannah Arendt* (New Haven, Conn. 1982).
51. Hannah Arendt, *The Origins of Totalitarianism* (New York, 1958, c. 1951), 459–460.
52. Hannah Arendt, "Understanding and Politics," *Partisan Review*, XX (July/August, 1953), 377.

53. Arendt, *The Origins of Totalitarianism,* 460.
54. *Ibid.,* 3.
55. *Ibid.,* 13, 15, 19, 21, 136.
56. *Ibid.,* 52–53, 354–355.
57. *Ibid.,* 25, 87, 229.
58. *Ibid.,* 152, 329.
59. *Ibid.,* 269–270, 292; Hannah Arendt, "The Concentration Camps," *Partisan Review,* XV (July 1948), 751–752.
60. Arendt, *The Origins of Totalitarianism,* 107–108, 155, 243–245, 318.
61. *Ibid.,* 35, 39, 237, 251, 256, 260–264, 357.
62. *Ibid.,* 232–235, 248, 317, 323–324, 336, 475.
63. *Ibid.,* 311–312, 314–315.
64. *Ibid.,* 159, 351–352, 384, 470–471.
65. *Ibid.,* 366–368.
66. *Ibid.,* 215–216. For a similar appraisal of the typical Stalinist functionary, see Rosenberg, "The Communist," *loc. cit.,* 2–5, 8.
67. Arendt, *The Origins of Totalitarianism,* 373–375, 383, 387.
68. *Ibid.,* 6, 344, 423, 426, 440, 444, 447–449, 465; Arendt, "The Concentration Camps," *loc. cit.,* 750.
69. Arendt, *The Origins of Totalitarianism,* 245, 314–315, 325–326, 454–457, 474–475.
70. *Ibid.,* 391–393, 411, 415, 458, 505.
71. "The 'Liberal' Fifth Column," *Partisan Review,* XIII (Summer 1946), 280–281, 283, 285–291.
72. *Ibid.,* 292. Barrett, apparently, is still proud of this essay; he reprints it as an appendix to his memoir of the period, *The Truants.*
73. "The Politics of Illusion," *Partisan Review,* XIII (November/December, 1946), 610–613, 616–618.
74. George Kennan, "The Sources of Soviet Conduct," in Walter Lippmann, *The Cold War* (New York 1972, c. 1947), 58, 61, 63–66.
75. *Ibid.,* 66, 68, 74–76.
76. Lippmann, *The Cold War,* 4, 22, 30, 51.
77. *Ibid.,* 6, 14–18.
78. *Ibid.,* 26, 30–31, 35, 52.
79. T.R.B., "Washington Wire," *New Republic,* CXVIII (March 22, 1948), 3. See also Michael Straight, "There Are Great Fears," *New Republic,* CXVIII (March 22, 1948), 6–7.
80. Michael Straight, "ERP: Aid to Peace . . . or Road to War?" *New Republic,* CXVIII (March 15, 1948), 12.
81. "Policy, Not Tactics, Needed in Berlin," *New Republic,* CXVIX (July 26, 1948), 5. For similar views, see "Our German Stake Is Worth Big Risks," *New Republic,* CXVIX (July 19, 1948), 10; and Frederick Ford, "New Marks, Old Mistakes in Berlin," *New Republic,* CXVIX (July 19, 1948), 11–12.
82. "The East-West Crisis," *New Republic,* CXVIX (October 11, 1948), 5–6.
83. "The Soviet Sphere Quakes," *New Republic,* CXVIX (July 12, 1948), 5.

84. Arthur Schlesinger, "Europe Takes Hope from ECA," *New Republic*, CXVIX (November 8, 1948), 19–20. See also Arthur Schlesinger, "Adding Guns to ECA Butter," *New Republic*, CXVIX (November 22, 1948), 19–21.

85. For examples of this argument, see "The North Atlantic Pact," *New Republic*, CXX (February 14, 1949), 5–6; "Should We Arm Europe?" *New Republic*, CXXI (August 15, 1949), 5–6; and Helen Gahagan Douglas, "Why I Voted for Arms for Europe," *New Republic*, CXXI (August 29, 1949), 9–10.

86. Samples of these criticisms can be found in the following articles: Michael Straight, "Truman Should Quit," *New Republic*, CXVIII (April 5, 1948), 1–5; Richard Strout, "Candidate in the White House," *New Republic*, CXVIII (April 5, 1948), 11–13; "Truman as Leader," *New Republic*, CXVIII (May 17, 1948), 13–26; and "The Democrats' Last Chance," *New Republic*, CXXIX (July 12, 1948), 11–20.

87. For a discussion of the formation and policies of the ADA, see Hamby, *Beyond the New Deal*, 151–152, 161–163, 168.

88. *Ibid.*, 245–246.

89. Helen Fuller, "For a Better World Right Now," *New Republic*, CXXIX (August 2, 1948), 13. For an earlier version of the same argument, see T.R.B., "Washington Wire," *New Republic*, CXVIII (January 12, 1948), 3.

90. James Wechsler, "The Liberal's Vote and '48," *Commentary*, IV (September 1947), 216–217, 221–222, 224–225.

91. Irving Howe, "The Sentimental Fellow-Traveling of F. O. Matthiessen," *Partisan Review*, XV (October 1948), 1125, 1128–1129.

92. James Burnham, "The Wallace Crusade," *Partisan Review*, XV (June 1948), 702–704.

93. Michael Straight, "Turnip Day in Washington," *New Republic*, CXXIX (July 26, 1948), 7.

94. T.R.B., "Washington Wire," *New Republic*, CXXIX (October 4, 1948), 4. See also T.R.B., "Washington Wire," *New Republic*, CXXIX (July 26, 1948), 3.

95. "1948: The New Beginning," *New Republic*, CXXIX (September 17, 1948), 32.

96. Eliot Cohen, "Citizen's Victory: Defeat of the 'Common Man,' " *Commentary*, VI (December 1948), 511–513.

97. T.R.B., "Washington Wire," *New Republic*, CXXIX (November 15, 1948), 3.

98. "It Was Not Magic That Won," *New Republic*, CXXIX (November 15, 1948), 6; Michael Straight, "Happy New Year!" *New Republic*, CXX (January 10, 1949), 6; "Damn the Torpedoes!" *New Republic*, CXXIX (November 15, 1948), 1.

3. Accommodation and Ambivalence

1. Irving Howe, "The New York Intellectuals," in *Decline of the New* (New York, 1970), 238.

2. See Christopher Lasch, *The New Radicalism in America* (New York, 1965), 316, 322.

3. See Alfred Kazin, *New York Jew* (New York, 1978), 62.

4. See David Caute, *The Fellow-Travellers* (New York, 1973), 289–291.
5. See John Diggins, *Up from Communism* (New York, 1977, c. 1975), 327.
6. William Barrett, "Culture Conference at the Waldorf," *Commentary*, VII (May 1949), 487, 491, 493. For a similar assessment, see Irving Howe, "The Culture Conference," *Partisan Review*, XVI (May 1949), 505–511.
7. Sidney Hook, "On the Battlefield of Philosophy," *Partisan Review*, XVI (March 1949), 251–253.
8. Sidney Hook, "Report on the International Day Against Dictatorship and War," *Partisan Review*, XVI (July 1949), 726–729; William Phillips, "America the Beautiful and Damned," *Commentary*, XII (November 1951), 507–508.
9. Hook, "Report on the International Day Against Dictatorship and War," *loc. cit.*, 731.
10. James Burnham, "Rhetoric and Peace," *Partisan Review*, XVII (November/-December, 1950), 861–863, 865–867, 870–871. Italics his.
11. "The Need is For a Democratic International," *New Republic*, CXX (March 28, 1949), 6.
12. William Barrett, "World War III: The Ideological Conflict," *Partisan Review*, XVII (September/October, 1950), 651–653, 656–657, 660.
13. See Caute, *The Fellow-Travellers*, 327; and "Congress in Berlin," *New Republic*, CXXII (June 16, 1950), 9.
14. Sidney Hook, "The Berlin Congress for Cultural Freedom," *Partisan Review*, XVII (September/October, 1950), 715, 718, 722.
15. Caute, *The Fellow-Travellers*, 298.
16. Seymour Lipset, *Political Man* (New York, 1963, c. 1960), xxi, xxv, xxxv.
17. Daniel Bell, *The End of Ideology* (New York, 1965, c. 1960), 16–17, 405. Italics his.
18. Arthur Schlesinger, "The Perspective Now," *Partisan Review*, XIV (May/-June, 1947), 242.
19. Arthur Schlesinger, *The Vital Center* (Boston, 1962, c. 1949), xii, 153.
20. *Ibid.*, 47.
21. Bell, *The End of Ideology*, 284.
22. *Ibid.*, 212, 224–226, 283; Lipset, *Political Man*, 82; Schlesinger, *The Vital Center*, 188.
23. Lionel Trilling, *The Liberal Imagination* (New York, 1953, c. 1950), vii–viii.
24. Bell, *The End of Ideology*, 300. For a similar observation, see Hannah Arendt, "Nightmare and Flight," *Partisan Review*, XII (Spring 1945), 259.
25. Reinhold Niebuhr, *The Irony of American History* (New York, 1952), 83; Reinhold Niebuhr, "Will Civilization Survive Technics?" *Commentary*, I (December 1945), 3, 6, 8. I have discussed Niebuhr's ideas in the 1930s at greater length in *Radical Visions and American Dreams* (New York, 1973), 141–150, 359–360. The best analysis of Niebuhr's intellectual development from the 1920s to the 1940s is Donald Meyer's *The Protestant Search for Political Realism, 1919–1941* (Berkeley and Los Angeles, 1961). From February through August 1950, *Partisan Review* conducted a symposium on "Religion and the Intellectuals." Though most of the participants were highly critical of the

religious impulse among writers, the need to discuss the issue in such depth testified to the significance of neo-orthodox Christianity in postwar America. Among the contributors to the symposium were James Agee, John Dewey, Sidney Hook, Alfred Kazin, Philip Rahv, William Phillips, Dwight Macdonald, Irving Howe, Allen Tate, W. H. Auden, William Barrett, Isaac Rosenfeld, Hannah Arendt, I. A. Richards, R. P. Blackmur, A. J. Ayer, Paul Tillich, James T. Farrell, Jacques Maritain, Meyer Schapiro, George Boas, Clement Greenberg, and Ernest van den Haag.

26. Schlesinger, *The Vital Center*, xxiii, 1, 56–57, 165.
27. Trilling, *The Liberal Imagination*, ix, xii–xiii, 94–96, 215.
28. *Ibid.*, xi–xii; Schlesinger, *The Vital Center*, 40; Niebuhr, *The Irony of American History*, 78–80.
29. Schlesinger, *The Vital Center*, 10, 173, 254; Arthur Schlesinger, "The Causes of the Civil War: A Note on Historical Sentimentalism," *Partisan Review*, XVI (October 1949), 981. See also Arthur Schlesinger, "Policy and National Interest," *Partisan Review*, XVIII (November/December, 1951), 709, 711.
30. Niebuhr, *The Irony of American History*, 145.
31. Trilling, *The Liberal Imagination*, 212–215.
32. Bell, *The End of Ideology*, 301–302, 393, 402, 404. See also Stephen Whitfield, "The 1950's: The Era of No Hard Feelings," *South Atlantic Quarterly*, LXXIV (Summer 1975), 296.
33. Daniel Boorstin, "Our Unspoken National Faith," *Commentary*, XV (April 1953), 327–329, 333. For a similar view, see Daniel Bell, "America's Un-Marxist Revolution," *Commentary*, VII (March 1949), 209.
34. Bell, *The End of Ideology*, 104, 112, 121.
35. Schlesinger, *The Vital Center*, 153–154, 174; Arthur Schlesinger, "The Politics of Democracy," *Partisan Review*, XVIII (March/April, 1951), 246.
36. Lipset, *Political Man*, 12–13, 77–78, 80–81, 292–293, 328–329; Bell, *The End of Ideology*, 108; Bell, "America's Un-Marxist Revolution," *loc. cit.*, 209; Daniel Bell, "Has America a Ruling Class?" *Commentary*, VIII (December 1949), 606.
37. Lipset, *Political Man*, 230, 234, 330, 444–445.
38. Bell, *The End of Ideology*, 66; Lipset, *Political Man*, 71.
39. Schlesinger, *The Vital Center*, 182–183; Bell, "Has America a Ruling Class?" *loc. cit.*, 603–604.
40. Niebuhr, *The Irony of American History*, 101, 104; Lipset, *Political Man*, xxiii.
41. Lipset, *Political Man*, 268–269; Seymour Lipset and Natalie Rogoff, "Class and Opportunity in Europe and the U.S.," *Commentary*, XVIII (December 1954), 564–566. A number of other writers agreed with this analysis. See William Grampp, "The Facts About 'Capitalist Inequality,'" *Commentary*, XI (June 1951), 515, 517; Granville Hicks, "How We Live Now in America," *Commentary*, XVI (December 1953), 507–509, 511; Robert Leckachman, "Our 'Revolution' in Income Distribution," *Commentary*, XX (August 1955), 133–135, 137, 139–140; and Monroe Berger, "The Business Elite: Then and Now," *Commentary*, XXII (October 1956), 371–372.

424   *Notes to pages 142–160*

42. Bell, *The End of Ideology,* 40–45, 89–90, 109, 398; Bell, "Has America a Ruling Class?" *loc. cit.,* 606.
43. Bell, *The End of Ideology,* 32.
44. Oscar Handlin, "Group Life within the American Pattern," *Commentary,* VIII (November 1949), 411–412.
45. Schlesinger, *The Vital Center,* 253; Lipset, *Political Man,* 52.
46. Handlin, "Group Life Within the American Pattern," *loc. cit.,* 411; Bell, "America's Un-Marxist Revolution," *loc. cit.,* 209; Lipset, *Political Man,* xxii.
47. Bell, *The End of Ideology,* 30.
48. Schlesinger, *The Vital Center,* 9, 186.
49. For an explicit statement of these ideals, see Schlesinger, *The Vital Center,* 248–249, 256.
50. Lipset, *Political Man,* 393–394, 430–433.
51. *Ibid.,* 185, 228–229.
52. *Ibid.,* 19–20.
53. *Ibid.,* 1, 67, 294–295; Bell, *The End of Ideology,* 280.
54. For a sustained and often devastating critique of the "pluralist" intellectuals, to which some of my comments in this and the following paragraphs are indebted, see Michael Rogin, *The Intellectuals and McCarthy* (Cambridge, Mass., 1967).
55. See John Higham, "The Cult of the 'American Consensus,' " *Commentary,* XXVII (February 1959), 93–99, for a contemporary but not so flattering assessment of this perspective.
56. Kazin, *New York Jew,* 15.
57. Richard Hofstadter, *The Age of Reform* (New York, 1960, c. 1955), 18.
58. Richard Hofstadter, *The American Political Tradition* (New York, 1954, c. 1948), xi; Hofstadter, *The Age of Reform,* 12–13, 15.
59. Hofstadter, *The American Political Tradition,* viii–x.
60. *Ibid.,* vi.
61. Hofstadter, *The Age of Reform,* 5–6.
62. Hofstadter, *The American Political Tradition,* 241, 277.
63. Hofstadter, *The Age of Reform,* 12.
64. *Ibid.,* 325, 327; Hofstadter, *The American Political Tradition,* vii.
65. Hofstadter, *The Age of Reform,* 7, 9, 16.
66. Hofstadter, *The American Political Tradition,* 231.
67. Hofstadter, *The Age of Reform,* 19–21.
68. Louis Hartz, *The Liberal Tradition in America* (New York, 1955), 28–31.
69. *Ibid.,* 5, 20, 32.
70. *Ibid.,* 3, 65–66.
71. *Ibid.,* 3, 6, 9, 140, 205.
72. *Ibid.,* 17–18.
73. *Ibid.,* 15, 47–49, 71, 101, 108, 114, 210, 230, 232.
74. *Ibid.,* 146–148, 151–155, 172–173, 176–177, 180, 189.
75. *Ibid.,* 205, 259–261, 264, 266–270.
76. *Ibid.,* 9–10, 59, 85–86, 250, 281.

77. *Ibid.,* 10–12, 175–176, 285–286.
78. *Ibid.,* 13–14, 255, 287.
79. *Ibid.,* 308.
80. John Kenneth Galbraith, *A Life in Our Times* (Boston, 1981), 30–31.
81. *Ibid.,* 284.
82. John Kenneth Galbraith, *The Affluent Society* (Boston, 1971, c. 1958), 4–5; Galbraith, *A Life in Our Times,* 354.
83. Galbraith, *The Affluent Society,* xvi, 92–94, 115, 118, 135, 162.
84. *Ibid.,* xviii–xix, 155–157, 163–164.
85. *Ibid.,* 3, 5.
86. *Ibid.,* 12, 19.
87. *Ibid.,* 141, 168–170, 250.
88. *Ibid.,* 106–108, 170–171, 174, 183–184, 211, 214–216.
89. *Ibid.,* 137, 146–147, 149, 151, 153. See also Galbraith, *A Life in Our Times,* 361.
90. Galbraith, *The Affluent Society,* xx, 127–128, 221.
91. *Ibid.,* 223.
92. *Ibid.,* xxiv.
93. *Ibid.,* 221, 225, 229, 248, 250–252.
94. *Ibid.,* 256–258.
95. *Ibid.,* 217, 267–268.
96. *Ibid.,* 274, 278, 280.
97. *Ibid.,* 275, 313, 316.
98. *Ibid.,* 262–266, 292–293. In 1958, Galbraith thought the passage of a guaranteed annual income plan in Congress was "beyond reasonable hope." Eleven years later, in the revised edition, it seemed to him "increasingly practical." Since American politicians in the 1980s still opposed such a plan, perhaps Galbraith's earlier assessment was more accurate. For that matter, the liberals' trust in Keynes and productivity, which Galbraith deplored in the 1950s, was replaced during the Reagan years by an even older faith in the doctrines of the free market and "trickle down" wealth—in other words, the "conventional wisdom" of Coolidge and Hoover.
99. *Ibid.,* 297, 299, 303, 307–308. Italics his.
100. *Ibid.,* 249.
101. See Dwight Macdonald, "London, 1957," in *Politics Past* (New York, 1970, c. 1957), 27–28. This essay originally appeared in *Encounter* (March and April, 1957).
102. Dwight Macdonald, "On the Proletariat as a Revolutionary Class," in *Politics Past,* 267–268; Dwight Macdonald, "The Responsibility of Peoples," in *Politics Past,* 71; Macdonald, "London, 1957," *loc. cit.,* 24. "On the Proletariat as a Revolutionary Class" originally appeared in *The Root Is Man* (1953); "The Responsibility of Peoples" originally appeared in *Politics* (March 1945).
103. Dwight Macdonald, "Bureaucratic Culture: Nicholas I and Josef I," in *Politics Past,* 223–228; Dwight Macdonald, "The Eisenstein Tragedy," in *Politics*

Past, 231. "Bureaucratic Culture: Nicholas I and Josef I" originally appeared in *Politics* (Spring 1948); "The Eisenstein Tragedy" originally appeared in *Partisan Review* (November/December, 1942).

104. Dwight Macdonald, "USA v. USSR," in *Politics Past,* 312; Dwight Macdonald, "The Eisenstein Tragedy: 2," in *Politics Past,* 236; Macdonald, "London, 1957," *loc. cit.,* 6. "USA v. USSR" originally appeared in *Politics* (Spring 1948); "The Eisenstein Tragedy: 2" originally appeared in *Politics* (October 1946).

105. Dwight Macdonald, "I Choose the West," in *Politics Past,* 197–200; Macdonald, "USA v. USSR," *loc. cit.,* 311; Macdonald, "London, 1957," *loc. cit.,* 5. See also Dwight Macdonald, "The Germans—Three Years Later," in *Politics Past,* 79; and Dwight Macdonald, "Truman's Doctrine, Abroad and at Home," in *Politics Past,* 190. "I Choose the West" was the title of Macdonald's speech in his debate with Norman Mailer at Mt. Holyoke College in the winter of 1952; "The Germans—Three Years Later" originally appeared in *Student Partisan* (University of Chicago, Winter 1949); "Truman's Doctrine, Abroad and at Home" originally appeared in *Politics* (May 1947).

106. Macdonald, "The Responsibilities of People," *loc. cit.,* 51, 61–62, 65, 71; Macdonald, "The Germans—Three Years Later," *loc. cit.,* 75–76; Dwight Macdonald, "A Way of Death," in *Politics Past,* 265. See also Macdonald, "Truman's Doctrine Abroad and at Home," *loc. cit.,* 190–192. "A Way of Death" originally appeared in *Politics* (Spring 1948).

107. Dwight Macdonald, "The Question of God," in *Politics Past,* 372–373; Macdonald, "London, 1957," *loc. cit.,* 28. "The Question of God" originally appeared in *Partisan Review* (May/June, 1950).

108. Macdonald, "The Responsibilities of People," *loc. cit.,* 61; Dwight Macdonald, "The Bomb," in *Politics Past,* 170, 178–179; Dwight Macdonald, "Notes on the Psychology of Killing," in *Politics Past,* 91; Macdonald, "London, 1957," *loc. cit.,* 29. "The Bomb" originally appeared in *Politics* (August and September, 1945); "Notes on the Psychology of Killing" originally appeared in *Politics* (September 1944).

109. Dwight Macdonald, "The Truth About the UN," in *Politics Past,* 298; Dwight Macdonald, "Gandhi," in *Politics Past,* 347–348; Dwight Macdonald, "Dorothy Day," in *Politics Past,* 350. "The Truth about the UN" originally appeared in *Politics* (November 1946); "Gandhi" originally appeared in *Politics* (Winter 1948); "Dorothy Day" originally appeared in *The New Yorker* (October 4 and 11, 1952).

110. Macdonald, "London, 1957," *loc. cit.,* 28, 31; Macdonald, "The Question of God," *loc. cit.,* 373.

4.   Conformity and Alienation

1. Hans Meyerhoff, "Offbeat Political Writing," *Commentary,* XXIV (November 1957), 465.

2. Seymour Lipset, *Political Man* (New York, 1963, c. 1960), 445. For a similar appraisal, see Norman Birnbaum, "America, A Partial View," *Commentary*, XXVI (July 1958), 42–44.

3. Lewis Coser, "American Notebook: Portraits and Problems," *Dissent*, IV (Summer 1957), 210.

4. Mary McCarthy, "America the Beautiful" in *On the Contrary* (New York, 1962), 11–12; Mary McCarthy, "Mlle. Gulliver en Amerique," in *On the Contrary*, 30. "America the Beautiful" originally appeared in *Commentary* (September 1947); "Mlle. Gulliver en Amerique" originally appeared in *The Reporter* (January 1952).

5. Dwight Macdonald, "America! America!" *Dissent*, V (Autumn 1958), 313. Italics his.

6. Delmore Schwartz, "The Grapes of Crisis," *Partisan Review*, XVIII (January/February, 1951), 12.

7. Dwight Macdonald, "Howtoism," in *Against the American Grain* (New York, 1962), 386; Coser, "American Notebook: Portraits and Problems," *loc. cit.*, 212. Macdonald's essay originally appeared in *The New Yorker* (May 22, 1954).

8. Schwartz, "The Grapes of Crisis," *loc. cit.*, 11.

9. Nathan Glazer, "The 'Alienation' of Modern Man," *Commentary*, III (April 1947), 378.

10. Leslie Fiedler, "The Ordeal of Criticism," *Commentary*, VIII (November 1949), 505–506.

11. Dwight Macdonald, "Abstractio Ad Absurdum," *Partisan Review*, XIX (January/February, 1952), 114.

12. Harvey Wheeler, "Danger Signals in the Political System," *Dissent*, IV (Summer 1957), 303.

13. Coser, "American Notebook: Portraits and Problems," *loc. cit.*, 211.

14. Daniel Bell, "Work and Its Discontents," in *The End of Ideology* (New York, 1965, c. 1960), 229–230, 232, 235, 256; Daniel Bell, "Adjusting Men to Machines," *Commentary*, III (January 1947), 88; Daniel Bell, "Meaning in Work—A New Direction," *Dissent*, VI (Summer 1959), 246.

15. Bell, "Work and Its Discontents, *loc. cit.*, 257; Bell, "Adjusting Men to Machines," *loc. cit.*, 85–87.

16. Bell, "Work and Its Discontents," *loc. cit.*, 244, 249, 251; Bell, "Adjusting Men to Machines," *loc. cit.*, 80, 86.

17. Bell, "Work and Its Discontents," *loc. cit.*, 239, 249, 255, 263; Bell, "Meaning in Work—A New Direction," *loc. cit.*, 245–247.

18. Bell, "Work and Its Discontents," *loc. cit.*, 254–255, 257, 259; Bell, "Adjusting Men to Machines," *loc. cit.*, 87.

19. Bell, "Work and Its Discontents," *loc. cit.*, 259; Bell, "Adjusting Men to Machines," *loc. cit.*, 87; Bell, "Meaning in Work—A New Direction," *loc. cit.*, 248.

20. Bell, "Work and Its Discontents," *loc. cit.*, 262–263, 268–270; Bell, "Adjusting Men to Machines," *loc. cit.*, 87; Bell, "Meaning in Work—A New Direc-

tion," *loc. cit.*, 243–245, 247–249. For a similar forecast of the benign effects of automation, see Arnold Rose, "Automation and the Future Society," *Commentary*, XXI (March 1956), 279–280.

21. William Newman, "Americans in Subtopia," *Dissent*, IV (Summer 1957), 260–261.

22. For an example of this charge, see Birnbaum, "America, a Partial View," *loc. cit.*, 44.

23. Newman, "Americans in Subtopia," *loc. cit.*, 256–257.

24. *Ibid.*, 258; Maurice Stein, "Suburbia—A Walk on the Mild Side," *Dissent*, IV (Summer 1957), 268, 272–274.

25. Newman, "Americans in Subtopia," *loc. cit.*, 263, 266.

26. Isaac Rosenfeld, "Life in Chicago," *Commentary*, XXIII (June 1957), 530–531.

27. Arnold Green, "Young America Takes Over the Colleges," *Commentary*, VII (June 1949), 524–525.

28. George Rawick, "The American Student: A Profile," *Dissent*, I (Autumn 1954), 395–397.

29. Mary McCarthy, "The Vassar Girl," in *On the Contrary*, 204; Robert Lynd, "Where Is the U.S. Going?" *New Republic*, CXXI (September 5, 1949), 17; Rosenfeld, "Life in Chicago," *loc. cit.*, 527. See also Birnbaum, "America, A Partial View," *loc. cit.*, 47. McCarthy's essay originally appeared in *Holiday* (May 1951).

30. Rawick, "The American Student: A Profile," *loc. cit.*, 397–398.

31. Green, "Young America Takes Over the Colleges," *loc. cit.*, 527–528, 532. Italics his.

32. McCarthy, "The Vassar Girl," *loc. cit.*, 205, 210. For a similar complaint, see Birnbaum, "America, A Partial View," *loc. cit.*, 47.

33. Green, "Young America Takes Over the Colleges," *loc. cit.*, 532–533.

34. McCarthy, "The Vassar Girl," *loc. cit.*, 208–209.

35. Green, "Young America Takes Over the Colleges," *loc. cit.*, 527, 529–531.

36. McCarthy, "The Vassar Girl," *loc. cit.*, 212, 214. See also Green, "Young America Takes Over the Colleges," *loc. cit.*, 531.

37. Rosenfeld, "Life in Chicago," *loc. cit.*, 527; Morris Freedman, "The Jewish College Student: 1951 Model," *Commentary*, XII (October 1951), 313.

38. Rosenfeld, "Life in Chicago," *loc. cit.*, 529.

39. *Ibid.*, 528.

40. For a sample of the journalistic concern, see Harrison Salisbury, *The Shook-Up Generation* (New York, 1958).

41. Harvey Swados, "Popular Taste and the Agonies of the Young," *Dissent*, V (Spring 1958), 174, 176–177.

42. Alfred Kazin, *New York Jew* (New York, 1978), 93.

43. Norman Mailer, *The Armies of the Night* (New York, 1968), 35.

44. Norman Podhoretz, *Making It* (New York, 1969, c. 1967), 219–220. See also Richard King, *The Party of Eros* (New York, 1973, c. 1972), 102; and Morris Dickstein, *Gates of Eden* (New York, 1977), 74–77.

, 45. Norman Mailer, "The White Negro," in *Advertisements for Myself* (New York, 1966, c. 1959), 312–313, 321, 327–328.

46. *Ibid.*, 313–317, 321.

47. *Ibid.*, 312, 327, 329.

48. Paul Goodman, *Growing Up Absurd* (New York, 1960), xiii, 15, 21–22, 28–29, 38, 137, 140, 145, 150, 152, 154.

49. *Ibid.*, x, 14, 160, 168–169.

50. *Ibid.*, 62, 65, 156.

51. *Ibid.*, 37, 41, 67, 134–135, 157, 162, 180, 193–195, 282–283.

52. *Ibid.*, 280–281.

53. *Ibid.*, 4, 6, 8–11, 47, 148.

54. *Ibid.*, xiv.

55. *Ibid.*, 12, 142, 229–233.

56. *Ibid.*, 13. Italics his.

57. For a brilliant discussion of the problems women faced, not only in the postwar years but throughout the twentieth century, see William Chafe, *The American Woman* (New York, 1972) and *Women and Equality* (New York, 1977).

58. Many of these points are elaborated in Kenneth Keniston's *Youth and Dissent* (New York, 1971).

59. For an extended analysis of the Frankfurt School's contributions to the study of mass culture, see Martin Jay, *The Dialectical Imagination* (Boston, 1973) chapter 6; and H. Stuart Hughes, *The Sea Change* (New York, 1975), chapter 4.

60. See Clement Greenberg, "Avant-Garde and Kitsch," *Partisan Review*, VI (Fall 1939), 39–49; Dwight Macdonald, "Soviet Cinema, 1930–1938," *Partisan Review*, V (July and August/September, 1938), 35–60; Dwight Macdonald, "Soviet Society and Its Cinema," *Partisan Review*, VI (Winter 1939), 80–94; and Dwight Macdonald, "Kulturbolschewismus Is Here," *Partisan Review*, VIII (November/December, 1941), 446–451. I have discussed the interest in popular culture during the 1930s in *Radical Visions and American Dreams* (New York, 1973), 263–268, 337–338.

61. Paul Lazarsfeld and Robert Merton, "Mass Communication, Popular Taste and Organized Social Action," in Bernard Rosenberg and David White, eds., *Mass Culture* (New York, 1957), 460. This essay originally appeared in Lyman Bryson, ed., *The Communication of Ideas* (1948).

62. Irving Howe, "The New York Intellectuals," in *Decline of the New* (New York, 1970), 227; Daniel Bell, "The Mood of Three Generations," in *The End of Ideology*, 312. Bell's essay originally appeared in *Encounter* (September 1959).

63. Podhoretz, *Making It*, 63–64.

64. For examples of this argument, see Henry Rabassiere, "Some Aspects of Mass Culture," *Dissent*, III (Summer 1956), 328–329; and Arnold Hauser, "Popular Art and Folk Art," *Dissent*, V (Summer 1958), 236.

65. Lipset, *Political Man*, 451. See also Bernard Berelson, "Who Reads Books and Why?" in Rosenberg and White, 122. Berelson's essay originally ap-

peared in the *Saturday Review of Literature* (May 12, 1951).

66. Clement Greenberg, "The Plight of Our Culture," *Commentary,* XV (June 1953), 566. See also Hauser, "Popular Art and Folk Art," *loc. cit.,* 231.

67. Gilbert Seldes, "The People and the Arts," in Rosenberg and White, 79. For a similar appraisal, see Arthur Brodbeck and David White, "How to Read 'Li'l Abner' Intelligently," in Rosenberg and White, 223. Seldes's essay originally appeared as a chapter in his book, *The Great Audience* (1951).

68. Rabassiere, "Some Aspects of Mass Culture," *loc. cit.,* 332.

69. Dwight Macdonald, "A Theory of Mass Culture," in Rosenberg and White, 59; Greenberg, "The Plight of Our Culture," *loc. cit.,* 564; Ernest van den Haag, "Of Happiness and of Despair We Have No Measure," in Rosenberg and White, 507–508, 518–519; Daniel Boorstin, *The Image* (New York, 1972, c. 1962), 13. Macdonald's essay originally appeared in *Diogenes* (Summer 1953).

70. Dwight Macdonald, "Masscult & Midcult," in *Against the American Grain,* 8–10, 32, 34. For an equally jaundiced view of the role of mass culture in a mass society, see Gunther Anders, "The Phantom World of TV," in Rosenberg and White, 359–361. Macdonald's essay originally appeared in *Partisan Review* (Spring and Fall, 1960); Anders's essay originally appeared in *Dissent* (Winter 1956).

71. Greenberg, "The Plight of Our Culture," *loc. cit.,* 563; S. I. Hayakawa, "Popular Songs vs. the Facts of Life," in Rosenberg and White, 393. Hayakawa's essay originally appeared in *Etc.* (1955).

72. Greenberg, "The Plight of Our Culture," *loc. cit.,* 565; Clement Greenberg, "Work and Leisure Under Industrialism," *Commentary,* XVI (July 1953), 54–55; Macdonald, "A Theory of Mass Culture," *loc. cit.,* 61, 64; Macdonald, "Masscult & Midcult," *loc. cit.,* 37, 50–51.

73. Paul Goodman, "Reflections on Literature as a Minor Art," *Dissent,* V (Summer 1958), 291–293; Boorstin, *The Image,* 145, 181, 189, 192, 198, 200–201, 204, 241, 249.

74. Greenberg, "Work and Leisure under Industrialism," *loc. cit.,* 58; van den Haag, "Of Happiness and of Despair We Have No Measure," *loc. cit.,* 505.

75. Goodman, "Reflections on Literature as a Minor Art," *loc. cit.,* 292; Macdonald, "A Theory of Mass Culture," *loc. cit.,* 65; Macdonald, "Masscult & Midcult," *loc. cit.,* 5–6; Dwight Macdonald, "Mark Twain," in *Against the American Grain,* 99. Macdonald's essay on Twain originally appeared in *The New Yorker* (April 2, 1960).

76. Macdonald, "Masscult & Midcult," *loc. cit.,* 28; Macdonald, "A Theory of Mass Culture," *loc. cit.,* 72; Greenberg, "The Plight of Our Culture," *loc. cit.,* 566.

77. van den Hag, "Of Happiness and of Despair We Have No Measure," *loc. cit.,* 509–513; Herbert Gans, "The Creator-Audience Relationship in the Mass Media: An Analysis of Movie Making," in Rosenberg and White, 318. For a similar argument, see Rolf Meyersohn, "Social Research in Television," in Rosenberg and White, 352–353.

78. Harold Rosenberg, "The Herd of Independent Minds," *Commentary,* VI (September 1948), 244–245, 248, 250–252.

79. William Phillips, "The American Establishment," *Partisan Review,* XXVI (Winter 1959), 112; Macdonald, "Mark Twain," *loc. cit.,* 102; Macdonald, "Masscult & Midcult," *loc. cit.,* 12–13; Greenberg, "Work and Leisure under Industrialism," *loc. cit.,* 54; Boorstin, *The Image,* 126–127.

80. Macdonald, "Masscult & Midcult," *loc. cit.,* 5; Irving Howe, "Notes on Mass Culture," in Rosenberg and White, 497, 499; Robert Warshow, "The Legacy of the 30's," in *The Immediate Experience* (New York, 1970, c. 1962), 38; Leslie Fiedler, "The Middle Against Both Ends," in Rosenberg and White, 543, 546–547; Dwight Macdonald, "The Triumph of the Fact," in *Against the American Grain,* 400–401; Theodor Adorno, "Television and the Patterns of Mass Culture," in Rosenberg and White, 476, 484; Boorstin, *The Image,* 121, 132–133, 147–148; Greenberg, "The Plight of Our Culture," *loc. cit.,* 565–566. See also Hauser, "Popular Art and Folk Art," *loc. cit.,* 233; and Leo Bogart, "Comic Strips and Their Adult Readers," in Rosenberg and White, 191. Howe's essay originally appeared in *Politics* (Spring 1948); Warshow's essay originally appeared in *Commentary* (December 1947); Fiedler's essay originally appeared in *Encounter* (1955); Macdonald's essay, "The Triumph of the Fact," originally appeared in *Anchor Review* (1957); Adorno's essay originally appeared in the *Quarterly of Film, Radio and Television* (1954).

81. Greenberg, "Work and Leisure under Industrialism," *loc. cit.,* 59; Greenberg, "The Plight of Our Culture," *loc. cit.,* 564; Dwight Macdonald, "By Cozzens Possessed," in *Against the American Grain,* 196; Dwight Macdonald, "Inside *The Outsider,*" in *Against the American Grain,* 223. Macdonald's essay on Cozzens originally appeared in *Commentary* (January 1958); his essay on *The Outsider* originally appeared in *The New Yorker* (October 13, 1956).

82. Macdonald, "Masscult & Midcult," *loc. cit.,* 38–41; Macdonald, "Inside *The Outsider,*" *loc. cit.,* 227–228; Dwight Macdonald, "Amateur Journalism," in *Against the American Grain,* 338; Dwight Macdonald, "Updating the Bible," in *Against the American Grain,* 272–273, 278; Dwight Macdonald, "Looking Backward," in *Against the American Grain,* 237. "Amateur Journalism" originally appeared in *Encounter* (November 1956); "Updating the Bible" originally appeared in *The New Yorker* (November 14, 1953); "Looking Backward" originally appeared in *Encounter* (June 1961).

83. van den Haag, "Of Happiness and of Despair We Have No Measure," *loc. cit.,* 517, 529–530; Hayakawa, "Popular Songs vs. the Facts of Life," *loc. cit.,* 400; Warshow, "The Legacy of the 30's," *loc. cit.,* 38. See also Hauser, "Popular Art and Folk Art," *loc. cit.,* 234.

84. Boorstin, *The Image,* 84–86, 91–97, 99, 101–103, 107, 109, 111–114, 116–117. See also Anders, "The Phantom World of TV," *loc. cit.,* 364.

85. Boorstin, *The Image,* 11–12, 35, 37, 39–40.

86. *Ibid.,* 14–17, 19–22, 30, 41, 43, 122, 156, 158, 162–164, 168.

87. *Ibid.,* 45, 47–49, 57, 60–61, 63, 211–213, 226–227. See also, Lazarsfeld and

Merton, "Mass Communication, Popular Taste and Organized Social Action," *loc. cit.*, 461–462.

88. Hortense Powdermaker, "Hollywood and the U.S.A.," in Rosenberg and White, 286, 289–291; Adorno, "Television and the Patterns of Mass Culture," *loc. cit.*, 479. See also, Lazarsfeld and Merton, "Mass Communication, Popular Taste and Organized Social Action," *loc. cit.*, 457–458. Powdermaker's essay originally appeared as a chapter in her book, *Hollywood, the Dream Factory* (New York, 1951).

89. Lazarsfeld and Merton, "Mass Communication, Popular Taste and Organized Social Action," *loc. cit.*, 464. Italics theirs.

90. Adorno, "Television and the Patterns of Mass Culture," *loc. cit.*, 476, 478; Lazarsfeld and Merton, "Mass Communication, Popular Taste and Organized Social Action," *loc. cit.*, 465, 472–473; Boorstin, *The Image*, 191–192; van den Haag, "Of Happiness and of Despair We Have No Measure," *loc. cit.*, 518; Howe, "Notes on Mass Culture," *loc. cit.*, 498. See also Murray Hausknecht, "The Mike in the Bosom," in Rosenberg and White, 376–377. Hausknecht's essay originally appeared in *Dissent* (Winter 1957).

91. Greenberg, "Work and Leisure Under Industrialism," *loc. cit.*, 61.

92. Boorstin, *The Image*, 3, 6, 240, 259–261.

93. Howe, "Notes on Mass Culture," *loc. cit.*, 499; Dwight Macdonald, "James Joyce," in *Against the American Grain*, 132; Macdonald, "Updating the Bible," *loc. cit.*, 283. Macdonald's essay on Joyce originally appeared in *The New Yorker* (December 12, 1959).

94. Rosenberg, "The Herd of Independent Minds," *loc. cit.*, 246, 252; van den Haag, "Of Happiness and of Despair We Have No Measure," *loc. cit.*, 517, 532–533; Macdonald, "Masscult & Midcult," *loc. cit.*, 56. See also Gans, "The Creator-Audience Relationship in the Mass Media: An Analysis of Movie Making," *loc. cit.*, 317.

95. Greenberg, "Work and Leisure under Industrialism," *loc. cit.*, 55; Clement Greenberg, "Art Chronicle: The Situation at the Moment," *Partisan Review*, XV (January 1948), 81–84; Macdonald, "A Theory of Mass Culture," *loc. cit.*, 63; Macdonald, "Masscult & Midcult," *loc. cit.*, 56, 61, 64, 70, 72–74; Macdonald, "Mark Twain," *loc. cit.*, 108; Dwight Macdonald, "James Agee," in *Against the American Grain*, 154; Macdonald, "By Cozzens Possessed," *loc. cit.*, 205; Macdonald, "Looking Backward," *loc. cit.*, 229, 236; Macdonald, "Amateur Journalism," *loc. cit.*, 346; Macdonald, Preface to *Against the American Grain*, x. Macdonald's essay on Agee originally appeared in *The New Yorker* (November 16, 1957).

96. William Whyte, *The Organization Man* (New York, 1957, c. 1956), 11–12.

97. *Ibid.*, 4.

98. *Ibid.*, 7–8, 32, 36, 40–42, 44, 50–51, 53–54, 57, 143, 387, 390.

99. *Ibid.*, 3–4.

100. *Ibid.*, 63, 78, 135–137, 147, 149, 152, 178, 225, 231–232, 358.

101. *Ibid.*, 14, 57–60, 65, 172, 245, 397, 400, 402, 404, 440, 448.

102. *Ibid.*, 13, 65, 184, 401, 440, 448. Italics his.

103. *Ibid.*, 14, 443, 447.

104. *Ibid.,* 12–15, 182, 184–185, 395, 448.
105. *Ibid.,* 8, 86, 102, 182, 232, 445, 447. For a contemporary critique of these tendencies in Whyte's argument, see Robert Lekachman, "Organization Men," *Commentary,* XXIII (March 1957), 275.
106. David Riesman, *The Lonely Crowd* (New Haven, Conn., 1961, c.1950), xxxii.
107. *Ibid.,* xv–xvi, xxix.
108. *Ibid.,* xxi, 18.
109. David Riesman, "Individualism Reconsidered," in *Individualism Reconsidered* (New York, 1964, c. 1954), 38, Riesman, *Individualism Reconsidered,* 122. "Individualism Reconsidered" originally appeared in William Loos, ed., *Religious Faith and World Culture* (1951).
110. Riesman, *The Lonely Crowd,* xxx.
111. *Ibid.,* 11, 17, 24, 39, 85. Italics his.
112. *Ibid.,* 14, 24, 41–42, 59, 92, 101; David Riesman, "How Different May One Be?" in *Individualism Reconsidered,* 266. This essay originally appeared in *Child Study* (Spring 1951).
113. Riesman, *The Lonely Crowd,* 18–21, 45–46, 48, 60–61, 63–65, 71, 79, 82, 129–130, 136–137, 234; David Riesman, "The Saving Remnant," in *Individualism Reconsidered,* 104–105; Riesman, "How Different May One Be?" *loc. cit.,* 266; David Riesman, "The Meaning of Opinion," in *Individualism Reconsidered,* 495. "The Saving Remnant" originally appeared in John Chase, ed., *The Years of the Modern* (1949); "The Meaning of Opinion" originally appeared in the *International Journal of Opinion and Attitude Research* (1949) and in *Public Opinion Quarterly* (1949).
114. Riesman, "How Different May One Be?" *loc. cit.,* 266; Riesman, *The Lonely Crowd,* 25, 47, 72–74, 81–82; Riesman, "The Saving Remnant," *loc. cit.,* 110, 112; David Riesman, "Movies and Audiences," in *Individualism Reconsidered,* 195. Italics his. "Movies and Audiences" originally appeared in the *American Quarterly* (1952).
115. Riesman, *The Lonely Crowd,* xxxvi, 206, 211, 214, 219, 222–223.
116. Riesman, "The Saving Remnant," *loc. cit.,* 114; Riesman, "Individualism Reconsidered," *loc. cit.,* 36–37; Riesman, *The Lonely Crowd,* xxxvi, xxxviii, 235. Italics his.
117. Riesman, "The Saving Remnant," *loc. cit.,* 106, 108, 118; David Riesman, "The Ethics of We Happy Few," in *Individualism Reconsidered,* 46; Riesman, *The Lonely Crowd,* 139; Riesman, "Individualism Reconsidered," *loc. cit.,* 37; David Riesman, "A Philosophy for 'Minority' Living," in *Individualism Reconsidered,* 55. "The Ethics of We Happy Few" originally appeared in *University Observer* (1947); "A Philosophy for 'Minority' Living" originally appeared in *Commentary* (November 1948).
118. Riesman, *The Lonely Crowd,* 31, 159; Riesman, "The Saving Remnant," *loc. cit.,* 101–102, 105.
119. Riesman, "The Saving Remnant," *loc. cit.,* 100, 116–117; Riesman, *The Lonely Crowd,* 242, 259.
120. Riesman, *The Lonely Crowd,* 251; David Riesman, "Values in Context," in *Individualism Reconsidered,* 18; Riesman, "The Saving Remnant," *loc. cit.,* 117.

"Values in Context" originally appeared in the *American Scholar* (1952).
121. Riesman, "Individualism Reconsidered," *loc. cit.*, 35; Riesman, "The Saving Remnant," *loc. cit.*, 117–120.
122. Riesman, *The Lonely Crowd*, xliv, 240, 247–248, 276, 304.
123. C. Wright Mills, *White Collar* (New York, 1956, c. 1951), xx, 321–322; C. Wright Mills, "The Structure of Power in American Society," in Irving Louis Horowitz, ed., *Power, Politics and People* (New York, 1967, c. 1963), 38; C. Wright Mills, "Culture and Politics," in Horowitz, 236–237; C. Wright Mills, *The Power Elite* (New York, 1959, c. 1956), 277; C. Wright Mills, "On Knowledge and Power," in Horowitz, 601; C. Wright Mills, "Liberal Values in the Modern World," in Horowitz, 189. "The Structure of Power in American Society" originally appeared in the *British Journal of Sociology* (March 1958); "Culture and Politics" originally appeared in *The Listener* (March 12, 1959); "On Knowledge and Power" originally appeared in *Dissent* (Summer 1955); "Liberal Values in the Modern World" originally appeared in *Anvil and Student Partisan* (Winter 1952).
124. Mills, "The Structure of Power in American Society," *loc. cit.*, 23, 25, 27–28, 31; Mills, *The Power Elite*, 3–4, 6–9, 11, 18, 28, 167, 199, 212, 215, 224, 229, 231, 267, 275, 286, 290, 293.
125. Mills, *The Power Elite*, 11, 15, 18–19, 62, 64–65, 67–70, 96–97, 278, 280–281, 283, 287, 292, 296; Mills, "The Structure of Power in American Society," *loc. cit.*, 29–30.
126. Mills, *White Collar*, 109, 111, 348–350; Mills, *The Power Elite*, 221, 296, 316–317, 355.
127. Mills, *The Power Elite*, 37, 243–246, 265–266, 336, 359; Mills, "The Structure of Power in American Society," *loc. cit.*, 30–33.
128. Mills, *The Power Elite*, 28–29, 46, 206, 210, 236, 254–255, 258–259, 262–263, 267–268, 306–310; Mills, "The Structure of Power in American Society," *loc. cit.*, 30, 32–33; Mills, *White Collar*, 322.
129. Mills, *White Collar*, xii, xvi–xvii, 71, 98, 108–109, 112, 114, 182–184, 186, 188, 219, 224–228, 233–238, 252; C. Wright Mills, "Diagnosis of Our Moral Uneasiness," in Horowitz, 332–333; C. Wright Mills, "The Competitive Personality," in Horowitz, 271; C. Wright Mills, "The Social Role of the Intellectual," in Horowitz, 300. "Diagnosis of Our Moral Uneasiness" originally appeared in the *New York Times Magazine* (November 23, 1952); "The Competitive Personality" originally appeared in *Partisan Review* (September/October, 1946); "The Social Role of the Intellectual" originally appeared in *Politics* (April 1944).
130. Mills, *White Collar*, xii, 111, 326–328, 347, 352–353; Mills, *The Power Elite*, 3, 261–262; C. Wright Mills, "The Big City: Private Troubles and Public Issues," in Horowitz, 397; C. Wright Mills, "The Middle Classes in Middle-Sized Cities," in Horowitz, 287, 290; Mills, "Liberal Values in the Modern World," *loc. cit.*, 187; Mills, "The Structure of Power in American Society," *loc. cit.*, 37. "The Big City: Private Troubles and Public Issues" was originally presented as a speech on the Canadian Broadcasting Company in

1959; "The Middle Classes in Middle-Sized Cities" originally appeared in the *American Sociological Review* (October 1946).
131. Mills, *The Power Elite*, 84, 297, 303–305, 314–315, 320–322; C. Wright Mills, "Mass Society and Liberal Education," in Horowitz, 353, 366–367; C. Wright Mills, "The Cultural Apparatus," in Horowitz, 406–407; C. Wright Mills, "Mass Media and Public Opinion," in Horowitz, 582; C. Wright Mills, "The Decline of the Left," in Horowitz, 229. "Mass Society and Liberal Education" originally appeared as a pamphlet published by the Center for the Study of Liberal Education for Adults in 1954; "The Cultural Apparatus" originally appeared in *The Listener* (March 26, 1959); "Mass Media and Public Opinion" was originally written in 1950 for the state department's Russian language journal *Amerika,* but its publication was prohibited by Soviet authorities; "The Decline of the Left" originally appeared in *Contact* (1959).
132. C. Wright Mills, "The New Left," in Horowitz, 256. This essay originally appeared in *New Left Review* (September/October, 1960).
133. Mills, *The Power Elite*, 338, 353; Mills, *White Collar*, 130–131, 135–136, 149, 151–152, 155, 159–160; Mills, "The Social Role of the Intellectual," *loc. cit.,* 299, 302; Mills, "The Decline of the Left," *loc. cit.,* 225, 229–231; C. Wright Mills, " 'The Power Elite': Comment on Criticism," *Dissent,* IV (Winter 1957), 25; C. Wright Mills, "The Professional Ideology of Social Pathologists," in Horowitz, 527; C. Wright Mills, "Two Styles of Social Science Research," in Horowitz, 556. "The Professional Ideology of Social Pathologists" originally appeared in the *American Journal of Sociology* (September 1943); "Two Styles of Social Science Research" originally appeared in *Philosophy of Science* (October 1953).
134. Mills, *White Collar*, 157, 159.
135. Mills, "The Social Role of the Intellectual," *loc. cit.,* 298–299; Mills, "The Decline of the Left," *loc. cit.,* 231–232; C. Wright Mills, "The Complacent Young Men," in Horowitz, 387. "The Complacent Young Men" originally appeared in *Anvil and Student Partisan* (Winter 1958).
136. Mills, "The Complacent Young Men," *loc. cit.,* 387–389; Mills, *The Power Elite*, 318–319; Mills, "The Big City: Private Troubles and Public Issues," *loc. cit.,* 395–397; Mills, "The New Left," *loc. cit.,* 253–254. Italics his.
137. Mills, "On Knowledge and Power," *loc. cit.,* 611; Mills, "The Decline of the Left," *loc. cit.,* 232–233, 235; Mills, "The Social Role of the Intellectual," *loc. cit.,* 300–302; Mills, *White Collar*, 159; Mills, " 'The Power Elite': Comment on Criticism" *loc. cit.,* 27. Italics his.
138. Mills, *The Power Elite*, 296, 353; Mills, "The Structure of Power in American Society," *loc. cit.,* 37–38.
139. Mills, "The New Left," *loc. cit.,* 259.

5. Are You Now, Have You Ever Been . . .

1. See David Caute, *The Fellow-Travellers* (New York, 1973), 304.
2. This phrase is taken from the title of an article in *Commentary*, XI (April 1951), 319–329, by Granville Hicks, an ex-Communist who presumably had learned.
3. The best accounts of McCarthyism's effects on its victims can be found in Walter Goodman, *The Committee* (New York, 1968); Stefan Kanfer, *A Journal of the Plague Years* (New York, 1973); David Caute, *The Great Fear* (New York, 1978); Larry Ceplair and Steven Englund, *The Inquisition in Hollywood* (New York, 1980); and especially Victor Navasky, *Naming Names* (New York, 1980).
4. For a description of how the loyalty oath program worked, see Navasky, *Naming Names*, 21, 29; Walter Goodman, *The Committee* (Baltimore, 1969, c. 1968), 195; and Garry Wills, Introduction to Lillian Hellman's *Scoundrel Time* (New York, 1977, c. 1976), 8–9.
5. Henry Wallace, "A Bad Case of Fever," *New Republic*, CXVI (April 14, 1947), 12–13. See also Alonzo Hamby, *Beyond the New Deal* (New York, 1973), 388.
6. Dwight Macdonald, "Truman's Doctrine, Abroad and at Home," in *Politics Past* (New York, 1970, c. 1957), 188–189; Wallace, "A Bad Case of Fever," *loc. cit.*, 13. Macdonald's essay originally appeared in *Politics* (May 1947).
7. Sidney Hook, "Liberalism and the Law," *Commentary*, XXIII (January 1957), 50, 52; Irving Kristol, "Liberty and the Communists," *Partisan Review*, XIX (July/August, 1952), 494; Robert Bendiner, "Civil Liberties and the Communists," *Commentary*, V (May 1948), 426; Leslie Fiedler, "McCarthy and the Intellectuals," in *An End to Innocence* (Boston, 1955), 60; Arthur Schlesinger, *The Vital Center* (Boston, 1962, c. 1949), 201, 212–214; Daniel Bell, "Status Politics and New Anxieties," in *The End of Ideology* (New York, 1965, c. 1960), 123; Richard Rovere, "Communists in a Free Society," *Partisan Review*, XIX (May/June, 1952), 345. See also Navasky, *Naming Names*, 43. Fiedler's essay originally appeared in *Encounter* (August 1954); Bell's essay originally appeared in *Encounter* (January 1956).
8. Schlesinger, *The Vital Center*, 210, 215; Bendiner, "Civil Liberties and the Communists," *loc. cit.*, 429.
9. Bendiner, "Civil Liberties and the Communists," *loc. cit.*, 425–426.
10. Alan Westin, "Libertarian Precepts and Subversive Realities," *Commentary*, XIX (January 1955), 4.
11. Schlesinger, *The Vital Center*, 210, 215–216; Rovere, "Communists in a Free Society," *loc. cit.*, 344; Bendiner, "Civil Liberties and the Communists," *loc. cit.*, 428.
12. Paul Kecskemeti, "How Totalitarians Gain Absolute Power," *Commentary*, XIV (December 1952), 545.
13. For a more detailed description of the testimony of Elizabeth Bentley and Whittaker Chambers, and their consequences for William Remington, Harry Dexter White, and Alger Hiss, see Goodman, *The Committee*, 244–249,

252, 254–259, 264–267, 286–287; Hamby, *Beyond the New Deal*, 379, 381, 384–385; Caute, *The Great Fear*, 56–61, 287–289; and Navasky, *Naming Names*, vii, 7. But by far the most comprehensive and persuasive analysis of the Hiss–Chambers case is Allen Weinstein's *Perjury* (New York, 1978).

14. See Navasky, *Naming Names*, 4, 8; and Hamby, *Beyond the New Deal*, 383, 385.

15. Much of this information is presented in Weinstein, *Perjury*, 71, 115, 125, 193, 312, 320–321, 522, 540.

16. Diana Trilling, "A Memorandum on the Hiss Case," *Partisan Review*, XVII (May/June, 1950), 486–487, 496–497, 500.

17. Harold Rosenberg, "Couch Liberalism and the Guilty Past," *Dissent*, II (Autumn 1955), 326.

18. Murray Kempton, *Part of Our Time* (New York, 1967, c. 1955), 27, 325–326.

19. Leslie Fiedler, "Hiss, Chambers, and the Age of Innocence," in *An End to Innocence*, 12, 17–18. This essay originally appeared in *Commentary* (December 1950).

20. *Ibid.*, 4. See also Morris Dickstein, *Gates of Eden* (New York, 1977), 42.

21. Fiedler, "Hiss, Chambers, and the Age of Innocence," *loc. cit.*, 5–6.

22. *Ibid.*, 21–22, 24; Philip Rahv, "The Sense and Nonsense of Whittaker Chambers," *Partisan Review*, XIX (July/August, 1952), 478.

23. Rosenberg, "Couch Liberalism and the Guilty Past," *loc. cit.*, 318–319, 321, 325, 327.

24. See Caute, *The Great Fear*, 62–69.

25. Leslie Fiedler, "Afterthoughts on the Rosenbergs," in *An End to Innocence*, 25–31. This essay originally appeared in *Encounter* (October 1953).

26. See Dickstein, *Gates of Eden*, 44.

27. Robert Warshow, "The 'Idealism' of Julius and Ethel Rosenberg," in *The Immediate Experience* (New York, 1970, c. 1962), 81. This essay originally appeared in *Commentary* (November 1953).

28. Fiedler, "Afterthoughts on the Rosenbergs," *loc. cit.*, 33, 38, 41, 43–45; Warshow, "The 'Idealism' of Julius and Ethel Rosenberg," *loc. cit.*, 72–74, 76, 79–80.

29. For a more extensive analysis of the Smith Act trials and their consequences for the Communist party in the 1950s, see Navasky, *Naming Names*, 4, 28–34; and Caute, *The Great Fear*, 185–215.

30. Roger Baldwin, "Liberals and the Communist Trial," *New Republic*, CXX (January 31, 1949), 8.

31. "The Communist Trial," *New Republic*, CXX (February 7, 1949), 6; "After the Communist Trial," *New Republic*, CXXI (October 24, 1949), 5–6.

32. Mary McCarthy, "No News, or, What Killed the Dog," in *On the Contrary* (New York, 1962), 35–36. This essay originally appeared in *The Reporter* (July 1952).

33. Kempton, *Part of Our Time*, 329, 331.

34. Fiedler, "Hiss, Chambers, and the Age of Innocence," *loc. cit.*, 23.

35. M. McCarthy, "No News, or, What Killed the Dog," *loc. cit.*, 36–38. Italics hers.

36. D. Trilling, "A Memorandum on the Hiss Case," *loc. cit.*, 498–499. For a

similar view, see Rovere, "Communists in a Free Society," *loc. cit.*, 343–344; and Schlesinger, *The Vital Center*, 119, 211–212, 218.

37. Sidney Hook, "Does the Smith Act Threaten Our Liberties?" *Commentary*, XV (January 1953), 64–65, 67–68, 71.

38. *Ibid.*, 73.

39. Robert Bendiner, "Has Anti-Communism Wrecked Our Liberties?" *Commentary*, XII (July 1951), 11–13.

40. Hook, "Does the Smith Act Threaten Our Liberties?" *loc. cit.*, 72.

41. Kecskemeti, "How Totalitarians Gain Absolute Power," *loc. cit.*, 545.

42. Bendiner, "Has Anti-Communism Wrecked Our Liberties?" *loc. cit.*, 16.

43. Caute, *The Fellow-Travellers*, 320–321, 323–324; Caute, *The Great Fear*, 414, 424.

44. See Goodman, *The Committee*, 327–328; and Caute, *The Great Fear*, 405–406.

45. Caute, *The Great Fear*, 406, 408–418, 422–424; Caute, *The Fellow-Travellers*, 321. See also Navasky, *Naming Names*, 58.

46. Schlesinger, *The Vital Center*, 207; Rovere, "Communists in a Free Society," *loc. cit.*, 345–346.

47. Sidney Hook, "Academic Integrity and Academic Freedom," *Commentary*, VIII (October 1949), 334. Italics his. See also Hook, "Liberalism and the Law," *loc. cit.*, 54.

48. The quotation from Norman Thomas can be found in Goodman, *The Committee*, 327; Hook, "Academic Integrity and Academic Freedom," *loc. cit.*, 331, 335, 337, italics his; Paul Hays, "Academic Freedom and Communist Teachers," *Commentary*, XXI (June 1956), 552.

49. Hook, "Academic Integrity and Academic Freedom," *loc. cit.*, 330, 334–335, 338.

50. *Ibid.*, 334, 339; Westin, "Libertarian Precepts and Subversive Realities," *loc. cit.*, 5–6, 8; Bendiner, "Civil Liberties and the Communists," *loc. cit.*, 430.

51. Henry Steele Commager, "Red-Baiting in the Colleges," *New Republic*, CXXI (July 25, 1949), 11–12.

52. *Ibid.*, 12–13.

53. Mary McCarthy, "The Contagion of Ideas," in *On the Contrary*, 49, 53. This essay was originally given as a speech to a group of teachers in the summer of 1952.

54. *Ibid.*, 54.

55. *Ibid.*, 52, 54.

56. Fiedler, "McCarthy and the Intellectuals," *loc. cit.*, 70, 76. Italics his.

57. Irving Kristol, " 'Civil Liberties,' 1952—A Study in Confusion," *Commentary*, XIII (March 1952), 229, 234. Italics mine.

58. *Ibid.*, 229–230, 236. See also Kristol, "Liberty and the Communists," *loc. cit.*, 496.

59. Rovere, "Communists in a Free Society," *loc. cit.*, 340–342, 346.

60. Alan Westin, "Our Freedom—And the Rights of Communists," *Commentary*, XIV (July 1952), 36–37.

61. *Ibid.*, 38.

62. M. McCarthy, "The Contagion of Ideas," *loc. cit.,* 44–45. Italics hers.
63. *Ibid.,* 45–46. Italics mine.
64. *Ibid.,* 45, 47.
65. For a more extended discussion of the confrontation between the House Un-American Activities Committee and the "Unfriendly Nineteen," see Goodman, *The Committee,* 207, 210, 216; Kanfer, *A Journal of the Plague Years,* 41, 74; Navasky, *Naming Names,* 80–82; Caute, *The Fellow-Travellers,* 309; and Ceplair and Englund, *The Inquisition in Hollywood,* 256.
66. Kempton, *Part of Our Time,* 182–183, 196, 204.
67. See Kanfer, *A Journal of the Plague Years,* 141; and Goodman, *The Committee,* 210, 213. But the most sensitive analysis of the Communist activities in and contributions to the film industry can be found in Ceplair and Englund, *The Inquisition in Hollywood,* chapters 1–7.
68. See Navasky, *Naming Names,* 83. The full text of the Waldorf statement is reprinted in Ceplair and Englund, *The Inquisition in Hollywood,* 445.
69. William Walton, "Rankin Puts It Plainly," *New Republic,* CXVII (December 8, 1947), 10.
70. Bendiner, "Civil Liberties and the Communists," *loc. cit.,* 427.
71. Martha Gellhorn, "Cry Shame . . . !" *New Republic,* CXVII (October 6, 1947), 21.
72. For a fuller account of the Hollywood Ten's convictions, jail terms, and subsequent activities, see Caute, *The Fellow-Travellers,* 309; Goodman, *The Committee,* 222–223; and Kanfer, *A Journal of the Plague Years,* 160.
73. See Navasky, *Naming Names,* x, 393.
74. See Kanfer, *A Journal of the Plague Years,* 75, 104–109; Goodman, *The Committee,* 300–301; and Navasky, *Naming Names,* 85, 88–89, 144, 152.
75. See Goodman, *The Committee,* 218, 301; Caute, *The Fellow-Travellers,* 325; and Navasky, *Naming Names,* 90, 335–336.
76. "Un-American Activities," *New Republic,* CXIX (December 13, 1948), 5–6.
77. James Burnham, "The Suicidal Mania of American Business," *Partisan Review,* XVII (January 1950), 55.
78. Louis Berg, "How End the Panic in Radio-TV?" *Commentary,* XIV (October 1952), 316–317, 322–324.
79. *Ibid.,* 321, 325.
80. Navasky makes a similar point in *Naming Names,* 88, 95.
81. See Kanfer, *A Journal of the Plague Years,* 3–5, 92; Navasky, *Naming Names,* 345; Caute, *The Great Fear,* 515, 530.
82. Alan Westin, "Do Silent Witnesses Defend Civil Liberties?" *Commentary,* XV (June 1953), 537–538, 540. Italics his.
83. Paul Hays, "Congress's Right to Investigate," *Commentary,* XX (November 1955), 444. Italics his.
84. Westin, "Do Silent Witnesses Defend Civil Liberties?" *loc. cit.,* 544.
85. Hook, "Liberalism and the Law," *loc. cit.,* 54; Westin, "Do Silent Witnesses Defend Civil Liberties?" *loc. cit.,* 539; Westin, "Libertarian Precepts and Subversive Realities," *loc. cit.,* 6.

86. Westin, "Do Silent Witnesses Defend Civil Liberties?" *loc. cit.*, 540–541.
87. Burnham, "The Suicidal Mania of American Business," *loc. cit.*, 60–61.
88. Hays, "Congress's Right to Investigate," *loc. cit.*, 442.
89. Westin, "Do Silent Witnesses Defend Civil Liberties?" *loc. cit.*, 541–543.
90. *Ibid.*, 543–544. For a fuller discussion of the legal implications of this dilemma, see Navasky, *Naming Names*, x, 34–35, 84; and Kanfer, *A Journal of the Plague Years*, 195. The best portrait of its effect on the individual witness is in Hellman, *Scoundrel Time*, 89–109.
91. Westin, "Do Silent Witnesses Defend Civil Liberties?" *loc. cit.*, 544, 546; Hays, "Congress's Right to Investigate," *loc. cit.*, 443.
92. Navasky quotes the blacklisted writer-director Abraham Polonsky on this very point in *Naming Names*, 279. See also p. 312.
93. Mary McCarthy, "Naming Names," in *On the Contrary*, 151–153. This essay originally appeared in *Encounter* (Spring 1957).
94. See Navasky, *Naming Names*, 317.
95. M. McCarthy, "Naming Names," *loc. cit.*, 152.
96. This statement was made by Donald L. Jackson, a Republican congressman and committee member from California. His words are reprinted in Goodman, *The Committee*, 299–300. See also Navasky, *Naming Names*, ix, 318.
97. Kempton, *Part of Our Time*, 209.
98. M. McCarthy, "Naming Names," *loc. cit.*, 153.
99. Michael Straight, "Trial By Congress," *New Republic*, CXIX (August 16, 1948), 6.
100. M. McCarthy, "Naming Names," *loc. cit.*, 153. Italics hers.
101. *Ibid.*, 154. Italics hers. See also Navasky, *Naming Names*, 28, 101, 322.
102. See Navasky, *Naming Names*, xix, xxi–xxiii, 28, 31.
103. See Kanfer, *A Journal of the Plague Years*, 186–187. Navasky describes the way Dmytryk, Rossen, Cobb, and Kazan changed their minds about testifying in *Naming Names*, xvii, 199–206, 232–238, 268–270, 302–304, 347, 373–374.
104. This motive was offered by the chairman of the committee, Harold Velde (Republican, Illinois), and is reprinted in Eric Bentley, ed., *Thirty Years of Treason* (New York, 1973, c. 1971), 579.
105. The words in quotation are taken from Davis's testimony on February 25, 1953, which is reprinted in Bentley, 581, 589–590, 598–601.
106. The words in quotation are taken from Boorstin's testimony on February 26, 1953, which is reprinted in Bentley, 602, 604–606, 608, 610–611.
107. The words in quotation are taken from Hicks's testimony on February 26, 1953, which is reprinted in Bentley, 618, 620, 622–623.
108. The quotations from *Where We Came Out* appear in Bentley, 623–624.
109. See Navasky, *Naming Names*, 58.
110. James Wechsler, *The Age of Suspicion* (New York, 1953), 268, 279, 305.
111. *Ibid.*, 290, 305.
112. *Ibid.*, 268–269, 278, 290, 293, 299, 304, 306. See also Navasky, *Naming Names*, 59.
113. Wechsler, *The Age of Suspicion*, 306.

114. *Ibid.*, 278.

115. Ceplair and Englund calculated that while fifty-eight people in Hollywood cooperated with HUAC and the clearance agencies, over two hundred did not. See *The Inquisition in Hollywood,* 379; also Navasky, *Naming Names,* 305.

116. I. F. Stone, "Must Americans Become Informers?" in *The Truman Era* (New York, 1973, c. 1953), 99. This essay originally appeared in the New York *Daily Compass* (July 11, 1951).

117. Lillian Hellman, *An Unfinished Woman* (New York, 1970, c. 1969), 228–229. See also Hellman, *Scoundrel Time,* 46; Navasky, *Naming Names,* 36–37; and Kanfer, *A Journal of the Plague Years,* 151.

118. Hellman, *Scoundrel Time,* 61, 95–96.

119. *Ibid.*, 99, 109.

120. *Ibid.*, 86, 90–91.

121. *Ibid.*, 103, 108.

122. *Ibid.*, 106.

123. See Caute, *The Fellow-Travellers,* 326.

124. The words in quotation are taken from Miller's testimony on June 21, 1956, which is reprinted in Bentley, 820, 822. Italics mine.

125. See Navasky, *Naming Names,* 216; and Goodman, *The Committee,* 394.

126. Robert Warshow, "The Liberal Conscience in *The Crucible,*" in *The Immediate Experience,* 200, 202; Robert Warshow, "Reply to Letters on Review of *The Crucible,*" *Commentary,* XVI (July 1953), 83. "The Liberal Conscience in *The Crucible*" originally appeared in *Commentary* (March 1953).

127. Arthur Miller, *The Crucible* (New York, 1964, c. 1953), 7–8.

128. *Ibid.*, 32–33, 94.

129. *Ibid.*, 69.

130. *Ibid.*, 97, 137, 140.

131. *Ibid.*, 141.

132. *Ibid.*, 141, 143.

133. On McCarthy's political demise, see Navasky, *Naming Names,* 23–24; and Caute, *The Great Fear,* 107–108.

134. Bell, "Status Politics and New Anxieties," *loc. cit.,* 119–120. This essay also appeared in revised form as the first chapter of *The New American Right.*

135. Seymour Lipset, "The Sources of the 'Radical Right,'" in Daniel Bell, ed., *The Radical Right* (New York, 1964, c. 1963 and 1955), 369–370. This volume enlarged upon *The New American Right* by adding essays written in 1962. The original essays were unchanged.

136. Fiedler, "McCarthy and the Intellectuals," *loc. cit.,* 47.

137. Dwight Macdonald, "The Triumph of the Fact," in *Against the American Grain* (New York, 1962), 416–420. This essay originally appeared in *Anchor Review* (1957).

138. Lipset, "The Sources of the 'Radical Right,'" *loc. cit.,* 336, 341–342; Bell, "Status Politics and New Anxieties," *loc. cit.,* 111; Seymour Lipset, *Political Man* (New York, 1963, c. 1960), 105.

139. Lipset, "The Sources of the 'Radical Right,'" *loc. cit.,* 344–346; Lipset, *Political Man,* 87, 92.

140. Richard Hofstadter, "The Pseudo-Conservative Revolt," in Bell, 89–90. This essay originally appeared in the *American Scholar* (Winter 1954–1955).

141. David Riesman and Nathan Glazer, "The Intellectuals and the Discontented Classes," in Bell, 110. This essay originally appeared in *Partisan Review* (Winter 1955).

142. Hofstadter, "The Pseudo-Conservative Revolt," *loc. cit.,* 76, 81–85, 87–88; Lipset, "The Sources of the 'Radical Right,'" *loc. cit.,* 309, 315, 338–339; Riesman and Glazer, "The Intellectuals and the Discontented Classes," *loc. cit.,* 114; Bell, "Status Politics and New Anxieties," *loc. cit.,* 111. See also Daniel Bell, "The Refractions of the American Past," in *The End of Ideology,* 98. This essay originally appeared in the *New Republic* (March 10 and 17, 1958).

143. Bell, "Status Politics and New Anxieties," *loc. cit.,* 111; Hofstadter, "The Pseudo-Conservative Revolt," *loc. cit.,* 90, 93; Lipset, "The Sources of the 'Radical Right,'" *loc. cit.,* 321, 339.

144. Lipset, *Political Man,* 169; Oscar Handlin, "How U.S. Anti-Semitism Really Began," *Commentary,* XI (June 1951), 541, 547–548; Fiedler, "McCarthy and the Intellectuals," *loc. cit.,* 57, 77; Bell, "Status Politics and New Anxieties," *loc. cit.,* 116–117; Peter Viereck, "The Revolt Against the Elite," in Bell, 167. Viereck's essay was originally given as a paper at the American Historical Association convention in December 1954.

145. Fiedler, "McCarthy and the Intellectuals," *loc. cit.,* 76; Lipset, *Political Man,* 170–173.

146. Riesman and Glazer, "The Intellectuals and the Discontented Classes," *loc. cit.,* 118–119; Hofstadter, "The Pseudo-Conservative Revolt," *loc. cit.,* 91–92; Lipset, *Political Man,* 113, 366.

147. Fiedler, "McCarthy and the Intellectuals," *loc. cit.,* 77, 84.

148. Lipset, "The Sources of the 'Radical Right,'" *loc. cit.,* 364.

149. Viereck, "The Revolt Against the Elite," *loc. cit.,* 162.

150. Riesman and Glazer, "The Intellectuals and the Discontented Classes," *loc. cit.,* 121, 126; Talcott Parsons, "Social Strains in America," in Bell, 228–229. Parsons's essay originally appeared in the *Yale Review* (Winter 1955).

151. Stephen Whitfield makes a similar point about McCarthy's image in "The 1950's: The Era of No Hard Feelings," *South Atlantic Quarterly,* LXXIV (Summer 1975), 294–295. For a full-scale critique of the intellectuals' analysis of McCarthyism's historical roots as well as of their efforts to describe its political and social constituency in the 1950s, see Michael Rogin, *The Intellectuals and McCarthy* (Cambridge, Mass., 1967).

152. M. McCarthy, "No News, or, What Killed the Dog," *loc. cit.,* 41.

153. Michael Harrington, "Liberalism—A Moral Crisis: The Committee for Cultural Freedom," *Dissent,* II (Spring 1955), 114–115, 121–122.

154. James Burnham, "A Letter of Resignation," *Partisan Review,* XX (November/December, 1953), 716–717.

155. For a fuller account of Oppenheimer's entanglement with McCarthyism, see both of Caute's works: *The Fellow-Travellers*, 334–339; and *The Great Fear*, 473–479.
156. See Navasky, *Naming Names*, 56–57; John Diggins, *Up From Communism* (New York, 1977, c. 1975), 330, 496; and Caute, *The Fellow-Travellers*, 329.
157. Michael Harrington, "The Post-McCarthy Atmosphere," *Dissent*, II (Autumn 1955), 292, 294. See also Harrington, "Liberalism—A Moral Crisis: The Committee for Cultural Freedom," *loc. cit.*, 117.

6. Endings and Beginnings

1. For a full account of the conflicts among *Commentary*'s editors between 1955 and 1959, see Norman Podhoretz, *Making It* (New York, 1969, c. 1967), 147–174.
2. Sidney Hertzberg, "The Crisis in U.S. Foreign Policy," *Commentary*, XVII (June 1954), 526; Paul Kecskemeti, "Reducing International Tension," *Commentary*, XX (December 1955), 520; Hans Morgenthau, "Khrushchev's New Cold War Diplomacy," *Commentary*, XXVIII (November 1959), 382–383.
3. Morgenthau, "Khrushchev's New Cold War Strategy," *loc. cit.*, 385–387; Martin Greenberg, "The New Deal Conservatives," *Commentary*, XVIII (November 1954), 483; Hertzberg, "The Crisis in U.S. Foreign Policy," *loc. cit.*, 526, 528.
4. Hertzberg, "The Crisis in U.S. Foreign Policy," *loc. cit.*, 525, 530–531.
5. See William Barrett, *The Truants* (New York, 1982), 37–38, 194–196. Barrett was and is extremely critical of the decline in Philip Rahv's passion for the Cold War and his continuing allegiance to Marxism. For these reasons, Barrett (who had been an associate editor of *Partisan Review* for nearly ten years) drifted away from the journal in the mid-1950s.
6. Diana Trilling and Philip Rahv, "America and 'The Quiet American,'" *Commentary*, XXII (July 1956), 66–67, 70–71.
7. Irving Howe, "This Age of Conformity," *Partisan Review*, XXI (January/February, 1954), 8–13, 15, 25, 29, 33; Irving Howe, " 'This Age of Conformity': Protest and Rejoinder," *Partisan Review*, XXI (March/April, 1954), 239. Italics his.
8. G. L. Arnold, "The Aftermath of War and the End of the Neo-Liberal Utopia," *Partisan Review*, XXII (Winter 1955), 96, 98; Henry Pachter, "Co-Existence Revisited," *Dissent*, VI (Summer 1959), 215; Irving Howe, "The Problem of U.S. Power," *Dissent*, I (Summer 1954), 216–217; H. Stuart Hughes, "A Politics of Peace," *Commentary*, XXVII (February 1959), 121, 123–124.
9. Hans Morgenthau, "The Lessons of World War II's Mistakes," *Commentary*, XIV (October 1952), 330–332.
10. For an example of these views, see Robert Langbaum, "Totalitarianism: A Disease of Modernism," *Commentary*, XIX (May 1955), 493.

11. G. L. Arnold, "Co-Existence: Between Two Worlds," *Partisan Review*, XXI (March/April, 1954), 154, 157–158.

12. Howe, "The Problem of U.S. Power," *loc. cit.*, 220. Italics his. See also Irving Howe, "Co-Existence: The Comedy of Tragedy," *Dissent*, II (Winter 1955), 4.

13. Emanuel Geltman, "Morality, Reality—And Peace," *Dissent*, V (Spring 1958), 110–111, 114; Henry Pachter, "A Bewildering Debate," *Dissent*, V (Spring 1958), 107–108.

14. Hughes, "A Politics of Peace," *loc. cit.*, 126.

15. Sidney Hertzberg, "Saving Asia for Democracy," *Commentary*, IX (April 1950), 326, 333; Hughes, "A Politics of Peace," *loc. cit.*, 123; Arthur Schlesinger, *The Vital Center* (Boston, 1962, c. 1949), 230–231.

16. Oscar Gass, "The United States and the Poorest Peoples," *Commentary*, XXV (February 1958), 93, 98; Hughes, "A Politics of Peace," *loc. cit.*, 124.

17. Howe, "The Problem of U.S. Power," *loc. cit.*, 211; Hughes, "A Politics of Peace," *loc. cit.*, 121.

18. Daniel Bell, *The End of Ideology* (New York, 1965, c. 1960), 403; Oscar Gass, "Liberal Capitalism and Socialism," *Commentary*, XXX (July 1960), 55.

19. Hughes, "A Politics of Peace," *loc. cit.*, 124.

20. *Ibid.*, 125. Italics his. For a similar argument, see A. J. Muste, "Co-Existence, Neutralism, Third Force," *Dissent*, II (Autumn 1955), 387, 391.

21. Hertzberg, "Saving Asia for Democracy," *loc. cit.*, 333.

22. Daniel Friedenberg, "A Journey to Cuba," *Dissent*, VII (Summer 1960), 283–285.

23. Henry Pachter, "A Foreign Policy," *Dissent*, VIII (Winter 1961), 7–8. For a less extreme defense of nationalism, see Hertzberg, "Saving Asia for Democracy," *loc. cit.*, 328; and "A New Policy for Asia," *New Republic*, CXXI (September 16, 1949), 6–7.

24. Bell, *The End of Ideology*, 403.

25. Seymour Lipset, *Political Man* (New York, 1963, c. 1960), 454–455; Howe, "The Problem of U.S. Power," *loc. cit.*, 214; Hertzberg, "Saving Asia for Democracy," *loc. cit.*, 327, 332.

26. Howe, "The Problem of U.S. Power," *loc. cit.*, 219.

27. Hughes, "A Politics of Peace," *loc. cit.*, 125.

28. *Ibid.*, 126; Gass, "The United States and the Poorest Peoples," *loc. cit.*, 96. The words in italics are Hughes's.

29. Irving Howe, "Notes on the Russian Turn," *Dissent*, III (Summer 1956), 309.

30. Dwight Macdonald, "The Great Thaw," in *Politics Past* (New York, 1970, c. 1957), 314. This essay originally appeared in *Encounter* (July 1956).

31. Lewis Coser, "Thought on 'Prosperous' Communism" *Dissent*, VII (Winter 1960), 21; Sidney Hook, "Socialism and Liberation," *Partisan Review*, XXIV (Fall 1957), 501.

32. Arnold, "Co-Existence: Between Two Worlds," *loc. cit.*, 155.

33. Macdonald, "The Great Thaw," *loc. cit.*, 314–316; Coser, "Thoughts on 'Prosperous' Communism," *loc. cit.*, 22.

34. Isaac Deutscher, "Communism Now: Three Views," *Partisan Review*, XXIII (Fall 1956), 510–511; Lewis Coser, "The New Turn in Russia," *Dissent*, III (Spring 1956), 125.

35. Macdonald, "The Great Thaw," *loc. cit.*, 317.

36. Howe, "Notes on the Russian Turn," *loc. cit.*, 312; G. L. Arnold, "Communism Now: Three Views," *Partisan Review*, XXIII (Fall 1956), 523.

37. Coser, "Thoughts on 'Prosperous' Communism," *loc. cit.*, 23–25.

38. Deutscher, "Communism Now: Three Views," *loc. cit.*, 517.

39. Hook, "Socialism and Liberation," *loc. cit.*, 503–504, 506, 510–511, 514; Irving Howe, "The Problem of 'National Communism,' " *Dissent*, IV (Spring 1957), 124.

40. Coser, "The New Turn in Russia," *loc. cit.*, 128; Irving Howe, "Communism Now: Three Views," *Partisan Review*, XXIII (Fall 1956), 526.

41. Deutscher, "Communism Now: Three Views," *loc. cit.*, 515–516.

42. Howe, "Communism Now: Three Views," *loc. cit.*, 527, 529; Howe, "Notes on the Russian Turn," *loc. cit.*, 310; Coser, "The New Turn in Russia," *loc. cit.*, 124–125; Arnold, "Communism Now: Three Views," *loc. cit.*, 520; Deutscher, "Communism Now: Three Views," *loc. cit.*, 512.

43. Howe, "The Problem of 'National Communism,' " *loc. cit.*, 122–123, 125–126; Howe, "Notes on the Russian Turn," *loc. cit.*, 312. Italics his.

44. Hook, "Socialism and Liberation," *loc. cit.*, 498.

45. Coser, "The New Turn in Russia," *loc. cit.*, 126, 128; Coser, "Thoughts on 'Prosperous' Communism," *loc. cit.*, 25; Howe, "Notes on the Russian Turn," *loc. cit.*, 309; Irving Howe, "Freedom and the Ashcan of History," *Partisan Review*, XXVI (Summer 1959), 267, 272; Macdonald, "The Great Thaw," *loc. cit.*, 317–318; Arnold, "Communism Now: Three Views," *loc. cit.*, 520.

46. Howe, "The Problem of 'National Communism,' " *loc. cit.*, 127; Irving Howe, "Intellectuals and Russia," *Dissent*, VI (Summer 1959), 299; Howe, "Notes on the Russian Turn," *loc. cit.*, 311; Irving Howe, "C. Wright Mills' Program: Two Views," *Dissent*, VI (Spring 1959), 194–195; Howe, "Freedom and the Ashcan of History," *loc. cit.*, 266. For a similar appraisal of Western relations with eastern European dissidents, see Norman Birnbaum, "Science, Ideology, and Dialogue," *Commentary*, XXII (December 1956), 573–574.

47. Norman Podhoretz, "The Jew as Bourgeois," *Commentary*, XXI (February 1956), 187.

48. Dwight Macdonald, "By Cozzens Possessed," in *Against the American Grain* (New York, 1962), 210–211. This essay originally appeared in *Commentary* (January 1958).

49. Robert Brustein, "Notes on a Suburban Theater," *Partisan Review*, XXVI (Fall 1959), 601, 603–604.

50. Alfred Kazin, "Psychoanalysis and Literary Culture Today," *Partisan Review*, XXVI (Winter 1959), 52; Norman Podhoretz, "The New Nihilism and the Novel," *Partisan Review*, XXV (Fall 1958), 578, 580.

51. Kazin, "Psychoanalysis and Literary Culture Today," *loc. cit.*, 45, 51, 53, 55;

Podhoretz, "The New Nihilism and the Novel," *loc. cit.*, 579.

52. Robert Brustein, "America's New Culture Hero," *Commentary*, XXV (February 1958), 123–124, 129.
53. *Ibid.*, 123, 126–127.
54. *Ibid.*, 125–128.
55. *Ibid.*, 128–129.
56. *Ibid.*, 129.
57. These quotations are taken, respectively, from Allen Ginsberg's poems "Howl" and "America," both published in 1956.
58. Diana Trilling, "The Other Night at Columbia: A Report from the Academy," *Partisan Review*, XXVI (Spring 1959), 230.
59. *Ibid.*, 221, 223–224.
60. *Ibid.*, 224–226, 228–229.
61. *Ibid.*, 228–230.
62. *Ibid.*, 230.
63. Norman Podhoretz, "The Know-Nothing Bohemians," *Partisan Review*, XXV (Spring 1958), 307–308, 313–314; Irving Howe, "Mass Society and Post-Modern Fiction," *Partisan Review*, XXVI (Summer 1959), 435.
64. Podhoretz, "The Know-Nothing Bohemians," *loc. cit.*, 310, 316, 318.
65. *Ibid.*, 318; Norman Podhoretz, "The Beat Generation," *Partisan Review*, XXV (Summer 1958), 476.
66. Barrett, *The Truants*, 156.
67. "A Word to Our Readers," *Dissent*, I (Winter 1954), 3–4.
68. Irving Howe, "America, the Country and the Myth," *Dissent*, II (Summer 1955), 242–244; Michael Reagan, "America as a 'Mass Society,'" *Dissent*, III (Fall 1956), 348.
69. Lewis Coser, "What Shall We Do?" *Dissent*, III (Spring 1956), 156, 160–161, 163.
70. Irving Howe, "The Quest for a Moral Style," in *Decline of the New* (New York, 1970), 155.
71. Lewis Coser and Irving Howe, "Images of Socialism," *Dissent*, I (Spring 1954), 130–138; Coser, "What Shall We Do?" *loc. cit.*, 161–164. See also Reagan, "America as a 'Mass Society,'" *loc. cit.*, 356; and Henry Rabassiere, "Confessions of an Old-Timer," *Dissent*, V (Winter 1958), 38, 40.
72. Norman Podhoretz, "The Issue," *Commentary*, XXIX (February 1960), 183–184.
73. Podhoretz, *Making It*, 209–210, 216–217.
74. *Ibid.*, 211, 218, 220, 229; Podhoretz, "The Issue," *loc. cit.*, 184.
75. Michael Harrington, "Our Fifty Million Poor," *Commentary*, XXVIII (July 1959), 19–22, 24; Michael Harrington, "Slums, Old and New," *Commentary*, XXX (August 1960), 120–121.
76. Harrington, "Slums, Old and New," *loc. cit.*, 118–119, 121–123; Harrington, "Our Fifty Million Poor," *loc. cit.*, 22–23, 25.
77. Harrington, "Our Fifty Million Poor," *loc. cit.*, 24–26; Harrington, "Slums, Old and New," *loc. cit.*, 123–124.

78. Coser, "What Shall We Do?" *loc. cit.*, 163.
79. See Samuel Lubell, "Racial War in the South," *Commentary*, XXIV (August 1957), 113–118; C. Vann Woodward, "The Great Civil Rights Debate," *Commentary*, XXIV (October 1957), 283–291; Oscar Handlin, "Civil Rights After Little Rock," *Commentary*, XXIV (November 1957), 392–396; C. Vann Woodward, "The South and the Law of the Land," *Commentary*, XXVI (November 1958), 369–374.
80. Michael Walzer, "The Idea of Resistance," *Dissent*, VII (Autumn 1960), 369–370.
81. *Ibid.*, 370.
82. *Ibid.*, 370–372; Michael Walzer, "The Politics of the New Negro," *Dissent*, VII (Summer 1960), 238, 242–243.
83. Walzer, "The Politics of the New Negro," *loc. cit.*, 243; Walzer, "The Idea of Resistance," *loc. cit.*, 370–372; Dwight Macdonald, "The Candidates and I," *Commentary*, XXIX (April 1960), 293; David Riesman and Michael Maccoby, "The American Crisis: Political Idealism and the Cold War," *Commentary*, XXIX (June 1960), 466.
84. H. Stuart Hughes, "End of an Epoch," *Partisan Review*, XXVII (Summer 1960), 568; Irving Howe, "Culture and Radicalism," *Commentary*, XXVII (May 1959), 457; Andrew Hacker, "The Rebelling Young Scholars," *Commentary*, XXX (November 1960), 404; Arthur Mitzman, "The Campus Radical in 1960," *Dissent*, VII (Spring 1960), 142.
85. Hughes, "End of an Epoch," *loc. cit.*, 568; Hacker, "The Rebelling Young Scholars," *loc. cit.*, 405–409.
86. Mitzman, "The Campus Radical in 1960," *loc. cit.*, 142, 144–147.
87. *Ibid.*, 147; Hacker, "The Rebelling Young Scholars," *loc. cit.*, 411–412.
88. William V. Shannon, "Eisenhower as President," *Commentary*, XXVI (November 1958), 390, 394, 398.
89. *Ibid.*, 390, 398.
90. Irving Howe, "Stevenson and the Intellectuals," *Dissent*, I (Winter 1954), 13, 15.
91. *Ibid.*, 13–14, 17–19. Italics his.
92. Karl Meyer, "Triumph of the Smooth Deal," *Commentary*, XXVI (December 1958), 462–463, 466–467; Lewis Coser, "A New Political Atmosphere in America?" *Dissent*, VI (Winter 1959), 11.
93. Irving Howe and Stanley Plastrik, "Notes on the Elections," *Dissent*, III (Fall 1956), 341–343. For a similar opinion, see William Newman, "Time Inc. Offers an Ideology," *Commentary*, XXVIII (December 1959), 477.
94. Norman Podhoretz, "The Issue: September 1960," *Commentary*, XXX (September 1960), a; Dennis Wrong, "Rockefeller as a Liberal Hero," *Commentary*, XXX (September 1960), 201–205; Macdonald, "The Candidates and I," *loc. cit.*, 288–292. Italics Macdonald's.
95. Irving Howe, "A New Political Atmosphere in America?" *Dissent*, VI (Winter 1959), 6.
96. Michael Walzer, "After the Election," *Dissent*, VIII (Winter 1961), 3.

97. Amitai Etzioni, "Neo-Liberalism—The Turn of the 60's," *Commentary*, XXX (December 1960), 473, 476–478; Howe, "A New Political Atmosphere in America?" *loc. cit.*, 5–7.
98. Walzer, "After the Election," *loc. cit.*, 3–4.

Bibliography

The following is not so much a formal or complete bibliography as a review of some of the more significant primary and secondary sources on which my own work has depended. I have not attempted to re-cite every entry in the notes, but rather to indicate those books that seem to me central to an understanding of American culture and social criticism in the 1940s and 1950s.

While scholars and journalists have written extensively about American diplomacy during and after World War II, the problems of domestic life have not received nearly the same attention. There are at least three books, however, that effectively describe the impact of the war on those who remained at home: Richard Polenberg's *War and Society* (Philadelphia, 1972), Geoffrey Perrett's *Days of Sadness, Years of Triumph* (New York, 1973), and John Morton Blum's *V Was for Victory* (New York, 1976). Among the many analyses of the origins and development of the Cold War, one of the best is still Stephen Ambrose's *Rise to Globalism* (Baltimore, 1971). For an important contemporary illustration of the debate over how the United States should respond to the challenges of the Soviet Union, see Walter Lippmann, *The Cold War* (New York, 1972, c. 1947), which includes George Kennan's classic explication of the policy of containment, "The Sources of Soviet Conduct." Joseph Goulden has provided an introspective and impressionistic interpretation of the nation's readjustment to the "peace" of the late 1940s in *The Best Years* (New York, 1976). The story is carried into the 1950s in Eric Goldman, *The Crucial Decade* (New York, 1960) and John Brooks, *The Great Leap* (New York, 1966). Though not primarily about the postwar years, two other books nonetheless offer memorable portraits of American politics and social mores in the 1950s: Garry Wills's *Nixon Agonistes* (Boston, 1970) and Tom Wolfe's *The Right Stuff* (New York, 1979).

On the tortured relationship between Western intellectuals and Communism, one of the most informative general treatments is David Caute's *The Fellow-Travellers* (New York, 1973). In the postwar years, however, the theme of disillusion has been predominant. Richard Crossman, ed., *The God That Failed* (New York, 1950) is an indispensable collection of statements by major American and European writers (André Gide, Richard Wright, Ignazio Silone, Stephen Spender, Arthur Koestler, and Louis Fischer) on why they first joined and then eventually broke with the Communist party. Two novels, Norman Mailer's *Barbary Shore* (New York, 1951) and Clancy Sigal's *Going Away* (Boston, 1962), further explain the reasons for attraction and disenchantment. Some American Communist party members have written poignantly about their own experiences and emotions as they departed: see George Charney, *A Long Journey* (Chicago, 1968); Joseph Starobin, *American Communism in Crisis, 1943–1957* (Cambridge, Mass., 1972); Al Richman, *A Long View from the Left* (New York, 1973); and Jessica Mitford, *A Fine Old Conflict* (New York, 1977)—the only comic account of the entire process. Vivian Gornick's *The Romance of American Communism* (New York, 1977) is based on interviews with former true believers, now nostalgic or embittered.

One reason, of course, that the American Communist party declined in numbers and influence was because of the effects of McCarthyism. Like foreign policy, this subject has been explored at considerable length. Among the general assessments, one might choose Richard Rovere, *Senator Joe McCarthy* (New York, 1959), an early but still standard biography; Athan Theoharis, *Seeds of Repression* (New York, 1971), one of the first "revisionist" efforts to trace the roots of McCarthyism to the Truman administration; Daniel Bell, ed., *The New American Right* (New York, 1955), discussed in the text; and Michael Rogin, *The Intellectuals and McCarthy* (Cambridge, Mass., 1967), a trenchant critique of Bell and his cocontributors.

The two trials that will always stand as the most representative and the most controversial of the McCarthy era are those involving Alger Hiss and the Rosenbergs. John Chabot Smith's *Alger Hiss: The True Story* (New York, 1976) tries to defend the innocence of his protagonist, but Allen Weinstein's *Perjury* (New York, 1978) makes an exhaustive and ultimately persuasive case for the prosecution. Similarly, Walter and Miriam Schneir seek to indict the government rather than the Rosenbergs in *Invitation to an Inquest* (New York, 1965), but Ronald Radosh and Joyce Milton in *The Rosenberg File* (New York, 1983) use documents released under the Freedom of Information Act to argue more convincingly for the couple's guilt though the authors deplore their execution. The most provocative fictional treatment of the events leading up to the Hiss case is Lionel Trilling's *The Middle of the Journey* (New York, 1947), while two equally compelling novels based on the Rosenbergs are E. L. Doctorow's *The Book of Daniel* (New York, 1971) and Robert Coover's *A Public Burning* (New York, 1977).

The mechanisms and consequences of the blacklist in every conceivable area of American life are comprehensively recounted in David Caute, *The Great Fear* (New York, 1978). Walter Goodman's *The Committee* (New York, 1968) focuses on the operations of the House Un-American Activities Committee. Stefan Kanfer has written sensitively about the repressions in the entertainment world in *A Journal of the Plague Years* (New York, 1973), as have Larry Ceplair and Steven Englund in *The Inquisition in Hollywood* (New York, 1980) though their book is especially valuable for its discussion of just what the Left actually did in and to the movie industry during the 1930s and the war years. The most complex and illuminating analysis of the effects of the blacklist can be found in Victor Navasky, *Naming Names* (New York, 1980). Yet ultimately there is no better way to understand the minds of the inquisitors, the informers, and the resisters than to read the excerpts of testimony before the congressional hearings contained in Eric Bentley, ed., *Thirty Years of Treason* (New York, 1971).

At the time, writers responded to McCarthyism from a variety of perspectives. To sample the reactions, one could begin with Murray Kempton's *Part of Our Time* (New York, 1955) which, though it is ostensibly a post-mortem on the radicalism of the 1930s, also reflects the attitude of intellectuals in the 1950s who were caught between their dislike of the McCarthyites and their disgust with the Communists. In the same vein, Leslie Fiedler's *An End to Innocence* (Boston, 1955) offers fascinating but ambivalent interpretations of McCarthy, Hiss, and the Rosenbergs. This ambivalence is underscored in James Wechsler's *The Age of Suspicion* (New York, 1953), his memoir of how it felt to be interrogated directly by the senator. Decades later, the liberals' plight was still being defended; see William O'Neill, *A Better World—The Great Schism: Stalinism and the American Intellectuals* (New York, 1983). The opinions and experiences of those who were unambiguously opposed to McCarthyism are reflected in Dalton Trumbo's *The Time of the Toad* (New York, 1972), originally a pamphlet published in 1949 by the Hollywood Ten, which in its revised version includes two additional essays written in 1956 and 1965; Trumbo's *Additional Dialogue* (New York, 1970), a collection of his letters written between 1942 and 1962; and Lillian Hellman's *Scoundrel Time* (New York, 1976), her recollections of her performance before

HUAC in 1952. Arthur Miller made informing the subject of three of his plays: *The Crucible* (New York, 1953), *A View from the Bridge* (New York, 1955), and *After the Fall* (New York, 1964). Similarly, Norman Mailer's *The Deer Park* (New York, 1955) deals in part with a movie director's decision to testify and thereby escape the blacklist, while Mary McCarthy's *The Groves of Academe* (New York, 1952) skillfully reverses the entire dilemma by presenting as its central character a professor who falsely claims to have been a Communist in order to keep his job at a liberal college.

In comparison with these examinations of particular events and crises, more general histories of postwar intellectual life are not as numerous. Among the most instructive sources are autobiographies. Everyone seems to be producing a memoir. So far the best are Norman Podhoretz's *Making It* (New York, 1967), Lillian Hellman's *An Unfinished Woman* (New York, 1969) and *Pentimento* (Boston, 1973), Alfred Kazin's *New York Jew* (New York, 1978), John Kenneth Galbraith's *A Life in Our Times* (Boston, 1981), William Barrett's *The Truants* (New York, 1982), Irving Howe's *A Margin of Hope* (New York, 1982), and William Phillips's *A Partisan View* (New York, 1984). There will be more.

For broader if briefer secondary interpretations of American culture and social thought since 1945, see the closing sections of Irving Howe's *World of Our Fathers* (New York, 1976) as well as his brilliant essay "The New York Intellectuals" in *Decline of the New* (New York, 1978), the final chapter of Christopher Lasch's *The New Radicalism in America* (New York, 1965), the concluding portions of Edward Purcell's *The Crisis of Democratic Theory* (Louisville, Ky., 1973), and the opening chapters of Morris Dickstein's *Gates of Eden* (New York, 1977). Alonzo Hamby has evaluated with great perception the evolution of postwar liberalism in *Beyond the New Deal* (New York, 1973). To gain some insight into what was happening on the opposite side of the political spectrum, see Ronald Lora, *Conservative Minds in America* (Chicago, 1971) and George Nash, *The Conservative Intellectual Movement in America* (Boston, 1976). The extraordinary impact of European émigrés on the American artistic, intellectual, and academic communities has been portrayed in Laura Fermi, *Illustrious Immigrants* (Chicago, 1968); Donald Fleming and Bernard Bailyn, eds., *The Intellectual Migration* (Cambridge, Mass., 1968); Martin Jay, *The Dialectical Imagination* (Boston, 1973); and H. Stuart Hughes, *The Sea Change* (New York, 1975).

Biographies and studies of particular groups of writers are growing in number. The last chapter of James Gilbert's *Writers and Partisans* (New York, 1972) deals with the postwar *Partisan Review*. John Diggins has provided a superb account of certain writers (Max Eastman, John Dos Passos, James Burnham, and Will Herberg) who moved from the left to the right in *Up From Communism* (New York, 1975). Peter Clecak has explored the ideas of C. Wright Mills, Paul Baran, Paul Sweezy, and Herbert Marcuse in *Radical Paradoxes* (New York, 1973). Richard King has done the same for Paul Goodman, Norman O. Brown, and Marcuse in *The Party of Eros* (New York, 1972). The Beat movement is sympathetically described in Lawrence Lipton, *The Holy Barbarians* (New York, 1959) and John Tytell, *Naked Angels* (New York, 1976). Two of the most illuminating portraits of individual lives can be found in James Atlas's *Delmore Schwartz* (New York, 1977) and Elisabeth Young-Bruehl's *Hannah Arendt* (New Haven, Conn., 1982).

With regard to primary sources for the postwar period, several authors collected their articles into books. Many of these have already been noted in the text. Among the most significant are David Riesman's *Individualism Reconsidered* (New York, 1954), Dwight Macdonald's *Politics Past* (New York, 1957) and *Against the American Grain* (New York, 1962), Daniel Bell's *The End of Ideology* (New York, 1960), and Mary McCarthy's *On the Contrary* (New York, 1962). In addition, Irving Louis Horowitz edited the essays of C. Wright Mills in *Power, Politics and People* (New York, 1963). For other examples, see James Baldwin, *Notes of a Native Son* (Boston, 1955); Murray Kempton, *America Comes of Middle Age* (New York, 1963), a sampling of his columns from the New York *Post* between 1950 and 1962; Irving Howe, *Steady Work* (New York, 1966), essays taken mostly from *Dissent* between 1953 and 1966; and I. F. Stone, *The Truman Era* (New York, 1973). On literary and larger cultural issues, three of the most revealing collections are Edmund Wilson's *Classics and Commercials* (New York, 1950); Lionel Trilling's *The Liberal Imagination* (New York, 1950); and Norman Mailer's *Advertisements for Myself* (New York, 1959), which contains "The White Negro." On modern painting, see Harold Rosenberg, *The Tradition of the New* (New York, 1959) and Clement Greenberg, *Art and Culture* (Boston, 1961).

Anthologies and collected essays or reviews are especially important in understanding the intellectuals' evaluations of the popular arts. For purposes of this study, the most useful have been Bernard Rosenberg and David White, eds., *Mass Culture* (New York, 1957), probably the broadest assortment of articles on the media; David White and Richard Averson, eds., *Sight, Sound, and Society* (Boston, 1968), which concentrates on movies and television; James Agee, *Agee on Film: Reviews and Comments* (Boston, 1964), which brings together his articles from the *Nation* and *Time* in the 1940s; Robert Warshow, *The Immediate Experience*

(New York, 1962), which republishes his classic essays, "The Westerner" and "The Gangster as Tragic Hero"; Manny Farber, *Movies* (New York, 1971); Pauline Kael, *I Lost It at the Movies* (Boston, 1965) and *Kiss Kiss Bang Bang* (Boston, 1968), each of which has some marvelously perceptive analyses of films and actors in the 1950s; and Dwight Macdonald, *On Movies* (Englewood Cliffs, N.J., 1969). Radio, television, and films were also the subjects of book-length assessments during the 1940s and 1950s. See for example Parker Tyler, *The Hollywood Hallucination* (New York, 1944); Martha Wolfenstein and Nathan Leites, *Movies: A Psychological Study* (New York, 1950); Gilbert Seldes, *The Great Audience* (New York, 1951); and Hortense Powdermaker, *Hollywood, The Dream Factory* (New York, 1951). But the two most influential interpretations of postwar mass culture in general were published in the early 1960s: Daniel Boorstin's *The Image* (New York, 1962) and Marshall McLuhan's *Understanding Media* (New York, 1964).

The major works of the intellectuals I have stressed are analyzed in the text. Among their books I have not treated are: Reinhold Niebuhr, *The Children of Light and the Children of Darkness* (New York, 1944); John Kenneth Galbraith, *American Capitalism* (Boston, 1952); Peter Viereck, *Shame and Glory of the Intellectuals* (Boston, 1953); and the following studies by C. Wright Mills—*The New Men of Power* (New York, 1948); *Character and Social Structure* (New York, 1953), coauthored with Hans Gerth; and *The Sociological Imagination* (New York, 1959). Finally, as the most vivid illustration of the contrast between the social criticism of the 1950s and that of the 1960s, see Michael Harrington's *The Other America* (New York, 1962). With the appearance of this book, a new decade had truly dawned and a new generation was about to emerge.

Index